Mamluks and Ottomans

Mamluks and Ottomans, dedicated to Michael Winter, aims to highlight aspects of variety and continuity in the history of the Middle East between the thirteenth and the eighteenth centuries CE.

The studies in this book look at the area from Istanbul through Syria and Palestine to Arabia, Yemen and Sudan. They demonstrate the great wealth of materials available, in a wide variety of languages, from archives and manuscripts, police records and divorce documents, through inscriptions and buildings to art works of every kind. The topics covered are equally varied:

- Sufism
- the festival of Nabi Musa
- religious institutions and their administration
- the politics of architecture
- royal biography
- social and military organization
- doctors and charity
- a Great Fire (a century before London's)
- pilgrimage guides
- land tenure
- medieval divorce
- confidence tricksters.

The contributors, from a dozen-odd institutions, show how much can be done and how much remains to be done in this field, making this book essential reading for those with research interests in Ottoman studies, Islam and Middle Eastern History.

David J. Wasserstein is Professor of History and of Jewish Studies at Vanderbilt University. He is the author of *The Rise and Fall of the Party-Kings* and *The Caliphate in the West*, and of numerous articles on topics in medieval Islamic and Jewish history.

Ami Ayalon is Professor of Middle Eastern History at Tel Aviv University. He is the author of *The Press in the Arab Middle East: A history*; *Reading Palestine: Printing and literacy 1900–1948*, and many articles on the modern political, social and cultural history of Arab societies.

Routledge Studies in Middle Eastern History

Mamluks and Ottomans

Studies in honour of Michael Winter

Edited by
David J. Wasserstein and
Ami Ayalon

Routledge
Taylor & Francis Group

LONDON AND NEW YORK

Transferred to digital printing 2010

First published 2006
by Routledge
2 Park Square, Milton Park, Abingdon, Oxon, OX14 4RN

Simultaneously published in the USA and Canada
by Routledge
270 Madison Ave, New York NY 10016

Routledge is an imprint of the Taylor & Francis Group

Typeset in Garamond by
Newgen Imaging Systems (P) Ltd, Chennai, India

British Library Cataloguing in Publication Data
A catalogue record for this book is available
from the British Library

Library of Congress Cataloging in Publication Data
A catalog record for this book has been requested

ISBN10: 0–415–37278–X (hbk)
ISBN13: 978–0–415–37278–7 (hbk)

ISBN10: 0–415–59503–7 (pbk)
ISBN13: 978–0–415–59503–2 (pbk)

Contents

Illustrations

Figures

Tables

Contributors

Reuven Amitai, the Hebrew University of Jerusalem
Benjamin Arbel, Tel Aviv University
Ami Ayalon, Tel Aviv University
Amnon Cohen, the Hebrew University, Jerusalem
Daniel Crecelius, California State University, Los Angeles
Joseph Drory, Bar-Ilan University, Ramat Gan, Israel
Daphna Ephrat, the Open University of Israel
Jane Hathaway, Ohio State University, Columbus, Ohio
Amalia Levanoni, University of Haifa
Donald P. Little, McGill University, Montreal
Rachel Milstein, the Hebrew University of Jerusalem
Carl F. Petry, Northwestern University, Chicago, Illinois
Minna Rozen, University of Haifa
Miri Shefer, Tel Aviv University
Boaz Shoshan, Ben Gurion University of the Negev, Beersheba, Israel
Amy Singer, Tel Aviv University
Hanna Taragan, Tel Aviv University
Gabriel Warburg, University of Haifa
David J. Wasserstein, Vanderbilt University, Nashville, Tennessee
Ursula Wokoeck, Tel Aviv University

Introduction

This book has a double aim. Unlike those who aim at two targets and miss both, we feel confident that we are giving no hostages to fortune in making this claim. The two are so closely intertwined with each other that their juxtaposition here seems only natural. In the first place, this is a collection of articles that have as their common theme the time and the area of the crossover from the later Mamluk period to the early Ottoman period in Egypt and the surrounding area. For a very long time, perhaps since the start of modern research on the period, there reigned the view that until 1516/1517 Egypt and the countries of the Fertile Crescent were ruled from within, that Arabic is the language of our principal sources for that era and that research has to concentrate on essentially local issues and problems. With the Ottoman conquest in 1516/1517, Egypt and the neighbouring lands become the obscure provinces of a huge empire with a faraway capital and faraway concerns; any interest their local problems may present to the student of history is minimal, and many if not most of the serious sources are in Ottoman Turkish. Such problems as are worthy of study are essentially different from those of the Mamluk period, despite the resurrection of Mamluk identity and strength in Ottoman Egypt and perhaps elsewhere in the region. Here are two distinct areas of study and research, as dissimilar as, say, Pharaonic and Ptolemaic Egypt.

Thus presented, the situation is seen in all its absurdity. Even if there had been little real continuity, it would be incumbent on us to enquire into the nature of the changes that occurred between Mamluks and Ottomans, to ask why such continuity was little or lacking, to wonder how the changes were effected. How much more true is this, given the vast range and depth of the continuity that actually existed. Yet the split has continued, even to this day, sustained by the paucity of scholars who possess an adequate command of the two languages and their resources. This dichotomous vision should be questioned – or, better still, discarded – if we are properly to understand the historical experience of Arabic-speaking societies in Egypt and the Fertile Crescent during the period from the fourteenth to the seventeenth centuries. One of our aims here, then, is to demonstrate, via a series of studies concentrated around that epochal date of 1516/1517, why it is so.

This ties our collection also to our second aim, which is to honour Michael Winter. Winter is one of those rare scholars with equal fluency in Arabic and in Ottoman Turkish, and one of those still rarer scholars who have chosen deliberately to use that double fluency in order to work across and over 1516/1517 and its outdated implications of closure and rupture. The recent collective *Cambridge History of Egypt* is divided into two volumes, one covering the period 640–1517, the other going 'From 1517 to the End of the Twentieth Century'. Only one contributor is represented with articles in both volumes. Michael Winter wrote the last article in volume 1, 'The Ottoman occupation', and the first in volume 2, 'Ottoman Egypt, 1525–1609'. (Those who wonder about the years 1517–25 must read both chapters.) We all write history with some awareness of what came next, which colours how we interpret the past; but Winter is unusual among historians of the Mamluks in his profound knowledge of what came after the closure of 1516/1517 and in using that knowledge to illuminate what he writes on the preceding period. A glance at the lengthy list of his publications shows a constant willingness to use his intimate familiarity with both eras to offer insight into each of them, based on an understanding of their interdependence. It also reveals his enviable command of the existing scholarship in the field with its different interpretations. This makes whatever he writes not only lucid and penetrating but also authoritative, and its reading a gratifying pursuit.

Michael Winter belongs to a generation of Israeli scholars with roots still in Europe. He was born in Czechoslovakia in 1934, and had the good fortune to move to Palestine before the outbreak of the War. He grew up in Haifa, attending the famous Réali high school, and in time pursued studies in Arabic and Middle Eastern history at the Hebrew University of Jerusalem. Later on, following a period of several years as an inspector in the Arab section of the Ministry of Education, he went to the United States for postgraduate work. At the University of California in Los Angeles he prepared his doctoral dissertation under the guidance of Gustav von Grunebaum, on the life and thought of 'Abd al-Wahhab al-Sha'rani, a sixteenth-century Egyptian Sufi thinker. Upon his return to Israel in 1972, he joined the faculty of the then young department of Middle Eastern and African History in Tel Aviv University, where he spent the rest of his career.

The dry facts of an academic life tell us little, though they may hint at much. The European background, as well as the period, point to a polyglot upbringing and a varied intellectual environment, producing a scholar who is at home as much in Ottoman archives as in discussions of German poetry. The Jerusalem training, followed by study with von Grunebaum, point to the rigor and thoroughness of the scholar's preparation for the tasks ahead, amply confirmed in Winter's writings and teaching themselves. All together serve to remind us both that scholarship is a humanistic and a humane activity, and that all of us who engage in it are links in a chain of tradition which ties us at once to the founders of our disciplines and to our students and in turn to their students, stretching on into the future.

In coming to consider the question of an offering to honour Michael Winter on his retirement – no, his pre-retirement – from active scholarship, we were thus faced with no difficult task: the obvious and only really appropriate offering was a collection of studies which should exemplify the leitmotif of Winter's career: the necessity to study Mamluk and Ottoman Egypt in their mutual interdependence.

We asked our authors to bear in mind the special interests of Michael Winter while preparing their contributions to this volume, and their variety testifies *inter alia* to the breadth of his own contributions to scholarship. These have ranged from classical Arabic literature to modern Islamic religious movements. In a volume like this we could not hope to offer representation of the entire range, and we chose very deliberately to restrict the volume to the Mamluk–Ottoman fulcrum which we see as representing most characteristically the central concerns of Winter's career. Another volume, in Hebrew, appearing simultaneously with this, presents a collection of studies on other subjects with which he has been concerned, in particular education in the Islamic world and religion in modern Islamic societies. In both volumes, the contributors have chosen to write about topics which Winter himself has addressed in the past. In both they have also reflected another aspect of his personality that he would certainly not wish to be forgotten – that of the teacher. In this, Winter has had actually two careers, the first as a teacher of Arabic (and later as an inspector of Arabic teaching) in schools in Israel, the second as an academic teacher and educator. All of our contributors are his colleagues and friends, but they are also, formally or otherwise, his students. In what they write here, they bear living testimony to his conviction of the truth of the Talmudic adage that 'it is not for us to finish the work, but neither are we free to desist from it'. In offering him the tribute of this collection, we remind him of the continuation of that sentiment, 'If you have studied much, then much reward will be given to you'.

Ami Ayalon
David J. Wasserstein
Tel Aviv, July 2005

1   Sufism and sanctity

The Genesis of the *wali Allah* in Mamluk Jerusalem and Hebron

Daphna Ephrat

The prominence of Sufism and the fascination exerted by holiness on the entire Sunni culture of the late medieval period have received considerable attention in current scholarship.[1] However, more attention needs to be drawn to the interrelationships between these phenomena and their concrete manifestations. In particular, further attempts should be made to define the link between the rise of Sufism as a legitimate version of *sunnat al-nabi* beginning in the fifth/eleventh century and the emergence of the Sufi saint, the *wali Allah*, as a charismatic figure within particular spatial frames. In this chapter I propose to inquire into this linkage through an examination of the lives and activities of the first generations of Sufi saints of Jerusalem and Hebron, broadly defined as those who lived in the cities during the Mamluk period (1250–1517).

Modern scholars, studying the evolution of Islamic sainthood in the context of the evolution of Sufi tradition and doctrine, offer extensive discussions of the role Sufism played in providing the theoretical basis for the rise of the Muslim holy man that can only be briefly summarized here. The attachment of Sufi shaykhs to the prophetic model through a recognized spiritual genealogy and their scrupulous observance of the *shari'a* and the *sunna* enabled them to embody the Prophet's personal charisma. At the same time, Sufi shaykhs drew their inspiration and legitimacy from the idea of a path (*tariqa*) by which to approach God, which implied that man was not only the creature and servant of God, but could also become His friend (*wali*). Gradually, a theory of sainthood (*wilaya, walaya*) developed. At its heart lay the idea of intercession; due to his nearness to God, the *wali* could intercede with Him on behalf of others, calling down divine grace (*baraka*) into the world during his lifetime or at his tomb.[2]

However, the key to our understanding of the linkage between the evolution of Sufism and the rise of the *wali Allah* lies in Sufism as a moral conduct, or ethical Sufism, as opposed to a mystical doctrine.[3] It was primarily through the actual manifestation of virtues (*manaqib*) usually ascribed to Sufis that men, and occasionally women, acquired the qualifications to attain closeness to the Divine. What placed them above all other believers was, thus, less their *ma'rifa* (mystical knowledge) than the extent of their outstanding *zuhd* (asceticism), their scrupulousness and self-control and other Sufi virtues, such as humility, generosity, and altruism, with which they were imbued. Moreover, in order to become both the believers' example of conduct to be followed as well as their intercessor before God, the *wali*'s life and activities, like those of any other holy man, must have been integrated in his natural and social environment.[4] In other words, in order to be recognized as a saint by the local community of believers, either in his lifetime or after his death, his figure must have been concrete and his virtues and extraordinary traits (*karamat*) publicly manifested. Similarly, the *wali* must have worked no less for the welfare (*maslaha*) of others than for his own personal perfection, fulfilling the spiritual and material needs of his fellow believers.

The quest for a charismatic benefactor acquired particular significance following the breakdown of the 'Abbasid state and the rise to power of alien regimes of military overlords beginning in the fifth/eleventh century (Seljuks, Ayyubids, Mamluks, Mongols). In the absence of stable institutions capable of providing protection, social identity and coherence, and with legal scholars at courts and *madrasas* increasingly associated with the official sphere, Muslims of all social categories turned to those whom they recognized as *awliya'* for spiritual guidance or to plead their case before God. The *awliya'* would often meet the spiritual and social needs and expectations of their fellow believers. They transmitted guidance and knowledge, cured diseases, distributed charity, and averted calamities, thereby assuming a variety of religious and social roles.[5]

Commonly perceived as a universal Islamic phenomenon, the emergence of the Sufi saint as a prominent figure must also have been the product of the concrete historical setting within which he was embedded. In the case of Mamluk Jerusalem and Hebron, it was influenced primarily by the cities' sanctity, by their long established position as centers of pilgrimage to universal and distinctive Muslim holy sites,[6] and by the proliferation of saintly tombs and Sufi lodges under the Mamluk regime. This proliferation led in turn to the intensification of social and religious life surrounding local *awliya'* of recognized virtue and their tombs.

Drawing on the biographies of the *awliya'* of this historical conjuncture, the analysis here revolves around the universal and the particular features of the Sufi saint, his cosmopolitan and his local affinities, the growth of a local following, and the transformation of his tomb into a center of public devotion. Composed in later periods, the accounts and narratives contained in the sacred biographies studied in this chapter convey the image of an ideal type of saint that was shaped after his death. In their endeavor to impose a normative homogeneity on the definition of the Muslim holy man, the religious scholars (*'ulama'*), authors of these texts, presented the *wali* in terms and expressions accepted by universal Islamic standards. Still, only by locating the ideal type of saint within a specific community could the norm become effective and the *wali*'s figure be commemorated. Accounts of saintly figures that had been related and transmitted by reliable reporters were carefully recorded, providing details about their lives and activities. Hence, notwithstanding the seemingly idealized and imaginary dimension of hagiographic narratives, their critical examination may uncover the *wali*'s peculiar traits and distinctive realities.[7]

Profile

There are no hagiographic or biographical compilations devoted to an individual Sufi saint or to groups of *awliya'* who lived in medieval Jerusalem and Hebron. The stories about their lives and miracles are incorporated in the pages of general biographical and hagiographic dictionaries and in obituaries (*wafayat*) concluding the accounts of major events in chronicles. Among the chronicles, *al-Uns al-jalil bi-ta'rikh al-Quds wal-Khalil* by the Hanbali judge Mujir al-Din al-'Ulaym al-Muqaddasi (d. 928/1521) is the most important source.[8] Covering the history of the two cities from the first Islamic century to the reign of Sultan Qayt Bay (d. 901/1495), a substantial part of *al-Uns* is devoted to recording and narrating the lives of their notables, scholars, Sufis, and saints. The abundant information about the lives of the *awliya'* and the examples given of their *baraka* shed light on their emergence as charismatic figures in the course of the Mamluk period.

In *al-Uns* and other compilations, the *awliya'* are commonly described as virtuous worshipers (*salihun*) and ascetics (*zuhhad*). A close examination of their biographies, however, reveals a rich variety of saintly figures. This variety refers both to the religious traditions the *awliya'* represented and to the avenues they pursued. Consequently, it is difficult to identify individual *awliya'* or groups of Sufi saints as belonging exclusively to one or another local spiritual path or religious association.

To begin with, because of their sanctity, Jerusalem and Hebron were from earliest times part of the *hajj* route and magnets for ascetics and Sufis from the entire Muslim world, who either settled or made extensive stays in them.[9] The endeavor to be in the immediate vicinity or under the aegis of the sanctuary, nourished by the traditions in praise of the cities that were developed and circulated mostly by early ascetics and mystics, intensified in the wake of the crusades. By then, Jerusalem and Hebron had been incorporated in the universal world of Islamic learning and devotion where a constant confluence between various religious traditions took place. Sufis, in particular, were linked to this universal world, traveling throughout the Islamic world in quest of guidance and trying to deepen their knowledge of "reality."[10]

Many Sufi saints in Mamluk Jerusalem and Hebron were immigrants, drawn to the cities from regions of the Muslim world as far apart as Spain and India, and representing the varied religious traditions they had already associated themselves with in their places of origin. Consider, for example, Burhan al-Din Abu Ishaq Ibrahim, a member of the famous Banu Jama'a family of Shafi'is, some of whom are said to have embraced the Qadiriyya method of spiritual guidance.[11] Born in Hama (in 596/1200), he traveled to Damascus where he studied jurisprudence (*fiqh*), acquiring mastery in the science pertaining to the mystical path (*'ilm al-tariq*) at the same time. He made a modest career for himself as a teacher of the prophetic traditions (*hadith*) in a number of places, although Hama remained his permanent home. Having made several pilgrimages to Mecca, he directed his steps finally to Jerusalem. He bade his fellow townsmen farewell, carried his shroud with him, and died in the city soon after his arrival there (in 675/1277).[12] 'Ala' al-Din 'Ali al-Ardabili al-'Ajami (d. 832/1428–29), whose *manaqib* and *karamat* were, according to Mujir al-Din, "too numerous to depict," is another example of a *wali* who settled in Jerusalem toward the end of his life. The son of a renowned mystic and miracle worker who had gained fame on his own merit, he succeeded his father as leader of the Sufis (*shaykh al-sufiyya*) in his home town of Ardabil. He then arrived in Damascus on his way to Mecca, accompanied by his many disciples and followers. After dwelling in Mecca for a while, he proceeded to Jerusalem where he died. He was buried in Bab al-Rahma cemetery in the presence of a large crowd. Erected by his closest disciples, his domed shrine (*qubba*) came to be a famous pilgrimage site.[13]

Greater Syria, it is also noteworthy, did not constitute the cradle of the major mystical paths that evolved in the course of the sixth/twelfth–seventh/thirteenth centuries. The overwhelming majority of the *tariqa*s that appeared on its soil during this period were branches of mystical paths that originated in other parts of the Muslim world, notably Iraq, eastern Iran, and Central Asia. There were but a few strictly local *tariqa*s in the towns and cities of Greater Syria as a whole,[14] and most *awliya'* in late medieval Jerusalem and Hebron do not seem to have been affiliated with any particular *tariqa*. Thus, when it appears in the texts, the word *tariqa* normally applies to a method of spiritual guidance practiced by a particular Sufi master, rather than designating an institutionalized Sufi brotherhood.

Finding its precedents in works that constitute the main tradition of Sufi historiography,[15] the figure of the savant Sufi saint appears to be the most prominent of all. This should not appear surprising if we bear in mind that the sacred biographies studied in this chapter were written by *'ulama'* for *'ulama'*. Accordingly, many *awliya'* are described as *al-'ulama' al-'arifin*, blending together the *'ilm* of the jurist and the *ma'rifa* of the mystic in their own education and in their teaching of others. Some were peerless (*afrad*) in their generation due to the spiritual stations (*maqamat*) and mastery of gnosis they attained, while others apparently did not gain importance as mystics. Some were spiritual masters (*murshid*s, *musalik*s), guiding aspirants who orbited around them, while others stressed individual salvation. Many are described as moderate ascetics, while a few others appear as extreme worshipers, totally separated from their natural and social environment. Some of the advocates of permanent and intense asceticism in Mamluk Jerusalem were affiliated with the Qalandar dervish path, which represented a new form of religious renunciation manifested in total poverty, begging or alms taking, homeless wandering, and celibacy.[16]

The full variety of religious traditions the *awliya'* represented emerges once we shift the emphasis from the supposedly unbridgeable differences and controversies between legalism and Sufism, or between the *fuqaha'* and the *fuqara'*, to the diversities and nuances within Sufism both as a mystical path and as a code of behavior. At the same time, by departing from the notions of popular religion in which the phenomenon of Muslim sainthood has been often submerged, we may advance our understanding of the concrete manifestations of the various dimensions of Sufism in different historical contexts. Indeed, during the Later Middle Period (broadly defined as the period from the Mongol invasions to the rise of the Ottoman Empire) the fluidity and diversity of Sufi belief and practice were revealed in their brightest light. Sober Sufism existed alongside the old traditions of mild and extreme asceticism, while various forms of saint veneration and dervish deviant pietism penetrated everywhere.

The long biographical entries that were devoted to *awliya'* who combined esoteric knowledge with the mastery of the legal sciences reasserted and nourished the rapprochement between legalism and Sufism. Together Sufi savants and legal experts are presented as active participants in the process of the formation of the Sunna, which began in the Muslim east and penetrated into Greater Syria during the sixth/twelfth century. They appear in our texts as arbiters of religious knowledge and practice, *al-'ilm wal-'amal*, and of the central moral tenet of "commanding right and forbidding wrong," *al-amr bil-ma'ruf wal-nahy 'an al-munkar*. Thus, for example, Abu Bakr 'Abd Allah al-Shaybani al-Shafi'i (d. 797/1394–95) was one of the greatest *awliya'* and *'ulama' al-sufiyya* who had acquired qualification in *'ilm* and advanced on the Path (*salaka tariq al-sufiyya*) in his home town of Mosul and in Damascus before settling in Jerusalem. Blending knowledge of the Divine Law with knowledge of True Reality (*jama'a bayna 'ilm al-shari'a wal-haqiqa*), he became an undisputed authority in *al-'ilm wal-amr*. People from all over al-Sham (Syria) visited him frequently (in his house located north of the wall of al-Aqsa), and followed all his instructions.[17]

The overwhelming majority of Sufi savants adhered to the Shafi'i rite of jurisprudence, the dominant Sunni rite in the Mamluk sultanate. Several among them simultaneously held the position of *mudarris* (teacher of the legal and Islamic sciences) in a teaching mosque or in a madrasa and that of *shaykh al-sufiyya* in the Sufi convent, the *khanqah*. Reflecting the social and intellectual assimilation of Sufis and Sufism into the mainstream of Muslim intellectual life, this combination was nowhere revealed more clearly than in the state-sponsored Salahiyya Shafi'i *madrasa* and *khanqah*, the most prestigious educational institutions of their kinds in Ayyubid and Mamluk Jerusalem. In addition, there were institutions in Mamluk Jerusalem in which the functions of the madrasa and *khanqah* were blended.[18] One testimony is provided by the dedication inscription of al-Dawidariyya *khanqah* (dated 695/1296–97), which explicitly declares that the institution was designed to serve a community of mystics (*al-ta'ifa al-sufiyya*) and students of the Shafi'i rite.[19]

Notwithstanding the growing combination of legalist and mystical learning, many among those who are designated as *awliya'* seem still to have oscillated between the two streams, seeking an alternative to religious attainment and devotion in the Sufi Way. Viewing the madrasa as the representative of formal knowledge, book learning, and worldliness, they would refrain from teaching or studying in the institution, or would resign their paid teaching positions at a certain phase of their lives. One of the most famous examples of this is that of Abu al-'Abbas al-Ramli al-Shafi'i, known as Ibn Arslan (d. 844/1440–41), the revered Qadiri mystic wayfarer (*salik*) and Shafi'i legal expert known mostly for his treatise on *fiqh*, *Matn al-zubad*. Relinquishing the positions of *mudarris* and mufti that he had held for a long period of time and moving from his home town of Ramla to Jerusalem, he devoted himself thereafter to advancing on the stages of the Path, training others to approach God more directly and intimately at the same time. Not only did he excel in mastery of the religious sciences, but he surpassed any other man in the entire Bilad al-Sham and in Egypt in his asceticism, pious practices, and moral conduct. Not a year passed without him dwelling by the sea (of Jaffa) spending days and nights in constant prayer publicly and in private, preferring obscurity and passionate love of God to ostentation, and refusing any worldly benefits and paid positions offered to him. He never cursed or abused anyone, never harbored feelings of hatred against anyone, and treated whoever tried to dispute with him with gentleness.[20]

Other *awliya'* are praised primarily for their inner struggle for personal perfection through constant *mujahada*, the struggle against one's passions and the drives of the lower soul. One such was 'Umar ibn al-Hatim al-'Ajluni, the famous *wali* of Hebron, designated in the introductory formula of his biography as *sahib al-mukashafat* (unveiling, direct witnessing of God), and *mujahadat*. He did not cut his hair and fingernails. Nor did he wash his body and clothes, until he knew the entire Qur'an by heart.[21] His contemporary in Jerusalem, al-Shaykh al-Salih Muhammad, was another *wali* known for his mortification of the flesh (*taqashshuf*), as well as his extreme purity in dietary matters (*al-halal al-mahd*), a prime characteristic of the extremely devout ascetic in medieval Islam.[22] He used to eat snakes and dung beetles, imagining the snakes as cucumbers and the dung beetles as grapes. Notables and commoners alike venerated him, as *karamat* and *mukashafat* were revealed in him. He had been seen among the pilgrims on the mountain of 'Arafat and in al-Quds al-Sharif on the morning following *'id al-adha*.[23]

While representing universal religious currents and possessing features that were common among their contemporaries throughout the Muslim world, it was due to the embodiment of their heroic virtues and practices within their specific community that these models of conduct became a focus of veneration. The following two stories, while conveying the retrospective, glorified image of the *wali* as constructed by the hagiographer, shed light on the identification of a "real" saint by the local community of believers at the same time. The first story concerns Shihab al-Din Abu al-'Abbas, the first *wali* whose biography appears in *al-Uns*, who attended the conquest of Jerusalem (by the Ayyubids, most probably in 1187) as one of the warriors while riding his ox:

> The ascetic worshiper, al-Shaykh Shihab al-Din [...] *al-zahid, al-salih*, was known by the surname of Abu Thawr. This is because he arrived in al-Bayt al-Muqaddas while riding an ox (Ar. *thawr*) [...]. In 595/1198, al-Malik al-'Aziz Abu al-Fath 'Uthman b. al-Malik Salah al-Din instituted as *waqf* for him a village in the vicinity of Bab al-Khalil (one of the nine gates of al-Haram al-Sharif). This is a small village with a cloister built during the Byzantine (Rum) period. Previously called Dayr Marqus, it is known now as the Dayr of Abu Thawr [...]. When he died, he was buried in this village, and his grave there is a well-known pilgrimage site. His descendants have been living there to this day.
>
> It is related about him that whenever he needed food, he used to write down his specific need, then place the paper around the ox's neck and send the ox to al-Quds. Roaming the city's streets, the ox would finally reach a seller who would provide the food requested. And this is one of his many *karamat*.[24]

The second story is contained in the biography of al-Shaykh Ibrahim al-Hudma (d. 730/1329–30), Kurdish in origin, who came to be one of the most revered *awliya'* of Hebron:

> [...] Coming to al-Sham from the east, he chose some land between al-Quds and al-Khalil to settle in, working and cultivating it. He became the object of *ziyara* [as] *karamat* were revealed in him. Towards the end of his life (he reached one hundred years), he married and was blessed with children who all came to be

known as virtuous worshipers. It is related that ten loaves of bread were bought for him daily in the market of Sayyidna al-Khalil (= Hebron) [...]. Preserved from the beginning of each week to its end, crumbled and seasoned, on the last day the bread was put in vessels and brought to his dwelling. He used to eat at once, abstaining from any nourishment during the rest of the week.[25]

The religious and social practices, sites and spaces that grew up around the transmission of the knowledge and guidance of these and other *awliya'* and the bestowal of their divine grace led to the emergence of local communities of disciples, companions, and devotees around them. Orbiting around the *wali* during his lifetime, these communities further consolidated around his tomb after his death.

Authority and following

The accounts of the lives and teachings of the *awliya'* do not indicate the existence of any organized community of Sufis in terms of modes of affiliation, initiation or confirmation of status by one specific individual. Similarly, the reception of the Sufi cloak, the *khirqa*, does not seem to signify unique affiliation to one particular master in order to benefit from his teaching, and even less to a fraternity, but the reception of one, and more frequently of many spiritual influences.[26] Nor do the accounts imply affiliation with a *tariqa* as a Sufi association. Rather, people are described as aspirants and followers of a certain *wali* who practiced his spiritual method (*tariqa*) through the transmission of ritual guidance, knowledge, and blessing, passing on his morals (*akhlaq*) at the same time. Indeed, as argued persuasively by Denis Gril and others, the emergence of local circles of devotees around a *wali* of recognized virtue came to be the prime manifestation of the consolidation of Sufism as a social phenomenon during the later medieval period.[27] Connection to the nascent local Sufi brotherhoods was thus through the cult of saints, which from the twelfth century on became central to the religious experience of Muslims throughout the Muslim world.

The sources at our disposal use the expression "*ahl al-tariqa*," or "*ahl al-tariq*," to designate the sets of people whom they describe as *ashab* (disciples), or *muridun* (novices), or *atba'* (followers) of a certain *wali*. Their accounts suggest the existence of two circles around him: one a small group, consisting of his disciples and companions, and another a wider circle of occasional visitors to his lodge or tomb who came to seek his blessing or simply to be close to him. No matter how fluid and informal the *wali*'s social networks might appear, references to the circles clustering around him indicate his spiritual, charismatic authority over his disciples and followers.

The renowned Ibn Arslan is a good example of a Sufi guide of well-established spiritual authority. Believers from various Muslim countries set out on journeys to visit him and the number of *talamidh* (disciples) and novices centering around him wherever he turned grew constantly. He educated a number of disciples (*jama'a*), advancing each aspirant on the Path in accordance with his spiritual state, regardless of his social status (*wa-shaghala kullan fima yara halahu yaliqu bihi fi al-najaba wa-'adamiha*). He then dressed a group of disciples from al-Sham and Egypt in his *khirqa*, and bestowed his *baraka* upon them.[28] His transmission of knowledge, as with other *awliya'*, extended to include many besides aspirants and novices. Even *awliya'* engaged in a struggle for their own spiritual perfection transmitted the fundamentals of religion to the people in general (*al-nas*), leading them in prayer or relating prophetic traditions to them. One such was the shaykh Shams al-Din Abu 'Abd Allah Muhammad al-Qurami (d. 788/1386). Praised by the people for his constant recitation of the Qur'an and prayer by night, many sought his transmission of *hadith*. At first he refrained, preferring spiritual retreat to leading public worship. But toward the end of his life he took the opportunity of his attendance at al-Aqsa mosque for the Friday congregational prayer to recite the sayings of the Prophet to a large crowd.[29]

Other *awliya'*, while living an ascetic life and avoiding association with the powerful, catered for the social needs of their fellow believers. One anecdote, in particular, illustrates this point. It tells of a disciple of Ibn Arslan who appealed for his help against acts of injustice (*mazalim*) inflicted by the district chief (*kashif*) of Ramla. The governor refused to deal with the case unless Ibn Arslan's supernatural forces were manifested in the palm trees standing in front of him. At that moment, the trees were uprooted by a sudden storm. Accompanied by his entourage, the governor then turned to Ibn Arslan in repentance. Attributing the miraculous deed to God alone, Ibn Arslan demanded that they should turn to Him and renew their religious belief.[30]

This last story provides us with another glance at the growth of the *wali*'s following. The more his virtues were manifested, the more his fellow believers turned to him; the more he met their spiritual and non-religious needs, the larger his following and authority became. A select few disciples and colleagues sought his spiritual advice in the hope of elevated mystical achievement for themselves. A much more numerous audience turned to him for instruction in the essentials of their religion, for guidelines in correct Islamic behavior, and for a word of blessing. In view of the *wali*'s growing local following, members of the cities' ruling and religious institutions joined in, fitting themselves into existing practices enacted by others. Participation of a Mamluk governor in saint veneration did not, of course, transform him into a native member of society, but it did provide an entry into the public sphere for him.

Disciples and people closely associated with the *wali* expressed their admiration and gratitude to him by clinging to him wherever he settled or traveled, by relating and recording stories about his life and miraculous deeds, and by erecting a tomb over his grave. Commoners provided the ascetic *wali* with the food necessary for his subsistence, while local governors established charitable endowments for the construction of his lodge and tomb, or set up the revenues of a village as *waqf* for his benefit. While experiencing their encounters with the Sufi saint in a variety of ways, believers of all social classes shared the belief in his ability to manipulate divine forces which shaped his perception as a charismatic figure. Whether seeking spiritual guidance or blessing, or to take part in the growing practices surrounding local holy men, they all flocked around whomever they believed to be their "channels to God," frequenting their lodges and tombs and attending their funeral ceremonies.[31]

Muhammad al-Qurami, whom we have just encountered, was one of the *awliya'* who are said to have become the spiritual poles (*aqtab*, s. *qutb*) of their generation; it is related that the *awliya'* turned to him, and the kings flocked to his doorstep.[32] Another, more detailed, noteworthy description of the *wali*'s prominent position in society is contained in the biography of al-Shaykh Muhammad b. 'Abd Allah (d. 844/1440–41) who arrived in Jerusalem and devoted himself to worship in al-Aqsa mosque. He made many pilgrimages to Mecca on foot, and many *karamat* and *mukashafat* were attributed to him. So highly regarded was he by the *'ulama'* of Jerusalem that they entrusted to him the keys of the Dome of the Rock. At the same time he is cited as an example of a *wali* who had complete authority (*satwa*) over the Sufis in the Salahiyya *khanqah*. His fame as a model of correct religious conduct spread far beyond the city's confines. It is related that whenever the famous shaykh Taqi al-Din al-Hasani arrived in Jerusalem it was only in his house that he dwelt and his food that he ate.[33]

With the passage of time, renowned Sufi guides and miracle workers established roots in Mamluk Jerusalem and its environs. Their positions as spiritual authorities eventually passed on to their closest disciples, sons, and other relatives. One such was al-Sayyid Badr al-Din (d. 650/1252), a member of a family of *ashraf*. He is described as a *qutb* of great renown; "all the *awliya'* of his generation obeyed him, and the high and low (*al-khass wal-'amm*) never ceased centering around him" (in his home in a village in Wadi al-Nusur west of al-Quds al-Sharif).[34] His son, al-Sayyid Muhammad (d. 663/1264–65), is described as one of those who attained elevated mystical states (*ahwal*) and spiritual perfection through *mujahadat* and firm intention (*'azm*) in worship. He guided a great number of people, and miraculous states were revealed in him.[35] Later, 'Abd al-Hafiz (d. 696/1296–97), Muhammad's son, is said to have guided a community (*jami'a*), eventually becoming the leader of the people of this spiritual Path in his lifetime (*intahat ilayhi ri'asat ahl hadhihi al-tariqa fi zamanihi*).[36] As the village in Wadi al-Nusur became too small to house al-Sayyid al-Badr's descendants, he preferred them to his own self. He therefore gave up the revenues from his land for their benefit, and moved to the village of Shafarat, later named by him Sharafat, after the *ashraf*, members of his family who settled and established roots there.[37] The most famous of them were al-Sayyid 'Ali and al-Sayyid Muhammad Baha whom Mujir al-Din describes as the "pillars" (*'amad*) of the Holy Land and its surroundings. It is related that notables and commoners frequented their residence, and a huge crowd sought their *baraka*. In their times, the Mamluk governor (*na'ib*) in al-Sham intended to institute the village of Sharafat as *waqf* for them. Refusing at first to accept the pious endowment, 'Ali eventually changed his mind in order that the land might serve the shepherds and cultivators.[38] As we shall see later, it was in this village that Dawud, the son of 'Abd al-Hafiz, erected a *zawiya* and a tomb where his descendants, all described as virtuous and charismatic figures, were buried.

Lodge and tomb

The dissemination of knowledge and guidance by the Sufi shaykh was not, of course, limited to any particular place, but occurred wherever he sat. Often, however, his circle (*halqa*) of aspirants would gather in his *zawiya*. Originally signifying particular corners of or spaces in large mosques, many *zawiya*s in late medieval Jerusalem and Hebron were independent buildings serving as a residence for their shaykh and as a forum for the transmission of his guidance and knowledge. The term "shaykh" of course meant Sufi master as well as teacher of the Islamic religious and legal sciences, and the shaykhs of the *zawiya*s listed in *al-Uns* sometimes taught *hadith*, jurisprudence, and other subjects in those very institutions or in *madrasas*.[39] However, in contrast with the royal institutions constructed over the course of the Mamluk period – the madrasa and the *khanqah* – the *zawiya* was usually, though not invariably, founded on private initiative by a shaykh who presided over it. Even when members of the ruling elite erected *zawiya*s or dedicated religious endowments to guarantee their perpetuation, their financing came from private sources for the benefit of a particular shaykh and his followers and successors.[40] Symbolizing the presence and authority of its first *Shaykh* and his successors, this realm of the Sufi saint often grew into a whole complex comprising a tomb, a minaret, a courtyard, an entrance gate, and presumably also a hall for ritual worship. Consider, for instance, the growth of the *zawiya* of al-Shaykh 'Ali al-Baka (d. 670/1271–72) whom Mujir al-Din designates as *"sahib al-zawiya bi-madinat sayyidna al-Khalil."* In 668/1269, a Mamluk provincial military governor (*amir*) constructed the *zawiya* for the sake of this ascetic *wali*, and several years later another *amir* erected a tomb over his grave. Finally (in 720/1320), the *na'ib* of al-Malik al-Nasir ibn Qalawun added an entrance gate and a minaret to the building.[41]

Two of the dominant *tariqa*s in Mamluk Jerusalem – the Bistamiyya and the Qalandariyya – had *zawiya*s erected by their shaykhs. Of them, that of the Bistamiyya (located in the northeastern part of the city) figures prominently in our sources. Originating in eastern Iran and spreading to various cities in Bilad al-Sham around the personalities of leading shaykhs,[42] the Jerusalem Bistamiyya had a recognized shaykh, designated in our sources as *shaykh al-bistamiyya*, or *sahib al-zawiya al-bistamiyya*. The first shaykh of this *zawiya* was 'Abd Allah al-Asadabadi al-Bistami (d. 794/1392), successor of al-Shaykh 'Ali al-Safi al-Bistami (d. 761/1360), one of the most famous Sufi guides and miracle workers of his time.[43] With successive generations of adherents to his *tariqa* buried by his side, his tomb became the nucleus of the Bistamiyya plot (*hawsh*) lying in the great Mamila cemetery west of the city. The dervish Qalandars, who had their origins in Central Asia, spread to Egypt and Syria during the first half of the seventh/thirteenth century. In Jerusalem, they converted an old church known as Dayr al-Ahmar in the middle of al-Mamila cemetery into their *zawiya*. Thereafter, a tomb complex grew up round about as an extension to the *zawiya*. The first mausoleum in this complex was built in 794/1391–92 for the founder of the *zawiya*, Shaykh Ibrahim al-Qalandari, by his admirer, a woman named Tunsuq.[44] By inhabiting their lodge in the cemetery area the Jerusalem Qalandars manifested the dervish striving for poverty (*faqr*).

It was the close association of the *zawiya* with the first *wali* of great renown buried in its complex that turned it into a sanctuary. Stories about miraculous events involved with the foundation of the complex reinforced its sacredness. This last point is nowhere illustrated more clearly than in the following story preserved in *al-Uns*:

> Dawud (son of 'Abd al-Hafiz) was one of the *awliya'* of extraordinary traits (*ashab al-karamat*). He lived in the village of Sharafat (where his grandfather, Badr al-Din had settled), which was inhabited by a few Christians, but not by any

Muslims apart from him, his family and his followers. Totally absorbed in worship, he was eventually revealed by God as a miracle worker. The reason for this was that the Christian villagers used to squeeze the grapes and sell their wine to Muslim sinners. Profoundly disturbed by this deed, he turned to almighty God. And from that time onwards, whenever the grapes were squeezed, the wine was turned into vinegar or, as some other people relate – to water. The Christians called him "magician" (*sahir*), and abandoned [the lands]. Having heard about the concern of the district tax collector (caused by the loss of revenues), Dawud leased the village's lands from him. He then erected a *zawiya* and a domed shrine there, where he and all of his descendants were buried.

One day a bird was seen approaching the *zawiya* rapidly, thereby causing the collapse of the building. The builder told Dawud about the occurrence. Dawud then ordered the rebuilding of the *zawiya*. [...] As the task had been completed and the bird approached the building again, Dawud pointed to it. At that moment the bird dropped dead behind the *zawiya*. When brought to him by his disciples at the lodge, it appeared as a man perfect in creation [...]. Dawud covered him in shrouds, prayed for him, and buried him in the shrine. [...] He said: "This is my cousin, Ahmad ibn al-Tayr, a man of the most noble intentions of all. God wished him to be the first to be buried in this shrine."[45]

By the end of the Mamluk period, the cities of Jerusalem and Hebron and their surroundings were dotted with complexes of Sufi lodges and saintly tombs, as evidenced in pilgrimage guides and travelers' accounts. Family and individual tombs were built side by side in successive generations in *zawiya*s or in the cemetery areas outside the cities' gates, clustering around a *wali* whose tomb had become an important focus of pilgrimage. One example relates to the tombs of Ibn Arslan and 'Abd Allah al-Qurashi (d. 590/1194) lying side by side. "Whoever invokes God's name while standing between the graves of Ibn Arslan and al-Qurashi, God will grant all his wishes," records Mujir al-Din.[46]

Sharing the belief that the invocation of God at the *wali*'s tomb is answered and that his *baraka* may be obtained simply by touching the stones over the grave, different segments of society played a role in the proliferation of saintly tombs. They would initiate the construction of new tombs or would attribute existing tombs to a renowned *wali*, whose place of burial remained unknown.[47] As saintly tombs proliferated, they were transformed into public space, the focus of forms of ritual common to the whole of the local communities.

During the Mamluk period, the *wali* became a most prominent figure in the cities of Jerusalem and Hebron and in Muslim urban and rural society as a whole. Shared by all local believers, saint veneration and the practices that grew up around it cut across social boundaries and blurred the distinctions between the so-called "popular" and "elitist" varieties of religion. At the same time, by being open to the active participation of the political authorities, saint worship, if it did not obliterate the barriers between the official and public spheres, at least rendered them bridgeable.

In their pursuit of holiness and of a model of conduct to be followed, Muslim believers generated and nourished an ideal type of saint embodying Shar'i-Sufi norms and values and apt to meet their spiritual and social needs and expectations. Biographers recorded and narrated the stories about the lives and miracles of the *awliya'*, glorifying them as saints and creating a reservoir of saintly figures for future generations. However, only through the localization of the ideal type of Sufi saint could his position as a charismatic figure become established and his commemoration be guaranteed. With regard to Mamluk Jerusalem and Hebron, this process of localization or appropriation of the universally recognized model was manifested in the consolidation of a large following around local *awliya'* and their successors, and in the proliferation of Sufi lodges and tombs throughout the cities and their rural environs. By portraying the life and activities of a Sufi saint within his community, authors of sacred biographies further reasserted his local affinities. Thus, while intensifying the cities' integration into the cosmopolitan world of Islamic piety surrounding saintly figures, the genesis of the Sufi holy man formed a most prominent part in the evolution of devotional Sufism as a focus of local communal life.

Notes

1 For a panoramic review of the prominence of Sufism and sainthood in the entire Muslim world of the late medieval period, see Albert Hourani, *A History of the Arab Peoples* (Cambridge, MA, 1991), pp. 153–7. For the development of visits to the graves of venerated holy persons into a fundamental aspect of Muslim spirituality, see Josef W. Meri, "The Etiquette of Devotion in the Islamic Cult of Saints," in *The Cult of Saints in Late Antiquity and the Middle Ages: Essays on the Contribution of Peter Brown*, James Howard-Johnston and Paul A. Hayward (eds) (Oxford, 1999), pp. 263–86; Richard W. Bulliet, *Islam: The View from the Edge* (New York, 1994), p. 174, notices the sixth/twelfth century as a milestone in this development. The most recent and comprehensive work on the growth of the cult of dead Muslim saints in the late medieval period is Christopher S. Taylor, *In the Vicinity of the Righteous: Ziyāra and the Veneration of Muslim Saints in Late Medieval Egypt* (Leiden (Islamic History and Civilization, Studies and Texts, 32), 1999). Although focusing on Egypt (1200–1500), Taylor provides observations of insight for our understanding of the evolution of the saint phenomenon as a whole. See also his extensive bibliography on this field.

2 Scholarship on Sufism as the theoretical foundation for the phenomena of sainthood is vast. The most recent and comprehensive contribution is Bernd Radtke and John O'Kane, *The Concept of Sainthood in Early Islamic Mysticism: Two Works by al-Hakim al-Tirmidhī* (Richmond, Surrey, 1996). Several recent studies have drawn our attention to Shi'i veneration of saints as a much more central part of religious doctrine and belief than in the Sunni case. Josef W. Meri, *The Cult of Saints Among Muslims and Jews in Medieval Syria* (Oxford, 2002), chapter 3, represents the most recent and extensive discussion of this topic.

3 Fritz Meier, "The Mystic Path," in *The World of Islam: Faith, People, Culture*, Bernard Lewis (ed.) (London, 1992), p. 118, points to this distinction (following the designation of classical Sufism by the eighth/fourteenth century Andalusian scholar Lisan al-Din Ibn al-Khatib as "mysticism of ethical behavior" (*al-tasawwuf al-khuluqi*). On the distinction between the mystical and moral dimensions of Sufism, see also Louis Brenner, "Separate Realities: A Review of Literature on Sufism," *International Journal of African Historical Studies* 5 (1972), p. 645.

4 Peter Brown makes this observation in his own revision of the rise of the holy man in late antiquity. As he himself admits, the models he used converged to attribute to the holy man a greater degree of separateness from his followers than he may actually have possessed; Brown, "The Rise and Function of the Holy Man in Late Antiquity, 1971–1997," *Journal of Early Christian Studies* 6:3 (1998), p. 368.

5 For general remarks on the roles assumed by the Sufi saint beginning in the sixth/twelfth century, see Ira M. Lapidus, *A History of Islamic Societies* (New York, 1988), p. 171. For a vivid picture of his various roles in the particular context of Palestinian rural communities, see Daniella Talmon-Heller, "The Shaykh and the Community: Popular Hanbalite Islam in 12th–13th Century Jabal Nablus and Jabal Qasyūn," *Studia Islamica* 79 (1994), pp. 103–20. See also Daphna Ephrat, *A Learned Society in a Period of Transition: The Sunni 'Ulama' of Eleventh-Century Baghdad* (Albany, 2000), pp. 144–7, for pious and charismatic leaders in the society of fifth/eleventh and early sixth/twelfth century Baghdad.

6 Lately, the sanctity of Jerusalem and its growth as a universal and Islamic pilgrimage center have received renewed scholarly attention. Important contributions include Amikam Elad, *Medieval Jerusalem and Islamic Worship: Holy Places, Ceremonies, Pilgrimage* (Leiden (Islamic History and Civilization, Studies and Texts, 8), 1995); Andreas Kaplony, *The Haram of Jerusalem 324–1099: Temple, Friday Mosque, Area of Spiritual Power* (Stuttgart, 2002).

7 This is in line with recent studies that seek to promote the use of hagiographic material as a valuable source for the study of the evolution and character of sainthood and the religious and social practices surrounding saintly figures within various spatial and temporal frames. For an eloquent discussion of this development in the field of Islamic studies, see Albrecht Hofheinz, *Internalizing Islam: Shaykh Muhammad Majdhūb Scriptural Islam and Local Context in the Early Nineteenth-Century Sudan* (doctoral dissertation, University of Bergen, 1996), vol. 1, pp. 140–4. An important implementation of this approach in the study of late medieval Sufism and sainthood is represented by Denis Gril in his extensive introduction to a hagiographic dictionary dedicated to seventh/thirteenth century Sufi masters; Gril, *La Risāla de Safī al-Dīn ibn al-Mansūr ibn Zāfir: Biographies de maîtres spirituels connus par un cheikh égyptien du VIIᵉ/XIIIᵉ siècle* (Cairo, 1986), pp. 1–79.

8 Mujir al-Din, *al-'Uns al-jalil bi-ta'rikh al-Quds wal-Khalil* (Baghdad, 1995).

9 See Elad, *Medieval Jerusalem*, pp. 65–6, for the sanctification ceremony of the *hajj* and the *'umra* from Jerusalem and the practice of combining the pilgrimage to Mecca with the visit to Jerusalem.

10 On the thriving cosmopolitan world of Islamic religious learning and devotion of the period from the fifth/eleventh century to the rise of the Ottomans, see especially Sam I. Gellens, "The Search for Knowledge in Medieval Muslim Societies: A Comparative Approach," in *Muslim Travellers: Pilgrimage, Migration, and the Religious Imagination*, Dale F. Eickelman and James Piscatori (eds) (London, 1990), pp. 55–63. For particular manifestations, see Joan E. Gilbert, "Institutionalization of Muslim Scholarship and Professionalization of the 'Ulamā' in Medieval Damascus," *Studia Islamica* 32 (1980), pp. 107–8; Éric Geoffroy, *Le Soufisme en Égypte et en Syrie sous les derniers Mamelouks et les premiers Ottomans: orientations spirituelles et enjeux culturels* (Damascus, 1995), pp. 81–2; Ephrat, *A Learned Society*, chapter 2.

11 See Kamal S. Salibi, "The Banū Jamā'a: A Dynasty of Shāfi'ite Jurists in the Mamluk Period," *Studia Islamica* 9 (1958), pp. 97–109.

12 Mujir al-Din, part 2, pp. 150–1. For a fuller biography, see Salibi, "The Banū Jamā'a," pp. 98–9, based on Mujir al-Din and al-Subki, *Tabaqat al-shafi'iyya al-kubra* (Cairo, 1324 AH), vol. 5, pp. 46–7.

13 Mujir al-Din, part 2, p. 169.

14 See Geoffroy, *Soufisme*, p. 216–39, for the origins and spread of the *tariqa*s in Greater Syria.

15 For the many precedents of this conjunction, most famously Abu Nu'aym's *Hilyat al-awliya'* and Hujwiri's *Kashf al-mahjub*, see Jawid A. Mojaddedi, *The Biographical Tradition in Sufism: The tabaqat Genre from al-Sulami to Jami* (Richmond, 2001), chapters 2 and 5.

16 The most recent and comprehensive study of the flourishing of deviant renunciation beginning in the seventh/thirteenth century is represented by A. T. Karamustafa, *God's Unruly Friends: Dervish Groups in the Islamic Middle Period 1200–1500* (Salt Lake City, 1994). For the Jerusalem Qalandariyya, see ibid., pp. 53–4, 100, no. 22; Geoffroy, *Soufisme*, p. 236. And see below on the Qalandari *zawiya* in Jerusalem.

17 Mujir al-Din, part 2, p. 164. See also Ibn Qadi al-Shuhba, *Tabaqat al-shafi'iyya* (Beirut, 1987), vol. 4, no. 683, pp. 300–1.
18 For examples of this blending in Mamluk Cairo, see Jonathan Berkey, *The Transmission of Knowledge in Medieval Cairo: A Social History of Islamic Education* (Princeton, NJ, 1992), pp. 57–9.
19 M. van Berchem, *Matériaux pour un Corpus Inscriptionum Arabicarum, deuxième partie, Syrie du sud, I: Jérusalem, Ville* (Cairo, 1922), 2131–14; al-'Asali, *Ma'ahid al-'ilm fi Bayt al-Maqdis* ('Uman, 1981), pp. 240–1.
20 See especially al-Sakhawi, *al-Daw' al-lami' li-ahl al-qarn al-tasi'* (Cairo, 1353 AH), vol. 1, pp. 282–3. See also Mujir al-Din, part 2, pp. 174–6; al-Nabhani, *Jami' karamat al-awliya'*, 2nd edn (Beirut, 1988), vol. 1, p. 533.
21 Mujir al-Din, part 2, p. 177.
22 For early manifestations of the recurring theme of purity in dietary matters, see Michael Bonner, *Aristocratic Violence and Holy War: Studies in the Jihad and Arab–Byzantine Frontier* (New Haven, CT, 1996), pp. 125–7 (in relation to the famous ascetic Ibrahim Adham, d. 161/777–78).
23 Mujir al-Din, part 2, p. 169.
24 Ibid., pp. 144–5.
25 Ibid., p. 153.
26 Denis Gril makes this point in light of the treatises of *khirqa* composed during the Mamluk period: "Sources manuscrites de l'histoire du soufisme à Dār al-Kutub: un premier bilan," *Annales Islamologiques* 28 (1994), p. 102.
27 Gril, *La Risāla*, p. 72. See also Ira Lapidus' observation that everywhere, from the tenth to the fourteenth centuries, individual Sufis and their followings of disciples and lay believers were the basic unit of Sufism; Lapidus, *A History*, p. 171. Several recent studies have shown that this observation is applicable to later periods as well. Thus, Nehemia Levtzion argues that, up to the eleventh/seventeenth century, most Sufi fraternities were diffusive affiliations, without a central organization, and without strong links between their members: "Eighteenth Century Sufi Brotherhoods: Structural, Organizational and Ritual Changes," in *Islam: Essays on Scripture, Thought and Society*, P. G. Riddell and T. Street (eds) (Leiden, 1997), pp. 147–6. In somewhat similar vein, Albrecht Hofheinz observes that in the Sudan people saw themselves as belonging to a particular brotherhood simply because they regarded a particular person as "their shaykh": Hofheinz, *Internalising Islam*, vol. 1, p. 18. For adherence to the shaykh rather than the *tariqa* as a social organization with regard to the Naqshbandiyya, see Arthur F. Buehler, *Sufi Heirs of the Prophet: The Indian Naqshbandiyya and the Rise of the Mediating Sufi Shaykh* (Columbia, SC, 1998), chapters 5 and 6.
28 al-Sakhawi, vol. 1, p. 282–4.
29 Mujir al-Din, part 2, p. 161. See also al-'Asqalani, *al-Durar al-kamina fi a'yan al-mi'a al-thamina* (Misr, 1966–67), p. 502.
30 al-Sakhawi, vol. 1, p. 286. See also Mujir al-Din, part 2, p. 175, for a slightly different version of the story.
31 See N. Z. Davis' important suggestion on the need to examine the range of people's relations with the sacred and the supernatural, so as not to fragment those practices, beliefs, and institutions which for different segments of the community of believers constitute a whole; "Some Tasks and Themes in the Study of Popular Religion," in *The Pursuit of Holiness*, C. Trinkhaus (ed.), (Leiden, 1974), pp. 312–3.
32 Mujir al-Din, part 2, p. 161; al-'Asqalani, p. 502.
33 Ibid., part 2, pp. 173–4.
34 Ibid., pp. 146–7.
35 Ibid., p. 147.
36 Ibid.
37 Ibid.
38 Ibid., pp. 148–9.

39 Thus, for example, *al-Nahwiyya zawiya*, an early seventh/thirteenth century establishment, made provisions for twenty-five students and their shaykh, with the stipulation that they would receive instruction in grammar and affiliate with the Hanafi school of law. See Mujir al-Din, part 2, p. 64; al-'Asali, *Ma'ahid al-'ilm*, p. 104. Several shaykhs of *al-Bistamiyya zawiya* taught in al-Salahiyya madrasa. One such was Shihab al-Din al-Halabi al-Bistami. See Mujir al-Din, part 2, p. 197.

40 Geoffroy makes this observation in *Soufisme*, p. 168. For the individual character of the pattern of establishing and endowing Sufi lodges and educational institutions in general, one governed by the considerations of particular local governors rather than the political endeavors of the Mamluk state, see Berkey, *The Transmission of Knowledge*, pp. 12, 58, 62, 129–30, 132. See also Leonor Fernandes, *The Evolution of the Sufi Institution in Mamluk Egypt: the Khanqah* (Berlin, 1988), pp. 16–32.

41 Mujir al-Din, part 2, pp. 149–50. For 'Ali al-Baka, see also Ibn Mulaqqin, *Tabaqat al-awliya'* (Cairo, 1973), no. 146, pp. 461–2.

42 For the establishment of the Bistamiyya in Jerusalem, see especially Geoffroy, *Soufisme*, pp. 232–3.

43 On al-Asadabadi, see Mujir al-Din, part 2, p. 162. For fuller biographical details, see Geoffroy, *Soufisme*, p. 233. For al-Safi, see Mujir al-Din, part 2, p. 157.

44 Geoffroy, Soufisme, pp. 235–6; Karamustafa, *God's Unruly Friends*, p. 54.

45 Mujir al-Din, part 2, pp. 147–8.

46 Ibid., p.175.

47 See the story about the great tomb in Mamila cemetery, which the people (*al-nas*) imagined to have been the grave of al-Wasiti, a revered wali to whom they ascribed many miraculous deeds. Mujir al-Din, part 2, p. 152.

2 The prince who favored the desert

Fragmentary biography of al-Nasir Ahmad (d. 745/1344)

Joseph Drory

The fate of youthful heirs to a powerful ruler is, by and large, precarious. In different cultures the same phenomenon recurs. Young princes, each born with a silver spoon in his mouth, their paths to supremacy seemingly assured, free from the need to earn their way into the pinnacles of power, are repeatedly deposed. Moreover, even when they show no indications of ambition and were ready to give up their status, they are still considered to be dangerous, lest someday they return to authority, or become instruments used by rivals to gain political control. Biblical, Roman, Byzantine or early Moslem chronicles of sovereigns' sons abound with stories of deliberate dismissal, at times brutal, at other times even mortal.

The political state of affairs which unfolded after thirty years of tight grip by the stern Mamluk Sultan al-Nasir Muhammad was no exception. A brief look at the career of al-Nasir Ahmad, one of the eight feeble sons of al-Nasir Muhammad who ruled Egypt, often quite nominally, during the years 740/1340–782/1380, may shed light on various aspects of the Mamluk polity, which has offered continual scope for Michael Winter's scientific curiosity and activity. His account exposes court life, military norms, transitory factions, bonds of loyalty, and personal aspirations of ambitious officers typical of the Mamluk sultanate in a less studied period. Although outwardly a variation on the theme of unfit inheritors, the story of al-Nasir Ahmad, rich in unprecedented peculiarities, unfolds slightly differently. It, however, reveals a wide range of human facets and unusual behavior, which reads like a thriller.

During his lifetime, al-Nasir Muhammad often sent his son Shihab al-Din Ahmad (born in 716/1316), even when he was a child, to the desert citadel and town of Karak, to accustom him to a true, knightly upbringing.[1] Karak was no random choice. From Ayyubid times, and more intensely under al-Nasir himself, in different phases of his political career, Karak was deemed a place for refuge and respite. During the Mamluk period, because of its relative remoteness, Karak became a punitive castle for delinquent officers, an unpretentious *niyaba* for elderly statesmen, or a private school for princes surrounded by a friendly and loyal population where the skills of chivalry could be acquired and practiced.

Only a few princes enjoyed such favor, and for shorter periods than Ahmad. It may be noted that Ahmad was called to Cairo only rarely and under special circumstances.[2] Spending so many years in Karak helped him cultivate trusting relations with its citizens and tribes. It also imbued him with affection for Karak (*mahabbat al-karak*).³ On the other hand, frequent absence from Cairo was bound to create a hostile or, at the very least, an unfriendly image of that city, its people and its establishment.

Shortly before al-Nasir Muhammad's death, he discussed the question of inheritance with two of his senior generals, who were trusted to implement his will. Two young sons were considered likely to succeed him. Abu Bakr who was favored (and confirmed) by the Sultan and by Qawsun, his son-in-law and trusted officer, and Ahmad whose candidacy was backed by Bashtak, another influential and haughty officebearer in the Mamluk court. Qawsun tried to further the cause of Abu Bakr, his nominee, or more accurately to forestall probable opposition by arguing that the father chose the son whom he knew best (*huwa awsa li-man huwa ahbaru bihi min awladihi*).⁴ As for Ahmad, he, in fact, was considered by al-Nasir Muhammad unqualified to rule.⁵ One is tempted to suppose that Ahmad agreed with his father's verdict.

In the turbulent days immediately after al-Nasir's death (in Dhu al-Hijja 741/May–June 1341) the ruler-designate, Abu Bakr, was proclaimed Sultan and given the title of his grandfather: al-Mansur. However, the real power was coveted by skilled and experienced generals of al-Nasir (*al-umara' al-kibar* or *al-akabir*) involved in parties, aspirations, struggles, strifes, coalitions, and mutual trials. Abu Bakr, less than 20 years old, was meant to be merely a puppet. When he tried to voice his own will, the veteran generals, led by Qawsun, were keen to lead him astray. Qawsun, a favorite of the late ruler, who had earned his credibility and trust and married one of his daughters, intended to take the office of "organizer of the state" (*mudabbir al-dawla*).⁶ He was concerned lest he be imprisoned by a too self-reliant Abu Bakr. Perhaps just an excuse, in any case it prompted Qawsun to detain Abu Bakr (on 21 Safar 742/5 August 1341) on the invented pretext of frivolous behavior. Abu Bakr was sent, together with six of his brothers, to distant Qus,⁷ where he was executed in Jumada II of that year/November 1341. In Abu Bakr's stead Qawsun, now the strong man in Egypt (who had already engineered the detention of his rival Bashtak) declared the 5-year-old Kuchuk as Sultan, while taking the function of custodian (*wasi*) and operating as vice-gerent, literally "substitute" (*na'ib al-sultan* or *al-saltana*).⁸

The leadership of Qawsun was far from being approved as a matter of course. Over the eight decades since the emergence of Mamluk rule, the Mamluk polity had come to regard ability and virtue, rather than origin or inheritance, as the key factors in gaining respect, obedience, command, and predominance: thus, other officers were driven to try their chances. On the other hand, this political practice, unique to the Mamluk system, found opponents within other Mamluk circles who adhered to and advocated the traditional inheritance through family relations as a decisive factor in selecting rulers. Even the more competent officers had to present credentials of long established descent. Qawsun, able as he was, must have taken the probability of disagreement into account.

The deportation of al-Nasir's son gave Qawsun's potential opponents a sharp weapon. The staunchest opposition to Qawsun was voiced by the ruler of northern Syria Aleppo, Tashtamur al-Saqi, nicknamed Hummus Ahdar. He maintained (in a letter to Qutlubugha al-Fakhri, his intimate associate) that as devoted servants to al-Nasir Muhammad – and he, indeed, proved to be a faithful Mamluk of the dead ruler[9] – they were forbidden to depose the son whom the master had chosen as his successor (*kayfa yaliqu bina, ma'shar mamalikihi, an nakhla'a ibnahu al-wahid min mulkihi alladhi nassa 'alayhi wa-qarrarahu*).[10] Other Mamluks in Egypt, disliking Qawsun, expressed similar sentiments. "We are the Sultan's servants, assets of his treasury. How can we abandon the son of our master and serve someone else?" (*nahnu mamalik al-sultan mushtara malihi kayfa natruku ibna ustadhina wa-nakhdumu ghayrahu*).[11]

Qawsun who had no scruples about sending the immediate heir al-Mansur Abu Bakr and his other brothers, hence theoretical contenders, to the southern town of Qus, after less than two months in power, found no grounds to release the elder brother Ahmad from the same fate. He recalled him to Egypt from Karak.[12] In reply, Ahmad, aware of the looming danger, stated his conditions. On 29 Rabi' I 742/12 September 1341, he responded that he would come only if the chief leaders of the state appeared in Karak where he could obtain their oath of allegiance (to obey his orders, let alone not harm him – assurance against the fate that had befallen his brother) and if his detained brothers were sent to the relatively nearby Karak rather than isolated Qus.[13]

Reasonable as these terms appear, it is more likely that Ahmad put them forward knowing that they would be rejected (so that he would have no need to comply) or in order to win time or some understanding among other decision-makers in Egypt. In the meantime, Ahmad, encouraged by the support of the people of Karak, sent letters to the governors of Syria wherein he described his fears.[14] Ahmad asked for refuge, reported his unwillingness to depart for Cairo, and held himself to be extremely unfortunate (*azhara lahum al-maskana al-za'ida*).[15] Several governors were touched (*raqqa lahu*) by his letters. However, some of these letters eventually reached Qawsun, the least desirable recipient.

When Ahmad, harboring no illusions and not given sufficient guarantees, failed to arrive, Qawsun asked his officers how to proceed and was advised by the ruler of Damascus to force him to come by besieging Karak.[16] This suggestion was eventually accepted.

The idea was bizarre enough: applying military might to force a designated ruler to leave his desert home and move to the palace in the capital. The sovereign was to be coerced to govern. One can easily judge what the ramifications of such a move might have been, in terms of the Sultan's authority and Qawsun's might, had it succeeded.

Qawsun dispatched a military mission to seize Ahmad. The troops, sent on 25 Rabi' II 742/7 October 1341, were led by Qutlubugha al-Fakhri, one of the ablest Mamluks of the late Sultan,[17] who at that period favored Qawsun.[18] It is recorded that this Fakhri was the only officer ready to carry out the task, something that everyone knew entailed a grave and gloomy future for the offspring of a prominent Sultan.

After some twenty days in the bleak, unpleasant climate of southern Jordan, faced with difficulties in provisioning his soldiers and harassed by the locals of Karak, Fakhri changed his mind (or at least his conduct).[19] Instead of fulfilling his orders, which he knew would definitely be followed by Ahmad's being sent into exile, and Qawsun's augmenting his influence and authority, he terminated his blockade. As a direct result, Fakhri unconditionally recognized Ahmad as Sultan,[20] disregarding the current uncommon situation. Fakhri was probably responsible for granting Ahmad the honorific al-Nasir, which he used in correspondence.[21] Since there was a reigning Sultan, al-Ashraf Kuchuk, in Cairo watched over by Qawsun, Fakhri's recognition of Ahmad was deemed mutinous, an explicit protest against existing legal order.

The mastermind behind this move was Tashtamur, the governor of Aleppo. He exploited his moral inspiration and influence to change Fakhri's allegiance and political adherence. Tashtamur, a close associate of Fakhri whom he regarded as his brother and whose fate he shared[22] – wrote to him, as mentioned earlier, that Mamluk bonds of loyalty to master and progeny are inflexibly enduring. Consequently, both of Qawsun's undertakings, removing one son, Abu Bakr, from what his father had destined for him and besieging another, Ahmad, were contradictory to the Mamluk ethos.[23]

Disapproval of Fakhri's surprising new declaration of loyalty centered mainly in Damascus, ruled by Altunbugha al-Salihi (formerly the governor of Aleppo, Gaza and after the arrest of Tankiz, the strong man of Damascus). Altunbugha supported Qawsun, and kept faithfully to this line until his final days. It was Altunbugha who encouraged the confused Qawsun to enforce Ahmad's obedience by besieging Karak.

The Syrian commanders were divided. One faction, composed of Tashtamur, Fakhri and other Damascene amirs, supported the "best legal" successor, though he was taking refuge outside the capital; another, consisting of Altunbugha and the governors of Tripoli, Safad and Hums, favored the existing power based on Cairo which commanded the resources of the state. From the latter's (de facto) point of view, the former (de jure) faction was intolerable.

The political question of the rightful heir to al-Nasir Muhammad was the key issue at stake in 742/1341–42 and divided the state's ablest senior officers. Qawsun, who was informed by Shati, the Bedouin leader of central Jordan, of his general Fakhri's betrayal, did not hesitate to let Altunbugha try and diminish the danger from the supporters of Ahmad. Thus, Altunbugha received permission to lead a campaign against Tashtamur, the governor who disagreed with Qawsun's treatment of the children of the previous Sultan, and who threatened to go to Karak in order to help his "master's son" (*ibn ustadhihi*).[24] Assisted by other Syrian rulers (Aruqtay in Tripoli, Aslam in Safad, the governor of Hums), Altunbugha headed on 5 Jumada II 741/26 November 1340 with his army to northern Syria, with the aim of routing Tashtamur. Tashtamur estimated that there were only a few loyal Mamluk supporters at hand and that his military power would fail in a confrontation. Disregarding the inconvenience, Tashtamur left Aleppo and sought refuge among the Rum Seljuqs in Asia Minor. He first headed towards Abulustayn (Elbistan), then to Qaysariyya (Qayseri).[25]

The derision of local castle-rulers along the route of flight provided Tashtamur with further evidence that he had no officers to rely upon and consequently he was unlikely to prove a match for Altunbugha. A further moral blow to Tashtamur was the hesitant stand of Tuquzdamur, the ruler of Hamat (of whose position Tashtamur had received a positive report[26]), due to feebleness more than out of political conviction.

Damascus, left without its regular army, was the chance Fakhri was waiting for. He entered the city, was joined by some deserting officers of Altunbugha who had remained behind, proclaimed (*da'a*) Ahmad as Sultan, swore the meagre military forces to loyalty to him, and established a bureaucratic administration.[27] In a nearby region, the governor of Gaza succeeded in seizing Qawsun's profitable sugar factory in the Jordan valley (Qasr Mu'in al-Din) harming both his finances and his morale.[28] As for financing his defiance, Fakhri used some methods which were not accepted: taxation ahead of schedule, confiscating orphans' resources (thus drawing the justified protest of the famous Qadi Taqi al-Din al-Subki) and extorting money from wealthy merchants.[29] Penalized officers (*battalun*) were permitted to return to military service, and were given financial support.[30]

Fakhri's troops waited at the crucial pass of Khan Lajin, north of the Syrian capital,[31] which Altunbugha, regardless of success, must inevitably cross on his return to Damascus. Sympathetic Bedouins were posted on the mountain ridges.[32] This strategic action proved to be a greater achievement than the conquest of (mostly empty) Damascus and was to reap fruit for Fakhri in the future.

Altunbugha reached Aleppo, plundered the property of the fleeing Tashtamur, and then headed back to Damascus, where Fakhri was on the alert. At a certain juncture, it seemed that a skirmish was unavoidable, but the army of Altunbugha, six times larger than Fakhri's, refused to fight.[33] Their refusal was followed by massive desertion (*mukhamara*) of officers to Fakhri (together with the able Bedouin chief of the Al Fadl, Sulayman b. Muhanna).[34] Altunbugha evaded a clash and found a way to flee southward to Gaza and prepare for a reunion, however humble, with Qawsun, his patron in Egypt.[35] Altunbugha's failure hastened the downfall of Qawsun's regime.

The defeat (or flight) of Altunbugha enabled Fakhri to enter Damascus for a second time, this time as a true victor. Reassured by jubilant popular approval, Fakhri renewed his preparations to install Ahmad in the sultanate. Damascus formally recognized Ahmad as Sultan.[36] His name was mentioned in the sermons,[37] coins bearing his name were struck, and royal emblems were prepared for an official procession to Cairo. Local Syrian governors, of Gaza,[38] Safad,[39] Hamat and Ba'albak supported Fakhri, the authorized governor of Damascus. Ahmad, though from afar, bestowed upon Fakhri the right to appoint governors in Syria, and named him viceroy of Syria (*kafil al-Sham*).[40] As for the call to leave Karak and come to Egypt, or at least to Damascus as a base before Egypt, Ahmad made it clear that without Tashtamur, the trustworthy mind behind this endeavor, there was no chance of his moving. We should not accept the pejorative interpretation expressed for example by Safadi that this was an excuse[41] for Ahmad not to leave Karak knowing how far and inconvenient it would be for Tashtamur to return from Asia Minor. Ahmad might be induced to insist on Tashtamur's arrival as a pre-requisite for his own carefully calculated travel, due to Tashtamur's approach and stance in favoring and sympathizing with Ahmad's anxieties and in defying Qawsun's methods. With Tashtamur at his side, Ahmad gained the self-confidence necessary to deal with the intriguing Egyptian Mamluk factions. From his refuge in Anatolian Qayseri Tashtamur was called to return safely to Damascus, an interim station before the final goal, the citadel of Cairo.[42] The political arena for Ahmad and his supporters now appeared brighter than before. Did Ahmad share the same assessment? To the Damascene notables who came to Karak to invite him to Cairo, and to be their approved sultan, Ahmad replied that this call was a ruse (*makida*) to arrest him so as to deliver him to Qawsun.[43]

Events in Egypt were no less stormy. Opposition to Qawsun increased. His loyal supporters were attacked, accusations were raised against him as aiming to get control of the state and of squandering money in order to cement his seizure of power. Soldiers poured into his stables and stole his horses. The mob in Cairo's streets demanded his downfall, and plundered his wealth. The fate of his (700) Mamluks was no less bitter.[44] Finally, beleaguered in the citadel, Qawsun surrendered (at the end of Rajab 741/December 1340). He was sent to Alexandria where he was detained and in Dhu al-Qaʿda of that year/April 1341 was killed, together with Altunbugha who remained his ally to the bitter end.[45]

Another delegation to Ahmad consisted of Egyptian officers (Jankali b. Baba, Baybars al-Ahmadi and Qimari Amir Shikar), bringing the pleasing tidings at the end of Rajab 741/December 1340 of Qawsun's political elimination. But their visit was of no avail.[46] Ahmad sent them back, two to Gaza and the third to the region of Safita (either Tall al-Safi, the Crusader's Blanche Garde, or al-Safi at the southern edge of the Dead Sea),[47] there to await further orders.

In Egypt, al-Ashraf Kuchuk, the infant Sultan, was deprived of his fictitious title and on 2 Shaʿban 741/21 January 1341, the sultanate of al-Nasir Ahmad was proclaimed in Egypt – for the time being an empty announcement. Fakhri, the lord of Syria, according to Ahmad's explicit definition, remained in Damascus awaiting the arrival of his Sultan. Now, when Qawsun was arrested Fakhri assumed he and Ahmad could move together in a glorious military procession decorated with symbols of royalty, as befitted a newly crowned Sultan. He was disappointed and enraged to find out that the meeting place had been changed to Gaza.[48] In low spirits he turned to Gaza, only to discover the generals, but no young Ahmad, for whom such a great persuasive effort had been orchestrated.[49]

Even when Ahmad's most esteemed supporters, the notables, judges, scribes, and officers who lingered in Gaza, dispatched letters via envoys urging him to hasten, Ahmad kept to his usual, doubting style. "It is impossible for the messengers to see him," was the formal answer given by the guards at Karak. Finally, a communication arrived saying that there was no need to wait in Gaza and that Ahmad would make his way, on his own terms, to Cairo.[50] The prince who systematically refused to approach Egypt, probably out of intense fear of being deceived, distrusted even his own well wishers, and found it difficult to rid himself of his doubts.[51] One gets the impression that Ahmad would scarcely have labeled Fakhri and his collaborators benefactors. Twenty days of Fakhri's siege in the service of the "evil-doer" Qawsun, who did not particularly favor Ahmad, could not suddenly be forgotten. The anxieties of the desert prince, deprived of a significant household in the seat of government, seem justified and understandable. The furious Fakhri, whose rage could not have been pacified easily, must have heard of Ahmad's behavior and thought over the aptitude of his candidate.[52]

Though declared Sultan already in early Shaʿban 741/January 1341 (after Qawsun's capitulation, and the release of Kuchuk), Ahmad took to the road only in Ramadan/February.[53] On 28 Ramadan 741/17 March 1341, the veiled Ahmad, dressed in Bedouin fashion (*ziyy al-ʿurban*), chose to cross the desert in the space of ten days (certainly by the Hajj road and not through Gaza) with a tiny group of ten people and to enter the capital, where he was to serve as successor to his all-powerful father. A declaration made by Ahmad accounts for his repeated negative responses: "I was not yearning for royalty, and found that place [i.e. Karak] adequate" (*ana ma kuntu atatalla'u ila al-mulk, wa-kuntu qani'an bi-dhalika al-makan*).[54]

The *'Id al-fitr* ceremonies which followed Ahmad's arrival are painted in the same cautious colors which had characterized Ahmad's lack of trust towards Egypt and the Egyptians. Amirs were not allowed to ascend to the citadel to greet their sultan and guards were stationed to deter too close an approach. The customary royal feast (*simat*) was not served. Contrary to tradition Ahmad did not show up at the festival prayer. Only among his men from Karak did Ahmad feel secure. They provided for all his social needs.[55]

Early speculations regarding Ahmad's suitability were expressed by Aydughmush, a high Egyptian officer, responsible for the royal horses. Suggestions to dismiss the asocial sultan were ruled out by Tashtamur, the officer most devoted to Ahmad's cause.[56] On 10 (or 12) Shawwal 741/29 or 31 March 1341, allegiance was officially sworn to Ahmad by the functionaries of the state, judges, the caliph, governors, bureaucrats, and prominent officers.[57] The 26-year-old Ahmad was publicly enthroned as Sultan of Egypt, the third son to inherit from his father.[58] But his elusive behavior, his avoiding being seen in public, an extreme consequence of what had befallen some of his relatives, kept continuing. Amirs were able to see him only twice a week, for no more than an hour. Outwardly, the state operated as usual. The main chancellery issued orders, made appointments, conducted correspondence and allocated money, while the royal court welcomed diplomatic missions from abroad.[59]

One subject which received special attention during the short period of Ahmad's stay in Egypt was the avenging of the misdeeds wrought by Qawsun, Ahmad's hated enemy, who was languishing in custody in Alexandria. Qawsun's wealth was confiscated. Legal proceedings were opened against the governor of Qus, who admitted that he had executed Abu Bakr (Ahmad's brother) under implied orders from Qawsun, an apology that did not save him from his own execution on 22 Shawwal 741/10 April 1341.[60] And – though Ahmad's direct involvement is not stated – Qawsun and Altunbugha were killed in prison.[61]

Ahmad also took the trouble to assign functionaries to the main offices. Especially annoying was his fondness for his unsuitable "team" from Karak. Their performance reinforced the local citizens' fears. These appointments were totally arbitrary and were more harmful than beneficial. They aggravated the bad feelings which the Egyptians fostered towards their new "excessively distrustful" and withdrawn sultan.[62] In any event, the key figure during Ahmad's sultanate was not an unknown from Karak but a man who had been famous since the previous decade. This was Tashtamur, who became the pitiable hero of Ahmad's reign.

At the beginning of the year, when Ahmad was besieged in Karak, it was Tashtamur who sent a letter of reprimand to Qawsun for instigating that shameful operation. Tashtamur was the man who convinced Fakhri to stop the blockade and to recognize Ahmad's right to rule, risking his name and reputation as a loyal officer (to Qawsun) and perhaps his career and life if the whole move had miscarried. Tashtamur was ready to travel from his northern principality in Aleppo to help save Ahmad when he was surrounded in Karak. He later went into exile in Anatolia when the governor of Damascus arranged a punitive delegation to his town. In all of these activities Tashtamur operated with commitment to the memory and legacy of his master, regardless of reward. This behavior suited someone who had served for ten years under al-Nasir, when Tashtamur, the ultimate Mamluk, gradually acquired that ruler's hard-to-win confidence. For the office of vice-gerent there was no candidate more suitable than Tashtamur. And yet, as *na'ib al-saltana* Tashtamur committed so many mistakes and behaved so recklessly that, within a short time, he paved the way to his own end.

A host of allegations were directed against Tashtamur. The *na'ib al-saltana* contradicted the sultan (*mu'aradat al-sultan*), cancelled his orders, had a patronizing attitude (*taraffu'*) towards officers and soldiers, ignored the amirs' recommendations and treated them impolitely. Furthermore, Tashtamur affirmed orders given by the sultan selectively, allowed petitions to the sultan to be delivered only in his presence and restricted the usually favoured trainees of the regime (*al-mamalik al-sultaniyya*). In one case Tashtamur rudely tore an honorary robe bestowed upon one of the amirs, apparently because it was conferred without his knowledge or consent. The vice-gerent promulgated new regulations, for example forbidding the amirs to enter the palace escorted by their mamluks. Ironically, this innovation facilitated Tashtamur's imprisonment at the end of Dhu al-Qa'da 741/May 1341, a move initiated by Ahmad himself, with the broad consent of angry, insulted and frustrated officers.[63] After nearly fifty days of mismanagement, Tashtamur was imprisoned. His days were numbered. So too were Ahmad's. The amir who had crowned him was the cause of his ruin.

In trying to elucidate Tashtamur's destructive and exasperating conduct, one can easily see it as over-devotion to the cause. Neither personal ambition nor any need to win respectability motivated Tashtamur, but rather empathy with Ahmad's anxieties and loyalty to his father's wishes, so recently abused by covetous amirs. Chronicles report only his critics' views, whereas his own remain unheard. Tashtamur's wish to supply a safety net for his prince provided many foes.

Immediately after the arrest of Tashtamur, other Mamluk amirs rushed to seize his comrade Fakhri, the ruler of Damascus, who had previously left Egypt. Ahmad, probably on his own initiative, instructed the governor of Gaza to guarantee Fakhri's confinement. News that he was already being trailed reached Fakhri in Salihiyya, east of the eastern Delta. He evaded arrest in his march along the Mediterranean coast of the Sinai but failed to reach Baysan. Leaving Jenin he was tempted to ask for shelter at the temporary encampment of Aydughmush, governor of Aleppo,[64] in 'Ayn Jalut, a station before the Jordan river crossing on the way to safe Damascus. The governor of Safad, Baybars al-Ahmadi, who had preceded Fakhri in the post, left his hilly town to join the fleeing governor of Damascus but arrived behind schedule.[65] Aydughmush proved an unreliable host. Pleasant at the start, he later seized Fakhri, to extradite him to Ahmad.[66]

One may reasonably ask why Ahmad behaved so ungratefully toward Fakhri, the man who labored arduously to bring him to power, with whom Ahmad had signed a contract of reconciliation, and who did not provoke the veteran Egyptian officers. A likely reason would be that Ahmad saw Fakhri as the man who forced him to leave his peaceful castle and compelled him to undertake the duties of rule for which he had little inclination. Fakhri was guilty of changing Ahmad's isolationist plans – for which he had to pay a bitter price. One might also suggest that political experience had taught Ahmad not to allow kingmakers too significant an authority.[67] The fate of Tashtamur offers further evidence for this conjecture.

A few days after the arrest of the chief rulers of Egypt and Syria, on 2 or 3 Dhu al-Hijja/19 or 20 May 1341, Ahmad was taking significant steps to leave Egypt. He collected a massive amount of his father's livestock (horses, cattle, sheep, poultry, birds of prey, and exotic animals), fleeced the state treasury, emptied chests of jewels, stole precious stones from his father's wealthy concubines, appropriated regalia of sovereignty (parasol [*qubba*], dagger [*nimjah*], and saddle-covering [*ghashiya*]) and removed riding accessories from the royal stables.[68] Ahmad was accompanied by his noteworthy prisoner Tashtamur, who was later joined by Fakhri after he was captured in the Esdraelon valley, and two major administrators: the inspector-general of the army, Shihab al-Din b. Abi al-Rakb (better known by his title *Jamal al-Kufat*) and the chief scribe, 'Ali b. Fadl Allah, a member of the renowned al-'Umari family. The group of Karakis who had previously escorted him to Egypt was also to depart with him. As his deputy governor Ahmad named Aqsunqur al-Salari, who as governor of Gaza several months before had lent him a helping hand. He was directed to confiscate the fortune of the two prominent prisoners, Tashtamur and Fakhri, and transfer it to Karak.[69] Ahmad, traveling at a record speed via the desert route, arrived in six days at Karak on 8 Dhu al-Hijja 742/14 May 1342.[70] The idea behind his absconding to Karak was not to give up the monarchy but rather to start ruling from Karak, the only place where he felt secure. Nothing attests to that aim better than Ahmad's wish to take the Caliph, a living emblem of royalty, from Cairo with him.[71] He managed to install him for some weeks in Gaza, as an interim station.[72]

In Karak Ahmad continued to act as a ruling sultan. To Egypt he sent written as well as oral orders, indirectly, via a Karaki mediator. There they reached the chief scribe who phrased them according to procedure, and they were then sent on to their destination. Correspondence with Syrian provinces followed the same pattern. Envoys from abroad wishing to deliver letters to Ahmad had to relay them through a mediator. Direct contact was strictly avoided.

Frequent calls from Egypt for Ahmad to come back, since political questions could scarcely be dealt with by what amounted to a vacancy in the rulership, were met with a deaf ear. Typical of Ahmad's perception of duty is his reply to the request of leading Egyptian politicians to move from Karak: "If I am the Sultan, let no one be superior to me (*in kuntu ana al-sultan fa-la ya'tamir 'alayya ahad*). I dominate Syria, Egypt is under my command. Wherever I choose to settle, so be it (*al-sham li wa-misr li ayyahuma shi'tu aqamtu bihi*)[73] [As for the needs of the state] I have appointed a deputy to fulfill the needs of the residents (*wa-qad aqamtu na'ib^an li-qada' hawa'ij al-ra'iyya*)";[74] or in other words: "I stay wherever I desire (*innani qa'id fi mawdi' ashtahi*).[75] Whenever I wish I will return to you (*ayya waqt aradtu ahduru ilaykum*)."[76]

On the other hand, Ahmad's unwarranted absence from Egypt noticeably diminished his authority. When he sent orders to Damascus to arrest Baybars al-Ahmadi, the former ruler of Safed who had aroused his suspicion, the local officers hesitated to comply with them. Baybars himself is quoted as declaring that, had Ahmad stayed in Egypt, he would have respected his directives, but not so as long as he resided in

Karak and was rumored to have committed misdeeds (*afa'il*), which may have been an allusion to political executions as well as to sexual decadence.[77]

In Karak, Ahmad ruthlessly executed his two prominent officers Tashtamur and Fakhri.[78] It is suggested that he did it out of rage or as punishment for these amirs who had compelled him to leave his secure shelter at Karak and risk political adventure, all of which was far from his natural inclinations and caused him trouble with the Egyptian politicians who saw him as a potential candidate for the sultanate. In Ahmad's eyes, execution was not too brutal a punishment for such misconduct. Nevertheless, public opinion viewed these executions not only as appalling but also as a sign of Ahmad's ingratitude, and they helped to reduce Ahmad's credentials and legality.[79]

In his absence, the Egyptian counselling officers (*arbab al-hall wal-'aqd* or *ashab al-mashwara*) chose another of al-Nasir Muhammad's sons as a sultan, this time al-Salih Isma'il (on 20 or 22 Muharram 743/25 or 27 June 1342). The citizens of Damascus, formerly Ahmad's supporters, after learning of his harsh behavior, also turned their backs on him. Though stripped of his royal title, Ahmad most likely remained satisfied in his beloved castle, among his favorite population, with familiar customs, hobbies, climate, and daily routine. However, even though he lacked all ambition, while in Karak he remained a menace, at least theoretically, lest he should return to Egypt, as his father had done in 709/1310. Even if he remained in Karak, some other contenders might manipulate his title and credentials to promote their cause in the Mamluk capital. No Egyptian politician could rule out that possibility.

The time, energy, and resources the state had to devote to eliminating the threat represented by Ahmad exceeded any positive contribution made by him during his time in power. This is reflected in the space allocated to the topic in the chronicles. Ahmad as an ex-sultan who throughout his short career had preferred not to leave Karak, still posed a more acute problem for Mamluk officialdom than when he was in power.

For more than two years after his enforced resignation in Muharram 743/June 1342, the Mamluk leadership did their utmost to bring Ahmad's supposed menace to an end. No fewer than seven military expeditions (*tajrida*) were sent to Karak for that assignment. These *tajarid*, each lasting several months, involved skilled military officers from Egypt, at times reinforced by associates from Damascus. Different strategies were tried, including communicating with the local Arab tribes, otherwise friendly to Ahmad, to gain their support. The expenditures for this project were huge, and covered various types of participants, soldiers and civilians alike.[80] The abortive sieges cost some officers their jobs. Only in 745/1344 was the aim finally achieved. With the help of a local citizen who defected to the government's side and knew the weak points of Ahmad's defense, the soldiers managed to enter the city and then to hit the wall of the fortress accurately. This enabled a squad of soldiers to penetrate and capture the reluctant yet exhausted Sultan (on 22 Safar 745/ 4 July 1344).[81] The soldiers arrested him, but still paid him respect. Ahmad, injured and notorious for his mistrust, refused even then to eat what he was offered by Egyptian soldiers, and would only eat from the hands of one of the few remaining loyalists.[82] It was his heir in office, the Sultan Salih Isma'il, who on his own decision (on 4 Rabi' I 745/16 July 1344), sent a mercenary to kill his half-brother clandestinely.[83] Ahmad's long-haired head was brought to the citadel in Egypt where it caused a sensation.

The judgment of historians on Ahmad is far from flattering. Ibn Iyas (d. 930/1524) writes that when he came to power he was expected to be a victorious lion (*layth ghalib*) or a luminous meteor (*shihab thaqib*) but after the disappointment he caused, people named him a crazy teacher (*mu'allim majnun*).[84] Ibn Hajar (d. 853/1449)[85] charges him with mismanaging (*sayyi' al-tadbir*) and with being constantly preoccupied with entertainment and drinking (*kathir al-lahw wal-inhimak fi al-shurb*)[86] although Safadi, his contemporary (d. 765/1363), portrays him as a person who caused harm to people's fortunes, religious values and souls.[87] Ibn Taghribirdi (d. 875/1470), deems Ahmad the worst of al-Nasir Muhammad's sons in conduct or behaviour (*sira*), to which frivolity (*khiffa*) and thoughtlessness (*taysh*) are to be appended.[88] Maqrizi (d. 845/1441), instead of stating his own assessment, cites al-Nasir Muhammad's warning to his eldest son, Ahmad: "Let him not enter Egypt ... for he will be a ground for the ruin of the monarchy (*sabab li-kharab al-mamlaka*)."[89]

The brief story of Ahmad mirrors the Mamluk state in the confused days following the death of one of its most forceful rulers, al-Nasir Muhammad. The vicissitudes of a prince who in under a hundred days changed from being invited to accept the monarchy to a detested public enemy reveal a sad son of a king, doomed to obligations for which he showed little taste and which he sought hopelessly to fulfil in his own uncompromising manner.

List of abbreviations

A'yan al-'Asr Khalil ibn Aybak al-Safadi (d. 764/1362), *A'yan al-'asr wa-a'wan al-qasr*, (ed.) A. Abu Zayd *et al.*, 6 vols, Beirut and Damascus, 1998.

Dhahabi Muhammad b. Ahmad al-Dhahabi, Muhammad b. 'Ali al-Husaini (d. 765/1363), *Min dhuyul al-'ibar*, (ed.) Muhammad Rashad 'Abd al-Muttalib, Kuwait, n.d.

Durar Shihab al-Din Ahmad b. 'Ali Ibn Hajar al-'Asqalani (d. 852/1448), *al-Durar al-kamina fi a'yan al-mi'a al-thamina*, (ed.) 'Abd al-Warith Muhammad 'Ali, Beirut 1997.

Ibn Iyas Shihab al-Din Muhammad b. Ahmad Ibn Iyas (d. 930/1523), *Bada'i' al-zuhur fi waqa'i' al-duhur*, (ed.) Mohammad Mustafa, Wiesbaden 1960–75.

Ibn Kathir 'Imad al-Din Isma'il b. 'Umar (d. 774/1372), *al-Bidaya wal-nihaya*, vol. 14, Beirut 1986.

Manhal Jamal al-Din Yusuf ibn Taghribirdi (d. 874/1469), *al-Manhal al-safi wal-mustawfi ba'da al-wafi*, (ed.) M. M. Amin, vol. 2, Cairo 1984.

Muqaffa Taqi al-Din Ahmad b. 'Ali al-Maqrizi (d. 845/1441), *Kitab al-muqaffa al-kabir*, (ed.) M. al-Ya'laoui, 8 vols, Beirut 1991.

Nujum Jamal al-Din Yusuf ibn Taghribirdi (d. 874/1469), *al-Nujum al-zahira fi muluk Misr wal-Qahira*, 16 vols, Cairo 1929–72.

Suluk	Taqi al-Din Ahmad b. ʿAli al-Maqrizi (d. 845/1441), *Kitab al-suluk li-maʿrifat duwal al-muluk*, (ed.) M. M. Ziyada and S. ʿAbd al-Fattah ʿAshur, 12 vols, Cairo 1934–73.
Tatimmat	Zayn al-Din ʿUmar b. Muzaffar ibn al-Wardi (d. 749/1348), *Tatimmat al-mukhtasar* (also known as *Taʾrikh Ibn al-Wardi*), Beirut 1970.
Wafi	Khalil b. Aybak al-Safadi (d. 764/1362), *Kitab al-wafi bil-wafayat*, (ed.) various scholars, 29 vols, Istanbul, Wiesbaden, 1931–.

Notes

(handwritten annotation: Abl Nasir d. 1341 Mohammed)

1 Maqrizi relates (*Suluk*, vol. 2, p. 272) that Ahmad first moved to Karak at the age of eight with a large treasure and a supervisor, to learn hunting and horsemanship (*furusiyya*).

2 In 731/1331 Ahmad went to Cairo for his circumcision, *Muqaffa*, vol. 1, p. 628. Then he was also promoted to the rank of Amir, *Suluk*, vol. 2, p. 335. In 738/1337, when he was 22, Ahmad was called to Cairo to be married to a daughter of an Amir, named Taʾirbugha (written also Zahirbugha, Tahirbugha), *Suluk*, vol. 2, p. 436.

3 Relying on *Aʿyan al-ʿasr* vol. 1, p. 370. *Nujum*, vol. 10, p. 72 phrases it in this way: Karak became a homeland (*watan*) for him.

4 *Wafi*, vol. 10, p. 143; *Nujum*, vol. 10, p. 20; *Muqaffa*, vol. 2, p. 425.

5 *Durar*, vol. 1, no. 745, p. 174; *Wafi*, vol. 8, p. 86.

6 *Suluk*, vol. 2, p. 551.

7 Abu Bakr was banished to the same house in Qus where his father al-Nasir had lodged the caliph al-Mustakfi in 737/1337, after expelling him from Cairo along with his children and family. Pious writers such as Ibn al-Wardi (*Tatimmat*, vol. 2, p. 474) regarded this as the vengeance of Providence, a just retribution against the sons for the disregard paid to the holy heir of the Prophet Muhammad by their father.

8 *Suluk*, vol. 2, p. 571.

9 When al-Nasir went on the Hajj in 732/1332, a risky journey for a politician, he left Tashtamur together with three other officers in his castle in Cairo, *Wafi*, vol. 16, pp. 437 ff. Tashtamur was entrusted with the disagreeable task of detaining the powerful Tankiz in 739/1338 in Damascus.

10 *Wafi*, vol. 16, p. 440; *Aʿyan al-ʿAsr*, vol. 2, p. 589.

11 *Suluk*, vol. 2, p. 575.

12 The rationalization for the call to Egypt had an air of self-righteousness. The ruler of Karak, a stepfather of Ahmad, sent a report to Qawsun in which he complained of Ahmad's defiance of his orders, and of his frivolous debauchery. Sympathizers from Karak – the ruler feared – might kill the complaining official who subsequently asked to be released from duty (*Nujum*, vol. 10, p. 23; *Suluk*, vol. 2, p. 573; *Muqaffa*, vol. 1, p. 630). Another report has it that it was rumored, on 22 Rabʿ II, that Ahmad was preparing to leave for Egypt. Either to avoid surprise or to introduce him majestically, as befits princes, a magnificent mission had to be sent (*Nujum*, vol. 10, p. 30).

13 *Nujum*, vol. 10, p. 24; *Suluk*, vol. 2, p. 573.

14 A letter addressed to Ahmad cautioning him against entering Egypt, signed by his wife (sister of the Amir Yahya b. Taʾirbugha was found in Rabiʿ I in the baggage of a roving Bedouin (*Suluk*, vol. 2, p. 574). Qawsun was enraged, and Ahmad's fears were further nurtured.

15 *Wafi*, vol. 8, p. 87.

16 The decision of the advisory officers (*umaraʾ al-mashwara*), *Suluk*, vol. 2, p. 574, was not approved by al-Mulk and Jankali who thought it advisable to wait and refrain from brutal actions (*Nujum*, vol. 10, p. 30). The two moderate officers advised Qawsun to end the affair by sending a chastising letter to Ahmad for his subversive activity. Qawsun acted as advised. Ahmad in reply claimed that the envoy (of Rabiʿ I) had used an insulting tone and that this had caused him to respond negatively. Apart from that, Qawsun – wrote

Ahmad – was a second father to him. Ahmad's diplomatic answer could not avert a harsher reaction, contrary to what was intended by al-Mulk and Jankali.

17 It is reported that Fakhri had a direct conduit to al-Nasir Muhammad. He also enjoyed exceptional tolerance despite his audacity. Fakhri's recommendations were always accepted. With regard to al-Nasir, a sultan notorious for his unhealthy suspiciousness, it is rather unusual. *Wafi*, vol. 24, no. 270, p. 255.

18 *Nujum*, vol. 10, p. 30; *Suluk*, vol. 2, p. 578.

19 *Nujum*, vol. 10, p. 33; *Suluk*, vol. 2, p. 580.

20 Signed a reconciliation treaty (*sulh*) with him (*Nujum*, vol. 10, p. 33).

21 Ibn Kathir, vol. 14, p. 194.

22 *A'yan al-'asr*, vol. 2, p. 587.

23 *Nujum*, vol. 10, p. 33; *A'yan al-'asr*, vol. 2, p. 589.

24 Ibn Kathir, vol. 14, p. 193; *Suluk*, vol. 2, p. 579.

25 *Suluk*, vol. 2, p. 582.

26 *Nujum*, vol. 10, p. 33.

27 *A'yan al-'asr*, vol. 2, p. 310; *Wafi*, vol. 24, no. 270, p. 257; *Suluk*, vol. 2, p. 584. A more detailed, favorable, description of different aspects of Fakhri's behavior is supplied by the contemporary Ibn Kathir, vol. 14, p. 198.

28 *Suluk*, vol. 2, p. 584.

29 Ibid.

30 *Nujum*, vol. 10, p. 35.

31 Ibid., p. 36.

32 They did not adhere exclusively to the Al Fadl chief who was a nomad in the Syrian desert. The governor of Safed, Ibn Subh, was requested to recruit Bedouin in the areas of Safad (Galilee) and Tripoli (*Suluk*, vol. 2, p. 584).

33 No reason for this transformation is given by the sources. Personal motives (discredit of Altunbugha, the personality of Fakhri), ideological grounds (abiding by the right of the sultan's son to succeed him), or a decline in motivation can all be suggested.

34 *A'yan al-'asr*, vol. 2, pp. 455–6.

35 The details of the crucial collision (Fakhri-Altunbugha) are hard to decipher. A great effort had been invested by both sides in avoiding fighting (Ibn Kathir, vol. 14, pp. 195–6). If there was any military clash at all (as *Suluk*, vol. 2, pp. 585, 586 might suggest), it was short, was not entitled to any identifiable name as a battle, and led to no casualties.

36 Ibn Kathir, vol. 14, p. 194.

37 According to *Tatimmat*, vol. 2, p. 475, the sermon declaring Ahmad a sultan was delivered in Damascus, Gaza and also in Jerusalem.

38 The assistance of Aq-Sunqur, the governor of Gaza, was most meaningful since he cut the communications between Egypt and Syria, or at least was able to relay their contents to Ahmad, whom he championed, *Wafi*, vol. 9, no. 4247, p. 313.

39 Aslam aided Altunbugha politically. As he headed to join his forces at Aleppo he was halted, at Qara, north of Damascus, by Fakhri and transferred his allegiance. *A'yan al-'asr*, vol. 4, p. 116; *Wafi*, vol. 9, no. 4211, p. 285; vol. 24, no. 270, p. 256.

40 *Wafi*, vol. 24, no. 270, p. 258.

41 *Wafi*, vol. 8, p. 87 (Ahmad) *ta'allala bi-hudur Tashtamur min al-bilad al-rumiyya*.

42 *Nujum*, vol. 10, p. 37.

43 Ibn Kathir, vol. 14, p. 198; *Wafi*, vol. 24, no. 270, p. 258.

44 *Suluk*, vol. 2, pp. 588–90.

45 *Nujum*, vol. 10, p. 44.

46 Ibid.

47 Ibid., p. 53.

48 Fakhri, in his frenzy, thought of transferring his formal allegiance to another, less unpredictable 'Abbasid candidate under whom an independent Syrian rule might be carried on (*A'yan al-'asr*, vol. 3, p. 278; *Muqaffa*, vol. 2, p. 633).

49 *Nujum*, vol. 10, pp. 55–6.

50 *Nujum*, vol. 10, p. 57.
51 The story of Ahmad agreeing to proceed to Egypt only after hearing – in a dream – the prophet Muhammad ordering him to leave Karak and undertake the responsibilities of the State (Ibn Kathir, vol. 14, p. 198) shows how difficult it was, at least for the citizenry, to have faith in his moves after such persistent reluctance.
52 *Nujum*, vol. 10, p. 57.
53 And the appointments he made for Hums and Damascus in Ramadan 742/February 1342, when still in Karak, Ibn Kathir, vol. 14, p. 199.
54 *Nujum*, vol. 10, p. 58; *Suluk*, vol. 2, p. 601.
55 *Suluk*, vol. 2, pp. 601–2.
56 *Nujum*, vol. 10, p. 60.
57 *Wafi*, vol. 8, p. 88, pointing out the rarity of having all the notable chiefs from Egypt and Syria present at his coronation; *Manhal*, vol. 2, p. 162.
58 *Nujum*, vol. 10, p. 60.
59 *Suluk*, vol. 2, pp. 603–6; cf. *Wafi*, vol. 9, no. 4236.
60 *Nujum*, vol. 10, p. 47; *A'yan al-'asr*, vol. 3, p. 187.
61 *A'yan al-'asr*, vol. 4, p. 139. The executioner was Shihab al-Din Ahmad b. Subh.
62 *Suluk*, vol. 2, pp. 605, 606, 618.
63 Ibid., pp. 606–7.
64 Who was active in eliminating Qawsun from positions of power. The stance of Aydughmush against Qawsun (cf. Ibn Iyas, vol. 1, pp. 493–4) apparently induced Fakhri to trust him.
65 Since Baybars, the governor of Safed, had left his town to meet Fakhri in his flight, a meeting which was forestalled, Ahmad became angry and suspicious (*haqada*) and ordered the arrest of Baybars (*Wafi*, vol. 10, no. 4848, pp. 353–5).
66 *Suluk*, vol. 2, p. 608.
67 Cf. R. Irwin, *The Middle East in the Middle Ages* (London and Sydney, 1986), p. 128.
68 *Nujum*, vol. 10, pp. 70–71; *Muqaffa*, vol. 2, p. 634.
69 *Suluk*, vol. 2, p. 610; *Nujum*, vol. 10, p. 68.
70 It is recorded by Ibn Iyas, vol. 1, p. 496 that Ahmad tried to obscure his objectives. No one knew where he was intending to go, and he thus created the impression that perhaps he meant to perform a pilgrimage. The fact that such an accusation is not transmitted by other sources, who tell quite the opposite, suggests the creation of an "anti-Ahmadi" tradition, painting the unpopular sultan in exceptionally black colors.
71 *Nujum*, vol. 10, p. 66.
72 Until Safar 743/5 July 1342, *Nujum*, vol. 10, p. 80.
73 *Muqaffa*, vol. 2, p. 634.
74 Dhahabi, p. 231.
75 *Nujum*, vol. 10, p. 69.
76 *Suluk*, vol. 2, p. 617.
77 Ibn Kathir, vol. 14, p. 201; *Suluk*, vol. 2, p. 626.
78 *Suluk*, vol. 2, p. 617; *Nujum*, vol. 10, p. 70; *Manhal*, vol. 2, p. 162. For the death of Fakhri the north Syrian historian Ibn al-Wardi shed no tears. Fakhri is accused of confiscating the fortunes of the citizens of Aleppo and (more ambiguously) of committing profane (*fawahish*) deeds, even in the month of Ramadan (*Tatimmat*, vol. 2, p. 478). Similar accusations are directed at Tashtamur whom Ibn Iyas (vol. 1, p. 504) defines as wicked and as an oppressor of the Egyptian population.
79 Ibn Iyas relates the horrible story of their cold-blooded elimination by Ahmad and lists this action as one of his gravest mistakes (Ibn Iyas, vol. 1, pp. 497, 504). *Manhal* (vol. 2, p. 162) reports people's feelings of repugnance (*nufur, istihash*) towards Ahmad on this account.
80 According to *A'yan al-'asr*, vol. 1, p. 374, no officer escaped being recruited for at least one, sometimes two, expeditions whereas civilians were subjected (*sukhkhira*) to carry fodder for the horses, food for the fighters, heavy bombardment machinery and other sorts of weapons for the siege.

81 *A'yan al-'asr*, vol. 1, p. 375; *Nujum*, vol. 10, p. 92.
82 *Suluk*, vol. 2, p. 661; *Nujum*, vol. 10, p. 92.
83 *Manhal*, vol. 2, p. 164; *Muqaffa*, vol. 2, p. 636; *Nujum*, vol. 10, p. 93.
84 Ibn Iyas, vol. 1, p. 495.
85 Ibn Hajar gives ample information about Ahmad in Karak during his father's lifetime from
    which one can deduce Ahmad's homosexual inclination towards good looking youngsters.
    He fell madly in love with one of them. The attempts of his father to control this politi-
    cally harmful predilection, as well as Ahmad's reactions, are also portrayed by Ibn Hajar.
    This enriches our knowledge about indulgent princes and their whims, beside giving some
    insight into Ahmad's character. Cf. *Muqaffa*, vol. 1, p. 628.
86 *Durar*, vol. 1, no. 745, p. 174.
87 *A'yan al-'asr*, vol. 1, p. 370.
88 *Nujum*, vol. 10, p. 72.
89 *Muqaffa*, vol. 2, p. 636.

3 Al-Nabi Musa – an Ottoman festival (*mawsim*) resurrected?

Amnon Cohen

Introduction

Al-Nabi Musa, near Jericho, was one of several shrines of historic Palestine, where, over centuries of Islamic rule, venerated Islamic prophets were commemorated and worshipped, while local traditions were gradually developed and transmitted to successive generations. Al-Nabi Salih in the district of Ramla, al-Nabi Hashim near Gaza, al-Nabi Rubin south of Jaffa, al-Nabi Yunis in the village of Halhul, north of Hebron, and al-Nabi Lut in the village of Bani Na'im, south of Bethlehem – these were all of local importance. Initially, al-Nabi Musa, too, may have been just such a peripheral shrine, gradually growing in importance, before becoming a focal point for large parts of Palestine as a whole (Figure 3.1).[1]

This predominantly religious importance acquired a different character in modern times, that of the emerging Palestinian national movement. The involvement over many years of the Jerusalemite Husayni family with the endowments established for the upkeep of the mosque of al-Nabi Musa was upgraded by Hajj Amin al-Husayni soon after the First World War. Not only did he personally take center-stage in the administration of the endowments, but he also took advantage of the growing political tension in Palestine in the early months of 1920 to turn the occasion of the Nabi Musa festivities, in the first days of April, into bloody acts of violence against the Jews in Jerusalem (Figure 3.2).[2]

From the end of Mamluk times, when the early parts of the complex were erected, to the dawn of the modern era stretched 401 years of Ottoman rule. The arbitrary dividing line that historians like to draw between these last two great stretches of Muslim history, in 1516–17, meaningful as it was in politics, urban history and many other fields, could not constitute a watershed in the popular customs and habits of the inhabitants of Palestine. For them, one Muslim ruler was simply replaced by another: neither the change from one legal school to another, from the Shafi'i to the Hanafi, nor the move of the capital, from Cairo to Istanbul, had any bearing on the festivities that had been conducted in and around the Nabi Musa complex for generations. For Michael Winter, whose doctoral dissertation focused on Mamluk Egyptian *mawlid* popular celebrations, and who in later years enlarged the scope of his academic research to include Ottoman Egypt and Syria, a discussion of the Palestinian equivalent of such a festival as Nabi Musa may be of both academic and personal interest.

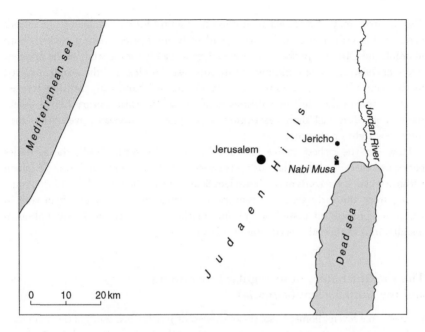

Figure 3.1 Map showing location of Nabi Musa.

Figure 3.2 Pilgrims at Nabi Musa, early 1920s.

Source: Ze'ev Vilnay Collection, the American Colony Collection, the Ben-Zvi Institute, Jerusalem.

Sources

The site itself may be regarded as an important source for its own history. In various parts of this walled-in complex we can identify inscriptions dating back to both Mamluk and Ottoman periods. These are relevant mainly for the study of the different stages of construction of buildings within this vast complex, and the people involved in this endeavor.[3] Some information may be gleaned from early Muslim written sources,[4] and in the Turkish *Seyahatname* of the seventeenth-century Evliya Çelebi there is an additional short description of the place.[5] European travelers too shed some new light on this site.[6]

However, the richest source for the history of the shrine itself, the activities performed there, and the relationship between it and the central and local Ottoman authorities are the records of the Jerusalem Shar'i court. The proceedings of this court dating from the early sixteenth century, the formative years of Ottoman rule in Palestine, provide an abundance of information that adds previously unknown insights into the actual functioning of this site.

The site: the nature of its regular functioning and the annual event (*mawsim*)

Located some seven kilometers south-south-west of Jericho, just south of the main road leading from this village to Jerusalem, overlooking the Jordan valley and the Dead Sea, al-Nabi Musa is built on a secluded spot, in the middle of the rising, barren plateau of the Judean Desert. The following short account of the complex is based on the minute description provided by Canaan less than a decade after the demise of the Ottoman Empire. It is composed of an extensive complex of buildings with large gates and may be divided into two parts: the sanctuary itself and the rooms surrounding it. The latter are separated from the first on three sides by an open space, the courtyard. The sanctuary itself is surrounded on the north and east by porches, and covers the supposed tomb of the prophet. The greater part of the complex is composed of rooms which serve to lodge visitors. Two mosques are attached to this complex. The second storey opens nearly everywhere on to a terrace which overlooks the courtyard. In the lower storey two large kitchens, as well as stables, storerooms, and woodrooms are to be found, besides the many rooms for pilgrims. East of the whole building is a cemetery, where those who die during the festival days are buried, as well as notables who die in Jericho and the 'Idwan tribesmen of Transjordan. The latter consider it a special blessing to be interred near this man of God. "Not a single tree is to be seen anywhere near the building, but large cisterns gather the rain-water for use in the feast-days," as summed up by Canaan in 1927, is still a precise description that holds true today.[7]

Historically speaking, the entire area lying east of the Jerusalem–Bethlehem line was a no-man's-land, where Jewish zealots in ancient days, Christian monks in Byzantine and later periods, or Muslim hermits during the long years of Muslim rule sought refuge from the tumultuous town and its distractions, finding peace and security in the many caves in the area. Under early and medieval Islamic rule, the entire region remained unpopulated, except for the occasional raids of the Bedouin tribes hovering in the desert. The same held true for the years of Ottoman rule, and although the new masters fortified their recent conquest of Jerusalem, turning it into a conspicuous walled city and a flourishing urban center, they did little to improve their grasp over this particular vast region adjacent to it, lying eastward, all the way to the Jordan valley. The annual caravans traveling from Damascus to and from the Hijaz followed the historical route that stretched east of the Jordan rift. On their way back, however, some pilgrims would branch off to visit "the first *qibla* and the third *haram*," that is Jerusalem.[8] Crossing the Jordan River near Jericho meant taking the shortest route to Jerusalem (Figure 3.3), that is, passing by the Nabi Musa complex. This implied adding two more aspects to the avowed aim of these pilgrims headed toward Jerusalem. On the one hand it meant that a visit could, and quite often would, be paid to this shrine. It offered shelter, food, and drink as well as a variety of religious services provided by the permanent inhabitants of al-Nabi Musa (the *khadim*, *shaykh* and various other religious personnel who collected steady salaries from the endowment, handsomely topped up by the occasional visitors). Second, the permanent staff could also provide information on road conditions ahead as well as security threats that were almost endemic to that area. The place thus became an unofficial safe halting station, just before pilgrims started the long, arduous climb to Jerusalem, exposed as they were to raids – or to the levying of ransom money – at the

Figure 3.3 The road past Nabi Musa.

Source: Ze'ev Vilnay Collection, the American Colony Collection, the Ben-Zvi Institute, Jerusalem.

hands of the nomadic population of the desert. The involvement of the authorities in the upkeep of the complex thus surpassed the religious duty to include also the provision of security by the state. Thus Muhammad Çelebi al-Naqqash, whose major assignments were the restoration of the walls of Jerusalem in the late 1530s and early 1540s, followed by the repair of the water conduit to Jerusalem, was entrusted towards the middle of the century with the refurbishing of the Nabi Musa complex. As in the case of the Jerusalem walls project, he was provided with adequate funds from the regular income of the governorate of Jerusalem, but al-Naqqash's premature death led to some complications in how this budget was laid out.[9]

Providing travelers with relative security throughout the year was, indeed, an important duty. However, al-Nabi Musa's claim to fame emanated from an annual event – the *mawsim*. Literally meaning "season, festive season," it assumed in the context of Palestine a different sense from the traditional festivities related to the Hajj pilgrimage: this took place in the month of April and lasted for approximately eight days. In other words, the Islamic nature of both the place and its traditional connotation notwithstanding, the "season" did not rotate through the solar year, as did other holidays, fixed according to the lunar calendar of Islam, but must have been established in accordance with much older regional traditions, based on a solar calendar quite possibly predating all monotheistic religions.

The timing of this *mawsim* coincided with the season of spring, which had always been, ever since pagan antiquity, the period of popular holidays. For the more structured religions of Judaism and Christianity, these are the days of Passover and Easter. Just like other believers, the Muslims of Jerusalem (as well as those residing in other parts of southern and central Palestine), needed a break from the dreary and miserable days of winter, hence their recourse to this organized outing to Nature. In a wider Islamic perspective this should be seen as a *ziyara* of a holy place, a shrine or a tomb of the venerated figure of Moses, *"kalim Allah,"* heavily imbued with religious connotations.[10] The main religious rationale of visiting such places lay in the hope and assumption that prayers made there would be more readily accepted by God, arriving as they did through this saintly channel. The *baraka* (blessing) associated with such a holy shrine might bring along with it positive results in earthly terms: healing for an ailing body or offspring to a barren womb were the most popular.[11] However, these, along with the regular prayers conducted in and around the Nabi Musa mosque, did not change the general atmosphere of a popular festival for all adult members of the family.

People converging on the Nabi Musa festival may have come well supplied with food, but during the days of the festival the place turned into a *simat*, that is, a free soup kitchen,[12] offering a free supply of food and drink to all comers. Out of the income of the endowment designated for the regular upkeep of this place, an impressive variety (and quantity) of foodstuffs was prepared in anticipation of the annual festival: rice and wheat, cooking butter (*samn*), molasses (*dibs*), pomegranates, chickpeas, lentils, raisins, cloves, salt and pepper, onion, and garlic. In order to cater for the masses that came, additional personnel was sent for: a cook and a baker, a miller, a siever, a water-carrier (*saqqa'*), a carpenter, a public-crier (the last two only "during the *mawsim*"). For distribution of the large quantities involved, several porters were brought in, and their services included the supply of utensils, blankets, firewood, lanterns, wicks, and olive oil.[13]

If food was a vital element, amusement seems to have been no less important. During the last days of December 1573, an exceptionally well-attended session was held at the Jerusalem court. The unusual presence of the governor (*sancak beyi*) of Jerusalem, accompanied by a variety of high-ranking military officers, religious dignitaries, and prominent members of local society, indicated wide public interest in the topic discussed. The reason for this gathering lay in a *firman* sent from Istanbul, ordering an official inquiry into the alleged conduct of the visitors to the Nabi Musa *mawsim*. Testimonies given at this session described a routine that was followed every year: the regular pilgrims who came there, accompanied by the junior and other dependent members of their household, servants, and other followers (*hum wa-atba'uhum wa-ta'ifatuhum*), also allowed "foreign" women to join them there. Notwithstanding this qualifying adjective, these women must have been quite well known in Jerusalem, for their full names are stated, as well as their professions: singers and players of popular musical instruments (tambourine – *daff*, and cymbals – *musannaj*). When the supervisors of the endowment, who seem to have been responsible for the entire festival, tried to deny this claim, a variety of eye-witnesses attested to the facts, leaving very little to our imagination. They described the "many" singers who pitched their tents on the roof of the mosque, or in close proximity to its entrance, entertained male company inside, played their loud music throughout the entire week, and performed ugly and despicable deeds, unworthy to be mentioned, at that holy shrine (*maqam sharif*).[14]

A less controversial amusement was performed in the open space adjacent to the complex. Mounted cavalry, as well as foot soldiers (all of them of Turkish origin, as their names reveal) from the retinue of the Jerusalem governor, joined in, mingling with the rejoicing crowds. However, they performed all kinds of mock and real training games, competed playfully at horseback riding, occasionally firing their guns in the air as part of the celebration, which sometimes ended in fatal accidents. The deliberate nature of the killing of a cavalry man by a janissary, as was claimed in court, was hard to prove when the case was brought before the Jerusalem Qadi, but there was no denial of the description provided there of an ambience of simulated military manoeuvres, competitions and other games that were held in broad daylight in close proximity to the bemused – but equally endangered – spectators.[15]

The sounds of shooting and singing, referred to above, convey the generally jovial nature of the gathering at al-Nabi Musa, created by the very assembling of the crowds and the sumptuous meals offered to all there by the *simat*. Another dimension of the overall picture is that of color. A list of objects that were stored in a repository in Jerusalem, to be issued by the supervisors of the endowment for the annual caravan – the *mahmal* – to the Nabi Musa *mawsim* included many drapes and curtains (*sitara*) of different fabrics (silk, cotton, Persian – *hurmuz*), and more conspicuously many colors (yellow, red, green, grey, black, etc.). The same repository also stored many pillows, mats, rugs and carpets, and flags – to be used for the comfort and enjoyment of the pilgrims on the road to the sacred place, then displayed at the site, to be returned, once the festival was over, in great pomp to Jerusalem.[16]

The popular occasion, undoubtedly not lacking elements of spontaneity, was basically a well-structured, organized event. The most important aspect of the provincial government's involvement was the provision of security. The soldiers, referred to earlier, may have been there at their own initiative, although their great numbers may indicate that at least some of them were there on duty. Conversely, in the spring of 1552, several members of the Ghudayya[17] family, usually associated with the custody of the site, reported an incident in which they went to meet with the Pasha of Jerusalem at al-Nabi Musa, this time without any armed guards from his retinue to protect them. They stayed there for a couple of days, waiting in vain, and when they started their climb to Jerusalem, they were attacked by nearby Bedouins who killed one of them. Eleven years later, about a month after the annual festival, reports reached Jerusalem to the effect that Haytham Bedouins had ambushed pilgrims close to al-Nabi Musa with the aim "of stealing their belongings." As a result the *subashi* of Jerusalem was ordered to raid the area, and the culprits were arrested.[18] A military presence, not just during the *mawsim* but on occasion throughout the year, was of crucial importance.

Another official role, this time of a religious nature, was the semi-permanent involvement of members of the Ghudayya family as custodians of al-Nabi Musa, as noted. The function of *nazir* of the endowment was created for the ongoing upkeep and supervision of this complex – yet another facet of the provincial authorities' well-established liaison with it. This link was maintained permanently by the qadi of Jerusalem who appointed, over the years, many members of this family to the supervision of the endowment. From correspondence between two religious dignitaries, read at the Jerusalem court in 1572, it emerges very clearly not only that a particular member of this family was appointed the responsible *shaykh* of the entire complex and supervisor (*nazir*) of its endowment, but that a document to this effect was issued by the *defterdar* of Damascus. As such, he was entrusted with making all necessary preparations for the approaching *mawsim*, for running its free soup kitchen, all of this "according to the old custom."[19] To confirm further the official role of this member of the Ghudayya family, the qadi authorized him to undertake any expenses necessary for the upcoming festival, even though the actual income earmarked for it had not yet arrived.

The official endowment deed, a copy of which must have been kept at al-Nabi Musa, has disappeared, nor has a copy of it yet been found in the court archives.[20] However, scattered references in the *sijill* indicate that much of its income derived from villages in the Jerusalem district: Tur Zayta (al-Tur), Dir Dibwan, Sur Bahir, Turmus 'Ayya, Jifna, Faghur, Fuqin, and even from Jericho. Some income derived from more distant locations, like Nablus, or from Bedouin tribes who collected *ghaf-fara* taxes.[21] This income was meant to be spent predominantly on the annual festival and the provision of free food for all visitors who arrived to celebrate the *mawsim* at al-Nabi Musa. However, the regular staff that were appointed there in various capacities (about 20 in all, most of them members of the Ghudayya family) were remunerated for their services by the endowment all year round.[22] The state treasury did not, however, wash its hands of its overall responsibilities: in the year 1562, for example, Bayram Beyi, a cavalry officer, serving in Jerusalem as a "feudal" lord (*za'im*), was granted by the central treasury in Istanbul a substantial sum of money

(400 *sultani* gold coins) as a special allocation, which he spent on urgently needed repairs at the site.[23] All of these were well-established, hence reliable sources of income – a crucial factor that guaranteed the permanent nature of the site and secured the ongoing activities there. They did not, however, preclude additional, impromptu donations by dignitaries who, like the governor of Cairo in 1556, sent in their contributions in the best tradition of Muslim charity.[24]

Conclusion

Historically speaking, al-Nabi Musa was an important site that provided the local population of central and southern Ottoman Palestine with significance in three dimensions: religious sanctity, security considerations, and popular-cultural tradition (Figure 3.4). A fourth dimension, the political, added only in the early twentieth century, under the British mandate (Figures 3.5 and 3.6), increased the centrality of the event meaningfully, then disappeared in the second half of that century, when the region came under Jordanian control. Modern Muslim rule – this time in Jordanian garb – elicited no defiance, and in any event the central Hashemite ruler would not have allowed any gatherings that could easily deteriorate (from the perspective of the central administration) into seditious behavior.[25] From 1967 onwards, under Israeli rule, though the ceremonies were not formally forbidden, the plateau adjacent to al-Nabi Musa became an area of regular military exercises, so that it could hardly tolerate a pilgrimage – annual or not – to the site. Most recently, since its

Figure 3.4 Pilgrims at Nabi Musa, early British mandate.

Source: Ze'ev Vilnay Collection, the American Colony Collection, the Ben-Zvi Institute, Jerusalem.

Figure 3.5 Nabi Musa, early years of British mandate.

Source: Ze'ev Vilnay Collection, the American Colony Collection, the Ben-Zvi Institute, Jerusalem.

Figure 3.6 Nabi Musa procession, 1928.

Source: Gershon Gera Collection, Ben-Zvi Institute, Jerusalem.

inclusion in the Palestinian Authority territories, a few cases of renewed religious activity at al-Nabi Musa have been reported. Judging by several available photographs, as well as other factual and circumstantial reports,[26] this renewed tradition should be viewed in the context of political developments among the Palestinians, as an attempt to highlight cultural-cum-political aspects of re-emerging Palestinian identity, based on solid historical tradition. The Husayni family, whose political relevance has diminished drastically (if not actually "disappeared," to use Ilan Pappe's expression) over the last few decades, may very well wish that the central role of Nabi Musa festivities should be resumed.[27] In view of the existing polarization between the overwhelming national trend of the Palestinian Authority (headed by Yasir 'Arafat, a scion of this family), and that of the rival, predominantly religion-oriented Hamas and Islamic Jihad, this comeback of al-Nabi Musa may have more to it than meets the eye. If so, it may be premature to evaluate how much popularity such an event could generate. For those who wish to resuscitate the *mawsim*, there is much to build on, going back to Ottoman and Mamluk tradition, but existing tensions and the different potential scenarios involved in its re-activation could well affect the outcome.

Notes

1 One may point out that neither the latter, nor any of the other shrines mentioned here, are related to in the new edition of *The Encyclopaedia of Islam*. For a very detailed description of the site and its feast (*mawsim*), as recorded from the days of the British Mandate, most probably preserved as it used to be during the long years of Ottoman rule, see Tewfik Canaan, *Mohammedan Saints and Sanctuaries in Palestine* (Reprint from the *Journal of the Palestine Oriental Society*, Jerusalem, 1927), pp. 193–214. For additional, valuable eye-witness accounts dating from the late Ottoman years see Salim Tamari and 'Issam Nassar (eds) *al-Quds al-'uthmaniyya fi al-mudhakirrat al-jawhariyya* (Jerusalem, 2003), pp. 56–62. See also Yehoshua Porath, *The Emergence of the Palestinian–Arab National Movement, 1918–1929* (Jerusalem, 1971; in Hebrew), pp. 5, 9.

2 Porath, op.cit., pp. 12, 77–9, 81, 168. See also Ilan Pappe, *Aristocracy of the Land: the Husayni Family* (Jerusalem, 2002; in Hebrew), pp. 118, 220–7.

3 Khalid Mahmud Mirar, *Maqam al-Nabi Musa* (Nablus, 1999). For photos of these inscriptions, as well as transcriptions of their texts, see ibid., pp. 54–66.

4 Mirar, op. cit., pp. 45–8. Joseph Sadan's thorough description and analysis of the traditional evidence for the Tomb of Moses ("Le tombeau de Moïse à Jéricho et à Damas: une compétition entre deux lieux saints principalement à l'époque ottomane," in *REI*, 49, 1981, pp. 59–99) should be consulted for his detailed bibliography of Arabic historical sources, as well as the yield of more recent academic research (e.g. that of L. A. Mayer). For several excerpts from the XIXth century Hebrew press of Jerusalem, as well as several present-day photographs, see Joseph Drory, "Le-korot hagigot Nabi Musa," in *Sal'it* (A/5, 1972, in Hebrew), pp. 203–8.

5 Evliya Çelebi, *Seyahat Name* (Istanbul, 1935), volume IX, pp. 4828–3.

6 W. H. Bartlett, *Jerusalem revisited* (London, 1855), p. 54; J. Finn, *Stirring Times* (London, 1878; Hebrew translation by Aharon Amir, Jerusalem, 1980), pp. 273–4, 433, 490, 576.

7 Canaan, pp. 194–5.

8 For a sketch of the main pilgrimage route, as well as several references to pilgrims who visited Jerusalem in addition to the traditional route to Mecca, see S. Faroqhi, *Pilgrims and Sultans, the Hajj under the Ottomans* (London, 1994), pp. XII, 29, 41, 129.

9 On al-Naqqash see my "The Walls of Jerusalem," in C. E. Bosworth, Charles Issawi, Robert Savory, A. L. Udovitch (eds), *The Islamic World, Essays in Honor of Bernard Lewis*

(Princeton, NJ, 1989), pp. 470–5. For the above episode see Proceedings (*sijill*) of the Jerusalem Shar'i court (henceforth JS), vol. 22, pp. 501–2.

10 Cf. "ziyara" in *EI²*. For a short historical description of the Nabi Musa *mawsim* see Mustafa ibn Kamal al-Din al-Siddiqi, *al-Hadra al-hissiya fi al-rihla al-qudsiyya* (MS at al-Khalidiya library, Jerusalem), pp. 13–14. See also: G. E. von Grunebaum, *Mohammadan Festivals* (London, 1988), pp. 76, 80–1.

11 For a variety of traditional popular beliefs in the blessing associated with al-Nabi Musa (e.g. the swallowing of wicks by sterile women to cure their condition), see Canaan, pp. 113, 184.

12 A term used to denote the regular nature of the daily provision of free food at the Machpela Cave in Hebron. Cf. A. Cohen and B. Lewis, *Population and Revenue in the Towns of Palestine in the Sixteenth Century* (Princeton, NJ, 1978), p. 113.

13 The quantities stated and the budget allocated by the supervisors of the endowment indicate a steady growth in the numbers of participants expected, for example, 1600 *qit'a* in April 1576, 3013 *qit'a* in 1584 (JS, vol. 56, p. 60, 544; vol. 64, p. 108). For a twentieth-century description of food distributed there see Canaan, pp. 204–6.

14 JS, vol. 55, p. 294. The permissive character of public singing, even when performed by male entertainers, was looked down upon and criticized by the religious establishment at that time (cf. my *The Guilds of Ottoman Jerusalem*, Leiden, 2001, pp. 52–6).

15 JS, vol. 66, p. 107. See also Canaan, pp. 208–9.

16 JS, vol. 57, pp. 96–7. Compare Canaan, pp. 197–200.

17 Members of this family were appointed to higher office, that of *naqib al-ashraf*, in the early years of the eighteenth century. As of the middle of that century they deliberately gave up this name and became known as "al-Husayni." For a detailed discussion see Adel Manna, "The rebellion of *Naqib al-Ashraf* in Jerusalem 1703–5," *Cathedra*, 53 (Jerusalem, 1989), pp. 72–3.

18 JS, vol. 25, p. 359; vol. 44, p. 285.

19 JS, vol. 54, p. 537.

20 One possible reason is that the *waqfiyya* originated in times pre-dating the Ottoman conquest of Palestine – see, for example, a reference to an order of the Mamluk sultan, Qansuh al-Ghuri, from mid-1508, stipulating the salaries of several religious functionaries at the site of al-Nabi Musa (JS, vol. 18, p. 528); cf. K. J. al-Asali, *Watha'iq maqdisiyya ta'rikhiyya* (Amman, 1989), vol. III, pp. 117–21.

21 JS, vol. 18, p. 50; vol. 22, p. 63; vol. 27, p. 274; vol. 46, p. 179. For details about this tax see Cohen and Lewis, pp. 56–8, 72, 129.

22 JS, vol. 18, p.10; vol. 31, p. 274.

23 JS, vol. 43, p. 459. See also JS, vol. 22, p. 501.

24 JS, vol. 31, p. 274.

25 This may serve as a correction to the footnote provided by Tamari and Nassar (p. 57, n. 2) to their recently published annotated text. See also Mirar, p. 105.

26 Mirar, pp. 105–06. See also: Israeli-Palestinian Interim Agreement on the West Bank and the Gaza Strip (28 September 1995), Article 32 (Religious Sites), paragraph 4.

27 Pappe, p. 374.

4 Some remarks on the inscription of Baybars at Maqam Nabi Musa

Reuven Amitai

In the framework of his biography devoted to the Sultan Baybars, Ibn Shaddad al-Halabi has a sizeable section describing the many achievements of this remarkable personality. In one sub-section, called "[The Chapter] on what [Baybars] – may Allah have mercy upon him – renewed in [or by] Holy Jerusalem,"[1] the author describes the following project:

> He built (*bana*) over the grave of Moses (*Musa*) – may Allāh have mercy upon him – [near] the "red hill" (*al-kathib al-ahmar*)[2] south of Jericho, a dome and mosque. He created an endowment (*waqf*) for it, for expenditures on its muezzin, prayer leader (*imam*), those who lived in its immediate vicinity and those who came to visit it.[3]

This is a general description of the complex known as Maqam Nabi Musa ("The Shrine of the Prophet Moses"), which is located some 1.5 km south of the Jerusalem–Jericho road, about 8 km southwest of Jericho (grid reference 1910.1327). The building has been described and analyzed elsewhere,[4] and thus a discussion of the site can be dispensed with here.

Ibn Shaddad's information is good as far as it goes but does not give us any details about when the building-complex was initiated, under what circumstances, when the work was executed, and what was its ultimate purpose. We must look elsewhere for more information. We are lucky, therefore, to have a long and detailed construction inscription on the building itself, giving many answers, albeit not necessarily complete ones, to the above questions. In conjunction with contemporary literary sources, we can find even fuller answers.

This long inscription, of relatively sophisticated design, was first deciphered and analyzed by L. A. Mayer in 1932.[5] Mayer's reading and description are good, and therefore there is no need for a full technical discussion of the inscription. His translation, however, was partial and inadequate, and a full one together with annotation is found below. My main purpose here is to return to the text and dwell on some of the matters upon which it touches, using various sources and modern studies to elucidate these points. For convenience I briefly describe the inscription and give the full text and translation (Figure 4.1a and b).

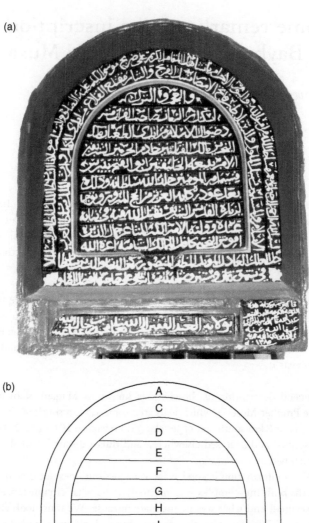

(a)

(b)

Figure 4.1 (a) The Inscription of Baybars at Maqam Nabi Musa; (b) Locations of the lines of the inscription.

Text (Figure 4.1a)

A بسم الله الرحمن الرحيم انما يعمر مساجد الله من آمن بالله واليوم الآخر أمر بإنشاء هذا المقام الكريم على ضريح موسى الكليم عليه الصلوة والتسليم مولانا السلطان الملك الظاهر الأ

B جلّ العالم العادل المؤيّد المظفر المنصور ركن الدنيا والدين السلطان

C الإسلام والمسلمين سيّد الملوك والسلاطين فاتح الأمصار مبيد الفرنج والتتار مقتلع القلاع من أيدي الكفار وارث الملك سلطان العرب

D والعجم والترك

E اسكندر الزمان صاحب القران مستر

F دّ ضوال الاسلام من أيدي الطغيان ملك

G البحرين مالك القبلتين خادم الحرمين الشريفين

H الآمر ببيعة الخليفتين ابو الفتح بيبرس

I قسيم امير المؤمنين خلّد الله سلطانه وذلك

J بعد عود ركابه العزيز من الحجّ المبرور وتوجّهه

K لزيارة القدس الشريف تقبّل الله منه في نيابة

L عبده وولّيه الأمير الكبير المثاغر جمال الدين

M آقوش النجيبى كافل الممالك الشاميّة أعزّه الله

N في شهور ثمان وستين وستمائة [من] الهجرة النبويّة على صاحبها أفضل الصلوة

O بولاية العبد الفقير الى الله تعالى محمد بن رحال عفا الله عنه

Translation (Figure 4.1b)

A   In the name of Allāh, the Merciful, the Magnificent. "They only shall manage Allah's places of worship who have believed in Allāh and the last day."[6] Ordered the building (*insha'*) of this noble sacred place over the tomb of Moses, the speaker (with God) – prayer and peace upon him, our lord, the Sultan al-Malik al-Zahir, the master

B   the most splendid, the scholar, the just, the heavenly assisted, the victorious, the triumphant, Rukn al-Dunya wal-Din, the Sultan

C   of Islam and the Muslims, master of kings and sultans, conqueror of the cities, annihilators of the Franks and Mongols, who wrests castles from the hands of unbelievers, heir to kingship, sultan of the Arabs,

D   Persians and Turks,

E   the Alexander of (his) time,[7] master of the stellar conjunction,[8] reclaimer of the

F   strayers of Islam from the hands of tyrants,[9] king of

G   the two *qibla*s,[10] servant of the two holy sanctuaries,[11]

H   he who commands to give the oath (*bay'a*) to the two caliphs,[12] Abu al-Fath Baybars,

I   associate of the Commander of the Faithful, may Allah make his rule last forever. This (was)

J   after the return of his noble mount from the pious pilgrimage (to Mecca), and his setting out

K   to visit Jerusalem. May Allah accept (this act) from him. (This was during) the governorship

L   of his slave and helper,[13] the great commander, the warrior on the frontier, Jamal al-Din

M   Aqqush al-Najibi, the governor of the Syrian provinces, may Allah grant him glory.

N   (This was in) the months of (the year) 668 (1269–70) [since] the prophetic *hijra*, may a most excellent prayer[14] be upon the one who carried it out.[15]

O   This was under the command/supervision of the slave in need of Allah, the exalted, Muhammad b. Rahhal (?),[16] may Allah forgive him.

I will first focus on the information regarding the establishment of the site. The inscription tells us what Ibn Shaddad left out: the date and general circumstances of the construction. This was sometime in 1268–69, after the Sultan had completed his pilgrimage to Mecca and then went on to Jerusalem. Yet, although this is an improvement over Ibn Shaddad and others who follow him, it does not give the full picture.

According to his biographies and various chronicles, Baybars had left for the Hajj in July 1269. He shrouded his movements in secrecy, as he was often wont to do. This was evidently directed towards both outside enemies and potential conspirators among his senior officers, who might take advantage of his absence. Making his way via Karak and Shawbak, he reached Medina on 25 Dhu al-Qa'da 667/26 July 1269, and from there he made his way to Mecca. Performing the necessary rituals of the Hajj, he was back in Karak on 30 Dhu al-Hijja 667/30 August. But unlike the impression gained from the inscription, the Sultan did not make his way directly to Jerusalem. Rather, he conducted a lightning inspection tour of Syria, maintaining secrecy and thus appearing without warning in various cities throughout the country. A modern biographer has written that "Baybars wanted to take his governors by surprise, his aim being that they should always and everywhere have to reckon on his sudden appearance."[17] He rode first to Damascus and then to Aleppo, in both places arriving unexpectedly. He then returned to the south, via Damascus again (13 Muharram 668/12 September 1269), and only then commenced the visit to Jerusalem and Hebron. Having completed his visit there he then set off for Egypt, arriving in Cairo on 3 Safar/2 October.[18] It was trips like this that helped make Baybars' legend.

I may add that, so far as I have been able to ascertain, no Arabic source emanating from the Mamluk Sultanate or outside it mentions the construction of Maqam Nabi Musa in this context, with the exception of the late fifteenth-century local chronicler, Mujir al-Din, who had recourse *inter alia* to the inscription itself. Even the trusted secretary and biographer of Baybars, Ibn 'Abd al-Zahir, who never misses a chance to extol his patron's virtues, reports in detail the Sultan's entire itinerary, yet skips over the event. There may be an explanation for this. The wording of the inscription says that the work was "ordered" after his return from the Hajj and "his setting out to visit holy Jerusalem" (*ba'd ... tawajjuhihi li-ziyarati al-quds al-sharif*). In other words, the Hajj had been completed, but Baybars had yet to reach Jerusalem.[19] Baybars, evidently somewhere on his way from Damascus and still not in Jerusalem, gave the order to construct an appropriate structure at a reputed site of the grave of Moses. We can speculate that he may even have passed by the site as he drew close to Jerusalem, and thus inspired (or perhaps prompted by someone in his entourage) gave the order commemorated in the inscription.

Be that as it may, from the inscription it appears that the actual work was supervised by Aqqush al-Najibi, governor of Syria from the early 1260s until 1271. The reference is not to greater Syria in its entirety but rather to Damascus and the related regions, including Jerusalem and its environs. This Aqqush was a veteran of the Salihiyya regiment, that is, the same regiment in which Baybars had served, and was thus Baybars' *khushdash*. Aqqush was part of the large group of senior Salihis who received important commands and senior ranks under Baybars early in his reign to shore up his rule; before receiving the governorship of Damascus, he had been *ustadar* (major-domo) in Egypt. In 1265, Aqqush had received a whole village on the Palestinian coast from Baybars as private property, as part of the general distribution of villages to officers in the region after the conquest of Arsuf and Caesarea. It appears that Baybars placed great trust in him, but in 1270, for reasons which are not clear, he was removed from office. He died in retirement in 1278.[20]

The appearance of a governor, provincial or local, in a sultanic inscription is a regular occurrence in this period. It is of some significance, since it appears that the governor was often the man directly responsible for carrying out the construction. In fact, I would suggest that this was an important reason why the construction work described here, unlike many others, is not described *en passant* in the annals. The Sultan, passing through, had given an order to initiate a building project. He may even at this time have given some consideration to the economic support for this project and its maintenance afterwards, by establishing a *waqf*. It is possible that he provided some general guidelines for the plan of the project. But, since Baybars had other matters on his agenda, he soon moved on to Jerusalem, leaving the governor to take care of matters. Thus, in the scheme of things, these projects were not important enough to warrant mention in the flow of the chronicles, or even in some of the Sultan's biographies, unless he himself actually took part in the work and its supervision, as in Safad in the aftermath of its conquest.[21] Only when the biographer summed up the Sultan's achievements, including his many building projects, did a specific construction get the mention that it deserved. Thus, the establishment of Maqam Nabi Musa is recorded by Ibn Shaddad al-Halabi,[22] but not by

Ibn 'Abd al-Zahir who did not devote a section to building projects in his panegyrical biography of Baybars.[23]

Like some of the other inscriptions of the period, the text gives the name of the individual who was evidently the chief professional builder at the site, or perhaps even the architect. The use of *"bi-wilaya"* is not unambiguous. It can mean both the office of minor local governor (i.e. a *wali*), or – as seems to be the case here – the responsibility for the construction project, usually a civilian. As an example of the former case, we have the recently discovered inscription from Qal'at Namrud (al-Subayba), also from the time of Baybars. There, an otherwise unknown Mamluk officer is mentioned after *"bi-wilaya."*[24] He may well have been the governor or commander of the fort, or just the officer supervising the project. In any event, after mentioning him, the inscription goes on to mention three civilian craftsmen: a certain *ustadh* (master), called a *muhandis*; a *mi'mar*; and the artisan who designed the inscription itself. It is clear that these terms had different meanings than in modern Arabic, but that is a matter beyond the scope of the present discussion.[25]

The usage of *"bi-wilaya"* in the present inscription, however, is probably closer to the latter practice, that is, describing the professional man in charge. We have a parallel for this usage in the inscription of Jisr ("bridge") Jindas near Lud, where 'Ala' al-Din 'Ali al-Sawwaq b. 'Umar is mentioned after *"bi-wilaya."*[26] Both Muhammad b. Rahhal and 'Ali al-Sawwaq appear to be civilian professionals. There is certainly no reason to assume that they are military men. I have not been able to identify Muhammad b. Rahhal, if that is indeed his *nasab*. (I have no better suggestion than Mayer's.)[27] We can, thus, only estimate his function at the site.

Let us turn to the various appellations and titles found in this inscription. I am not referring to the integral parts of the Sultan's name: "al-Malik al-Zahir Rukn al-Dunya wal-Din Abu al-Fath Baybars," to which could be added the *nisba*s "al-Bunduqdari" and "al-Salihi," not found in the current inscription. To anyone familiar with the period, these are regular titles and part of the then prevalent royal protocol.[28] What interests me here are the other panegyric descriptions. Many of these terms are found in Ayyubid epigraphy, and some of these go back to the Seljuqs via the Zengids.[29] These titles can be broken down into three major categories: those which describe the Sultan as a just and powerful Muslim ruler, those which portray him as a mighty Jihad warrior, and those which show his power and majesty. These categories, or course, are not mutually exclusive. In the first category, that of a just Islamic ruler, we have such titles as *al-'alim* and *al-'adil*, as well as *khadim al-haramayn al-sharifayn, al-amir bi-bay'at al-khalifayn*, and of course, *qasim amir al-mu'minin*. The holy-warrior component is seen in *al-mu'ayyad, al-mansur, fatih al-amsar, muqtali' al-qila' min aydi al-kuffar*, and – perhaps most evocatively – *mubid al-faranj wal-tatar*.[30] For the third category of just plain power and majesty, there is *sayyid al-muluk wal-salatin, warith al-mulk, sultan al-'arab wal-'ajam wal-turk*, and *iskandar al-zaman sahib al-qiran*. Virtually all of these titles are found at least once in another of the many inscriptions, and many are found in almost every one. I would suggest that the most important of these many titles was *qasim amir al-mu'minin*. It is the only one to be placed after his name, it is found in most of his inscriptions, and it is the one appellation which is found on Baybars' coins. Without a doubt, his official position as sultan, granted to him by two 'Abbasid caliphs, with the added title of "associate of the caliph," was the most important of his various claims to legitimacy.

The cumulative effect of all of these terms and titles is to give the picture of a tough fighter in the name of Islam, an impression certainly strengthened by Baybars' behavior on the battlefield and in day-to-day affairs. Perhaps no less important than his image as *mujahid*, "holy warrior," and a just Muslim sultan, is that of the *Heerkönig*, to use P. M. Holt's very apt term.[31] In other words, Baybars' role as the commander leading his troops into battle, and being the greatest of fighters' is an important component of his identity and the image he was trying to produce. Echoes of this are clearly seen in the present inscription.

The titles used in the inscription at Maqam Nabi Musa have an uncanny resemblance to those found in an inscription from 664/1266. This is a long inscription describing the foundation of the mausoleum of a hero of early Islam, Khalid b. al-Walid, just north of Hums. Most of the titles found in the Nabi Musa inscription are found in the earlier one.[32] It is clear that the composer of the later text had the earlier inscription in mind when he prepared his copy. Perhaps they were composed or executed by the same person. One might ask if more than just the earlier inscription was an inspiration for Maqam Nabi Musa. Comparing the two structures might be an interesting line of inquiry.

One more comment about the inscription: I have often wondered what was the point of some Arabic inscriptions, which are located in positions that make reading them very difficult if not nearly impossible. At the same time, they are often written in such a stylized manner that even a trained epigrapher has trouble deciphering them. This is a point worthy of further enquiry and thought. In any event, the present inscription is different. It is placed relatively low, is accessible to the eye, and the style of the writing does not pose much of a problem. Here, at least, the inscription was intended to be read, and the visitor to the Maqam had the opportunity to peruse its contents and to meditate on its message of power and piety.

Notes

1 [dhikr] ma jaddadahu – rahimahu allah – bil-Quds al-sharif.
2 This refers to a location mentioned in a *hadith*: "Had I been there, I would have shown you his tomb on the side of the road below the heap of red sand" (*Sharh*, to Muslim, *Sahih* [Bulaq, 1283], 5:131, chapter *Fada'il*, par. *min fada'il Musa*, cited by L. A. Mayer, "Two Inscriptions of Baybars," *Quarterly of the Department of Antiquities of Palestine*, 2 (1932), p. 29, note 3, who also discusses other traditions related to the site or the grave of Moses). Due to the red soil of the area, local tradition, according to Mayer, identified this "red sand" with this particular location. In Hebrew, this area is referred to as "Ma'aleh Adumim," a name which derives from the red soil of the region.
3 'Izz al-Din ibn Shaddad al-Halabi, *Ta'rikh al-Malik al-Sahir (Die Geschichte des Sultan Baibars)*, (ed.) A. Hutayt (Wiesbaden, 1983), p. 351. This is the basis for the following, shorter reports: Khalil b. Aybak al-Safadi, *al-Wafi bil-wafayat* (ed.) H. Ritter *et al.* (Wiesbaden, 1931–), vol. 10, p. 341; Muhammad b. Shakir al-Kutubi, *Fawat al-wafayat* (Cairo, 1951–53), 1:168. Mayer, "Two Inscriptions," p. 30, was not aware of Ibn Shaddad's passage, or any other before that of al-Kutubi (1363).
4 Shmuel Tamari, "Maqam Nabi Musa," *Assaph: Studies in Art History* (Tel Aviv), Section B, vol. 1 (1980), pp. 167–90; Sefi Ben-Yosef (ed.), *Israel Guide: The Judean Desert and the*

Jordan Valley (Jerusalem, 1979), pp. 134–5; Mayer, "Two Inscriptions," p. 27, note 2, gives a review of relevant sources, travel literature and academic studies which had been published up to the date of his own study (1932). See also the article by Amnon Cohen in this volume.

5 See the article mentioned in note 2; the text was reprinted in E. Combe, J. Sauvaget and G. Wiet (eds), *Répertoire chronologique d'épigraphie arabe (RCEA)* (Cairo, 1931–), vol. 12, (no. 4612), pp. 141–2.

6 Qur'an 9:18. Translation from R. Bell, *The Qur'an* (Edinburgh, 1937), vol. 1, p. 175.

7 This reflects the great prestige accorded to Alexander the Great and the popularity of the Alexander legend in medieval Islamic culture. See W. Montgomery Watt, "al-Iskandar," *EI2*, vol. 4, p. 127; W. L. Hanaway, "Eskandar-nama," *Encyclopaedia Iranica*, vol. 8, pp. 609–12.

8 Meaning, it would seem, that he was born "under a lucky star"; *qiran* means the "conjuncture of two stars" (J. G. Hava, *Al-Faraid Arabic–English Dictionary* (rpt, Beirut, 1970), p. 602). See also R. Dozy, *Supplément aux dictionnaires arabes* (Leiden, 1881), vol. 2, p. 347; cf. Max Freiherr von Oppenheim and M. van Berchem, *Inschriften aus Syrien, Mesopotamien und Kleinasien*, vol. 1 (= *Beiträge zur Assyriologie und Semitischen Sprachwissenschaft*, VII, (1) (Leipzig, 1909), pp. 4–8, esp. 7, who translated this expression, found in earlier inscriptions of Baybars, as "der unter glücklichen Umständen geborene"; for this inscription, see note 32. One might also note the allusion to the previous expression, for two reasons: (1) The root of *al-qiran* is the same as Dhu al-Qarnayn ("the master of the two horns"), Alexander's sobriquet in the Islamic world; (2) and more importantly, in popular works – at least – Alexander was known as *sahib al-qiran* (Hanaway, "Eskandar-nama," p. 612). Thus, the comparison of Baybars to Alexander is emphasized.

9 This may refer to those Muslims, soldiers, and civilians, who had fled to the Sultanate from the Mongols during the reign of Baybars.

10 The two directions of prayer: Mecca and Jerusalem, which had been the first – and soon superceded – *qibla*.

11 Mecca and Medina.

12 Early in his regime, Baybars had twice given refuge and subsequently given an oath of allegiance to scions of the 'Abbasid family: al-Mustansir, who was then killed in an ill-advised campaign to Iraq, and then al-Hakim. On these matters, see P. M. Holt, *The Age of the Crusades: The Near East from the Eleventh Century to 1517* (London and New York, 1986), pp. 92–3; for a more detailed rendition and analysis, see S. Heidemann, *Das Aleppiner Kalifat (AD 1261): vom Ende des Kalifates in Bagdad über Aleppo zu den Restaurationen in Kairo* (Leiden, 1994).

13 Arabic text: *wali*, which Mayer translates as "regent."

14 Mayer, pp. 29 and 32, suggested that a word was effaced in the original inscription (or the copy which he used), but a close examination shows that there was no word at the extreme left of line N, but rather a floral decoration as on the extreme right.

15 This refers, of course, to the prophet Muhammad.

16 On this reading, see below.

17 Peter Thorau, *The Lion of Egypt: Sultan Baybars I and the Near East in the Thirteenth Century*, tr. P. M. Holt (London and New York, 1992), p. 199, citing Shafi' b. 'Ali, *Husn al-manaqib al-sirriyya al-muntaza'a min al-sira al-zahiriyya*, (ed.) 'A-'A. al-Khuwaytir (Riyad, 1976), p. 148.

18 Thorau, *Lion of Egypt*, p. 199, who does not mention anything about the erection of the *maqam* of Moses. The main source for this itinerary is Ibn 'Abd al-Zahir, *al-Rawd al-zahir fi sirat al-malik al-zahir*, (ed.) 'A-'A. al-Khuwaytir (Riyad, 1396/1976), pp. 359–60, who is closely followed by al-Nuwayri, *Nihayat al-arab fi funun al-adab*, vol. 30, (ed.) M. 'Abd al-Hadi Shu'ayri (Cairo, 1410/1990), pp. 166–70; a shorter version is found in al-Maqrizi, *Kitab al-suluk li-ma'rifat duwal al-muluk*, (ed.) M. M. Ziyada (Cairo, 1934–74), vol. 1, pp. 581–3 (translation in M. Quatremère, *Histoire des sultans mamlouks de l'Égypte* (Paris, 1837–42), vol. 1, pt. 2, pp. 70–5). Shafi' b. 'Ali, p. 148, provides a most terse summary. Many authors virtually skip over this whole circuit to Syria, or mention Damascus

and Aleppo without noting the trip to Jerusalem. See, for example, Badr al-Din al-'Ayni, *'Iqd al-juman fi ta'rikh ahl al-zaman*, vol. 2, (ed.) M. M. Amin (Cairo, 1408/1988), p. 57; Ibn al-Dawadari, *Kanz al-durar wa-jami' al-ghurar*, vol. 8, (ed.) U. Haarmann (Freiburg–Cairo, 1971), p. 141; al-Yunini, *Dhayl mir'at al-zaman fi ta'rikh al-a'yan* (Hyderabad, 1954–61), vol. 2, p. 430. I suspect that all three of these last mentioned sources are derived from the now lost account in the annals of Ibn Shaddad's biography. A short, but complete itinerary, evidently independent of other authors, is provided by Abu al-Fida', *al-Mukhtasar fi ta'rikh al-bashar* (Istanbul, 1286/1869–70), vol. 4, pp. 5–6.

19 Mujir al-Din al-Hanbali, *al-Uns al-jalil bi-ta'rikh al-Quds wal-Khalil* (Amman, 1973), vol. 1, p. 102, writes that the Sultan built the *qubba* (cupola) "upon his return from the Hajj and during his visit to Jerusalem" (*'inda 'awdihi min al-hajj wa-ziyaratihi bayt al-maqdis*). This passage, however, is clearly derived from the inscription itself (as Mayer, p. 32, noted), and cannot represent independent testimony. Mayer suggests that another passage by Mujir al-Din (vol. 2, p. 87) on the construction of the site is not based on the inscription, but has an independent source. There is, however, nothing in this latter passage which indicates information gathered from any other source besides the present inscription.

20 Ibn 'Abd al-Zahir, 222; Safadi, vol. 9, p. 323; Ibn al-Dawadari, vol. 8, p. 93; Reuven Amitai-Preiss, "The Mamluk Officer Class during the Reign of Sultan Baybars," in Yaakov Lev (ed.), *War and Society in the Eastern Mediterranean, 7th–15th Centuries* (Leiden, 1997), pp. 267–300, esp. p. 294; Mayer, "Two Inscriptions," p. 31, wrongly wrote that Aqqush "passed into the service of Baybars," thus misrepresenting the nature of their relationship.

21 Ibn 'Abd al-Zahir, pp. 263, 280.

22 The first half of the annals from Ibn Shaddad's biography has been lost, so it is impossible to tell whether he inserted a description of the construction of this site into the flow of the narrative. I suspect, however, that he probably skipped this incident, and even Baybars' trip to Jerusalem, as seen by some of the sources mentioned in note 17, who often cite Ibn Shaddad for the events of these years.

23 As mentioned earlier, the account of the Sultan's activities at this time in the biography by Shafi' b. 'Ali is very concise, and thus it is no surprise that the project at Nabi Musa is not mentioned at all.

24 R. Amitai, "An Arabic Inscription at al-Subayba (Qal'at Namrud) from the Reign of Sultan Baybars," *Israel Antiquities Authority Reports*, no. 11 (Jerusalem, 2001), pp. 110, 112.

25 See ibid., pp. 116–17.

26 *RCEA*, vol. 12, pp. 174–5 (nos 4660–1).

27 Mayer, in his *Islamic Architects and their Works* (Geneva, 1956), does not mention this individual, perhaps since his father's name is uncertain, or it was not unequivocal that he was a contruction professional, and not a military man or other type of official.

28 Amitai, "An Arabic Inscription at al-Subayba," pp. 110–11.

29 For Seljuq inscriptions (from Damascus, 475/1082): *RCEA*, vol. 7, pp. 214–19 (nos. 2734–7). For Nur al-Din b. Zengi (from Aleppo, 543/1149), *RCEA*, vol. 7, pp. 246–8 (no. 3137); (from Damascus, 551/1156). For an example of Ayyubid protocol, see the inscription from al-Subayba, from 627/1230, in R. Amitai, "Notes on the Ayyubid Inscriptions at al-Subayba (Qal'at Nimrud)," *Dumbarton Oaks Papers*, 43 (1989), pp. 114–15 (no. II).

30 In other inscriptions, this is often accompanied, usually at the end, by *wal-arman* ("and the Armenians").

31 P. M. Holt, "The Position and Power of the Mamlūk Sultan," *Bulletin of the School of Oriental and African Studies*, 38 (1975), pp. 237–49, esp. p. 246.

32 Von Oppenheim-van Berchem, *Inschriften aus Syrien, Mesopotamien und Kleinasien*, pp. 4–8, esp. 5–6; *RCEA*, vol. 12, pp. 104–06 (nos 4556–7); cf. vol. 12, pp. 128–30 (no. 4593), which contains a summary of the *waqf* document at the same site, again with many similar titles.

5   Sign of the Times

Reusing the past in Baybars's architecture in Palestine

Hanna Taragan

In the year 1274, al-Malik al-Zahir Baybars, the first Mamluk ruler (658–77/1260–77) ordered the construction of a porch (*riwaq*), to be attached to the tomb of Abu Hurayra (also known as the tomb of Rabban Gamliel) in Yavne, some 20 kms south of Jaffa.[1] Featuring a tripartite portal and six tiny domes, the porch had two arches decorated with cushion voussoirs and one with a zigzag frieze (Figure 5.1). Baybars also installed a dedicatory inscription, naming himself as the builder of the *riwaq*.[2]

Baybars's choice of Yavne could perhaps be explained by the fact that the coastal towns lay in ruins, or alternatively by Yavne's location on the main road from Cairo to Damascus. It seems, however, that above and beyond any such strategic or administrative considerations, Baybars focused on this site in order to disseminate his political and religious messages, institutionalizing the power of the Mamluk dynasty in general and legitimizing his own rule in particular.

Abu Hurayra had been revered since the beginning of Islam, particularly among the Sunnis. His main claim to fame was that he transmitted 3,500 *hadith*s of Muhammad. For the Muslim population and pilgrims, the many tombs of the Prophet's Companions (*sahaba*) and other holy men acquired the status of specific sites on the map as holy places.[3] A visit to any of them was believed to grant the pilgrim their blessing. We also learn from the author of Baybars' biography, Ibn 'Abd al-Zahir (d. 692/1292), that the Sultan himself sometimes rode to the tomb of Dihya al-Kalbi, another of the Prophet's Companions.[4]

Abu Hurayra, the Prophet's mythological friend, attained a special status during the Mamluk period, both in popular lore and among the rulers.[5] By adding the porch and the lofty foundation inscription to the tomb, Baybars created a type of reliquary shrine, thus effectively exploiting the memory or cult of Abu Hurayra, in order to associate it with himself. Abu Hurayra, however, had actually been buried in Medina. The fact that we find a tomb bearing his name in Yavne epitomizes Baybars' exploitation of Muhammad's illustrious Companions, as well as various military commanders and biblical figures such as Abraham, Moses and King David, not only for the purpose of glorifying holy sites but also in order to establish a clear link between the illustrious past and the consolidated Muslim identity associated with his own figure and his new dynasty.

After all, al-Malik al-Zahir Baybars al-Bunduqdari, first of the Mamluk rulers, was not born a Muslim. Like most Mamluks, he had been bought as a slave, converted to

Figure 5.1 Yavne, tomb of Abu Hurayra/Rabban Gamliel. Facade with friezed arches.

Islam and conscripted into the army. His path and claim to legitimacy lay in presenting himself as a devout defender and exalter of Islam, conducting *jihad* against the infidels. Baybars indeed served as Sultan of Islam and the Muslims. In 1261 he was declared by al-Mustansir (a descendant of the 'Abbasids, brought to Cairo by Baybars) as deputy of the Caliph and leader of Jihad.[6] He was the first to dispatch the *mahmal* (the covering of the Ka'ba) to Mecca in 664/1266;[7] he appointed *qadis* to the four legal schools in the city;[8] and, most importantly, he waged intrepid war against the Crusaders and the Mongols. By establishing an affinity between past ideas and memories and present events, Baybars made deliberate and shrewd use of historical references in his Palestine-based architecture.

The addition of a portal to the existing tomb typifies Baybars's building policy in Palestine: he constructed very few religious edifices from the foundation, and preferred to restore and refurbish existing buildings, such as Maqam Nabi Musa near Jericho.[9] At times he also changed their function from church to mosque, as in Ramla, Gaza or Lydda (Lod).[10] He rehabilitated the tombs of the patriarchs in Hebron[11] and added units, as in the tomb in Yavne. To paraphrase remarks by J. Winter and E. Sivan on collective memory in the twentieth century, Baybars thus 'gathered bits and pieces of the past' and 'joined them together in the public. The public is the group that produces, expresses and consumes collective remembrance'.[12]

Allusion to historical references in art history has been a common practice in many cultures. As early as fifty years ago Richard Krautheimer examined the links between an archetypal building and its copies in western medieval art.[13] *Translatio*, according to his perception, enables the 'transformation' of an old structure into a new one, without the latter becoming an exact imitation. Often a single element or even a name was sufficient to evoke a connection with the prototype. In Islamic art, however, historical references to the past or its recycling acquired a particular meaning. The notion of *isnad* or *sanad* is derived from the root *s-n-d*, meaning 'to lean' or 'to rely on'. It generally refers to a chain of authoritative sources on which a certain piece of information or knowledge, mainly from the prophetic and other 'traditions' (*hadith*), is based. This chain of transmission often begins with the founding generation, mainly with the Prophet and his Companions. The acts and sayings of all these authorities have a unique significance as models for subsequent generations. In Islamic art and literature, this form of historicism and its derivatives (revival of archaic forms, continuity, copying, adoption, etc.), in which models of the past lend canonical status to later works of art and architecture, may be regarded as a metaphorical *isnad*.

What were the modes of action used by Baybars in order to shape a visual memory that would connect his name and deeds to the glorious past? Why did he choose or embrace one particular memory rather than another? What was the range of associations he wished to articulate or the spectrum of emotions he wanted to evoke and how did his subjects understand, interpret and employ the past?

According to Baybars' biographer, Ibn Shaddad 'Izz al-Din (d. 684/1285), Baybars was well aware of the potential use that could be made of architecture and its language for political goals:

> When he, may God protect him with His grace, learned that the durability of buildings would fulfill for their builder the role of longevity and revive their name if forgotten, and that the fame of the builder would shine through such eternal [structures], he preoccupied himself with constructing [buildings, such as] earlier potentates had been unable [to build], and set up what [earlier] craftsmen had failed [to create]: chambers of edifices of this world and the hereafter, Allah would reward him who erected them.[14]

Furthermore, following the Ayyubids in their perception of Jihad, Baybars also expressed his identification with Islam both through wars against the infidel enemy and through accelerated construction for bequeathing and disseminating Sunni Islam: *masjids*, *madrasas*, *mashhads*, etc.[15] It should be noted that Baybars' building enterprise was by no means an exceptional phenomenon, but rather one congruent with the spirit of the time which presented him as a ruler loyal to Islam and its essence. Buildings, whether newly consecrated or renewed, sprang up all over Syria and Palestine.

The periods of the Zangids (Zangi 521–41/1127–46; Nur al-Din 549–69/1154–74) and Ayyubids (589–658/1193–1260) and primarily the period following the conquest of Damascus (570/1174) and the unification of Syria by Nur al-Din, witnessed a 'Sunni revival', whose motto was the dissemination of religious teaching and the extirpation of heresy (*nashr al-'ilm wa-dahd al-bid'a*).[16] The construction of *madrasas*, *khanqas*, *zawiyas*, *mashhads* and mausoleums was an integral part of that 'revival'. In Aleppo under the Ayyubids, for example, hundreds of such structures were erected.[17] This wave of religion-oriented construction and activity continued to flourish during the twelfth and thirteenth centuries. Rulers were not the only builders; the *'ulama'* too were involved in this activity, lending it further legitimacy (especially through the establishment of *waqf*). We hear of great willingness and enthusiasm on the part of various sectors of society – amirs, princes, clerks, women, Sufis, storeowners, craftsmen – to welcome the creation of new sites and donate money towards their construction, renovation and maintenance.[18]

We have already noted Baybars' creative 'affinity' to the memory of the *sahaba* and the beginnings of Islam, such as through the additions of a *riwaq*, a portal and an inscription to the tomb of Abu Hurayra in Yavne. In this context, it is interesting also to note his use of Biblical and/or Qur'anic figures. In the wake of his victory over the Mongols at 'Ayn Jalut in 658/1260, he ordered the construction of a commemorative monument (*mashhad*). Its construction was documented by Ibn 'Abd al-Zahir:

> When God had given him victory over the Mongols at 'Ayn Jalut, and since this place was holy and God has mentioned it in His sacred Book in the story of Talut and Jalut, and since the sultan realized the dignity of this place, for which God had reserved this sacred victory, he decided to construct a monument there, in order to show the significance of the gift of God, and the shedding of the enemy's blood in that place. He issued orders to the deputies in Syria with regard to this.[19]

The above excerpt reflects the reasons for the construction of that victory monument by Baybars, in the eyes of his contemporaries. The first sentence alludes to God's favouring Baybars, giving him the power to defeat the Mongol enemy (*tatar*),[20] where the second seeks to link that victory to the memory of the Biblical–Qur'anic story – that took place also at 'Ayn Jalut – describing Saul (*Talut*) fighting the Philistines and David's (*Da'ud*) battle against and victory over Goliath (*Jalut*) (see Judges 7 and 1 Samuel 17:31, as well as Qur'an, 2:249–251). The Qur'anic story, however, differs from the Biblical one in linking Gideon's trial by water and his battle against the Midianites to the battles of King Saul against the Philistines and David against Goliath.[21]

If Baybars indeed constructed a commemorative structure at 'Ayn Jalut, no traces have remained to attest to this. The term *mashhad* in this case may not indicate a building, but possibly a monument. In any case, the important point is that Baybars employed all the components of the Biblical–Qur'anic myth to convey an essence of war against the infidels (*jihad*). The ancient tale of David fighting Goliath was interwoven into the story of Baybars' own current war against the Mongols, thus blurring the boundaries between past and present, real and mythical, expanding and processing the kernel of truth. The different times, spaces and narratives all merge, and the factual core acquires epic dimensions, rendering the story larger than life. In this way, Baybars employed the past to colour the story of the present battle and in particular to present himself as its hero.

According to Winter and Sivan, the goal of keeping collective memory alive is the glorification of the regime. 'All political leaders massage the past for their own benefit.'[22] Even if we do not all concur fully with these assertions, in this specific case they are congruent with the reality described earlier.

Gratitude to God can already be seen as a fundamental motif at Saladin's Qubbat al-Nasr at the Horns of Hattin.[23] Some regard Baybars' construction of the commemorative monument as a continuation of the one built by Saladin following the latter's victory over the Crusaders in 1187. According to Sivan, there is an 'historical determinism' in Muslim belief guaranteeing that if the Muslims follow Saladin and other heroes of the twelfth and thirteen centuries, they are bound to score victories, and the Mamluks perceived themselves as Saladin's successors, certainly as far as Jihad was concerned.[24]

If in the instances mentioned earlier Baybars chose the Prophet's companions as well as Biblical–Qur'anic figures as models from the past, elsewhere, he also 'used' the memory of the Umayyad period in a well-planned and focused manner. He thus turned to the era of conquests against the Byzantines, adopting certain elements from the architecture and ornamentation traditions to serve his purposes. The conquests of the seventh and eighth centuries have always been extolled both in the ideology and the collective memory as attesting to Islam's moral and intellectual pre-eminence to this very day.[25] It is no coincidence that immediately upon the conquest of Safad, for example, Baybars built a hypostyle mosque in the city, the so-called Red Mosque, al-Jami' al-Ahmar (674/1274–75).[26] Construction of mosques of this type prevailed in the Umayyad period (and also evoked the memory of the House of the Prophet Muhammad in Medina), with the Great Mosque of Damascus constituting a likely prototype. The hypostyle mosque soon attained symbolic status, and throughout the Middle Ages mosques in this style were erected wherever Islam made a new conquest and its victorious presence was to be declared for all to see.[27]

Construction of the Red Mosque in Safad also takes us back to the first monumental hypostyle mosque Baybars built in Cairo between 1266 and 1269 (Figure 5.2). This mosque was built in the Husayniyya area, north of the Fatimid gates of Cairo, Bab al-Futuh and Bab al-Nasr.[28] It is of gigantic dimensions, with each exterior wall measuring approximately 100 metres in length and monumental portals protruding from their centres. In both these hypostyle mosques (Safad and Cairo), Baybars added elements that reinforce their declarative purpose as 'conquering mosque'. In Safad he added the portal (Figure 5.3) with its decorative elements and inscription, alongside his grandiose use of stone and stone *muqarnas*, whereas in Cairo he added three portals crowned by inscriptions, a dome and numerous spolia. The importance assigned by Baybars to the portal element is likewise evinced by the *mashhad* of Abu Hurayra in Yavne, where the cushion voussoir frieze adorns the arches of the portal similarly to the main portal of Baybars' Great Mosque in Cairo.

Baybars' emphasis on the portals of his monumental buildings is evinced not only in the concrete examples familiar to us, but also in the written sources, such as an inscription in the mosque of Ramla commemorating his conquest of Jaffa. This appears in the survey of inscriptions (the *RCEA*) where Combe, Sauvaget and Wiet maintain that the inscription was located in the White Mosque in Ramla.[29] According to another source, the inscription came from the Great, or 'Umari, Mosque, originally a Crusader church situated near the market of Ramla (I have

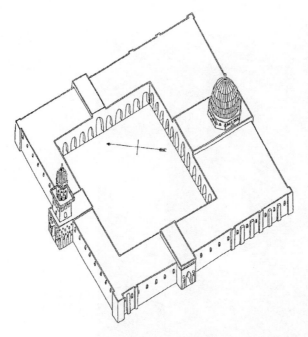

Figure 5.2 Cairo, the Great Mosque of Baybars al-Bunduqdari (1266–69), axonometric view.

found no trace of such an inscription at either site):

> In the name of God the Merciful, the Compassionate... gave power to his servant... who has trust in him... who fights for Him and defends the faith of His Prophet... Sultan of Islam and the Muslims, Baybars... who came out with his victorious army on the 10th of the month of Rajab from the land of Egypt, resolved to carry out *jihad* and combat the intransigent infidels. He camped in the port city of Jaffa in the morning and conquered it, by God's will, in the third hour of that day. Then he ordered the erection of the dome over the blessed minaret, as well as the gate of this mosque... in the year 666 of the Hijra [1268 C.E.]. May God have mercy upon him and upon all Muslims.

The example just mentioned demonstrates how the construction of a portal was intended to symbolize Baybars' triumphs over the Crusaders. Our knowledge of the portal of the Great Mosque in Cairo, for example, must rely on two biographies of Baybars written during his lifetime and under his patronage – one by Muhyi al-Din Ibn 'Abd al-Zahir, the other by Ibn Shaddad 'Izz al-Din – as well as on a third record, written two centuries later by Maqrizi (d. 845/1441). They all dwell on Baybars' special request, prior to his destruction of Jaffa in 666/1268, that the portal of his new Great Mosque be identical to the portal of the Zahiriyya Madrasa at Bayn

Figure 5.3 Safad, the Red Mosque (1274–75). The Portal.

al-Qasrayn in Cairo, built by Baybars himself in 660/1261–62, and that the dome match that of the mosque of the Imam al-Shafi'i, built by the Ayyubids in 1211.[30] In all other respects, Baybars gave the architect a free hand. From these texts we thus learn that the elements of the portal and the dome were of central importance to Baybars.

In these chronicles, the portal appears to figure as a metonym for a comprehensive idea. When the portal element is noted by the chronicles as a separate and emphasized item in Baybars' building activity – sometimes in conjunction with the dome and/or minarets – it is afforded a special role among the other elements of the building. In the case in point, it signifies the victory of Islam and of Baybars himself over the enemy. One should bear in mind that portals and gateways were already used to constitute a declaration of the patron's power and victory in the eastern and western Roman and Christian Empires and from the early Islamic period on. We find clear examples of this in the monumental entrance gates to the Umayyad palaces and to the prayer hall of the Great Mosque of Damascus as well as in the city gates of Baghdad, Fatimid Cairo, etc.

If the portals of the hypostyle mosques in Safad and Cairo were indeed a bearer of Baybars' political and religious message, the inscriptions declare this publicly. Even when the foundation inscription is merely a 'banal formulation',[31] it nonetheless perpetuates both the metaphorical quality of the mosque portal and the name of the ruler inscribed on it, and thereby automatically links the two. Anyone passing by or through the portal would be able to read it, and the name of Baybars would be impressed on his mind. In a culture that did not permit visual images of the ruler or patron who had endowed the building, unlike in Christian edifices and portals, the written word – the ruler's name in this case – became a surrogate means of extolling his deeds. The Mamluks in Syria kept up this practice, which had originated in the Ayyubid period with Nur al-Din (541–69/1146–74). The latter, in the wake of the battles against the Crusaders at Edessa, Antioch and Tripoli, had his epithets as a warlord of the Jihad inscribed in Arabic on the portals of the buildings that he erected. These emphasized his dedication to the holy war against the infidels as well as his affirmation of Sunni orthodoxy.[32]

The foundation inscription appearing on the portal of a mosque or other edifice thus clearly proclaimed the ruler's agenda. The same applies to the Mamluk revival of the Byzantine mosaic technique that adorned the walls of the Umayyad Dome of the Rock in Jerusalem, as well as the Umayyad Great Mosque in Damascus. Both the technique and the images reappeared in the Mamluk era, in Baybars' own tomb (*Qubbat al-Zahiriyya*) erected in Damascus (Figure 5.4), whose construction was completed by Qalawun (1281) after Baybars's death.[33] Mosaics were also likely employed in Baybars's Qasr al-Ablaq which has not survived.[34]

The execution of numerous mosaic repairs and renovations at the Dome of the Rock and in Damascus in the early part of the Mamluk era, between 1260 and 1340, reveals the Mamluks' knowledge of the Umayyad (originally Byzantine) technique. Baybars himself carried out restoration and renovations at the Dome of the Rock in 1261[35] and in 1269, he reconstructed the mosaics in Damascus.[36] Flood contends that Baybars invested 20,000 dinars in these renovations. Ibn Shaddad 'Izz al-Din asserts that Baybars had seen the poor condition of the mosaics, but that the money was, in fact, intended to replace the marble there.[37] Either way, Baybars, like Qala'un after him, was certainly aware of the beauty and prestige of the Umayyad mosaics.[38] Here, once again the legitimacy of Mamluk rule was consolidated by connecting the present with the glorious past by means of adoptive references, in this case by transmitting the Umayyad aura to the Mamluks. In this way, the Mamluk victory over the Crusader Christians appears to have been put on par with the Umayyad victories over the Byzantine Christians.

One of the forms of 'dialogue' between a victorious culture and a conquered one is via spolia. The modern concept of spoils of war refers among other things to the reused parts or materials of architectural construction that are taken from a demolished enemy building to be erected or incorporated elsewhere, usually at the site where the victor has chosen to declare the victory (imperial structures, religious

Figure 5.4 Damascus. Mausoleum of Baybars al-Bunduqdari (Zahiriyya Madrasa 1277–81). Mosaic work. Courtesy of Hans-Ulrich Kuhn, Tübingen.

structures, etc.) and present it in public; to proclaim victory over the enemy by destroying the latter's legacy, while underscoring the legitimacy of the new reign or religion.[39]

The use of spolia in Baybars' monuments had a two-fold function: practical and symbolic. In the former, for example, the wood for the dome of Baybars' great mosque in Cairo constituted a reuse of material brought from Jaffa, following the third major campaign (666/1268) that started with the capture of the town of Jaffa on the coast. The marble slabs and wood from the citadel were shipped to Cairo. The Sultan's orders were to use the marble for the *mihrab* and the wood for the *maqsura* of the mosque of the *Husayniyya*.[40] In this context, it is also important to note the conversion of churches into mosques in Ramla, Lydda and elsewhere – a practice that may also come under the category of spolia.[41]

Regarding symbolic spolia, Baybars, as has been seen, had the arches of the portal complementing the tomb of Abu Hurayra decorated with cushion voussoirs and a zigzag frieze (Figure 5.1). Generally speaking, Islamic art forms were not interpreted in writing during medieval times, and it is therefore not certain why Baybars adorned the arches with the cushion voussoir, or what this motif conveyed. We can venture an answer to this question only on the basis of a close reading of the work of art itself, by decoding its specific imagery and formal language within the context of its strictly art-historical models or visual symbols.

Figure 5.5 Jerusalem, Holy Sepulchre. Doors and windows adorned with cushion voussoir.

A significant early example of the cushion voussoir frieze from the early twelfth century is found on the south facade of the Holy Sepulchre in Jerusalem (Figure 5.5) framing the doors and the double windows in the first and second stories. The motif was invested there with a site-specific significance and, like the ground plan and other elements of the building, the frieze became a canonic model for future churches.[42] A direct model for the cushion voussoir in the Abu Hurayra *riwaq* was found by Clermont-Ganneau at the end of the nineteenth century in the Crusader architecture of Yavne itself.[43] Yavne shifted between Muslim and Crusader rule until the final Muslim conquest in 1244. In the early twelfth century, a Crusader church was built on the tell opposite the tomb of Abu Hurayra and one of its doors was adorned with a cushion voussoir.

Incorporation of the cushion voussoir in important Crusader buildings as well as in Baybars' addition to Abu Hurayra's tomb in Yavne and in his great mosque in Cairo (Figure 5.6) suggests that Baybars had borrowed the motif from Christian architecture as spoils, trophies taken from the Crusader churches (even though the cushion voussoir first made its appearance in a defined sculptural form on Bab al-Futuh, one of the three gates of the city of Cairo, in 1087–92). The facades of both Muslim and Crusader buildings in medieval Palestine thus visually reflect the power struggle between the two religions in this country from the eleventh through the fourteenth centuries.[44]

The question that arises at this point is how Baybars' subjects – the local populations in the provinces of Palestine and Syria that were governed from Cairo – received and

Figure 5.6 Cairo, the Great Mosque of Baybars al-Bunduqdari. Portal arch adorned with cushion voussoir.

interpreted the explicit and implicit messages of their new ruler. In other words, how did Baybars convey his messages to that community? It was here, I believe, that Baybars' shrewd use of regional practice steeped in historical reference (cushion voussoir, glass mosaics, the use of local buildings already invested with sanctity, revival of the hypostyle mosque, etc.) came into play as a factor facilitating identification by signifying continuity and evoking a sense of familiarity. Repetition and simulation, absorption of aura through proximity and virtual spoliation were how Baybars set out to endow contemporary architecture with historical reference.[45]

Notes

1 L. A. Mayer, I. Pinkerfeld and J. W. Hirshberg, *Some Principal Muslim Buildings in Israel* (Jerusalem, 1950), pp. 20–4, fig. 9–10, 11; H. Taragan, 'Politics and Aesthetics: Sultan Baybars and the Abu Hurayra/Rabbi Gamliel Building in Yavne', in Asher Ovadiah, (ed.), *Milestones in the Art and Culture of Egypt* (Tel-Aviv, 2000), pp. 117–44. Andrew Petersen, *A Gazetteer of Buildings in Muslim Palestine* (part 1) (Oxford, 2001), pp. 313–16.

2 M. van Berchem in Ch. Clermont-Ganneau, *Archaeological Researches in Palestine during the Years 1873–1874* (London, 1869), II, p. 177.

3 M. J. Kister, 'Sanctity Joint and Divided: on Holy Places in the Islamic Tradition', *Jerusalem Studies in Arabic and Islam*, 20 (1996), p. 42.

4 Muhyi al-Din 'Abd al-Zahir, *al-Rawd al-zahir fi sirat al-malik al-zahir*, edited and translated by S. F. Sadeque, in *Baybars I of Egypt* (Oxford–Decca, 1956), p. 172.

5 Boaz Shoshan, 'High Culture and Popular Culture in Medieval Islam', *Studia Islamica*, 83 (1991), pp. 67–107.

6 Maqrizi, *Kitab al-suluk li-ma'rifat duwal al-muluk*, M. M. Ziyada and S. 'Abd al-Fattah 'Ashur (eds) (Cairo, 1970–73), I, p. 544.

7 Ibid.

8 P. M. Holt, 'The Position and Power of the Mamluk Sultan', *BSOAS*, 38, part 1 (1975), pp. 243–7.

9 Ibn Shaddad, *Ta'rikh al-malik al-zahir*, A. Hutayat (ed.) (Wiesbaden, 1983), p. 351. S. Tamari, 'Maqam Nabi Musa Near Jericho', *Cathedra* 11 (1979), pp. 153–80 (Hebrew). See also J. Sadan, 'The Tomb of Moses (Maqam Nabi Musa), Rivalry between Regions as to their Respective Holy Places', *The New East (Ha-Mizrah he-Hadash)*, XXVIII (1979), pp. 22–8 (Hebrew); J. Sadan, 'The Maqam Nabi Musa Controversy as Reflected in Muslim Sources', *The New East (Ha-Mizrah he-Hadash)*, XXVIII (1979), pp. 220–38 (Hebrew). Yehoshu'a Frenkel, 'Baybars and the Sacred Geography of Bilad al-Sham: A Chapter in the Islamization of Syria's Landscape', *Jerusalem Studies in Arabic and Islam* 25 (2001), pp. 153–70.

10 Ibn Shaddad, p. 352. As for Lydda which was partially destroyed by Baybars and rebuilt as a mosque in 1268, see Petersen, *Gazetteer* (n. 1), p. 35.

11 Ibn Shaddad, p. 350.

12 Jay Winter and Emmanuel Sivan (eds), *War and Remembrance in the Twentieth Century* (Cambridge, 1999) p. 6. See also M. Halbwachs, *On Collective Memory*, trans. by Lewis A. Coster (Chicago, IL 1992); Jacques Le Goff and Pierre Nora (eds), *Constructing the Past. Essays in Historical Methodology* (Cambridge, 1985).

13 Richard Krautheimer, 'Introduction to an Iconography of Medieval Architecture', *Journal of the Warburg and Courtauld Institutes* 5 (1942), pp. 1–33.

14 Ibn Shaddad, p. 339.

15 R. S. Humphreys, 'Ayyubids, Mamluks and the Latin East in the Thirteenth Century', *Mamluk Studies Review* 2 (1998), pp. 8–9. See also C. Hillenbrand, *The Crusades: Islamic Perspective* (New York, 2000), p. 211.

16 Daniella Talmon-Heller, 'Society and Religion in Syria from the Reign of Nur al-Din to the Mamluk Occupation (1154–1260)' (PhD dissertation, Hebrew University of Jerusalem, 1999), p. 10 (Hebrew).

17 Yasser Tabbaa, *Construction of Power and Piety in Medieval Aleppo* (Pennsylvania, 1997), p. 183.

18 Christopher Taylor, *In the Vicinity of the Righteous: Ziyara and the Veneration of Muslim Saints in late Medieval Egypt* (Leiden, 1999) p. 9.

19 Ibn 'Abd al-Zahir, *al-Rawd al-zahir fi sirat al-malik al-zahir*, p. 91. English translation by Sadeque, *Baybars I of Egypt*, pp. 115–16.

20 Thomas Leisten, 'Mashhad al-Nasr: Monuments of War and Victory in Medieval Islamic Art', *Muqarnas* 13 (1996), pp. 7–26.

21 Moshe Sokolow, 'Goliath and 'Og in Midrash and Hadith', *Sefunot* 1 (16) (1980), pp. 49–58 (Hebrew); see also Frenkel, 'Baybars and the Sacred Geography', p. 157.

22 Winter and Sivan, *War and Remembrance*, pp. 6–7.

23 Zvi Gal, 'Saladin's Dome of Victory at the Horns of Hattin', in B. Z. Kedar (ed.), *The Horns of Hattin* (Jerusalem and London, 1992), pp. 213–15.

24 E. Sivan, 'Jihad: Myth and History', *Alpayim* 11 (1995), p. 16 (Hebrew); C. Hillenbrand, *The Crusades, Islamic Perspectives* (New York, 2000), p. 235.

25 Fred M. Donner, 'The Sources of Islamic Conceptions of War', in John Kelsay and James Turner Johnson (eds), *Just War and Jihad* (New York and London, 1991), pp. 53–4; Sivan, 'Jihad', p. 15.

26 Mayer, Pinkerfeld and Hirschberg, *Buildings in Israel* (n. 1), pp. 44–6, figs 46–51; Hanna Taragan, 'Doors that Open Meanings: Baybars's Red Mosque at Safad', in M. Winter and A. Levanoni (eds), *The Mamluks in Egyptian and Syrian Politics and Society* (Leiden, 2004), pp. 3–20.

27 O. Grabar, 'The Iconography of Islamic Architecture', in P. Soucek (ed.), *Content and Context of Visual Arts in the Islamic World* (Pennsylvania and London, 1988), p. 55; B. O'Kane, 'Monumentality in Mamluk and Mongol Art and Architecture', *Art History* 19/4 (1996), p. 514.

28 J. Bloom, 'The Mosque of Baybars al-Bunduqdari in Cairo', *Annales Islamologiques* 18 (1982), pp. 44–78.

29   E. Combe, J. Sauvaget, G. Wiet, *Répertoire chronologique d'épigraphie arabe* (Cairo, 1943), pp. 123–4.

30   Ibn Shaddad, p. 346; Maqrizi, *Kitab al-mawa'iz wal-i'tibar bi-dhikr al-khitat wal-athar* (Beirut, 1959), pp. 299–300.

31   S. Blair, *Islamic Inscriptions* (New York, 1998), pp. 29–42.

32   Y. Tabbaa, 'Monuments with a Message: Propagation of Jihad under Nur al-Din', ibid., pp. 223–4. See also another opinion by C. Hillenbrand, 'Jihad Propaganda in Syria from the Time of the First Crusade Until the Death of Zengi: The Evidence of Monumental Inscriptions', in K. Athamina and R. Heacock (eds), *The Frankish Wars and Their Influence on Palestine* (Birzeit, 1994), pp. 60–70.

33   On the images of the buildings represented, for example, in the mosaics of the Great Mosque in Damascus and reappearing in the tomb of Baybars in certain variations, see Nasser Rabbat, 'The Mosaics of the Qubba al-Zahiriyya in Damascus: A Classical Syrian Medium Acquires a Mamluk Signature', *ARAM* 9–10 (1997–98), pp. 227–39; B. Flood, 'Umayyad Survivals and Mamluk Revivals: Qalawunid Architecture and the Great Mosque of Damascus', *Muqarnas* 14 (1997), pp. 57–79.

34   The architect Ibrahim ibn Ghanim who planned Baybars' tomb in 1281 is also the person who built the palace at Qasr al-Ablaq, and he is probably responsible for the installation of the mosaics in both edifices. See Nasser Rabbat, *The Citadel of Cairo: A New Interpretation of Royal Mamluk Architecture* (Leiden, 1995), p. 167.

35   On this see Flood (n. 33, p. 66) quoting Mujir al-Din 'Abd al-Rahman b. Muhammad, *Kitab al-uns al-jalil bi-ta'rikh al-Quds wal-Khalil* (Baghdad, 1995), pp. 433–4.

36   On the mosaics in Damascus that were restored by Baybars see K. A. C. Creswell, *Early Muslim Architecture* (2nd edn, New York, 1979), I, I p. 346; Flood, pp. 66–7.

37   Ibn Shaddad, pp. 355–6.

38   During the Bahri period (1250–1382) the Mamluks used glass mosaics also in various prayer niches such as the *mihrab*s of the Qalawun complex (1284), the mosque of Sitt Hadak (1339–40), and others. All these *mihrab*s used the same glass mosaic technique in the conch in similar patterns which consisted of vegetal and floral motifs and are modeled after Umayyad prototypes found in the Dome of the Rock.

39   H. Saradi, 'The Use of Ancient Spolia in Byzantine Monuments: The Archaeological and Literary Evidence', *International Journal of the Classical Tradition* 3 (1997), pp. 395–423; Beate Brenk, 'Spolia from Constantine to Charlemagne: Aesthetics versus ideology', *DOP*, XLI (1987). D. Kinney, 'Spolia: Damnatio and Renovatio Memoriae', in *Memoirs of the American Academy in Rome* 42 (1997), pp. 117–48.

40   Ibn Shaddad, *Ta'rikh al-malik al-zahir*, p. 346.

41   Hillenbrand, *Crusades* (n. 15, p. 286): 'The appropriation of the sacred monuments of another faith that are still in daily use and their transformation, with the visible signs of one's own religion, is an even greater humiliation. It is more than mere military occupation – it is an invasion and desecration of religious sanctity, trespassing on sacred monumental symbols of a faith.'

42   N. Kenaan-Kedar, 'Local Christian Art in Twelfth Century Jerusalem', *Israel Exploration Journal* 23 (1973), pp. 225–7; (ead), 'Armenian Architecture in Twelfth-Century Crusader Jerusalem', *Assaph* 3 (1998), pp. 77–92, (ead), 'Symbolic Meaning in Crusader Architecture: the twelfth-century dome of the Holy Sepulchre Church in Jerusalem', *Cahiers Archéologiques* 14 (1986), pp. 109–17.

43   Ch. Clermont-Ganneau, II, p. 179.

44   H. Taragan, 'Politics and Aesthetics', pp. 126–7; R. Ousterhout, 'Architecture as Relic and the Construction of Sanctity: the stones of the Holy Sepulchre', *Journal of the Society of Architectural Historians* 62 (2003), pp. 18–19.

45   This chapter is an expanded version of a lecture I delivered at the Israel Academic Center in Cairo in November 2001, reported in an abridged form in the Center's bulletin.

6   A fourteenth-century Jerusalem court record of a divorce hearing

A case study*

Donald P. Little

This is not so much intended to be a detailed analysis of an individual document from the Haram collection as it is a case study of a sample representing the Arabic pieces as a whole. Although I will certainly analyze this particular document from the standpoints both of form and content, my purpose will be to use it as an example of the practical, methodological problems that a scholar encounters, and must try to solve, in using such records as sources for social, institutional – including legal and judicial – political, and even cultural history of the Mamluks during the late fourteenth century. I hope I will be indulged if I take a personalized approach since my remarks inevitably reflect my own problems in learning to use these sources, and I freely admit that after some twenty-five years of hard work I am still having difficulty in reading and interpreting the documents and that solutions are still elusive. Moreover, I have recently become aware of what at least one scholar familiar with the Ottoman archives has labeled as

> the dangers of "document fetishism." By this exotic-sounding term we mean the tendency to reproduce more or less verbatim the statements of our primary sources and associated unwillingness to use logic and/or experience of the relevant milieu to interpret them....[1]

This peril is even more important for Mamluk, as opposed to Ottoman, documents, since so few of the former have survived, impeding statistical analysis. In any case, I will try to situate my document in the milieu of a provincial Mamluk court.

I shall begin by placing this document, a record from a Shafi'i court in Jerusalem, dated 5 Dhu l-Hijja 795/12 October 1393 – almost exactly 610 years ago – into context; otherwise, as an isolated item, its significance would be limited. First of all, what are the Haram documents, and how does our document, which I have classified as (#653) in my catalog,[2] fit into them? The Haram collection, so-called because it was discovered locked away in the Islamic Museum at al-Haram al-Sharif in 1974–76, consists of 883-plus documents, almost all of which are written in Arabic and pertain to affairs in Jerusalem in the late eighth/fourteenth century; the rest are written in Persian and in what I call Persianate Arabic and have nothing whatsoever to do with Jerusalem. Since many, no fewer than 265, bear the name of a particular Shafi'i judge and many others seem to refer to him if only indirectly, I believe that the collection constitutes the remnants of a Shafi'i court archive, in particular the papers of this judge but augmented with earlier and a very few later materials. Despite its small size, this collection is extremely important, because it is virtually the only Muslim judicial archive, partial though it may be, to have survived in the Islamic world prior to the Ottomans. Before that time, scholars are almost wholly dependent, as is well known, on literary sources – mainly chronicles and biographical dictionaries – for their knowledge of Islamic history. Although the Haram collection contains only a minute fraction of the records preserved in the Ottoman archives, it nevertheless gives us a glimpse at the history of Mamluk Jerusalem not afforded by other sources. Here we will focus on institutional, judicial history in general, and the Shafi'i court in partic- ular. For the most part, studies of Muslim judicial institutions and practices have been based on theoretical works of jurisprudence and are highly abstract, describing for the most part what the *fuqaha'* construed as the ideal norms for the constitution and practice of the courts and their officials, without taking into account how these norms were interpreted and implemented, if indeed they were implemented, by individuals.[3] Now, for the first time, we have some of the records of an identifiable judge about whom a small but intriguing amount of information has been recorded in literary sources. This judge, named Sharaf al-Din Abu al-Ruh 'Isa b. Jamal al-Din Abi al-Jud Ghanim al-Ansari al-Khazraji al-Maqdisi, belonged to a long line of a prominent family of scholars in Jerusalem and served in several official capacities in Palestine: deputy judge of Nablus (781–85/1380–83); chief judge in Jerusalem and its districts (793?–97/1390?–95); Shaykh al-Khanqah al-Salahiyya and Nazir al-Maristan al-Salahi, the principal Sufi and medical institutions respectively in the city; as well as Nazir al-Awqaf al-Mabrura – supervisor of the pious endowments of the city. Obviously, then, Sharaf al-Din must have been one of the most important civilian officials in Jerusalem during the first half of the last decade of the fourteenth century. Nevertheless, his character and reputation were subject to conflicting interpretations. In the standard history of Islamic Jerusalem compiled by Mujir al-Din al-'Ulaymi (b. 810/1406), Sharaf al-Din is depicted as a beneficent judge, popular among Jerusalemites because of his act in making an endowment property available for agricultural use, thereby increasing its revenue, for the *waqf*.[4] But, according to another, contemporary historian, Ibn Qadi Shuhba (d. 851/1448), Sharaf al-Din was a shady figure:

> A man of reprehensible conduct . . . Sharaf al-Din devoured the money belonging to pious endowments and the people, so that the inhabitants of Jerusalem com- plained against him several times and wrote unfavorable reports about him . . . When Sari al-Din became *qadi* [in Damascus] the people complained to him regarding Sharaf al-Din, whereupon Sari al-Din sent a messenger to threaten him. The people rejoiced when Sharaf al-Din was stricken with colic and died overnight . . . in 797/1395. The day after his death, a letter from the sultan arrived, ordering that he be investigated and bastinadoed at the Haram, but God had protected him with his death.[5]

Added to this subjective charge of Sharaf al-Din's corruption in a literary source is a documentary accusation in the Haram papers that he had filched some carpets from the Dome of the Rock for his own use (#71)! There is also a court record of a case, published by me, which indicates that Sharaf al-Din's rulings may have been influenced by personal, extra-judicial considerations.[6] Although the verdict on his probity as a judge has not yet been decisively determined, this is certainly one of the considerations that should be borne in mind by scholars who try to interpret his activities from the Haram documents. From a broader point of view, it is also clear that study of the documents must be supplemented with reading of the literary sources not just for biographical data, but for such indications found in the passage quoted that judges in Jerusalem during this period were subject to the oversight of judges in Damascus as well as that of the sultan himself in Cairo, who was soon to relieve the chief qadi of Damascus of the responsibility of appointing provincial judges and do so himself.

Again, so as not to examine (#653), a type of court record, in isolation, we should look at other types of records of cases, transactions, and procedures in which Sharaf al-Din was engaged and which survive in the Haram collection. Of these, by far the most numerous are the estate, or probate, and inventories. The 423 specimens of these have been studied in a book by Huda Lutfi, *al-Quds al-Mamlukiyya: A History of Mamluk Jerusalem Based on the Haram Documents*,[7] and several of these have been published elsewhere. These consist of inventories, authorized by the Shafi'i court, that is, Sharaf al-Din, conducted by witnesses who list the assets of a person dying or dead, for the purpose of establishing his or her estate and its heirs, including the Mamluk state. Sometimes, it should be noted, the authorization was granted by the Hanafi judge in concert with Sharaf al-Din. This is not at all unusual. As I have shown elsewhere, judges of three of the four *madhhabs* – Shafi'i, Hanafi, and Hanbali – both in Jerusalem and in Damascus often cooperated by conveying records and rulings from one court to another.[8] Furthermore, we know that a Maliki served as court clerk or notary in Sharaf al-Din's Shafi'i court. In any event, the participation of Sharaf al-Din in the issuance of estate inventories and the public sale of chattels from the estates was usually limited to authorization and appointment of the inventory agents, but sometimes he was involved in court certification of these notarial documents as was the case with other types of transactions and contracts.

More to our purpose, there were several types of documents recording various ways in which judges acted in a judicial capacity, some of which have been published. Perhaps the simplest, and most unusual, of these is the petition–decree (*qissa-marsum*), involving a process whereby an individual submitted a request to an official for his intervention or for appointment to office. Normally, these petitions were made to secular officials, most notably the sultan himself or one of his high-ranking officers, as a kind of extra-judicial, *mazalim* appeal, and for these reasons they are not covered in notarial manuals such as *Jawahir al-'uqud wa-mu'in al-muwaqqi'in wal-shuhud* ("The Nature of Contracts and the Aid of Judges, Notaries, and Witnesses") by the fifteenth-century Shafi'i *faqih*, Shams al-Din Muhammad al-Asyuti,[9] but are discussed in chancery handbooks. Nevertheless, as the attached specimen, Haram (#215) (see Figure 6.1), shows, a judge, in this case Sharaf al-Din's superior in Damascus, could be and was addressed for his help in this manner and format. In this document[10] Sutayta, an abandoned wife in Jerusalem, complains in 798/1395 to

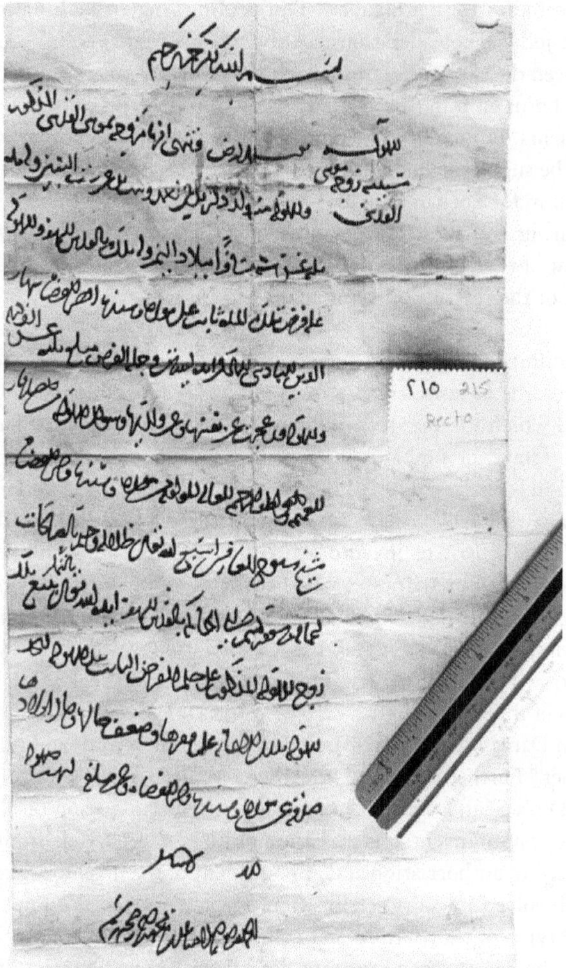

Figure 6.1 Haram (#215) recto.

a chief judge in Damascus that her husband had been absent for thirteen years in Yemen without paying the maintenance of thirteen thousand dirhams owed to her and her children for that period and requests the judge to authorize the sale of the husband's property in Jerusalem in order to provide that maintenance. A glance at (#215) shows immediately that it has been cast in the format of a chancery petition, with the name of the petitioner in the upper right-hand margin, and much conspicuously unutilized space in the right-hand margin and between the lines of the petition. On the back of the petition is found the judge's response (see Figure 6.2), cast in the form of a decree, headed by his identifying *'alama (ahmadu Llah ta'ala* = I praise God the Exalted) with the date at the bottom (*sabi' al-Muharram sanat thaman wa-tis'in wa-sab' mi'al*7 Muharram 798/22 October 1395), and the use of lots of blank space. The use of stereotyped phrases is evident in both the petition and the decree. In the former, the conventional "slave (*mamluka*) kisses the ground and reports (*tuqab-bil al-ard wa-tunhi*)" and "petitions from the all-embracing bounties and merciful benevolences ... a gracious decree to the magistrate in Jerusalem the Noble ... as a bounty from our Lord and Master (*wa-su'al al-mamluka min al-sadaqat al-'amima wal-'awatif al-rahima ... marsum karim ila al-hakim bil-Quds al-Sharif ... sadaqatan 'an*

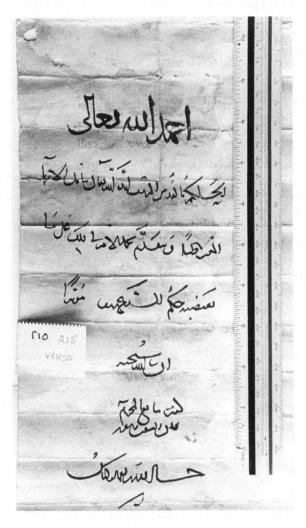

Figure 6.2 Haram (#215) verso.

Mawlana wa-Sayyidina...)." In the decree, "The magistrate in Noble Jerusalem... should give consideration to this report... and that the matter therein be treated according to what the edict of the noble law requires (*al-hakim bil-Quds al-Sharif... yata'ammal al-inha'... wa-yataqaddam bi-haml al-amr fi dhalik 'ala ma yaqtadihi hukm al-shar' al-sharif...*)." The fact that this document survived in Jerusalem indicates that it and the petition were sent from Damascus to Jerusalem. Substantively, these documents are of interest to us in the context of judicial procedure from the indications that a document from a Maliki judge in Jerusalem is adduced in support of a petition to the Shafi'i Chief Judge of Damascus to give instructions to the Shafi'i Chief Judge of Jerusalem. Again, we have evidence of close cooperation between judges of the four *madhhab*s in Damascus and Jerusalem. But the question of why this particular petition-decree format should have been adopted rather than another remains open, especially since there were other procedures and formats available to claimants, for example, the *su'al-marsum* (petition-court record), of which there are six specimens in the Haram collection, two of which I have published.[11]

With document (#616) (see Figures 6.3 and 6.4), we are back in the Shafi'i court of Sharaf al-Din and in the realm of documents described by al-Asyuti. This document is of special interest because it attaches various ancillary documents, including an oath at the bottom of *recto*, plus a legal acknowledgment (*iqrar*) and a court certification on *verso*. Here it is to be stressed that all these documents conform closely to the models prescribed by al-Asyuti in his notarial manual and that study of that work is essential to deciphering and interpreting the Haram documents. (#616) *recto* (see Figure 6.3) contains a petition (*su'al*) from a Jerusalem commoner requesting a court record (*mahdar*) from Sharaf al-Din's court attesting that the petitioner had deposited copper currency with a shopkeeper in Jerusalem. This part of the document appears at the head of *recto*. Note that like the chancery-style petition, it places the name of the petitioner in the right-hand margin and labels him the stereotypically lowly "slave (*mamluk*)."[12] The conventional phrase, "kisses the ground and reports," identical to that in (#215) discussed earlier, appears here too. The response to the petition is couched in another conventional format, not, however, a decree, but a testimony (*shahada*), in which it is established that the petitioner has produced witnesses to verify his claim:

> Those who affix their signatures, or have them written with their permission, at the end, give testimony of which they are informed, competent, and without doubt or skepticism... (*shahida man wada'a khattahu akhirahu wa-man yuktabu 'anhu bi-idhnihi shahadatuhum biha 'alimun wa-laha muhaqqiqun la-yashukkun wa-la-yartabun...*).

On the basis of this signed testimony by no fewer than five witnesses, the judge Sharaf al-Din has ruled that the present court record be written, granting the claimant's petition. This ruling appears in the form of the phrase "let it be written (*li-yuktab*)" written with a thick pen in the upper-left margin. This is followed by Sharaf al-Din's signature motto, "Praise be to God, I ask Him for success (*al-hamdu lillah wa-as'aluhu al-tawfiq*)." The *mahdar* is concluded at the bottom with the

Figure 6.3 Haram (#616) recto.

signatures of the five witnesses, written in the prescribed notarial style: "I witnessed its contents (*shahida* or *ashadu bi-madmunihi*)." After each of these witnessing clauses the judge has written his endorsement in a thick pen with the phrase, "he was witness before me (*shahida 'indi*)." In order to establish the absolute legitimacy of this transaction and the verdict, a ruling, called a *tawqi'*, is written in the right hand margin, perpendicular to the text of the *mahdar*, with the standard phrase, written with a thick pen by the court notary, in this case a Maliki, "Let there be witnesses to its certification....Let there be an oath (*li-yushhad bi-thubutihi...li-yuhlaf*)." Accordingly, below the signatures appears an oath (*half*) taken by the claimant before two signatory witnesses that he had indeed made the claimed deposit. This oath was undoubtedly legally necessary since the consignee of the deposit had died and could not verify or deny the claim, and it is classified by al-Asyuti as an oath of entitlement

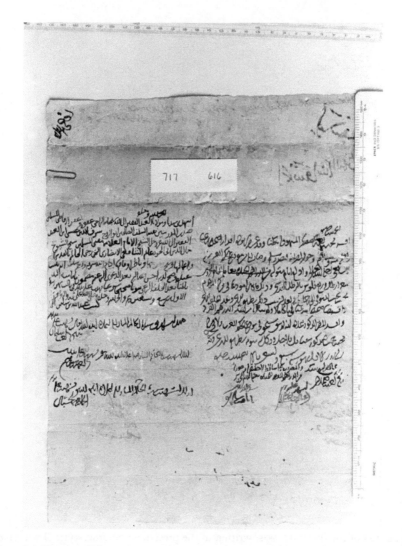

Figure 6.4 Haram (#616) verso.

with a witness (*yamin al-istihqaq ma'a al-shahid*).[13] That the judge has agreed to the validity of the claim and that it should be certified is indicated by a phrase, called in notarial parlance "claim motto (*'alamat al-da'wa*)," written on the upper-left corner of *verso*: "it was claimed in its (legal) manner (*udd'iya bihi bi-tariqihi*)."

This transaction continues on *verso* (see Figure 6.4) with two further documents. First an attestation (*ishhad*), written in standard judicial format, whereby Sharaf al-Din calls on no fewer than five legal witnesses to certify the contents of the court record and the oath on *recto*. This they do by appending their signatures in legally prescribed witnessing clauses such as those set down in al-Asyuti's manual. This took place in late December 1394, a few days after the drafting of the court record. Six days later, in a formal *iqrar* witnessed by two signatories, the claimant acknowledges that he had received his deposit in full and that he had no further claim on the estate of the deceased consignee nor on the court depository where the deposit had apparently been stored until the claim was legally resolved. This set of documents written on the front and back of the piece gives ample evidence of the complex legal procedures that could be involved in presenting, deciding, and certifying a case. Again it is to be stressed that these procedures are recorded in close conformity with those laid down in al-Asyuti's manual for judges and notaries. But the question remains open as to whether the document accurately reflects what actually happened in the court or whether the judge wanted the record to conform to the standard legal format in order to give it legitimacy.

Finally, a third way in which claimants and litigants could gain access to a judge and solicit and receive his judgment is illustrated by a third type of Haram document, called a *da'wa* (claim), recorded in the form of a court record (*mahdar*) as described by al-Asyuti. Three documents of this type I have published elsewhere and to characterize them, I shall quote myself, relying, as always, on al-Asyuti. A *da'wa*

> is a record of an action heard in court in which a plaintiff presents a claim for the consideration and judgment of a judge. A claim may or may not involve another party, i.e. a defendant...; in either event, it is incumbent upon the plaintiff to produce evidence in support of his claim, which the defendant, if there be one, can contest with his own witnesses or which he can deny with an oath. It is the function of the judge to determine whether the plaintiff has established his claim in a legal and valid manner and, if necessary, to give a formal pronouncement to that effect which is then recorded for the benefit of the court archives and for the successful party in the case.[14]

The question immediately arises as to how a *da'wa* differs from a *su'al/mahdar*. Unfortunately, this question I cannot answer with any asssurance, except to suggest that the former can be legally contested by defendants, whether real or fictional, whereas the latter is normally not; that the *da'wa* involves litigation in other words, and that a *su'al/mahdar* normally does not. In any event, the present document, (#653) *recto* and *verso*, does involve two litigants whose conflicting claims and evidence are heard before and judged by Sharaf al-Din al-Shafi'i. Since this document has not been published, I shall transcribe and translate the two parts in full.

Haram document (#653) *recto* (see Figure 6.5).
Transcription

Heading

١ جرى ذلك كذلك

٢ كتبه عيسى بن غانم الشافعي

٣ لطف الله به

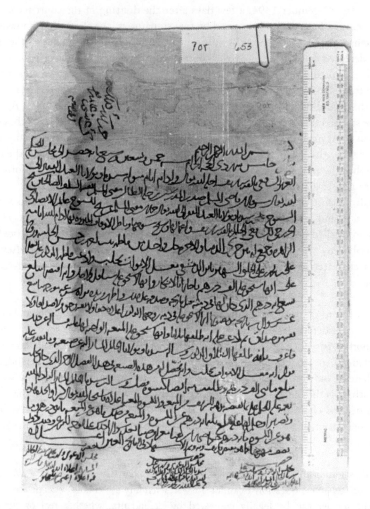

Figure 6.5 Haram (#653) recto.

Text

١ بسم الله الرحمن الرحيم

٢ بتاريخ خامس شهر ذي الحجة الحرام سنة خمس وتسعين وسبعماية حضر الى مجلس الحكم

٣ العزيز الشافعي بالقدس الشريف اجله الله تعالى وادام ايام متوليه سيدنا ومولانا العبد الفقير الى

٤ الله تعالى شرف الدين قاضي المسلمين صدر المدرسين رحلة الطالبين مفتي المسلمين بقية السلف الصالحين شيخ

٥ الشيوخ عيسى بن سيدنا ومولانا العبد الفقير الى الله تعالى جمال الدين مفتي المسلمين شيخ الشيوخ غانم الانصاري

٦ الخزرجي الشافعي الحاكم بالقدس الشريف واعمالها وشيخ شيوخها وناظر الاوقاف المبرورة بها ادام الله ايامه

٧ الزاهرة وجمع له بين جزي الدنيا والاخرة كل واحد من فاطمة بنت احمد بن حسن الحلبية وزوجها

٨ علي بن محمد بن علي الحلبي الشهير بابن الدمشقي مغسل الاموات بحلب وادعت فاطمة المذكورة على بعلها

٩ علي انها تستحق عليه الف درهم فاجابها بالانكار وانها لا تستحق عليه شيا قل ولا جل وانه اقبضها مبلغ

١٠ تسعماية درهم الذي كان لها في ذمته قبل تاريخه فصدقته على ذلك واظهر من يده براة شرعية مؤرخة بتاسع

١١ عشر شوال سنة تاريخه من مضمونه انها لا تستحق عليه في ذمة زوجها المذكور اعلاه ولا بقية من حق ولا صداقا ولا

١٢ بقية من صداق ثم ادعت عليه انه طلقها ثلاثا وانها تستحق عليه المتعة الواجبة لها عليه فساله عن ذلك

١٣ فاعترف بانه طلقها الطلاق المذكور وساله سيدنا ومولانا الحاكم المشار اليه عن صنعته وما يقدر به عليه

١٤ فذكر انه مغسل الاموات بحلب وانه تحصل له من هذه الصنعة في هذا الفصل الاخر الذي كان بحلب

١٥ مبلغ مايتي الف درهم وطلبت منه ايضا كسوة فصل وسالت سيدنا الحاكم المشار اليه ادام الله

١٦ نعمته عليه الحكم عليه بما يقتضيه مذهبه الشريف من المتعة والكسوة المعينة اعلاه فاستخار الله تعالى كثيرا واتخذه هاديا

١٧ ونصيرا وحكم لها عليه مبلغ ثلثماية درهم عليه الكسوة والمتعة من ذلك ما هو عن المتعة مايتي درهم وما

١٨ هو على الكسوة ماية درهما حكما صحيحا شرعيا معتبرا مرضيا يعد سوالها ذلك على الوجه الشرعي وذلك دون

١٩ نصف مهرها كما هو مقتضى الشرع الشريف وبه وسم الاشهاد في التاريخ المعين اعلاه

٢٠ (ا) حضرت

٢١ مجلس الدعوى وشهدت على

٢٢ سيدنا الحاكم المشار اليه ايده الله بما [نسب] اليه

٢٣ اعلاه في تاريخه كتبه عبد الرحمان بن احمد النابلسي

٢٠ (ب) حضرت

٢١ مجلس الدعوى وشهدت على

٢٢ سيدنا الحاكم المشار اليه اعلاه ايده

٢٣ الله تعالى بما فيه اعلاه في تاريخه

٢٤ كتبه عبد الله بن محمد بن حامد

٢٠ (ت) حضرت

٢١ مجلس الدعوى وشهدت على سيدنا الحاكم

٢٢ المشار اليه اعلاه ايده الله تعالى بما نسب اليه

٢٣ فيه اعلاه كتبه عيسى بن احمد العجلوني

Translation

Heading written perpendicular to text, in upper left corner

1   That took place in that manner
2   Written by 'Isa b. Ghanim al-Shafi'i,
3   May God be gracious to him

Text

1   In the name of God, the Compassionate, and Merciful.

2   On 5 Dhi al-Hijja the sacred, 795 (12 October 1393) there came to the esteemed court

3   of the Shafi'i (magistrate) in Jerusalem the Noble, may God the Exalted ennoble him and perpetuate the days of his agent, Our Master and Lord, the Servant Needy of

4   God the Exalted, Sharaf al-Din, Judge of the Muslims, Chief of the Teachers, Goal of the Seekers, Mufti of the Muslims, Survivor of the Virtuous Forefathers, Shaykh of

5   Shaykhs, 'Isa son of Our Lord and Master the Servant Needy of God the Exalted Jamal al-Din, Mufti of the Muslims, Shaykh of Shaykhs, Ghanim al-Ansari

6   al-Khazraji al-Shafi'i, Magistrate in Jerusalem the Noble and its districts, Shaykh of its Shaykhs and Supervisor of its Blessed Endowments, may God perpetuate his radiant days

7   and combine for him rewards of this world and the next, Fatima bint Ahmad b. Hasan al-Halabiyya and her husband

8   'Ali b. Muhammad b. 'Ali al-Halabi, known as Ibn al-Dimashqi, washer of corpses in Aleppo. The said Fatima claimed against her husband

9   'Ali that she was entitled to 1000 dirhams from him. He answered her, denying that she was entitled to anything great or small and that he had paid her the amount of

10 900 dirhams for which he had been indebted to her before the date of this document. She confirmed this, and he produced a legal quittance, dated 10 Shawwal of the current

11 year (19 August 1393), stating that she was not entitled to financial obligation from her said husband, no claim or partial claim, no dower, *sadaq,*

12 or partial dower. Then she claimed against him that he had repudiated her three times so that she was entitled to the indemnity (*mut'a*) obligatory for her from him. (The judge) asked him about that,

13 and he acknowledged that he had performed the mentioned repudiation. Our Lord and Master, the mentioned magistrate, asked him about his work and how it was valued.

14 The husband stated that he was a corpse washer in Aleppo and that during the last period that he was in Aleppo he had earned

15 200,000 dirhams. She also requested from him severance clothing (*kiswat al-fasl*) and asked Our Lord the mentioned magistrate, may God perpetuate

16 His benefaction to him, for a judgment against him according to that which his noble school requires of an indemnity and the clothing specified above. He beseeched God the Exalted for proper guidance and adopted him as guide and

17 helper and judged that he owed her 300 dirhams for the clothes and the indemnity, 200 for the latter, and

18 100 for the former, in a true, legal, considered, executable judgment following her request for that in the legal manner. Moreover, that is irrespective of (*duna*)

19 half of her nuptial gift (*mahr*) as the noble law requires. The attestation was endited on the specified date.

20a I was present	20b I was present	20c I was present
21a at the claim session and was witness to	21b at the claim session and was witness to	21c at the claim session and was witness to Our Lord, the mentioned magistrate,
22a Our Lord the mentioned magistrate, May God support him in what [is attributed] to him	22b Our Lord, the mentioned magistrate may he be supported by	22c may God the Exalted support him in what is attributed to him
23a above on its date. Written by 'Abd al-Rahman b. Ahmad al-Nabulsi	23b God the Exalted in what is above on its date	23c above, Written by 'Isa b. Ahmad al-'Ajluni.
	24b Written by 'Abd Allah b. Muhammad b. Hamid.	

(#653) *verso* (see Figure 6.6). Transcription

١ جرى ذلك كذلك
٢ كتبه عيسى بن غانم الشافعي
٣ لطف الله به

١ بتاريخ العشر الاول من شهر ذي الحجة سنة خمس وسبعماية اقر نورالدين على الزوج المذكور باطنا اقرارا شرعيا طوعا وهو بمجلس
٢ الحكم العزيز الشافعي المشار اليه باطنا ان زوجته فاطمة المذكورة باطنا تستحق ذمته مبلغ ماية درهم نصفها خمسون درهما فضة معاملة عن كسوة
٣ فاصل واحد استحقاقا شرعيا وصدقته على ذلك واقرت انها قبضت منه المبلغ المعين اعلاه والمتعة المقدرة باطنا وجملته ثلثماية [درهما]
٤ قبضا تاما كاملا وافيا وانها لا تستحق بعد ذلك في ذمته دينا ولا عينا ولا جليلا ولا حقيرا [من حقوق] الزوجية ولا غيرها الى تاريخه وبه شهد في تاريخه

٥
(ا) اشهد عليهما بذلك
٦ كتب عيسى بن احمد العجلوني

٥ (ب) اشهد عليهما بذلك
٦ كتب عبد الرحمان بن احمد النابلسي

٥ (ت) شهدت عليهما بذلك
٦ كتبه احمد بن محمد الخلال

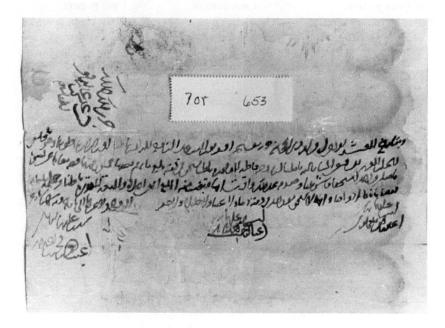

Figure 6.6 Haram (#653) verso.

Translation
Heading written perpendicular to text, upper left corner

1   That took place in that manner
2   Written by 'Isa b. Ghanim,
3   May God be gracious to him

Text

1   On the first tenth of Dhi al-Hijja 795/8–17 October 1393, the husband
    mentioned on *recto* acknowledged in
2   the Noble Shafiʻi Court mentioned on *recto* that his wife Fatima mentioned on
    recto is legally entitled to a financial obligation from him of 100 dirhams, half
    being 50 dirhams, of silver in circulation for one set of severance clothing.
3   She confirmed him in that and acknowledged that she had received from him
    the amount specified above as well as the indemnity calculated on *recto*, totalling
    300 dirhams,
4   completely, entirely, and sufficiently and she was not entitled thereafter from his
    financial obligation to any debt or chattel, great or small [from the rights of
    marriage] or otherwise up to the date of this document. This was witnessed on
    this date.

| 5a I am witness to the two of them in that. | 5b I am witness to the two of them in that. | 5c I was witness to the two of them in that. |
| 6a Written by 'Ali b. Ahmad al-'Ajluni | Written by 'Abd al-Rahman b. Ahmad al-Nabulsi | 6c Written by 'Abd al-Rahman b. Muhammad al-Khalal (?) |

These two *da'wa*s are written in the same format but not by the same hand. Here, perhaps, is a good place to remark that the scripts are obviously not easy to decipher since they are written cursively, without the distinguishing consonantal dots, and often carelessly, with the result that it would be extremely difficult to read them if we did not have a good idea of their content and stereotyped words and phrases. Again al-Asyuti comes to our rescue by providing samples which contain the standard phrases used in the various types of legal documents. At any rate, the *da'wa* on *recto* is longer and more complex than that on *verso*, so we shall focus on the former. A *da'wa* always bears the judge's endorsement, either his motto signature or one of several phrases such as appears here, "That took place in that manner (*jara dhalika ka-dhalika*)." Why one endorsement may be used rather than another I have not been able to determine since our guide, al-Asyuti, is not clear on this point. In any event the endorsement signifies the judge's approval of the content of the *da'wa* as a record of what transpired in his court. The text always begins with the date of the court session, and in cases initiated by individuals, the name of the presiding judge, complete with his titles, follows. These for our judge Sharaf al-Din al-Shafi'i take up no fewer than four lines of the text on (#653) *recto* and include not only honorifics customarily bestowed on a chief judge but also titles indicating his other offices in Jerusalem as well. The use of these titles indicates, I believe, the importance of protocol and its observance in the recording of court procedures. Then come the names of the two principals: the plaintiff, Fatima, and the defendant, 'Ali, her husband, a washer of corpses. Both are from Aleppo but seem to be presently resident in Jerusalem since it is there that they go to court. Then the claims of the plaintiff are presented, followed by the defendant's defense. The plaintiff then asks for the judge's judgment (*hukm*) according to his legal school. Then, in standard legalese, the document indicates that the judge considered the matter, with the phrase, "He beseeched God the Exalted for proper guidance and adopted Him as Guide and Helper and judged...(*fa-stakhara Llah ta'ala kathiran wa-ttakhadhahu hadiyan wa-nasiran wa-hakama*...)." The document ends with the witnessing clauses of three witnesses to the effect that they attended the court session and attested that the court record accurately reflected what had transpired. Again, I would stress that this is standard format as presented in notarial manuals and was followed by the enditer of our document.

The question of the substance of the document is somewhat problematic for a variety of reasons. The proceedings are not described in detail but only in general terms; the language is occasionally ambiguous; at least one of the statements seems on the surface implausible; probably most importantly, no reference is made to the basis on which the judge gave his final opinion. Nevertheless, the document gives valuable insight into the way questions arising from marriage and divorce could be handled in a pre-Ottoman court. In a nutshell, the wife, Fatima, claims in court that she was entitled to 1,000 dirhams from her husband, 'Ali, for a prior financial obligation (*dhimma*). Unfortunately, the nature of this obligation is not specified; consequently, we do not know whether it was a part of her (deferred) dower or her maintenance or perhaps a loan that she had made to him. This charge 'Ali counters with the claim that he had already paid her 900 dirhams, to which Fatima agrees, and 'Ali produces a document of legal quittance (*bara'a*), dated two months previously, to the effect that Faflima no longer had any financial claim on him whatsoever, including dower (*sadaq*). Since, however, dower is specified, perhaps the claim does refer to the deferred portion of her dower. But the case sounds peculiar. Why did Fatima bring this charge if she agreed that 'Ali had already paid her 900 of the 1,000 dirhams and that he had a legal quittance to that effect? Perhaps because she wanted court cognizance of the partially redeemed debt before she proceeded to her next claim. Or, perhaps, she simply did not know how 'Ali would plead. But, in the meantime, what had happened to the missing 100 dirhams, and why would Fatima, and the quittance, agree that she had no further claim on this particular debt if 100 dirhams were missing? But then Fatima charges that since 'Ali had repudiated her three times, this being a valid form of divorce, he owed her an indemnity, called *mut'a* (not to be confused with the Shi'i Muslim form of temporary marriage, also designated by this term). Again there is no dissent between the couple as 'Ali acknowledged that he had indeed performed the triple repudiation. That being the case, Judge Sharaf al-Din questioned 'Ali about his profession and its remuneration. As a corpse washer, 'Ali replies, he had earned the astounding sum of 200,000 dirhams during his last stint in Aleppo. This at a time when *fiqh* professors were making 3,600 dirhams a year, and janitors 180, at the Madrasa-Khanqah of Sultan Barquq in Cairo![15] Nevertheless, it should be recognized that 695 was a disastrous plague year in Syria and that according to the historian Ibn Sasra, in Aleppo

> from the beginning of the epidemic to its end three hundred and sixty thousand persons died...One hundred and fifty thousand died from within the city, and the remainder from outside of the city and its vicinity.[16]

Although these figures are undoubtedly greatly exaggerated, as Michael Dols points out,[17] they do make 'Ali's claimed salary sound slightly less preposterous.

More importantly, what were the legal issues involved? Surprisingly enough, there are references in both the primary and the secondary legal literature on the payment of an indemnity (*mut'a*) by a husband to a repudiated wife. These references are complex. A deceptively simple formulation is found in al-Nawawi's *Minhaj al-Talibin*, compiled in the late thirteenth century, as follows:

> A woman repudiated before or after consummation of marriage, to whom the law does not allow half dower, may demand a pecuniary indemnity called motah. This is so also in the case of separation, at any rate when this separation is not

the result of anything for which the woman is responsible. It is recommended that the motah should never be less than thirty drahmans, and where the parties cannot agree as to the amount of the motah, the decision rests with the court, which takes into account the condition of both the litigants. Some authorities maintain that the court should have regard to the husband's condition only; some only to that of the wife; others admit no legal minimum, provided that the motah consists of something that can form the basis of a legal obligation.[18]

Since the document specifies later that Sharaf al-Din questioned the defendant about his financial means and gave judgment on the basis of the requirements of his school, he may well have been aware of this opinion by one of the leading scholars in Shafi'i *fiqh*. Al-Asyuti, in his chapter on marriage (*nikah*), also discusses *mut'a* briefly, stating that there are discrepancies in the positions of the various legal schools on this issue. According to Abu Hanifa, al-Shafi'i, and Ahmad b. Hanbal, he says, "The woman who is repudiated before cohabitation (*masis*) and payment of maintenance (*fard*), is entitled only to *mut'a* ...," that is, not, presumably, to her dower. But, according to al-Asyuti, Ibn Hanbal opines elsewhere that she is "entitled to half of the fair bride price (*mahr*)." Moreover, according to the same source, Ibn Hanbal and Abu Hanifa hold that *mut'a* "is obligatory for every repudiated woman," while al-Shafi'i maintains that it is "incumbent on every living husband for a repudiated wife for whom half the bride price is not obligatory."[19] Reference to Schacht's *Introduction to Islamic Law* reveals that a husband who has consummated his marriage with a wife and later repudiates her must pay her the full bride price but

> If repudiation takes place before consummation, the wife has the right to half the stipulated *mahr* (or, if no *mahr* was stipulated, to an indemnity which is called *mut'a* and consists of a set of clothing ...[20]

More recently, Yossef Rapoport has discussed in detail the issue of *mut'a* in theory and practice as it evolved in early Islamic Egypt and he concludes that around the ninth century and thereafter it "became obsolete when it became common practice to defer a portion of the *sadaq* until death or divorce ... and its payment was left to the discretion of husbands."[21] Clearly, however, our document indicates that the theory and practice of *mut'a* were still alive in late fourteenth-century Jerusalem and therefore deserve further study.

As if these formulations were not sufficiently ambiguous, our particular case is further complicated by the fact that Fatima demands not just an indemnity from her husband but something termed *kiswat fasl/fasil* as well, which I take to mean severance clothing due to her from the maintenance her husband owes her. I have found no references to such an entitlement in the legal literature that I have examined so far. A further element of uncertainty is introduced by the clause stating that Sharaf al-Din's judgment was made to award Fatima 200 dirhams as indemnity and 100 for the clothing "irrespective of half her bridal gift (*duna nisf mahriha*)." On the other hand, she acknowledges on *recto* that after receiving the indemnity and the clothing she is not entitled in any way to any "rights of marriage (*huquq al-zawjiyya*)."[22]

Obviously, it is impossible to tell from the generalized legal language of the document the basis of Sharaf al-Din's judgment. It is my opinion that the jurisprudence on this issue was so ambiguous that Judge Sharaf al-Din must have used considerable judicial discretion in his verdict. Although it is certainly plausible to infer that indemnity may have been awarded because 'Ali repudiated his wife before cohabiting with her, this inference cannot be established with any certainty from the document itself or from the jurisprudential literature. Obscurity, of course, is a common feature of court records. Here is what Leslie Peirce observes on the basis of her study of sixteenth-century Ottoman records from 'Ayntab:

> But the court record is not a transparent text. It cannot be read as a complete and faithful account of what went on at court, nor can the speech recorded in the register be assumed to be a verbatim account of what people said.... Rather than a reflection of 'reality,' the written record is a constructed representation after the fact, recomposing events and acts of speech.... The judge's principal job in authoring the written record was to summarize, that is, to extract and record the elements of the proceedings that were essential to satisfying the requirements of correct legal procedure. The written record of a case, shaped by these requirements, is consequently not a mirror of human events and emotions, but rather a prism transforming separate streams of experience into a narrative focussed to satisfy a particular set of requirements.[23]

Nevertheless, it would certainly seem that Judge Sharaf al-Din in this case did try to act in conformity with Shafi'i jurisprudence, most manifestly in his concern for awarding an indemnity well within with the husband's means.

The *da'wa* on *verso*, court recognition that Fatima had received the amounts awarded to her, though simple, is also somewhat peculiar. Normally such a record would take the form of an acknowledgment (*iqrar*). Why the judge decided to adopt the *da'wa* format when no disputable claim was involved is not apparent. But it is good, I think, to end with perplexity, since we are pondering difficulties that arise from the use of documents as historical texts. Obviously there are no easy solutions, no clear-cut methodology for analyzing these records, so that at this stage, as far as the Haram documents are concerned, it is only with the cumulative publication and analysis of as many of the documents as possible that we can learn what we want to know, even at the risk of being labeled document fetishists.

Finally, a brief comment on the social significance of our documents. In two cases under discussion, what emerges most clearly is the conspicuous presence of women before a judge in some capacity or another. In both instances, the judge heard pleas from women, one in the form of a formal petition, the other in a court claim. In the first, involving a husband absent in Yemen, the judge promised to look into the matter and to rule accordingly; in the second, the judge, following his understanding of the jurisprudence involved, ruled in favor of the woman plaintiff. That women of apparently humble status in late fourteenth-century Jerusalem had ready and sympathetic recourse to its judges and courts is no longer earthshaking in light of recent scholarship on the status of medieval Muslim women but is interesting nonetheless.

And yet to stress the significance of women and to ignore men would be misleading. Although judgment went against the husband 'Ali he did, after all, have his day in court and his defense was heard and apparently weighed by the judge in rendering a verdict.

Notes

* A summary of this chapter was presented at a conference on "Dynamism of Muslim Societies," held 5–8 October 2001, in Kisarazu, Chiba, Japan. I am pleased to dedicate this version to Michael Winter.
1 Suraiya Faroqhi, *Approaching Ottoman History: An Introduction to the Sources* (Cambridge, 1999), pp. 1–2.
2 Little, *A Catalogue of the Islamic Documents from al-Haram ash-Sharif in Jerusalem* (Beirut, 1984), p. 268.
3 But for a study of some activities of Jerusalem courts and judges based on Mujir al-Din al-'Ulaymi's chronicle, see my article "Communal Strife in Late Mamluk Jerusalem," *Islamic Law and Society*, VI (1999), pp. 69–96.
4 *Al-Uns al-jalil bi-ta'rikh al-Quds wal-Khalil* (Amman, 1983), II, 127.
5 *Ta'rikh Ibn Qadi Shuhba*, (ed.) 'Adnan Darwish, I (Damascus, 1977), 565.
6 Little, "Two Fourteenth-Century Court Records from Jerusalem concerning the Disposition of Slaves by Minors," *Arabica*, XXIX (1982), pp. 41–2.
7 Berlin, 1985.
8 See Little, "Documents Related to the Estates of a Merchant and His Wife in Late Fourteenth Century Jerusalem," *Mamluk Studies Review*, II (1998), pp. 173–7.
9 Muhammad Hamid al-Fiqi (ed.), 2 vols (Cairo, 1955).
10 Published by Little, "Five Petitions and Consequential Decrees from Late Fourteenth Century Jerusalem," *Arab Journal for the Humanities*, LIV (1996), pp. 359–65.
11 Nos. 616 and 654. Little, "Two Petitions and Consequential Records from the *Haram* Collection," *Jerusalem Studies in Arabic and Islam*, XXV (2001), pp. 171–94.
12 Carl Petry has misconstrued this term in a petition to mean "a female member of the Mamluk elite," and has therefore misinterpreted a divorce case as involving "class prerogatives." See his "Conjugal Rights versus Class Prerogatives," in *Women in the Medieval Islamic World: Power, Patronage, and Piety*, (ed.) Gavin Hambly (New York, 1998), pp. 227–40.
13 Al-Asyuti, *Jawahir*, II, 317.
14 Little, "Two Court Records," p. 22, where nos. 649 and 650 are published. Cf. Little, "Haram Documents related to the Jews of Late Fourteenth Century Jerusalem," *Journal of Semitic Studies*, XXX (1985), pp. 243–57, for (#335), a court record of a hearing conducted in the presence of Sharaf al-Din at the order of the viceroy of Damascus.
15 Felicitas Jaritz, "Beitrag," to *Madrasa, Hanqah und Mausoleum des Barquq in Kairo* (Glückstadt, 1982), pp. 150–1, 154.
16 *A Chronicle of Damascus 1389–97*, trans. William M. Brinner (Berkeley, CA, 1963), p. 183. I am indebted to Boaz Shoshan for this observation.
17 *The Black Death in the Middle East* (Princeton, NJ, 1977), p.181.
18 *Minhaj et Talibin: A Manual of Muhammadan Law according to the School of Shafii*, trans. E. C. Howard (London, 1914), p. 313.
19 *Jawahir*, II, 45.
20 Oxford, 1964, p. 167.
21 "Matrimonial Gifts in Early Islamic Egypt," *Islamic Law and Society*, VII (2000), p. 21.
22 Although this phrase is obliterated in this document, I have reconstructed it from other documents.
23 "She is in Trouble...and I will Divorce Her': Orality, Honor, and Representation in the Ottoman Court of 'Aintab," in Hambly, *Women*, pp. 272–3.

7 The hoax of the miraculous speaking wall

Criminal investigation in Mamluk Cairo

Carl F. Petry

Among the myriad anecdotes reported in the voluminous chronicle literature describing Cairo and Damascus in the Mamluk period appears an intriguing – and at first glance wryly amusing – case of fraud conceived and implemented by a woman, her jurist husband and their Sufi accomplice during the latter eighth/fourteenth century. The hoax was so spectacularly successful that it provoked widespread unrest throughout the Mamluk capital. The case involved an ingenious ruse in which a wall of a house owned by a local Hanafi jurist allegedly spoke miraculously, responding to questions put to it by individuals high and low concerned over personal crises or their future. The incident achieved a degree of notoriety sufficient to warrant its description decades later by three eminent chroniclers of Cairo: al-Maqrizi, Ibn Hajar al-'Asqalani, and Ibn Taghri-Birdi.[1] Al-Maqrizi, whose version is the earliest of the three, also produced the most nuanced discussion of events. His portrayal of both participants and their actions hints at his own perception of mispropriety by the culprits, and the assiduous detective work by the individual who solved the case. Ibn Hajar's version, following Maqrizi's, is shorter, but includes a satirist's derision of the affair. His imputation of guilt differs somewhat from his predecessor's. And he alone described how the hoax was carried out. Ibn Taghri-Birdi, who may have assumed his readers' familiarity with Maqrizi's rendition, provided the tersest account of the three. He nonetheless added a second short satire deriding the hoax, and focused his remarks on its ultimate prosecution by the atabak of Cairo.

The incident was noted during the construction of an inventory of crime and criminal violence as reported in significant works of chronicle literature during the Mamluk period. The period covered during the search extended roughly from the mid-eighth to the mid-tenth hijri centuries (c.1350–1550 CE). I collected roughly 1,100 cases, ranging over a diverse array of criminal activity.[2] Of the several fields of crime collated, fraud emerged as a prominent category. The incident discussed below emerged as one of the more elaborately recounted (by these authors). Its portrayal by the three historians reveals their sentiments (and biases) about deceit, its consequences for social disorder, and the corruption of public trust by its perpetrators. With regard to procedure, translations of the three versions of the hoax are followed by commentaries on themes discernible in the authors' agendas, and contrasts in their assignment of primary culpability on the offenders' part.

Translations

Maqrizi, *Kitab al-Suluk*, 3: 361, line 8:

A grotesque event occurred during the month of Rajab (781 = October–November 1379). An individual who heard cases as a Hanafi witness among the hearing stations at the Square of the Festival Gate in Cairo was known as al-Shihab Ahmad ibn al-Fishi. Upon entering his dwelling near the Azhar Mosque, he heard a voice from a wall saying to him: "Fear God, and be courteously intimate with your wife." Seeing no one, he believed that a jinn was speaking to him. When he informed his companions, they accompanied him to his house whereupon they heard the speech emanating from the wall. The speaker responded to their queries but remained invisible. They too assumed that a jinn was addressing them. When they gossiped about their experience, both Cairo and Misr were aroused. People came from all over to Ibn al-Fishi's house to hear the wall speak. They began to tell the wall their allegations, and it addressed them. What they said most was: "Good Heavens, greet the speaking wall!" The populace verged on infatuation over this, and brought to that wall many perfumed items. (Even) the virgin came to it from her private quarters.

(As news of this affair spread,) the muhtasib of Cairo, Jamal al-Din Mahmud al-'Ajami, rode to this Ibn al-Fishi's dwelling to verify what the wall said. He had (previously) delegated one of his aides to investigate him. Now, at the house was a raised terrace, and beneath it a stable where a soldier (policeman?) was stationed. He (the soldier) was also put in charge of him (Ibn al-Fishi). When the aide came up to the wall and addressed it, it answered him. The aide then ordered the wall razed, but it responded: "Demolish, for it will fall on nothing; nor do I care." And indeed when he razed the wall he found nothing. The aide returned to his house much amazed. Since discord (over the affair) was now escalating among the populace, the muhtasib consulted with his colleagues as to a course of action. He (then) dispatched someone (the aide) to investigate whether the wall ceased speaking after its demolition the first time. [Apparently the wall had been rebuilt after the aide's initial interrogation.] His delegate found the wall talking as it had prior to its demolition. The muhtasib was perplexed by this.

This market inspector was both astute and bold. His career had seen both good and bad days, but overall no positive fortune had come his way. Not that his actions failed to invoke popular praise, since when he supervised a charitable trust he caused its destitution due to his lavish distributions to its beneficiaries. Indeed, when he held the inspectorship in Cairo, prices dropped – while they rose upon his dismissal. The populace fretted, and demanded his reinstatement due to the prosperity brought on by his good deeds. As the saying goes: "To be sparing with beneficence diminishes prosperity."

When the muhtasib's delegate returned and informed him that speech continued from the wall, he gathered his associates and convened them before it. They recited several verses from the Qur'an. The muhtasib then summoned the owner

of the house, saying: "Tell the speaker that the Qadi Jamal al-Din greets you."
The owner duly said: "Oh revered Sir, the Qadi greets you." The wall replied:
"And to him peace, with God's mercy and blessing." The muhtasib then said:
"Ask it how long will this calumny go on?" It replied: "Until God the All-High
wishes." The muhtasib then turned to the owner, saying: "Tell it that what you
do riles the people, and is not beneficial." The wall replied: "No speech remains
after this," and fell silent. They addressed it as "Esteemed Shaykh" but it spoke
no more. Its tone had been harsh, indicating that its words were not human.
When he despaired over talking with it, it ceased to acknowledge him.
Meanwhile, the dispute among the people over the wall intensified. They had
begun to regard it as an object of veneration. They now assembled before it
routinely, declaring to it all sorts of fantasies. The muhtasib's visit had occurred
on Monday the 12th (presumably of Rajab = 24 October). Thereafter, the wall
recommenced addressing the people. Its notoriety grew so that even officers and
notables came to it with food and other offerings – to Monday the third of
Sha'ban (14 November).

The muhtasib now resolved to unravel this ruse. He schemed against Ibn
al-Fishi incessantly until the latter acknowledged that the affair was a hoax. On
that day, the muhtasib rode to Ibn al-Fishi's house, accompanied by a group of
aides. He apprehended him along with his wife and a Sufi mendicant, revered
by the people, who lived with them. This Sufi was known as al-Rukn 'Umar. He
returned with them to his house. Upon interrogation, the wife informed the
muhtasib that it was she who had spoken (from behind the wall). Her motive:
her husband, Ibn al-Fishi, had afflicted her intimacy, and she (therefore) had
beguiled him with an allegation that the jinn had recommended her (to him).
She had persisted with this ruse against him until he was influenced by her. She
then informed her husband of her trick. He realized that she should persist with
the faked speech so that they might gain fame and riches. She agreed with him
to continue with the hoax, so that events progressed as they did.

The muhtasib rode to the Amir al-Kabir and informed him of what the wife
had confessed. The Amir arrested her, the husband and the shaykh 'Umar (who
had connived) with them. The Amir flogged the two men with the bastinado,
while the wife was lashed with a cane some 600 strokes. He then ordered all
three fastened on a camel. They were paraded throughout Cairo and Misr on this
Monday (the third) – an ignominious day. During it the people's weeping over
the wife was widespread, for she had been mounted on a camel with her hands
stretched out and nailed on wooden stocks, her head shawled and her face veiled.
Such a crucifixion was unprecedented for a woman. With regard to the muhtasib, it was arranged that he descend (from the Citadel) with a robe of honor that
had been bestowed on him. The masses heightened their revilement of him due
to their anger concerning her.

This Ibn al-Fishi had previously been meeting with the Amir al-Kabir
wearing a woolen shawl on his head. He would present him with morsel of *ka'k*,
saying: "The Shaykh of the wall, Muhammad, sent this to you." He would then
take the Amir's hand in his and shake it, saying: "Fear God and treat the
commoners justly." The Amir was influenced by his words. The Shaykh 'Umar

al-Rukn subsequently went to the Amir after al-Fishi. He had attained renown for withdrawing to the roof of the Mosque of 'Amr ibn al-'As where he dwelled for thirty years. The populace had frequented him there – amirs, notables and others – seeking the blessing of his prayers on their behalf, until the affair of speech from the wall had become well-known. He then came to Ibn al-Fishi and attended him. The people gathered to him. When the Amir al-Kabir received 'Umar al-Rukn and honored him, he set about his chicanery and (then) departed. Now, when the muhtasib ascended the two culprits to the Amir, and apprised him of their fraudulent acts, the latter's anger heightened against them. When they confessed to their heinous ruse, events took their course.

Among other deceits disclosed during this episode: Ibn al-Fishi's wife claimed that several days prior to the inquest she had, during her sleep, beheld herself preaching on a *minbar*. One of the knowledgeable dream interpreters with whom we (al-Maqrizi) were contemporaneous deciphered this vision as a profound infamy, since the wife by her nature was qualified neither to mount the *minbar* nor to preach the *khutba*. And so it was that she rode the camel a whole day while nailed – her fate a warning to the people for such behavior. We seek God's protection from an evil judgment.

Ibn Hajar al-'Asqalani, *Inba' al-ghumr*, 1: 198, line 4:

On the first of Rajab (781 = 13 October 1379), a rumor spread among the populace that someone was speaking from behind a wall. The people obsessed over this throughout Rajab and Sha'ban, believing that the speaker was either a jinn or an angel. A typical statement: "Oh Lord, preserve us, for the wall talks." In response (the poet) Ibn al-'Attar said:

> Oh you who speak unseen from a wall,
> Appear, unless this act be false.
> For people do not hear tongues of walls,
> For it is said that walls have (only) ears.

Then Jamal al-Din the muhtasib pursued the incident and probed the facts until he discovered the truth of it. He first went to the house and heard the speech from the wall. He ordered the soldier to lurk near the site (to keep watch). He beat the (owner's) servant to force a confession. He (then) ordered the wall razed, which was done.

They subsequently returned but heard the speech as before. The muhtasib attended another time and ordered the one who addressed the speaker to say: "This is what upheaval causes among people. How long will it last?" He (the wall speaker) replied: "After this day, nothing remains," and went off. But then he (the muhtasib) learned that he (the speaker) had resumed. The muhtasib's conviction strengthened that the case was fabricated. He persisted with his investigation until he learned the covert facts of the matter.

To wit: he discovered an individual called the Shaykh Rukn al-Din 'Umar (associated) with another named Ahmad al-Fishi, who had colluded with him in this affair. The two had instructed Ahmad al-Fishi's spouse how to speak from behind the wall through a gourd, so that the voice would come out strangely – not resembling normal human sounds. The muhtasib communicated the case to Barquq (the Amir al-Kabir), who nailed them down after flogging their legs with the bastinado and the woman below her legs. Many people felt great pain for them. The muhtasib Jamal al-Din was granted a robe of honor because of his investigation.

It was said that this case originated from the wife's jealousy of her husband. She had connived with the Shaykh 'Umar that he speak to her from behind the wall from a gourd, and prevent him (her husband) from mistreating her. He bored (a hole in) the wall so that nothing remained of it but its (outer) shell. He then installed the gourd and spoke from behind it. He spoke to him (her husband) at night in that detestable voice, saying: "Oh Ahmad, fear God and associate intimately, and favorably, with your wife, for she is a pious woman." After he did that repeatedly, the husband was frightened and reconciled with her. When this affair went on for some time and the two had come to terms, the wife apprised her husband of the ruse. It then opened a trove of income for them. The people hastened to Ahmad al-Fishi's house to hear the voice. The woman arranged that it would be she who did the talking (behind the wall).

The muhtasib was motivated to investigate their case because the speech that was heard yielded no information about anything missing, nor an incident to come. Al-Rukn 'Umar had resided in the Mosque of 'Amr ibn al-'As for thirty years in good standing. The populace had revered him and visited him. Their trial occurred on the second of Rajab (14 October). The aforementioned Ahmad was a respected jurist, seated near the Azhar Mosque, close by the Zawiya of Ibn 'Atta'.

Ibn Taghri-Birdi, *al-Nujum al-Zahira*, 11: 172, line 14:

In this year (Rajab 778, November–December 1376), a peculiar event occurred in Egypt with regard to speech from a wall. To wit: at the outset of Rajab, a person's speech emanated from a wall in the house of the honorable Shihab al-Din Ahmad al-Fishi al-Hanafi, near the Azhar Mosque. All who proceeded to this wall and asked something of it received a response. It would address them with eloquent words. The people crowded to it; notables of the regime repaired to the wall and addressed it. The populace were obsessed with the site, abandoning their workplaces to swarm around the aforementioned house. (Consequently,) the intelligentsia heightened their scrutiny of the phenomenon, examining all events involved with it. Yet they did not obtain any information about it.

The populace were perplexed by the peculiar affair, until the Qadi Jamal al-Din Mahmud al-Qaysari al-'Ajami, muhtasib of Cairo, arrived at the house. He investigated the affair with every power vested in him, so that he razed a section of the wall. No sign of anyone was disclosed. The speech continued each day to the third of Sha'ban (16 November). The masses now verged on worshipping at the site, frequently calling out: "For Heaven's sake, the wall is speaking."

Government officials feared the situation would get out of hand. The affair alarmed them, until it was discovered that the one who was speaking was the spouse of the owner of the dwelling. The Atabak Barquq was informed of that. He then summoned her along with her husband. When they presented themselves, the woman denied the accusation, but he flogged her and she confessed. He then ordered her nailed. Another individual was nailed with her, by the name of 'Umar. He was responsible for inciting the people to assemble before her. Subsequently, Barquq lashed the husband and this 'Umar with the bastinado. The two were paraded around Misr and Cairo. Then they (all?) were released after serving a term in prison. With regard to this affair, the Shaykh Shihab al-Din ibn al-'Attar said, in short verse:

> Oh speaker from the wall who is unseen,
> Appear, unless this deed be false.
> We did not hear tongues in walls,
> For it is said that walls have (only) ears.

Another said:

> In the dwelling of al-Fishi the mortals returned marveling
> over a speaker from a wall whose caprice persisted.
> All of them they flogged in cold irons,
> since the owner of the house was aware of him within.

Commentary

Al-Maqrizi: domestic deceit, popular unrest, gendered blasphemy

At the outset, Maqrizi placed special emphasis on the disruptive consequences of the loquacious wall. He began his comments about the hoax with a statement on turmoil stemming from the scheme hatched by Ibn al-Fishi, his spouse and the Shaykh 'Umar, noting how rapidly word spread about the wall's miraculous capacity to speak. Maqrizi concluded his opening statement with a stock phrase about the virgin woman, stereotypically the most closeted individual in this society, departing her secluded quarters unchaperoned to address the wall. He then went on to discuss the intrepid investigator, Jamal al-Din al-'Ajami, market inspector of Cairo. Maqrizi depicted the muhtasib as incorruptible and esteemed among the populace for his rigorous enforcement of commercial standards. Maqrizi commented that al-'Ajami was generous to a fault, depleting the principal of charitable trusts when distributing their proceeds to needy recipients. Although al-'Ajami may not have stinted in his beneficence, he apparently gained little in the way of promotions from his profligacy since Maqrizi saw no upward trajectory in his career – prior to the wall scandal. Al-'Ajami's zeal intensified as his suspicion heightened. After placing the owner of the house under surveillance by an aide and a soldier (presumably serving as a local gendarme), al-'Ajami eventually uncovered the elaborate ruse, and extracted confessions from all three suspects. Maqrizi did not explain how al-'Ajami solved the case. But he mused at length over its insidious context.

The context involved deceit evolving from a rather simple – and maudlin – motive: unrequited passion. The wife (never named) of an established Hanafi jurist, prompted by advice from a Sufi shaykh of some local standing, hid behind a wall in their home and spoke to her husband as a spirit, admonishing him to resume conjugal intimacy with her. Yet Maqrizi chose to focus on the darker implication of gender impropriety as the root malfeasance underlying the disruption that ultimately ensued from this ploy. Maqrizi described Ibn al-Fishi's wife as the ruse's initial instigator, whose frustration over personal neglect was readily supplanted by ambition and greed that led to massive fraud. The wife's primary culpability was brutally apparent in the incident's formal prosecution, following al-'Ajami's disclosure of the ruse. The muhtasib conveyed the three suspects to the Grand Amir (the Atabak in Ibn Taghri-Birdi's version), who heard the charges in his capacity as penultimate appellate judge, answerable only to the sultan. The Amir convicted all the suspects. While sentencing the men to flogging, he subjected the wife to an unusually severe penalty: 600 cane strokes – a potentially life threatening trauma. The display of the culprits on camels that followed was a routine act of public degradation imposed on criminals of this ilk. But the fastening (literally nailing) of the wife to some sort of wooden stocks amounted to an effective crucifixion, and Maqrizi noted that such a shocking chastisement was unprecedented for a woman.[3]

Maqrizi hardly exonerated the two male offenders. He described in detail how Ibn al-Fishi and al-Rukn 'Umar had exploited the haunted wall to gain the ear of the Grand Amir himself. His ire kindled by his own chagrin over being duped by the ruse, the Amir condemned the men to beating and stripped them of their positions. Maqrizi commented on the loss of prestige they suffered in consequence of their crime: the enduring stigma for violation of public trust. But Maqrizi singled out the wife, who starkly emerged in his rendition as the transgressor of accepted behavioral boundaries. Maqrizi concluded the affair by relating the wife's disclosure, presumably under interrogation, of her dreams about preaching the Friday *khutba* publicly from a *minbar*.

Even imagining such an act in one's sleep was blasphemous for a woman according to a reputed dream interpreter, and Maqrizi regarded the wife's indulgence in clandestine fantasy as the crime meriting her likely death sentence by crucifixion. Fraud that had deceived so many among the populace succeeded because it was instigated by an individual who had defied divinely ordained norms of conduct, even if secretly.

Maqrizi thus displayed no empathy for the three offenders. He noted that the inspector al-'Ajami, who might expect to win the Grand Amir's favor for astutely unraveling a complex case – and gain the stature of a stalwart defender of the public interest that had previously eluded him, was indeed rewarded by his superior. Apparently ignoring widespread sympathy among the populace over the wife's fate as unduly cruel, the Amir elected to bestow the customary robe of honor on the muhtasib before his descent from the Citadel. Maqrizi thus tantalizingly juxtaposed al-'Ajami's success against the public's consternation over disclosure of the hoax and their lachrymose compassion for its perpetrators. How did these issues fare at the pens of Maqrizi's successors?

Ibn Hajar: domestic spat, adroit ploy, sullied stature

In contrast to Maqrizi, Ibn Hajar attributed blame for the ruse primarily to the two male plotters: the jurist Ahmad ibn al-Fishi and the Sufi Rukn al-Din 'Umar. He initiated his remarks by noting how rapidly rumors spread about the haunted wall. He then quoted satirical verses by a local poet, Ibn al-'Attar, who hinted at widespread suspicion over the credibility of supernatural speech emanating from the wall. Like his colleague, Ibn Hajar praised the muhtasib's persistence. Alarmed over the heightening of popular unrest, al-'Ajami doggedly probed the case until he discovered its plot. At this stage, Ibn Hajar inserted details about the ruse and investigation omitted by Maqrizi: the soldier–gendarme covertly watched Ibn al-'Fishi's house and subsequently beat a confession from a servant. But the groom either divulged no clue or was genuinely ignorant of the plot, apparently, since neither his flogging nor demolition of the wall disclosed a culprit.

When al-'Ajami finally succeeded in uncovering the ruse, the key figure implicated by Ibn Hajar turned out to be the Shaykh Rukn al-Din. It was he who had colluded with Ibn al-Fishi to proceed beyond a domestic ploy to hoodwink the populace. Uniquely among the three chroniclers, Ibn Hajar described the procedure for implementing the ruse.[4] The shaykh had been the one who first addressed Ibn al-Fishi's wife from behind the wall, his voice shockingly distorted and amplified by its transmission through a gourd (presumably when she was ready for conjugal relations with her husband). Ibn Hajar asserted flatly that the sordid affair which followed grew from Ibn al-Fishi's abuse and neglect of his wife. Although the wife readily apprised her husband of the trick and willingly replaced the shaykh as the hidden speaker, Ibn Hajar pointed to Rukn al-Din as the one who had perceived its lucrative potential for deluding people. Regardless of their social stations, all were gullible and thus ripe for fleecing.

Ibn Hajar restricted the prosecution to the two men by the Atabak and future sultan Barquq (Maqrizi's Amir al-Kabir) after the inspector brought the suspects before him. Paralleling Maqrizi's version, Ibn Hajar also claimed that the Atabak granted al-'Ajami a robe of honor for resolving the case and diluting the public's furor. He dwelled on the shaykh's fall from grace, stating that he had resided in the Mosque of 'Amr as a renowned guardian of piety for 30 years. Revered status accrued over a lifetime was thus lost in an irresistible moment of greed. Rukn al-Din's fellow conspirator, Ibn al-Fishi, ostensibly shared his disgrace. But did the two manage to surmount their humiliation and regain their positions? The final commentator had new twists to add.

Ibn Taghri-Birdi: the facility of gullibility

Latest of the chroniclers, Ibn Taghri-Birdi accentuated the notoriety of the miraculous wall, and the eagerness of both notables and commons to accept its speech as supernatural. He depicted Ibn al-Fishi, owner of the house, as a jurist whose reputation was respected, and thus not suspected of mendacity or fraud by the public. Ibn Taghri-Birdi acknowledged the muhtasib as the sleuth who discerned the hoax. He described him also as a qadi, and likely sharing Ibn al-Fishi's Hanafi affiliation due to the Iranian and Anatolian origins indicated by his nisbas. Yet Ibn Taghri-Birdi discussed the offenders' prosecution solely in the context of a hearing by Barquq (similarly titled Atabak, the future sultan). According to Ibn Taghri-Birdi, it was he who forced confessions from Ibn al-Fishi's wife and, presumably, from her co-conspirator 'Umar (no mention of his status either as a shaykh or a Sufi). Ibn Taghri-Birdi claimed that, although the wife did the speaking, 'Umar was responsible for spreading word about the wall itself and inciting the populace to gather before it.

Ibn Taghri-Birdi's depiction of the culprits' fate departs from his predecessors' portrayal in detail as well as brevity.[5] He stated that the wife and 'Umar, as primary instigators, both suffered the nailing, while Maqrizi limited the more severe crucifixion to the former. But the public flogging seems to have been reserved for the two men, with no subsequent mention of the wife's final punishment. He did use the third person plural rather than the dual when noting the offenders' release after serving time in jail. Whether Ibn Taghri-Birdi actually meant to include the wife is unclear. As indicated previously, he may have assumed his readers' familiarity with Maqrizi's and Ibn Hajar's more replete accounts of the incident. But if so, his lack of comment on Maqrizi's heated condemnation of the wife's transgressions remains enigmatic. Whatever his motive, Ibn Taghri-Birdi wished to leave his audience musing over verses by pundits who satirized the affair. His quotation from Ibn al-'Attar diverged only slightly from Ibn Hajar's. The second, unnamed, employed no clever usages but simply commented on the offenders' culpability and deserved punishment.

Retrospective

All three historians embellished a common theme: evolution of the hoax from a private domestic matter into a massive public fraud. Once the perpetrators comprehended its extraordinary potential, they put aside their personal differences to concentrate on refining their techniques and reaping the profits and stature that were so readily proffered. The chroniclers pointedly observed how avidly the populace, both elite and commons, fell for their scheme. It was the tumult resulting from their infatuation, to use Maqrizi's term, over the wall that caught al-'Ajami's notice, and thereby spurred his investigation.

But the aspect of this hoax that rivets the contemporary reader's attention was clearly Maqrizi's implication of the wife's primary culpability as a violator of behavioral norms deeply embedded in the popular mind. Her willingness to delude her husband, despite his neglect, itself tarnished her role as a submissive spouse obliged to accept whatever condition he imposed on her. Such duplicity on her part, as Maqrizi would imply, thus paved the way to the subsequent fraud that disrupted Cairo's public order and embarrassed the Grand Amir, who ranked as second political authority of the sultanate. The wife's admission to her fantasy over preaching the *khutba* openly in a mosque, extracted under duress, Maqrizi added to confirm her blasphemous delusions. These were the inevitable consequences of an ego gone off on a wild tangent.

It is therefore Maqrizi's version, closest to the incident chronologically, that moves inexorably from the ludicrous ingenuousness of the original domestic squabble to the dreadful final outcome of the wife's crucifixion. That Maqrizi's successors chose not to dwell on this theme of gendered transgression is truly enigmatic, if one assumes their knowledge of Maqrizi's rendition. Without inclusion of the wife's guilt for crimes far surpassing her wiles to settle a personal dispute, the incident remains at the level of an inane hoax – one that easily succeeded in duping so many people from all social levels because of the credulity natural to the human species. Ibn Hajar and Ibn Taghri-Birdi either presupposed their readers' knowledge of Maqrizi's depiction, and decided not to elaborate on it, or elected to ignore it to highlight the tragi-comic dimension of the affair by confining their remarks to its domestic aspect and the masses' capacity for deception. If the latter hypothesis more closely encompasses their intent, then the selectivity of facts by which historians of the Mamluk period sought to impart their take on themes vital to the message they wanted to convey is starkly revealed in an event such as the miraculous speaking wall.

Notes

1 Taqi al-Din al-Maqrizi, *Kitab al-suluk li-ma'rifa duwal al-muluk*, vol. 3, (ed.) Sa'id 'Ashur (Cairo, 1970); Shihab al-Din Ibn Hajar al-'Asqalani, *Inba' al-ghumr bi-anba' al-'umr*, (ed.) Hasan Habashi (Cairo, 1971); Jamal al-Din Ibn Taghri-Birdi, *al-Nujum al-zahira fi muluk al-Qahira*, (ed.) Ahmad Zak al-'Idwi (Cairo, 1929–52). I wish to acknowledge the assistance with the translation offered by my colleague, J. O. Hunwick. A second eye is vital to such an exercise, especially an eye as informed as his.

2 A crime is defined here as an act deemed sufficiently menacing or disruptive to warrant investigation, subsequent prosecution, and eventual punishment by the legal and military authorities. This distinction separates criminal acts from other kinds of social violence that passed without formal inquiry. The 1,100 cases were selected from a larger group of violent incidents according to this criterion of inclusion in the broader study. Data on crime collected from narrative chronicle literature of the Mamluk period (the earliest surviving registers of cases from criminal courts date from the decades following the Ottoman conquest) have been compared with analyses of criminal activity occurring in medieval Europe and China. Such studies as Barbara Hanawalt, *Crime and Conflict in English Communities, 1300–1348* (Cambridge, 1979); Guido Ruggiero, *Violence in Renaissance Venice* (New Brunswick, 1980); Edward Muir and Guido Ruggiero (eds), *History from Crime* (Baltimore, 1994); Lenman Gatrell (ed.), *Crime and the Law: The Social History of Crime in Western Europe since 1500* (London, 1980); James Inciardi and Charles E. Faupel (eds), *History and Crime: Implications for Criminal Justice Policy* (Beverley Hills, 1980); Eric H. Johnson, *The Civilization of Crime: Violence in Town and Country since the Middle Ages* (Urbana, 1996); Derk Bodde and Clarence Morris (eds), *Law in Imperial China* (Philadelphia, 1973); Philip Huang, *Civil Justice in China* (Stanford, 1996) have revealed many parallels with the prosecution of crime in the medieval Islamic world. Fraud is certainly represented as a category in these studies, but did not assume the prominence that emerged from the Mamluk-period narrative data.

3 Crucifixion (literally "nailing"; sometimes translated as "scourging") was frequently imposed on men during the Mamluk period as punishment for homicide, rebellion or treason, and was restricted largely to members of the military elite. To my knowledge, its infliction on a woman is restricted to this case, although a definitive count through all incidents included in the broader study has yet to be completed.

4 With regard to Ibn Hajar's discussion of the technique that produced the distorted voice, he may have had access to sources about the ruse unknown to Maqrizi. Why the latter would have omitted such an intriguing detail from his otherwise more replete version if he had known about it remains inexplicable.

5 Ibn Taghri-Birdi's date for the incident differed from his predecessors by three years. He provided it without comment or correction of the earlier versions. Its occurrence suggests that he used sources differing from theirs – but without identification.

8 *Awlad al-nas* in the Mamluk army during the Bahri period

Amalia Levanoni

Researchers of the Mamluk period are in full agreement regarding the career the Mamluks chose for their sons, *awlad al-nas*; they trained their children mainly for one of two careers of the elite: as clerks in the civil elite or as soldiers in the Mamluk army. This chapter will focus on the Mamluk sons who chose a military career. David Ayalon clearly links the service of the *awlad al-nas* to the *halqa*, the auxiliary corps of the Mamluk army. He thinks that the Mamluk sons' chances of promotion were thin when compared to those of the purchased Mamluks. They were kept out of the latter's units and restricted to the far inferior *halqa*. However, Ayalon notes, there were sons of amirs who attained amir rank in the army, but no higher than Amir of Forty. During the second period of rule of al-Nasir Hasan (755–62/1354–61), sons of Mamluks attained the rank of *muqaddam alf*, commander of a thousand, but this was out of the ordinary and unique to this particular sultan. During the Circassian period, the sons of Mamluks are totally identified with the *halqa* and their status declined with it.[1] Ulrich Haarmann also thinks that the *awlad al-nas* who entered the army usually served in the *halqa*.[2] But in contrast to Ayalon, Haarmann thinks that they succeeded in advancing through the ranks and attained senior posts in the army, but only on condition that they had an advocate behind them and the right friends at court. There was, of course, a correlation between the political status they attained and their part in the *iqta'* land allocation system. From the 1370s, the members of the Qalawunid house, the *asyad*, amassed vast economic power through the *iqta'at* they took for themselves. Sultan Barquq, the first Circassian sultan (784–801/1382–99), restored the lands held by the *asyad* to the *iqta'* system with the establishment of the *diwan al-mufrad*, a bureau that dealt with payments to the Mamluks he purchased, as part of the introduction of a new division of the sultanate's resources.[3] In *A Turning Point in Mamluk History*, I had noted the gradual but constant increase in the entry of sons of Mamluks into the army during the Turkish, Bahri, period, with military and economic status equal to that of the purchased Mamluks.[4] In this chapter, I shall attempt to show that the heightened status of the sons of the Mamluks during this period, particularly the sons of the amirs, was not sporadic but the consequence of a deliberate policy of the Qalawunid sultans, those who succeeded in maintaining effective rule, and the Mamluk factions that were fighting for the remnants of the Turkish hegemony in the Mamluk sultanate.

During the rule of Baybars and Qalawun, the recruitment of sons of Mamluks, *awlad al-nas*, into the Mamluk army ranks, when it occurred, was a rare exception. During this period there were 11 amirs who were sons of Mamluks – 8 in Egypt, 2 in Damascus and 1 whose whereabouts are unknown.[5] Although the rank of others is not mentioned, 2 out of 10 were amirs. As the sources usually attach importance to the rank of amir of one hundred and seldom fail to mention it and as none of the six were famous amirs, it may be assumed that none held the rank of amir of one hundred. This confirms not only that the entry of sons of Mamluks into the army was extremely limited during this period but also that the status of those who were recruited remained low.[6] Sons of Mamluks were usually granted an allocation of money, meat, bread and fodder until they reached adulthood when they became eligible for recruitment as soldiers in a designated unit of the *halqa*.[7] It was Qalawun who, out of respect for his Bahri Mamluk colleagues, inaugurated a special unit in the *halqa* for sons of Mamluks, which he called 'al-Bahriyya'. That is, he recruited those who were found idling in Cairo 'and gave them a wage and *iqta'at* in the *halqa*'.[8] Furthermore, the *iqta'at* granted to the sons of Mamluks in the *halqa* were clearly inferior to those granted to the Royal Mamluks.[9]

Qalawun was insistent on these conventions even concerning the sons of his most eminent amirs. Amir Turuntay, who was *na'ib al-saltana*, and Amir Kitbugha, *na'ib al-ghayba*, each got his offspring married to the offspring of the other and petitioned Qalawun to grant *iqta'at* in the *halqa* to their sons. Qalawun refused on the grounds that they had not reached adulthood, 'fearing that it would be said that he had granted *iqta'at* to young men [*khashyat^{an} an yuqala a'ta al-sibyan akhbaz*]'.[10]

After Qalawun's death in 689/1290, Egypt was thrown into a state of political instability and turmoil which continued until al-Nasir Muhammad's third accession to the sultanate (709/1310), and it was during this period that a power struggle between the dominant Mamluk amirs ensued. Even though they failed in their efforts to take the sultanate, these amirs effectively continued to run the affairs of the state, behind the nominal rule of Qalawun's sons.[11] The controlling position of the amirs in high government offices became a determining factor in the increase in number of sons of Mamluks who were recruited into the army and their enhanced status – they were made holders of *iqta'at* and given high command in battle. The sources reveal thirty-nine amirs who were sons of Mamluks at that time.[12] Eleven of them participated in battle at command level, the most prominent among them, relative to *iqta'* size, being Nasir al-Din Ibn Baktash al-Fakhri who a year prior to his father's death in 706/1306 had been granted, at his own request, his father's *iqta'* which was that of a commander of one thousand. Others were 'Ali Ibn Aybak al-Khazindar and Muhammad Ibn Qarasunqur, who both reached their positions because of their fathers' influence.

During al-Nasir Muhammad's third reign, the recruitment of Mamluk sons increased. The names of ninety-three amirs who were sons of Mamluks can be collated from the sources dealing with this period.[13] However, as the information that the sources contain on the number of Sultani Mamluks who served the various sultans is incomplete, it remains difficult to assess the relative significance of the sons of the Mamluks in each of the periods under discussion.[14]

That, compared with the two earlier periods, the standing of the sons of the Mamluks was greatly enhanced during al-Nasir Muhammad's third reign is further-more demonstrated by the ranks they held, the *iqta'at* they were granted and the mil-itary and administrative positions they held. During al-Nasir Muhammad's rule, 9 of the 93 sons of Mamluks were amirs of one hundred, 7 in Cairo and 2 in Damascus. Seven of these amirs were commanders of one thousand, hence holding senior com-mands in the army. Muhammad Ibn Taybars al-Waziri was one of the commanders of one thousand who commanded a garrison that left Egypt to join the Syrian forces in the conquest of Malatya in 715/1315.[15] Amirs who were sons of Mamluks and held the ranks of amir of ten and amir of forty are reported to have been commanders of units involved in military campaigns during the rule of al-Nasir Muhammad. The three sons of Baybars al-Hajib, for example, marched with their father in his cam-paign to Mecca to put down the revolt led by Sharif Humayda in 719/1319.[16]

Obviously, the award of the rank of amir of one hundred was accompanied by the grant of a suitable *iqta'*. Husayn Ibn Jandarbak attained special status with al-Nasir Muhammad, for on his arrival in Egypt he received the *iqta'* of Amir Aslam who was amir of one hundred and commander of one thousand. After his death in 728/1327, 'the sultan was exceedingly distraught (*wa-janna al-sultan jununahu ila al-ghaya*) and granted *iqta'at* in the *halqa* to his (Husayn's) Mamluks, awarded them wages, awarded amirates to several of his relatives, and granted an honorarium to his wives, daughters and relatives'.[17] In 738/1337, the sultan gave Yalbugha al-Yahyawi, the son of Tabita, a magnificent, specially commissioned palace, and it would appear that this was in addition to his *iqta'*. In the following year he was granted al-Manzila in the Ushmum district in addition to his *iqta'*, and the sultan heaped expensive gifts upon him 'so that he would wonder at his munificence (*hatta yata'ajjaba min in'amihi 'alayhi*)'.[18] Several amirs of ten and amirs of forty whose names appear in the list of sons of Mamluks are mentioned in the chronicles as having been granted an *iqta'* together with their ami-rate. Thus the sons of Arghun al-Na'ib returned their *iqta'at* in Egypt when they were posted to Aleppo together with their father in 727/1327, but they received others in their place in Aleppo.[19] On the death of 'Ali Ibn Qutlubak al-Fakhri in 731/1331, his *iqta'* was granted to al-Nasir Hajj Ibn Tuquzdamur al-Hamawi,[20] and when Muhammad Ibn Malikshah died, in 727/1327, his *iqta'* was transferred to Bakman.[21]

Further evidence that the sons of Mamluks held *iqta'at* as valuable as those granted to the *khassakiyya* Mamluks can be found in a unique list compiled by Ibn al-Dawadari (d. *c.*736/1335) as part of a description of al-Nasir Muhammad's preparations for his *hajj* in 732/1332. In this list, Ibn al-Dawadari enumerates the amirs left behind in Egypt when al-Nasir Muhammad and his retinue embarked on the Hajj. These amirs were bidden to provide carpets which, it seems, were used at the departure and return ceremonies in honour of the sultan. The size of the carpet that each amir had to pro-vide corresponded to the amount of his *'ibra*, the land tax levied according to the holding's size and quality: 'and the size of these carpets was determined according to the *'ibra* (*fa-inna hadha* [!] *al-busut qurrira* [!] *'ala al-'ibar*)'.[22] The list mentions eight amirs who were sons of Mamluks. Using this carpet quota as a yardstick, a comparison between the *iqta'at* held by these amirs and those held by their Mamluk peers who had identical rank shows that the sons of Mamluks were not at all discriminated against with regard to *iqta'* grants. Thus, for example, the *iqta'* of 'Umar Ibn Arghun al-Na'ib was equal in size to that of Tuqtamur al-Salihi, both of whom were amirs of forty and were commanded to provide 67 cubits of carpet.[23] The *iqta'* of Muhammad Ibn Jumaq, who was not the son of a Mamluk but a relative of the sultan, was equal in size to that of 'Ali Ibn al-Agha'i or al-Aghani both of whom were amirs of forty and who provided 84 cubits of carpet. The *iqta'* of Balaban al-Sinani, who was also an amir of forty, was smaller than that of al-Agha'i, and he had to provide 74 cubits of carpet.[24] 'Ali Ibn Salar was an amir of ten and Aqul al-Hajib an amir of forty, yet both had to provide 67 cubits.[25]

The appointment and advancement paths of the sons of Mamluks during the rule of al-Nasir Muhammad were often identical to those used for his Sultani Mamluks. Muhammad Ibn Baktamur al-Husami was the son of a senior amir who was awarded the rank of amir of ten well before he was ready for military service, that is, upon the death of his father in 729/1328, when he was only 13 years old.[26] Thirty-five of the ninety-three sons of Mamluks who received appointments during al-Nasir Muhammad's reign were the sons of amirs who were currently serving in the army, and with the exception of Yalbugha al-Yahyawi, whose father attained fame thanks to his son, all were the sons of senior amirs who were close to al-Nasir Muhammad. There are several examples which demonstrate how the high status of the fathers was a decisive factor when al-Nasir Muhammad awarded amirates to the sons. Amir Ahmad Ibn Baktamur al-Saqi was awarded the rank of amir of one hundred in 726/1325 when he was but 13 years old and his father a very senior amir in the service of al-Nasir Muhammad.[27] The three sons of Aydughmish were awarded amirates by virtue of being their father's sons: 'And [Aydughmish's] status in the eyes of his master al-Malik al-Nasir was unassailable (*wa-kana makin^{an} 'inda ustadhihi*) and he awarded amirates to his three sons, Amir Hajj Malik, Amir Ahmad and Amir 'Ali.'[28] Tankiz, *na'ib al-Sham*, had attained such lofty status that al-Nasir Muhammad would not make decisions without first consulting him. At Tankiz's urging his son 'Ali was awarded an amirate in 732/1331. In the case of his two other sons, Muhammad and Ahmad, who were also made amirs during their father's lifetime, al-Nasir Muhammad even claimed that he himself could only benefit from their promotion.[29]

This leads us to an important development where we find that the award of amirates to the sons of amirs, especially senior amirs, after al-Nasir's death laid the foundations for a new political nobility in the Mamluk army. Out of a desire to protect his government, al-Nasir Muhammad consolidated his links with the amirs not only through according them political and military status but also by forging links through marriage. The result was an intricate web of relationships woven by al-Nasir Muhammad and his relatives through marriage to the sons and daughters[30] of his amirs, which in turn created a new class of amirs' sons who were blood relations of the Qalawunids. This kinship gave the amirs' sons a noble status even for a claim to rule. In the period that followed the death of al-Nasir Muhammad, the idea of handing over the reins of government to the amirs' sons, or at least handing over the power of decision to the amirs who were related by marriage to al-Nasir Muhammad, was to play a certain role, as will be seen later.[31]

Between 741/1341 and the fall of the house of Qalawun in 784/1382 there were some 257 amirs who were sons of Mamluks.[32] The increase in the numbers of sons of Mamluks joining the army[33] typified the entire period, not only that of Sultan al-Nasir Hasan, who openly encouraged during his second reign the advancement of the sons of Mamluks in preference to the Mamluks.[34] The enhanced status of the sons of Mamluks was clearly manifested in the *iqta'at*, administrative positions and military commands they held. The dominant amirs who managed government affairs behind the Qalawunid sultans also awarded high amirate rank to their sons, a suitable *iqta'* granted with the rank. In 748/1347, the son of Yalbugha al-Yahyawi, about 7 years old, was already one of the amirs of forty in Egypt.[35] Tashtamur Hummus Akhdar awarded the rank of commander of one thousand and the concomitant *iqta'* that had belonged to Baybars al-Ahmadi to his son (742/1341).[36] Arghun al-Kamili, the *na'ib* of Aleppo, 'had a three-year old son who was amir of one hundred and commander of one thousand and on al-Kamili's death his *taqdima* was added to the *niyaba iqta''.*[37] Al-Ashraf Sha'ban (764–78/1363–76) increased significantly the share of the *asyad* in the *iqta'* allocation.[38]

At least forty-four of the sons of Mamluks who were awarded amirates during this period were made commanders of one thousand a figure which does not include those commanders of one thousand who were sons of sultans.[39] The latter were awarded the rank already from Baybars' time when they were heir-apparent so as to make their status stand out from that of the other sons of the sultan.[40] Sons of amirs had now come to hold the most senior administrative positions. In 769/1367, Khalil Ibn Qawsun was appointed to the rank of *atabak al-'asakir* by Sultan al-Ashraf Sha'ban and Nasir al-Din Muhammad Ibn Aqbugha As was al-Ashraf Sha'ban's *ustadar*, an office carrying immense political power.[41] Sons of amirs became vice-sultans of both small and large provinces in Egypt and Syria.[42]

At the same time, many of the amirs who were sons of Mamluks held military command posts and appear in the sources as active army officers in battle.[43] Most of these battles were between rival Mamluk factions. Thus we find 'Umar Ibn Arghun al-Na'ib as one of the three commanders of a 4,000 strong cavalry force which left Egypt in 742/1342 to subdue Sultan al-Nasir Ahmad, who had fortified himself at Karak.[44] Khalil Ibn Qawsun led an army to put down a mutiny against his father-in-law, Amir Shaykhu, who was at that time administering government affairs (758/1357).[45] In 767/1365, Khalil was one of the commanders who rose against Amir Yalbugha al-'Umari, who held the reins of rule behind Sultan al-Ashraf Sha'ban, and was one of the central figures in the rebellion against al-Ashraf Sha'ban in 769/1367.[46] In this rebellion, Amir Asandamur promised the sultanate to Khalil Ibn Qawsun as he was al-Nasir Muhammad's grandson and his own daughter's son. The rebellion was unsuccessful, but the fact that 'a great host (*jam' kabir*)' of Mamluks joined the rebel forces proves that, although daughters of Mamluk sultans were formally not eligible for rule, the status of their sons from marriages with amirs was by now built on foundations strong enough to make their claim to rule not seem at all farfetched.

A further indication of this may be found in the attempt that was made to seize the sultanate for Ahmad Ibn Yalbugha al-'Umari. Amir Aynabak, who together with Qaratay had earlier ousted al-Ashraf Sha'ban (778/1376), wanted the sultanate for

Ahmad. The caliph did not accede to their claim on the grounds that al-'Umari was not of the house of Qalawun, and remained adamant even when Aynabak proffered the claim that Ahmad was indeed of Qalawun's house as his mother had become pregnant by al-Hasan Ibn Qalawun and while with child had married Yalbugha al-'Umari. Here, again, the claim for Ahmad's legitimacy for rule was based on his tie of kinship with the house of Qalawun.[47] Further proof of the strengthening of the position of the sons of Mamluks was the emergence of a third generation of Mamluks. During the rule of al-Nasir Muhammad there were 2 amirs who were the grandsons of Mamluk amirs, a number which was to rise to 36 in the period between the death of al-Nasir Muhammad and the ascent of Barquq.[48]

This phenomenon of the increase in the numbers of second- and third-generation sons of amirs in the ranks of the Mamluk army and the reinforcement of their status was not only the result of the great power accumulated in the hands of the amirs but also of the army's ethnic structure in this period. The sources show that in the second half of the fourteenth century and the beginning of the fifteenth, the Turkish Mamluks, who had been the dominant factor in the Mamluk army, almost completely disappeared from the slave markets due to various causes in their countries of origin. In Egypt itself the Black Death (749/1348) decimated the Mamluk soldiers.[49] It is worthy of note that the damage inflicted by epidemics on the Mamluk population was far more severe than that suffered by the local population since the latter was better used to local conditions.[50] The continued existence of the Turkish factor as an important entity in the Mamluk army was therefore contingent upon fresh importation of Mamluks from their country of origin, the area of the Golden Horde, that was dominated at the time by the descendants of Genghis Khan. Its population, however, had dwindled in the second half of the fourteenth century, *inter alia* in the wake of the Black Death, and it was hardly able to provide the manpower required for its rulers' army. Thus, for example, Khan Jani Bek (742–58/1342–57) forbade the export of Mamluks from his country to Egypt.[51] His death was followed by internal power struggles between the descendants of Genghis Khan that diminished even further the resources and population of the Golden Horde. Even after the unification of the Golden Horde under the rule of Tokhtamish (d. *c*.802/1399) with the assistance of Timur (Tamerlane d. 807/1405) who invaded central and west Asia and unified them under his rule, the struggles did not cease. Because of his own conflict with Timur, for thirty years Tokhtamish waged war against the Timurid governors in the country. Timurid attacks on the Golden Horde severely injured its economy and caused its final disintegration.[52] The fifteenth-century historian Muhammad b. 'Abd al-Rahman al-Sakhawi (d. 902/1497) says that as a result of these wars, the Golden Horde became a wilderness and that during this period the importation of Mamluks to Syria and Egypt was forbidden.[53] Shihab al-Din al-Qalaqashandi (d. 821/1418) relates, in the encyclopaedic manual that he compiled at the beginning of the fifteenth century, that only a few Turks remained in the Mamluk army, those Turkish Mamluks that had survived from previous generations, and their sons.[54] In contrast with the decline of military manpower of Turkish origin, the Circassians reached Egypt without difficulty, both as freemen and as Mamluks purchased in the slave markets.[55]

The absence of importation of Turkish Mamluks might well explain the introduction of sons of Mamluks into the army. Indeed, many of the *awlad al-nas* included among the amirs in 791/1389 were sons and grandsons of Turkish Mamluks.[56] This increase in the numbers of sons of Mamluks at this period was not a mere happenstance; it coincided with the ethnic struggles for hegemony in the Mamluk army. The Mamluk factions that fought against Barquq viewed his rise to power as a sign of change in the ethnic character of the sultanate, a shift of the hegemony from Turkish to Circassian hands.[57] By their utterances at least, these factions defined themselves as an ethnic group fighting for the house of Qalawun that symbolized the Turks' place in the Mamluk sultanate.[58] It would appear, then, that the increase in the entry of the Mamluks' sons into the army, particularly in the second half of the fourteenth century, was not only because of the position their fathers held at court but also part of a deliberate effort, at least on the part of the Turkish elements in the sultanate including the house of Qalawun, to create support bases for the preservation of the old regime.

Notes

1 David Ayalon, 'Studies on the Structure of the Mamluk Army', *Bulletin of the School of Oriental and African Studies*, XV (1953), pt. I, pp. 203–28; pt. II, pp. 448–76 (reprinted in his *Studies on the Mamluks of Egypt* (London, 1977), no. I), pp. 456–9.

2 Ulrich Haarmann, 'The Sons of Mamluks as Fief-Holders in Late Medieval Egypt', in T. Khalidi (ed.), *Land Tenure and Social Transformation in the Middle East* (Beirut, 1984), pp. 142–4.

3 Ibid., pp. 162–3.

4 Amalia Levanoni, *A Turning Point in Mamluk History, The Third Reign of al-Nāṣir Muḥammad ibn Qalawun 1310–1341* (Leiden, 1995), pp. 42–52.

5 Al-Nuwayri, *Nihayat al-arab fi funun al-adab*, Leiden University Library, Ms. Or. 2M, 2N, 2O, 19B: 19B, fol. 38a; 2N, fols. 5a, 8b, 9b; Ibn al-Furat, *Ta'rikh al-duwal wal-muluk*, (ed.) Q. Zurayq (Beirut, 1942), vol. IX: VII, pp. 168, 169, 171, 219, 237, 239, 251, 285; al-Yunini, *Dhayl mir'at al-zaman* (Hyderabad, 1954–61), vols I–IV; Topkapi Saray Ms. Ahmet no.2007/E3, 2907/E4, I, p. 204; al-Maqrizi, *Kitab al-suluk li-ma'rifat duwal al-muluk*, (ed.) M. Ziyada and S. 'Abd al-Fattah 'Ashur (Cairo, 1930–73), vols I–IV, I, pp. 677, 696, 709.

6 On the Mamluk conception of the position of the *awlad al-nas* in the Mamluk army, see Haarmann, pp. 142–4; Ayalon, 'The Mamluk Army', pt. II, pp. 456–8; 'Mamlukiyyat: A First Attempt to Evaluate the Mamluk Military System', *Jerusalem Studies in Arabic and Islam*, II (1980), pp. 328–9.

7 Al-Maqrizi, *Kitab al-mawa'iz wal-i'tibar fi dhikr al-khitat wal-athar* (Cairo, 1987), II, p. 216.

8 Ibn al-Dawadari, *Kanz al-durar wa-jami' al-ghurar*, (ed.) H. R. Roemer, 'Abd al-Fattah 'Ashur and U. Haarmann (Cairo, 1960–72), VIII, p. 303; Maqrizi, *Suluk*, I, p. 658.

9 Ayalon, 'The Mamluk Army', pt. II, p. 457.

10 Maqrizi, *Khitat*, II, p. 216.

11 Kitbugha, Lajin and Baybars al-Jashankir ascended to power but their reigns were very short: Robert Irwin, *The Middle East in the Middle Ages* (London, 1986), pp. 88–9, 90–4.

12 Baybars al-Mansuri, *Zubdat al-fikra fi ta'rikh al-hijra*, (ed.) D. S. Richards (Beirut, 1998), pp. 262–3, 332, 349, 367, 428; *al-Tuhfa al-mulukiyya fi al-dawla al-Turkiyya* (Beirut, 1987), p. 168; Ibn al-Dawadari, IX, pp. 34, 88, 135, 170, 174; Khalil b. Aybak as-Safadi, *al-Wafi bil-wafayat*, (ed.) 'A. Amara and J. Sublet (Wiesbaden, 1980), II p. 398; IX, p. 489; X, pp. 283, 398; al-Nuwayri, 2N, fols 3a, 5a, 8b, 58a, 70b; 2O, fols 2b, 31a, 37a,

50a, 51a; Ibn Hajar al-'Asqalani, *al-Durar al-kamina fi a'yan al-mi'a al-thamina*, (ed.) M. S. Jadd al-Haqq (Cairo, n.d.), II, p. 71, 306; III, p. 70; al-Yunini, 2907/E3, fols 13b, 19b, 45a, 47a; 2907/E4, fols 4a-b, 18a, 25a; *Suluk*, I, pp. 847, 939, 940, 947; Ibn Taghri-Birdi, *al-Nujum al-zahira fi muluk Misr wal-Qahira* (Cairo, 1963–72), vols VII–XVI, VIII, pp. 241, 255; Ibn Taghri-Birdi, *al-Manhal al-safi wal-mustawfi ba'da al-wafi*, (ed.) M. M. Amin (Cairo, 1993), Bibliothèque Nationale (Paris), mss. arabes nos. 2070, 2072; Dar al-Kutub (Cairo) Ms. 1928, II, M. M. Amin (Cairo, 1988); Ms. Topkapi Saray (Istanbul) Ahmet A2912/4, A2911/4, A2912/4, fols 122b, 206b, 222b, 227b, 253b; K. V. Zettersteen, *Beiträge zur Geschichte der Mamlukensultane* (Leiden, 1919), pp. 118, 153; Musa b. Muhammad b. Yahya al-Yusufi, *Nuzhat al-nazir fi sirat al-Malik al-Nasir*, (ed.) A. Hutayt (Beirut, 1986), p. 321; Ibn al-Furat, VIII, pp. 168, 169.

13 Al-Yusufi, pp. 119, 159, 234, 235–6, 321, 367, 411, 416; Shams al-Din al-Shuja'i, *Ta'rikh al-Malik al-Nasir Muhammad Ibn Qalawun al-Salihi wa-awladihi*, ed. Barbara Schäfer (Wiesbaden, 1977), pp. 17, 28, 33, 39, 41, 44, 49, 50, 54–6, 66, 73, 80, 89, 94–5, 97, 121, 142, 148, 157–8, 168, 175, 179–80, 182, 192, 195–6, 200, 213, 220, 223, 232–3, 239, 241, 244, 247, 250–1, 256–7, 267, 273; *Durar*, I, p. 418; II, pp. 70, 173, 177–8, 230, 306, 309, 316; III, pp. 98, 100, 103–4, 127, 338–40, 343, 469; IV, pp. 79, 212–13; Ibn Hajar al-'Asqalani, *Inba' al-ghumr bi-abna' al-'umr fi al-ta'rikh* (Hyderabad, India, 1976), vol. I–VII, I, p. 164; III, p. 84; al-Nuwayri, 2O, fols 2b, 3a, 31a, 37a, 39a, 48a, 50a, 51a, 60a, 67b–68a, 73a, 81a, 82a, 85a, 110a, 119a, 122a, b; 19B, fols 9b, 38a, 97a, 114a, 115a, 119a–b, 123a, 124b, 127b, 128b, 130a, 133a, 138a, 139a, 143b; Zettersteen, pp. 48, 118, 147, 153, 157, 160, 162, 165–6, 169, 174, 177, 180, 182, 199, 201, 205–6, 208, 210, 215, 216–18; Ibn al-Dawadari, IX, pp. 34, 180, 206–7, 212, 216, 225, 239, 281, 284, 357, 366–9, 371; *Wafi*, II, pp. 255, 310; III, p. 170; IX, p. 285; X, pp. 193, 300, 330; XII, pp. 348–9; XIII, p. 398; *Nujum*, IX, pp. 14, 43, 74, 103, 106, 198, 232, 262, 269, 280, 282, 286–7, 300, 306, 327; X, pp. 10, 77, 100, 103, 119, 128, 135, 317; XI, p. 140; *Manhal*, I, p. 257; 1928, fols 378a–b, 432b; *Suluk*, II, pp. 75, 111, 146–7, 169, 191, 194, 230, 238, 249–50, 257, 281–2, 287, 313–14, 326, 332, 338, 352, 358, 426, 461, 610, 621, 730, 747; *'Iqd*, A2912/4, fols 342b, 370a, 387b. In order to remove all doubt that amirs who were sons of Mamluks served in the *halqa* during al-Nasir Muhammad's rule, a number of examples can be found that clearly demonstrate a distinction between amirs of ten, amirs of forty, amirs of one thousand and *muqaddamu al-halqa*. In times of war, *muqaddamu al-halqa* were given command of forty *halqa* soldiers (al-Qalqashandi, *Kitab subh al-a'sha fi sina'at al-insha'* (Cairo, 1913–19), IV, p. 16) and those of amirate rank served with the Royal Mamluks (al-Nuwayri, 19B, fols 96b, 97a–b, 125a; al-Shuja'i, p. 35; *Suluk*, II, pp. 498–9).

14 Ayalon, 'The Mamluk Army', pt. I, pp. 222–8.

15 Al-Nuwayri, 2O, fol. 73a.

16 Ibid., fols 119a–b. See also Jariktamur Ibn Bahadur (*Suluk*, II, p. 418), Samghan Ibn Sunqur al-Ashqar (*Suluk*, II, p. 191), Muhammad Ibn al-Shamsi and 'Ali b. Qarasunqur (*Suluk*, II, p. 194) and 'Ala' al-Din b. Qarasunqur (al-Nuwayri, 2O, fol. 81b).

17 Al-Nuwayri, 19B, fols 119a–b; *Wafi*, IX, p. 285; XII, p. 349.

18 *Durar*, V, p. 212; *Suluk*, II, pp. 438, 463; *Nujum*, X, p. 185.

19 Al-Nuwayri, 19B, fols 115b, 130a.

20 *Nujum*, IX, p. 286.

21 *Suluk*, II, p. 327.

22 Ibn al-Dawadari, IX, p. 369; *Suluk*, II, p. 356. On a similar case see *Suluk*, II, pp. 871–2. For '*ibra*, see H. Halm, *Ägypten nach den mamlukischen Lehensregistern* (Wiesbaden, 1979–82), I, pp. 40–2.

23 *Suluk*, II, pp. 338, 498.

24 Al-Nuwayri, 19B, fols 97a, 103b, 123a.

25 Al-Nuwayri, 2O, fols 48a; *Suluk*, II, 260.

26 *Suluk*, II, p. 314. See also the case of Tabita's son, Yalbugha al-Yahyawi, *Nujum*, IX, p. 133; X, p. 185.

27 *Wafi*, VI, p. 267; X, p. 196.

28 *Nujum*, IX, p. 100; *Wafi*, IX, p. 489.

29 *Durar*, II, pp. 56, 57; III, p. 104. For another example, see al-Yusufi, pp. 119, 137.

30 Ibn al-Dawadari, IX, pp. 358, 380; Mufaddal Ibn Abi al-Fada'il, *al-Nahj al-sadid wal-durr al-farid fima ba'da ta'rikh Ibn al-'Amid*, (ed.) S. Kortentamer (Freiburg, 1973), pp. 17, 37, 51, 98; al-Shuja'i, 18, 29, 33–4, 42–4, 74, 111, 140, 160, 240, 247, 252–4; *Wafi*, IV, pp. 370–1; VIII, p. 86; IX, p. 311; X, pp. 197, 251, 299–300; *Durar*, I, pp. 422, 494; II, p. 77; III, p. 341; V, p. 127; *Manhal*, 2070, fols 172b–3b; 2072, fol. 37a; *Nujum*, XI, p. 292; *Suluk*, II, pp. 237, 249, 272, 283, 296, 333, 346, 407, 417, 432, 436, 460–1, 492, 497–8, 754–5; III, p. 152; al-Yusufi, p. 363.

31 *Wafi*, IX, p. 219; *Manhal*, II, p. 425. For an outstanding example, see *Suluk*, II, pp. 151–3.

32 *Inba'*, I, pp. 3, 7, 160, 164, 167, 189, 205; II, pp. 130, 254; III, p. 84; *Khitat*, II, p. 55; *Suluk*, II, pp. 563, 571, 590, 594, 600, 603, 605–7, 609–10, 621, 643, 645, 661–2, 672, 681, 684, 699, 709, 730–1, 737, 742, 754, 768, 849, 857, 868–9, 875, 895, 903, 905, 916; III, pp. 34, 41, 51, 61, 63, 66–7, 75, 84, 90–1, 99–100, 104–5, 110, 117–18, 120, 144–5, 151, 153, 158, 161–2, 182–3, 185, 219, 226, 232, 258, 262, 267–8, 274–5, 277, 288–9, 290, 296, 304, 308–9, 311, 313–14, 317, 333, 341, 344, 356, 360, 368, 371, 377, 380, 385–9, 391–2, 400, 404, 410, 441, 460, 467, 471, 523, 611, 648, 652–4, 671, 680–1, 687; *Manhal*, I, pp. 247, 257; II, pp. 268, 436; III, pp. 99, 217; IV, p. 263; 2070, fols 69a–b; 2072, fols 108a–b; 1928, fols 432b; *Nujum*, X, pp. 10, 17–18, 57, 68, 77, 88, 93, 100, 119, 135, 168, 194, 220, 228, 253, 290; XI, pp. 30–1, 33–4, 45, 47, 51, 54, 62–4, 71, 106, 110, 124, 141, 150, 155, 161, 179–80, 194, 202, 209, 236, 244, 279, 281, 301, 317, 321–2, 335, 340–1, 344–6, 352, 382–3; XII, pp. 10, 16, 24; *Durar*, I, pp. 29, 115, 164, 315, 339, 373, 420, 422, 472; II, pp. 15, 179, 306, 309–10, 314–15; III pp. 98, 100–1, 105, 126–8, 244, 351; IV, pp. 12–13, 17, 268; V, p. 149; *Wafi*, III, pp. 170–1; X, p. 302; XII, p. 398; Ibn Qadi Shuhba, *al-I'lam bi-ta'rikh al-Islam*, (ed.) 'A. Darwish (Damascus, 1977), III, pp. 6, 10, 19, 31, 74, 109–10, 124, 144, 154, 174–5, 201, 204–5, 249, 264, 288, 301, 330–1, 355, 363–4, 366, 390–1, 409–10, 493; Sharaf al-Din Yahya Ibn al-Ji'an, *Kitab al-tuhfa al-saniyya bi-asma' al-bilad al-misriyya*, (Cairo, 1898), pp. 15, 19, 22, 30, 34, 42–3, 46–7, 50, 53–5, 67, 73–5, 77–9, 83, 85, 89, 91, 97, 99, 101, 109, 113, 116–17, 120–1, 123, 127, 129, 131–4, 137, 151, 155, 157–8, 162–4, 168–9, 173–5, 177, 179, 183, 185, 187–8, 190, 192–3; al-Shuja'i, pp. 148, 157–8, 168, 175, 179, 192, 195–6, 220, 223, 232, 239, 241, 244, 247, 251, 257, 266–7, 273; al-Yunini, 2907/E3, fols 47a, 55b.

33 On the position of Mamluks' sons, *awlad al-nas*, in this period, see Haarmann, pp. 145–6; Halm, I, pp. 1–2.

34 Haarmann, pp. 162–3.

35 *Manhal*, 1928, fol. 342b.

36 *Suluk*, II, p. 606.

37 Ibid., p. 895. For further examples of Mamluks' sons who were fief-holders, see *Wafi*, X, p. 302; *Durar*, II, p. 15; III, p. 100; V, p. 212; *Nujum*, X, pp. 185, 194, 217, 220, 317; XI, pp. 31, 49, 54, 150, 155, 180, 341; *Suluk*, II, pp. 606, 621, 672, 709, 737, 903; III, pp. 54, 63, 90–1, 100, 145, 153, 161, 258, 288, 296, 308–9, 341, 371, 387, 389; Ibn Qadi Shuhba, pp. 204, 355, 409–10; 493; *Manhal*, II, p. 436; 2070, fols 69a–70b; 1928, fol. 432b; *Wafi*, III, p. 170; X, p. 302; *Durar*, I, p. 29; al-Shuja'i, pp. 175, 192, 196, 213, 232, 247, 251.

38 *Suluk*, III, p. 63; *Manhal*, 2070, fols 29a–b; *Nujum*, X, p. 317; XI, p. 342.

39 *Suluk*, II, pp. 609–10, 684, 709, 769, 895, 903; III, pp. 41, 63, 90, 100, 145, 151, 153, 258, 296, 308, 333, 387, 389, 523, 605; *Nujum*, X, pp. 194, 317; XI, pp. 31, 45, 47, 49, 62–4, 155, 161, 180, 209, 341; Ibn Qadi Shuhba, pp. 19, 74, 204, 289–90, 299, 355, 567; *Manhal*, III, p. 99; *Durar*, III, p. 127.

40 *'Iqd*, A2912/4, fol. 90b; *Suluk*, III, pp. 43, 63.

41 Ibn Qadi Shuhba, p. 204; *Nujum*, XI, p. 63; for further examples of sons of amirs holding administrative positions, see ibid., pp. 51, 150, 161, 234, 341; Ibn al-Ji'an, pp. 78, 133;

Durar, III, p. 98, 127; IV, p. 268; *Suluk*, III, pp. 75, 84–5, 91, 100, 144–5, 182–3, 268, 290, 309, 356, 360, 377, 389, 400, 467, 471, 523, 652; Ibn Qadi Shuhba, pp. 19, 204; al-Shuja'i, pp. 148, 273; *Manhal*, III, p. 99.

42 *Suluk*, III, pp. 267; Ibn Qadi Shuhba, p. 204. For further examples, see *Inba'*, I, p. 164; *Suluk*, II, p. 905; III, pp. 63, 67, 84, 91, 145, 226, 308, 360; Ibn Qadi Shuhba, p. 19; *Durar*, III, p.101; IV, pp. 13, 17, 268; *Nujum*, XI, pp. 51, 63, 124; *Inba'*, I, p. 164; al-Shuja'i, p. 192; *Manhal*, III, p. 99.

43 *Suluk*, II, pp. 610, 645–6, 709, 868, 903; III, pp. 51, 63, 67, 158, 161, 274–5, 311, 317, 344, 360, 391, 404; *Nujum*, X, pp. 68, 88, 135; XI, p. 54; *Durar*, II, p. 306; *Manhal*, II, p. 268.

44 *Suluk*, II, p. 646.

45 *Suluk*, III, p. 34. For other battles in which he took part, see *Suluk*, II, pp. 610, 709; III, pp. 105, 110, 274–5, 311.

46 Ibid., III, pp. 104–5, 151–3.

47 *Suluk*, III, p. 309.

48 al-Shuja'i, pp. 121, 157, 220, 266; Zettersteen, p. 217; Ibn al-Dawadari, IX, p. 225; *Manhal*, 1928, fols 346a, 432b; *Suluk*, II, pp. 875, 905; III, pp. 120, 161, 185, 289, 341, 389, 593, 654, 685; *Nujum*, XI, pp. 71, 106, 150, 299, 317, 321–2, 345–6; XII, p. 10; Ibn Qadi Shuhba, pp. 19, 109, 154, 264, 391, 535; Ibn al-Ji'an, pp. 19, 47, 65, 78, 113, 120, 127, 131, 155, 164, 169, 171; *Durar*, II, p. 179; V, p. 149; *Inba'*, I, p. 420; II, p. 130; III, p. 73.

49 *Suluk*, II, p. 781. See also M. W. Dols, 'The General Mortality of the Black Death in the Mamluk Empire', in A. L. Udovitch (ed.), *The Islamic Middle East, 700–1900: Studies in Economic and Social History* (Princeton, NJ, 1981), pp. 397–428.

50 David Ayalon, 'The Plague and its Effects Upon the Mamluk Army', *Journal of the Royal Asiatic Society*, 1946, pp. 67–73.

51 Al-Shuja'i, p. 214.

52 J. J. Saunders, *The History of the Mongol Conquest* (London, 1971), pp. 165–6; M. E. Yapp, 'The Golden Horde and its Successors', in *The Cambridge History of Islam*, P. M. Holt, Ann K. S. Lambton and Bernard Lewis (eds), (Cambridge, 1970), vol. 1, pp. 498–9.

53 Shams al-Din Muhammad b. 'Abd al-Rahman al-Sakhawi, *al-Daw' al-lami' li-ahl al-qarn al-tasi'* (Beirut, n.d.), II, p. 325

54 Al-Qalqashandi, IV, p. 458.

55 David Ayalon, 'The Circassians in the Mamluk Kingdom', *Journal of the American Oriental Society*, 69/3, 1949, pp. 135–7; David Ayalon, 'Aspects of the Mamluk Phenomenon', *Der Islam*, 53, 1976, pp. 208–9.

56 See for example Ibn al-Furat, IX, pp. 67–8, 97–101.

57 See Amalia Levanoni, 'Al-Maqrizi's account of the Transition from Turkish to Circassian Mamluk Sultanate: History in the Service of Faith', in Hugh Kennedy (ed.), *The Historiography of Islamic Egypt (c.950–1800)* (Leiden, 2001), pp. 93–105.

58 See for example Ibn al-Furat, IX, pp. 64–5, 101–2.

9 Popular Sufi sermons in late Mamluk Egypt

Boaz Shoshan

It is now generally accepted that during the Mamluk period Sufism in Egypt and Syria was largely integrated into the life of Muslim communities. Geoffroy's exhaustive work on Sufism in the late Mamluk and early Ottoman periods makes it amply clear that *fiqh* and *tasawwuf* intermingled and that Sufi scholarship was gradually gaining ground and embraced by the ulema as well as the political rulers.[1] As Geoffroy and others point out, it is in a scholar such as Suyuti (849–911/ 1445–1505), himself a Shadhili,[2] that this development is manifested. Thus, concerning the theological concept of the 'supreme name' (*al-ism al-a'zam*) the Egyptian savant goes so far as to give Sufi writings priority over other interpretations. Elsewhere, in a special *fatwa* entitled *Amal al-fikr fi fadl al-dhikr* Suyuti considers *dhikr*, the Sufi ritual of invocation,[3] superior to other forms of worship; 'unveiling' (*kashf*)[4] is preferable to vision through dreams (*ru'ya*).[5] Geoffroy sees in Suyuti's *al-Hawi lil-fatawi* another step in the evolving relationship between Sufism and Islamic culture in general, in that for the first time the former features as a recognized branch of knowledge and queries about Sufi matters are regarded as equal to those dealing with juristic issues. Michael Winter argued quite some time ago that Sufism influenced Egyptian 'Ulama' in the early Ottoman period and that some of the most distinguished men of letters then were practising Sufis. In Syria as well, many high-ranking ulema became followers of Sidi Ali b. Maymun, the originally Moroccan, important propagator of Sufism in Syria.[6] Geoffroy lists several men who combined *shari'a* and *haqiqa*, that is, conventional legal learning and the Sufi gift of experiencing 'true reality'.[7] This, one should note, did not start in Ottoman time. My reading of Mamluk sources has taught me that the association of *fiqh* and *tasawwuf* in the careers of many learned individuals was a widespread phenomenon in the fifteenth century CE and possibly earlier. It certainly merits a systematic study of the rich biographical data.

All this, clearly enough, is at the level of the intellectual elite. With respect to the Islam of the people I have argued elsewhere that, although we know relatively little about it, Sufism in all likelihood immensely influenced it, at least in the case of medieval Cairo.[8] It is pertinent to note here that although Geoffroy has impressively amassed material on the world of the Sufis and their socio-religious role (a fact that makes his work truly definitive) the vast field of relationship between the Sufis and 'the people' still remains little known. The French scholar points out the frequent association between the Sufis (*fuqara'*) of the Ahmadiyya order (Ahmad al-Badawi's disciples), such as Shaykh Muhammad Badr al-Din Ibn Sa'idi (d. 928/1522) and the people.[9] It is especially in the type of the ecstatic 'possessed' (*majdhub*), Geoffroy's 'fou de Dieu', who is capable of predicting the future, and possessor of a beneficent force of divine origin (*baraka*)[10] that Geoffroy sees the link between Sufis and ordinary Egyptians and Syrians.[11] One should add the numerous examples of veneration of shaykhs, crowded festive celebrations (especially *mawlids*) that were conducted by and for Sufi saints, the popular ascription of miracles (*karamat*)[12] and benevolent deeds to Sufi leaders as all links between the Sufi sphere and ordinary believers.[13]

I believe we have reached the point where this particular domain of the Sufi-people nexus is pretty much exhausted in terms of possible research. However, one generally neglected aspect of this nexus that deserves further study, and which may provide some compensation for the scarcity of historical data, is the sermons that Sufi shaykhs delivered at mosques and other religious institutions. It has been pointed out that Sufis, the Shadhilites at the forefront,[14] gradually undermined the monopoly that the Hanbalites had enjoyed as popular preachers.[15] Noteworthy in this respect is the Sufi concern with preaching to women. Thus Ahmad al-Zahid (d. 819/1416) of the Suhrawardiyya order[16] preached exclusively to women and according to one report left sixty quires of his sermons.[17] Another Sufi preacher who had women among his listeners was Ibn al-Hamawi. In 1489 he urged them to increase their modesty by changing their headcovers, a call that, interestingly enough, aroused some storm in scholarly circles.[18] From Sidi 'Ali b. Maymun we get a sense of the importance of preaching to women. His disciple 'Ali b. 'Atiya, also known as Alwan al-Hamawi, at the time the most prominent Sufi writer in Syria, refers to a special category of preachers who desired to please their female audience.[19]

Most sermons, even the large number ascribed to the Ahmad al-Zahid, have not survived. However, there are some exceptions. We have in manuscript form the *Majalis al-bulqiniyya* by Siraj al-Din al-Bulqini (d. 805/1403), a leading Shafi'i of a notable family who was the most celebrated jurist of his age and at the same time an associate of Muhammad al-Hanafi the Shadhilite (d. 847/1443).[20] Geoffroy, who considers Sufi sermons as evidence of the rapprochement between the Sufis and the ulema, pays only scant attention to their actual content on the pretext that they deserve a separate study.[21] I myself have devoted some pages to the sermons of the thirteenth-century Shadhilite Ibn 'Ata' Allah al-Iskandari, and to his *Taj al-'arus* in particular. As I noted, beside conventional themes Ibn 'Ata' Allah included *dhikr* and the virtues of Sufi shaykhs as specific Sufi topics of instruction to the public.[22]

In this chapter I wish to turn to another collection of sermons that remains neglected: *al-Rawd al-fa'iq fi al-mawa'iz wa'l-raqa'iq* [*sic*] ('The Superior Meadows of Preaching and Sermons') by Shu'ayb al-Hurayfish. In the lack of identifying data it is difficult to establish the author's/compiler's identity. One possibility is that the name is an abbreviation for 'Abdallah b. Sa'd (or Sa'dallah)[23] b. 'Abd al-Kafi 'The Egyptian', surnamed 'al-Harfush', as well as 'Ubayd (d. 801/1399), who was known for his *karamat*[24] and, according to one source, was 'author of Hurayfish's book of sermons' (*sahib kitab al-hurayfish fil-wa'z*).[25] However, the addition al-Danashuri in a Paris manuscript of the work[26] suggests an entirely different identification, namely, that the author was an Egyptian Sufi who lived in the latter part of the fifteenth and early part of the sixteenth century.[27] Be that as it may, the work was repeatedly printed at the end of the nineteenth and beginning of the twentieth century.[28]

Here, as in the past, my study is premised on the assumption that texts written for the purpose of instruction, be they modern school textbooks or medieval sermons, are of invaluable importance as indicators of the 'spiritual nourishment', in fact of the *culture* of the people studied. In the words of a prominent student of this subject, 'sermons are the surest index of the prevailing religious feeling of their age'.[29] Although other categories of material (celebration, veneration, etc., in the case of medieval Egypt) tell us mainly about institutional/structural aspects of popular religion, the study of *mawa'iz* directs us at the terra incognita that popular *ideas* and *beliefs* are and may enlighten us about the details of their contents.

It is pertinent at the outset to make a few observations about the general character, structure, and recurrent patterns of the *Rawd*. It consists of fifty-six sessions (*majalis*) that impress the reader as corresponding to actual sessions/sermons. This impression is heightened by several indications. One is the repeatedly direct address that the author/compiler makes in almost all sessions to his 'brethren' (*ikhwani*)[30] and, more seldom, to the 'folks of righteous Sufis' (*ma'shar al-fuqara' al-sadiqin*), simply *fuqara'*,[31] and, quite significantly, to the 'folks of merchants' (*ma'shar al-tujjar*), not necessarily just in a metaphoric sense but possibly in reference to the social category that the listeners consist of. Another indicator is that the collection is replete with verses and rhythmical prose as if to make the text more congenial to untrained ears.[32] The sermon-like style is particularly striking, for example, in passages in which each line is preceded by the exclamation word *Ah* ('oh').[33] Finally, the enormous number of tales, many of them of a fantastic nature, could possibly indicate a preference for them in texts directed at large audiences. One should add that despite the repetitive heading of quite a few *majalis* they have not been organized in separate sections. In other words, there are, for example, no fewer than seven hagiographic chapters entitled 'The Glorious Deeds (*manaqib*) of the Righteous (*salihin*)' dispersed through the book. This could suggest that the editing of the work has kept their original order intact.

About two-thirds of the *majalis* treat subjects that concern the ordinary Muslim. These thirty-odd sessions in turn can be divided into two groups: sermons about theological themes and sermons that call for the practice of certain duties. The rest have a particular Sufi intent. In what follows I shall be more specific on some of the contents.

To begin with the theological issues that feature in the *Rawd*, they range between the 'merits of the Ka'ba' (*fada'il*), through the 'Wailing and those who wail for the fear of the Almighty' (*al-buka' wal-bakkayin min hashiyat Allah*) to the discussion of death and description of Hell. I take as an example for closer observation the sixth session that enumerates the 'merits of Laylat al-Qadr', on which the Qur'an is believed to have been revealed.[34] It typically starts with benediction and praise to God in *saj'*. The Almighty, through the long chain of deeds that emanated from Him, distinguished Laylat al-Qadr as 'better than a thousand nights', as the night when the 'gates of Heaven are opened, the angels descend with good tidings (*bisharat*) to those people who stay awake and celebrate it (*man ahyaha min al-anam*)'. This is the night when God is believed to forgive sins and 'cover the blemish (*satr al-'uyub*)', to purify the hearts and satisfy the needy (*hawa'ij al-sa'ilin*). The text then turns to the five possible interpretations of the term *qadr* and to the debate over which of the nights of Ramadan Laylat al-Qadr actually refers to. Also, the 'circumstances of revelation' (*asbab al-nuzul*) of the relevant Qur'anic verses as regards the night are reproduced. A plastic description of Laylat al-Qadr that is ascribed to the Prophet is related. According to this, the angels carry four banners (*liwa'*), one of which they place on Muhammad's grave, one on Tur Sinin, a third one on the Meccan *haram* and the fourth in Jerusalem (Bayt al-Maqdis). The angel Gabriel then pays visits to the homes of all believers. At dawn (*fajr*) he is the first to ascend back to Heaven, he shadows the sun with his wings and invites each of the angels to join him. They all then pray for the sake of the believers and ask forgiveness (*istighfar*) for those who have repented during the previous year. At the end of Laylat al-Qadr God declares Ummat Muhammad absolved from all its sins.

At this point, the author supposedly turns to his audience with the typical address *ikhwani*. Here, unlike the earlier material in this session that has been reproduced from a variety of sources, his original contribution appears to start. The gist of this session's concluding part is the relevance of what has been said before to the specific audience to whom he directs his message. A plea is made to the listeners to repent on this special night, as all their fortunate predecessors in the past had repented on the occasion of Laylat al-Qadr. A prayer to God to 'place the needy (*sa'ilin*) at His gate and give the poor/Sufis (*fuqara'*) shelter' concludes the session. A variety of metaphorical illustrations are employed, such as the 'sea' from which the 'ship of the miserable' (*safinat al-masakin*) is rescued but in which the sinners are doomed to drown.

Let me now move on to the second category of *majalis* in the *Rawd*, the one treating the performance of religious duties. The duties discussed are significantly limited. We find the so-called Five Pillars and, in addition, the well-known practice of visiting graves (*ziyarat al-qubur*). For the purpose of the present occasion one can take, as an example, the very first *majlis*, entitled 'The Merits of Blessing the Prophet and Uttering the Basmala'. It starts with a series of metaphors culled from the world of economics that could be interpreted not simply as a random choice but as part of a social appeal. Thus the author describes himself as offering to his audience 'merchandise' (*bida'ati*) for sale. He then puts the following question to his supposed listeners:

> Which profit is larger than this, which trade (*tijara*) is more lucrative? Oh, folks of merchants (*ma'shar al-tujjar*), those who desire to gain a dirhem or a dinar! If it were said to you that in a certain town there is the prospect for a twofold profit, wouldn't you rush to pack it in? How much more so when the trustworthy (*al-sadiq al-amin*) [Muhammad] has announced his profitable merchandise.

The analogy, the author goes on, is that, like an extremely profitable investment, blessing the Prophet, that is, saying the formula *salla Allah 'alayhi wa-sallam* only once would bring upon the Believer a ten-fold blessing from God. Another reward for blessing the Prophet is an immediate forgiveness (*ghafr*), as exemplary tales prove.

That blessing the Prophet carries enormous reward is illustrated in the following exemplum. A young man died the death of an evildoer (*fahsh*), rejecting any thought about repentance (*tawba*) regardless of his mother's urgings to this effect. After his death she had a dream and saw him being tortured, then another dream and by that time his lot was improved. To her question what had caused the change for the better the deceased son explained that he benefited from the death of someone like him who, in contradistinction, repented and blessed the Prophet twenty times. The lesson, as the young men puts it to his mother, is that 'blessing the Prophet is light in the hearts, a negation of sins (*takfir lil-dhunub*) and mercy (*rahma*) to both the living and the dead'.

Let us briefly consider also the 'visiting of graves' that recent research has meticulously elucidated in the case of late medieval Egypt.[35] The *majlis* devoted to the subject in the *Rawd* throws light from a somewhat different angle. Thus, one could argue that we learn much about the *mentalité* that is involved in the conceptualization of death and, for example, blurs the Western/modern clear separation between the living and the dead. That the living are able to converse with the dead is a well-known topos. What I find noteworthy is that in the extraordinary tales that are reproduced in the session devoted to *ziyarat al-qubur* not only the dead can act as intercessory to the living but also vice versa. As a result, those who inhabit the graves can, through the acts of their living relatives, be saved from their fate in Hell.[36] Thus the didactic message of the importance of righteous conduct gains an additional dimension.

Finally, I turn to the Sufi material in the *Rawd*. It should be noted at the outset that Sufism features not only in specific sessions but also in the general sessions already referred to. This is variously manifested. For one, the authorities that the compiler relies upon for his exemplary tales are occasionally Sufi figures. This is true, for example, of the ninth-century Dhu al-Nun al-Misri[37] who is the source of several tales.[38] The celebrated Abu Yazid al-Bistami (d. *c.*262/875)[39] and the Baghdadi ascetic Junayd (d. 298/910)[40] are sources as well, as are unidentified Sufis (*ba'd al-sufiyya*)[41] or the synonymous 'righteous men' (*salihin*).[42] The Sufi dignitaries and others mentioned earlier are not only sources but also the very heroes of tales they authorize. Thus, in a fantastic tale Junayd sets out for the Hajj but his camel subverts his intention by persistently pursuing the direction of Constantinople. Junayd succumbs only to find out that he has been sent on a divine mission to cure a (Byzantine) princess of the mental illness that had debilitated her. Junayd performs the task by converting her to Islam, and since success in this case is contagious, he converts the king and the queen as well. As if this were not sufficient, the wish of the princess to die as a martyr (*shahida*) is fulfilled shortly afterwards.[43] In another tale in a chapter on the Pilgrimage the semi-legendary Rabi'a al-'Adawiya[44] is the heroine. She is able to intercede for all the pilgrims in a Hajj she took part in.[45]

Unmistakable Sufi notions are not only discussed in what may be characterized as the *Rawd*'s specifically Sufi *majalis* but in sessions that are not recognizable as such. Thus the Sufi 'love of the Lord' (*mahabba*), to which a special session is devoted (see later), also features in a chapter that deals with the Qur'an.[46] The notion of the *faqir* and his special status is recurrent. They are, as the Prophet is believed to have said, the first to enter Paradise, preceding the rich by 'half a day', which actually means by no less than five hundred years.[47] They are the best of His creatures (*safwat khalqihi*) and the richest of them, chained by their *mahabba* and resistant to the devil's government.[48] Or the Sufi ritual of *dhikr* finds place in a treatment of the Hajj in the form of the following aphorism:

He who lights up the torch of *dhikr* the banners become visible to him,
And he who emigrates to the desert of desire the tents show to him.[49]

To linger a little longer on this Sufi notion of Invocation, in the above mentioned session on 'Blessing the Prophet' we are told about a servant who had lived hedonistically, was constantly drunk and refused repentance. Nevertheless, when he died he was seen enjoying the best of Paradise (*arfa' maqam*), a surprising result he explained by his participation in a session of *dhikr* (*majlis al-dhikr*) in which he learned the importance of blessing the Prophet.[50]

As for the sessions that are specifically devoted to Sufi concepts and themes, I have already noted the predominance of the *manaqib al-salihin* and *manaqib al-awliya'* that amounts to over half a dozen of the sessions. Obviously, what we have here is numerous hagiographic tales. If we turn to the fourth session in the *Rawd*,[51] one tale has it that a slave offered in the market for sale is infamous for his 'madness' (*junun*). However, upon interrogation it is revealed that this insanity is only apparent to the ignorant (*jahil*) and that the real cause for the man's peculiar spasms is the Sufi 'love' (*mahabba*) that spreads in the body like intoxication (*khamar al-mahabba*). The source of this tale, one 'Abd al-Rahman b. al-Muhadhdhab, then realizes that the slave is actually a saint (*min awliya'*) and purchases him. The slave's virtues instantly emerge as he refuses to enter his master's house so as not to violate the household's privacy. The food that is sent to him at the gate he does not touch but abstains from eating it. At night he stays awake and immerses himself deeply in prayer and wailing. Among the words he utters is justification of his torment ('*adhab wa-naqm*). As a result he is set free. The motif of the insane as a Sufi in disguise (*fi al-batin min al-muhibbin wa-fi al-zahir min al-majanin*) recurs in another tale.

The righteous Sufis also undergo extraordinary experiences, not to say miraculous ones, such as the one who was carried in an instant from Jerusalem to the Ka'ba to perform the pilgrimage by four young men who, it turns out, were disguised angels. In a special session devoted to the righteous women (*al-salihat al-tayyibat al-sabirat*), for example, we read of the ninth-century Sufi Sirri al-Saqati (?) who encountered a maid (*jariya*) imprisoned in the asylum (*bimaristan*) for insanity. As in the tale on the 'insane' male Sufi related above, so here too the discrepancy between the *zahir* and the *batin* soon emerges. As the maid demonstrates her Sufi virtues of *mahabba* and ecstasy (*wajd*) the Sufi recognizes her sainthood and releases her from captivity.[52]

One theme that still deserves our attention is *mahabba*, possibly the most recurrent Sufi notion in the *Rawd*. In the special *majlis* devoted to it[53] the Sufi 'love' of God is repeatedly characterized as reserved only to the privileged. It is light (*nur*) to the knowledgeable and elevated ('*arif, khawass*) but fire (*nar*) to the ignorant or simpleminded (*jahil, 'awamm*). That *mahabba* could indeed be fatal we learn from a tale about a session (*majlis*) conducted by Dhu al-Nun al-Misri in the presence of the fantastic figure of 70,000 people. On that occasion the Sufi ascetic spoke about the 'love of God' (*mahabbat Allah*) and the 'lovers and their characters' (*muhibbin*). After eleven of the audience died and many fainted, the Egyptian Sufi was told by his disciple (*murid*) that he 'had burnt their hearts by invoking the love of God and that perhaps he should have calmed them down by speaking of the love of human beings' (*mahabbat al-makhluqin*). Dhu al-Nun expressed his deep sorrow but also his hope that those hurt would see bliss (*hana'*).

'(S)ermons take us to water but do not let us drink', observed a self-critical student of medieval Christian preaching, admitting that we never know how much the audiences of popular preachers assimilated and to what extent they were actually influenced.[54] This caveat is true even when we are told, for example, that Ibn 'Ata' Allah's sermons 'had great influence on people's hearts and souls'.[55] After all, this could have been a biased assessment. But this is as closely as we can reach historical reality. So while we certainly lack the tools to estimate the *Rawd*'s impact, its survival is of significance and cultural value.

Notes

1 Eric Geoffroy, *Le Soufisme en Égypte et en Syrie: sous les derniers mamelouks et les premiers ottomans, orientations spirituelles et enjeux culturels* (Damascus, 1995).
2 See art. 'al-Suyuti', *EI2* (E. Geoffroy).
3 See art. 'Dhikr', *EI2* (L. Gardet); J.-C. Garcin, 'Histoire, opposition politique et pietisme traditionaliste dans le husn al-muhadarat de Suyuti', *Annales islamologiques* 7 (1967), esp. pp. 81–7.
4 See art. 'Kashf', *EI2* (L. Gardet).
5 See art. 'Ru'ya', *EI2* (T. Fahd).
6 Michael Winter, 'Sheikh Ali Ibn Maymun and Syrian Sufism in the Sixteenth Century', *Israel Oriental Studies* 7 (1977), pp. 302–3.
7 Geoffroy, 154–6. For the Sufi *haqiqa* see art. 'Hakika', *EI2* (L. Gardet).
8 Boaz Shoshan, *Popular Culture in Medieval Cairo* (Cambridge, 1993), p. 10.
9 Geoffroy, p. 147.
10 See art. 'Baraka', *EI2* (G. S. Colin) and most recently Josef W. Meri, 'Aspects of *Baraka* (Blessing) and Ritual Devotion among Medieval Muslims and Jews', *Medieval Encounters* 5 (1999), pp. 46–69.
11 See examples in Geoffroy, pp. 329–33. See also p. 118–19.
12 See art. 'Karama', *EI2* (L. Gardet).
13 Shoshan, pp. 10–12, 16–22.
14 See art. 'Shadhiliyya', *EI2*.
15 Garcin, 'Histoire', pp. 81–2; Winter, 'Sheikh Ali Ibn Maymun', p. 307; Shoshan, p. 12.
16 See art. 'Suhrawardiyya', *EI2* (F. Sobieroj).
17 Shoshan, p. 13; Geoffroy, p. 159.
18 Shoshan, p. 13.
19 Winter, pp. 299, 300.
20 Geoffroy, p. 159. For Bulqini see art. 'Bulkini', *EI2* (H. A. R. Gibb). For further examples of preachers see Geoffroy, pp. 159–60.
21 Geoffroy, pp. 157–8.
22 Shoshan, pp. 13–6.
23 Though not Shiayb, as in William M. Brinner, 'The Significance of the Harafish and their "Sultan"', *Journal of the Economic and Social History of the Orient* 6 (1963), p. 210, following *GAL*, II, p. 228.

24 Sakhawi, *Daw'*, vol. V, p. 20; Sakhawi, *Tibr*, p. 349. See also al-'Asqalani, *Inba'*, vol. II, p. 73; Brinner, 'Harafish', p. 199. He allegedly foretold the Frankish invasion of Alexandria in 767/1365.

25 Ibn al-'Imad, *Shadharat al-dhahab fi akhbar man dahab* (Cairo, 1350–1/1931–2), vol. III, p. 7.

26 Frontispiece of BN ms. arabe no. 1306.

27 See on him Sha'rani, *al-Tabaqat al-kubra*, vol. II, pp. 67, 83, who mentions Muhammad al-Hurayfish ad-Danushari as one of his teachers, whom he visited at his home in Danushar in 915/1509–10.

28 *GAL* II, 177, S II, p. 229.

29 Mark Pattison. For references see Shoshan, p. 90, n. 47. For the use of medieval sermons for studying popular Christianity, see for example, Alexander Murray, 'Religion among the Poor in Thirteenth-Century France: The Testimony of Humbert de Romans', *Traditio* 30 (1974), pp. 285–324.

30 See in particular *Rawd*, p. 83. I have used the Maktaba 'Alamiyya edition (Cairo, n.d.).

31 For example, ibid., pp. 2–3.

32 It is noteworthy that this Alwan al-Hamawi criticized popular preachers for using poetry, 'which is the devil's Quran in the house of God'. See Winter, p. 299.

33 *Rawd*, p. 54.

34 Ibid., pp. 36–40.

35 Christopher S. Taylor, *In the Vicinity of the Righteous: Ziyara and the Veneration of Muslim Saints in Late Medieval Egypt* (Leiden, 1999).

36 *Rawd*, for example, pp. 20–1.

37 See on him art. 'Dhu'l-Nun, Abu'l-Fayd', *EI2* (M. Smith).

38 For example, pp. 8, 112, 116, 117, 118.

39 Ibid., p. 9. See on him art. 'Abu Yazid al-Bistami', *EI2* (H. Ritter).

40 See art. 'Djunayd', *EI2* (A. J. Arberry).

41 For example, pp. 3–4, 123.

42 For example, pp. 18, 34.

43 Pp. 60–1.

44 P. 36. See art. 'Rabi'a al-'Adawiyya al-Kaysiyya', *EI2* (Margaret Smith and Ch. Pellat).

45 *Rawd*, p. 46.

46 Ibid., pp. 7–8.

47 Ibid., pp. 2–3.

48 Ibid., p. 72.

49 Ibid., p. 44: *man awqada misbah al-dhikr lahat lahu al-'alam wa-man tagharraba fi badiyat al-shawq zaharat lahu al-khiyam.* I take it to intend *dhikr* to be superior.

50 Ibid., pp. 3–4.

51 Ibid., pp. 22–6.

52 Ibid., pp. 226–7.

53 Ibid., pp. 194–201.

54 D. L. d'Avray, *The Preaching of the Friars: Sermons Diffused from Paris before 1300* (Oxford, 1985), p. 259.

55 Shoshan, p. 12, for similar statements as regards other preachers.

10 Physicians in Mamluk and Ottoman courts

Miri Shefer

Abu Zakariyya Yahya Ibn 'Abd Allah (d. 1483–84), Head of the Orthopaedists and Surgeons in Egypt under the Mamluk sultanate, began his career as a barber and circumciser. He nevertheless rose to serve two sultans – al-Zahir Khushqadam (r. 1461–67) and Qaytbay (r. 1468–96) – and several important military office holders (*amirs*) as their private physician. That he profited handsomely from his career is evident from the many properties listed in the charter for his charitable endowment (*waqfiyya*). According to his biographer, al-Sakhawi, Abu Zakariyya's residence was 'magnificent', and his wealth was on a scale comparable to that of an *amir* of the time.[1]

Ahi Çelebi (d. 1523–24) was the personal physician to four Ottoman sultans – Mehmed II (r. 1451–81), Beyazid II (r. 1481–1512), Selim I (r. 1512–20) and Süleyman I (r. 1512–66). His considerable wealth is revealed in his welfare charities. He founded a mosque in Istanbul and two *madrasa*s in Edirne, which were funded by dozens of shops, rooms for rent, gardens and hamams in various towns and taxes he was entitled to collect from various villages.[2]

Other members of the medical profession were less successful. The Mamluk oculist Shihab al-Din al-Shawi became rich only after he left his profession and took a position at the mint.[3] A Jewish physician from Qalyub (north of Cairo) writing to his wife about his new clinic in the big city assured her that the public response had been good; however, his fellow physicians were so competitive that he dared not leave his practice even for one day to visit her and check on her sore eyes. Maybe this was just an excuse on behalf of the husband, but apparently he thought it was a convincing one. Another physician did not buy even 'one thread' of a new suit for two years, and his children suffered from hunger. While there were Jewish physicians who could contribute generously to charity (at least three pieces of gold; it is instructive that these rich physicians were lumped together with merchants on the contributors' list), one physician paid only one dinar, the same as several dyers, practitioners of a craft considered very low on the social scale. Another physician contributed 1.5 dinars, the same as some shopkeepers.[4] For comparison, the lowest paid workers in Egypt earned a monthly salary ranging from 1.2 to 2 dinars in the period between the eleventh and the fourteenth centuries; and specialized workers could earn a monthly salary of up to six dinars in the same periods.[5]

Compare their situation with that of Mikha'il, a Jewish physician from Damascus, who is the subject of a ferman, an Ottoman imperial decree, dated Saturday, 5 Rabi' I 1024/6 April 1615. The sultan, Ahmet I (r. 1603–17), issued a decree to the Qadi in Damascus complying with a request from Yunus, the head physician in the Syrian province. Yunus had petitioned the sultan on behalf of Mikha'il. The Jewish doctor was very competent (*kemal-i hezaqet*), argued Yunus, but his current financial situation was bad and bitter. Mikha'il was so poor (*feqir-iil-hal*) that he could not pay his taxes (*'avariz ve niizul*). The Syrian head physician interceded on Mikha'il's behalf at the Imperial court. He asked the Sultan to exempt Mikha'il from paying these taxes and thus deliver him from his misery. The Sultan now ordered the Damascene judge to lead an enquiry into the matter. If indeed the facts were as described by the head physician, the judge should grant the Jewish doctor exemption from paying taxes. He should make sure that no one intervened and defied the Sultan's wishes and report immediately back to Istanbul how he carried out this order.[6]

These biographies reveal how different the life stories of physicians could (and still can) be. There is no doubt that the heroes of the first two biographies belonged to an elite group. Although the other two examples do not necessarily tell the story of losers (who do not figure much in our sources anyway), they nevertheless reflect more ordinary fates.

That physicians played an important role in Muslim societies and could enjoy very high status is almost a commonplace of modern writing. However, we should ask what it was that made them part of an elite? And to which elite did they belong? In sum, how could physicians become success stories? In this chapter I deal with one specific example of physicians as part of elite circles in a pre-modern Muslim society, namely, medical doctors at court. As a case study, I compare biographies of physicians to the Mamluk and Ottoman sultans and sketch some characteristics of their career at court.

Not that the Mamluks and Ottomans were the first to employ medical doctors at their courts. One source of the twelfth century credits Ibn Sina (d. 1037) with being the first physician ever to serve rulers. According to al-Bayhaqi, before Ibn Sina physicians kept their distance from the gates of palaces.[7] However, Ibn Sina too was hardly the first doctor to serve a Muslim monarch. Yet there are several reasons for lumping the Mamluks and Ottomans together. Mamluk and Ottoman court cultures had some similarities, the outcome of joint Turkish and Arab Muslim traditions. In both courts we can find Arabic-speaking doctors serving sultans of Turkic origins. And in some cases we can establish that these were even the same physicians: Mamluk physicians in Cairo who later served the Ottomans in Istanbul. This trend is especially conspicuous at the beginning of the sixteenth century after Selim I conquered the Mamluk Sultanate. Upon leaving Cairo for Istanbul, the sultan took with him several leading physicians along with other prominent Cairenes;[8] other Mamluk physicians sought Ottoman patronage on their own initiative. Last but not least on the list of reasons to compare physicians in the Mamluk and Ottoman courts is Michael Winter's long-standing interest (one of many) in the transformation of the Middle East from the Mamluks to the Ottomans.

How could a physician gain a footing in the patron's house? How could an anonymous member of the herd make himself noticed by an influential patron? It seems that the roads to the patron's gate were numerous. Physicians were a very heterogeneous group in terms of their family, educational and vocational backgrounds. Those in power tried to set criteria for entry into their realm and thus to maintain closed ranks. They failed. In this context we should understand some of the famous medical rivalries in history when each side tried to invoke self-serving claims concerning medical excellence and professional ethics.[9] There was no real exclusiveness in the medical realm. Rarely was there formal hierarchy or guild-type associations. In consequence a medical career was open to all, and success within the reach of everyone with luck.

The image emerging from biographical dictionaries suggests that in social terms physicians practising within the large disciplines, natural (internal) medicine (*tibaba*), surgery (*jiraha*) and ophthalmology (*kihala*), enjoyed higher esteem, whereas bone-setters, cuppers (*fassad* or *hajjam*), a dealer in spices and drugs (*'attar*), a maker of syrups (*sharabi*) and the barber/circumciser (*muzayyin*), were regarded as artisans not very different from others with whom they shared a booth at the market place. However, one's original speciality was not always a stumbling block. Although most prominent physicians were either internalists or surgeons, oculists and bloodletters could also gain entry to their ranks. They certainly appeared as part of the entourage of important figures. Sixteenth- and seventeenth-century salary lists from the Ottoman imperial palace bear witness to the fact that oculists were part of the medical corps at court (although, it is true, with lower salaries).[10]

Michael Chamberlain, speaking of the *'ulama'* in medieval Damascus, says that 'books were also emblems of prestige for the elite [...] Many of those with a claim to learning wrote at least one book, and some wrote hundreds'.[11] Physicians composed books and presented them to rulers and important medical figures as a means to win the approval of people who could determine their professional futures. The fate of a physician arriving in a new city from afar depended completely upon his ability to win acceptance among his local peers, and so gain broader assent to his professional credentials and claims to status in his field. It was 'an exercise in affirmation, a claim to valid status as a scholar worthy of esteem and respect in his field'.[12] Such was the case of Ibn Sallum (d. 1670), an Arab physician from Aleppo who became the head physician (*hekimbaşı*) of the Empire and an intimate of Sultan Mehmet IV (r. 1648–87).[13] Ibn Sallum presented his works to the Sultan who rewarded him with a fur coat, a ceremonial gift of patronage, for his famous tract *Ghayat al-itqan fi tadbir badan al-insan* on therapy and hygiene ('The Greatest Thoroughness in Treatment of the Human Body').

Although medical careers were open to many, it is clear that those with family 'in the business', so to speak, would be likely to have a smoother path than those without such advantages. Having successful physicians as relatives made it easier to find good teachers either within the family or outside, and to start building connections. Indeed, families of physicians were widespread in the pre-modern Middle East.[14] The Qaysunizades, a family of Egyptian physicians, are one example out of many for this phenomenon. The first Qaysunizades served the Mamluks, but then were taken by

Selim I to Istanbul. Members of the family served the sultans as their personal doctors till the beginning of the seventeenth century.[15]

Talab al-'ilm – the process of seeking knowledge – which usually entails extensive travelling, was common among seekers of medical knowledge as a lot rode on the reputation of one's teachers. As in other branches of scholarship, the identity of one's teachers figured heavily in any evaluation of one's qualifications. Having a famous physician for a teacher boosted one's career options, even more so when the teacher in question was a man of consequence at court. It is quite common to find in Mamluk and Ottoman biographical dictionaries long lists of names of teachers and students of the famous medical doctors included in their collections.

Here, however, we can note a difference between the Mamluk and Ottoman physicians. Scholars from Egypt, it seems, rarely made long travels outside Egypt. Most of them were concentrated in the scholarly centre of Cairo. Physicians from Anatolia, on the other hand, were apparently more willing to invest time and effort to travel outside their regions in order to study with renowned teachers. This difference may reflect the different degree of self-importance which Muslims in Anatolia and Egypt attached to themselves and their position in the Muslim cultural hierarchy. We can find an example in Emir Çelebi (d. 1638), one of the most renowned physicians of his era. He was born in Anatolia but studied medicine in Cairo, and he stayed on there as head physician in the Qalawunid hospital. He later became the personal physician of Sultan Murat IV (r. 1624–40).[16] I am not aware of a parallel life story for a Mamluk court physician.

Most prominent physicians at court were Muslims. Although a great many non-Muslim doctors practised privately, positions at court were usually given to Muslims or converts. It has been suggested that the Mamluks, for example, were less tolerant of *dhimmi*s in the medical profession than previous dynasties had been, like the Ayyubids who employed numerous Christian doctors.[17] Certainly during the first Ottoman centuries there were several Christian and Jewish physicians who rose to eminence in the Ottoman court. But from the seventeenth century onwards, their numbers and importance shrank.[18] Hekim Ya'qub (d. 1481), an Italian Jew who immigrated to Istanbul, illustrates this. He was appointed a personal physician to Mehmed II, but only when he converted in his old age to Islam was he able to accumulate real power. He then won the position of a vizier with the title of *paşa*.[19] A *ferman* from 1574 explicitly ordered a vacant position among the court doctors to be filled with a Muslim. The decree explained that as the number of Jewish physicians at court was higher than that of Muslims, the situation should be reversed. It is instructive that whereas the previous holder of the position, a Jewish physician by the name of Firuz who passed away, earned thirty akçe (silver coins) per diem, his replacement, a Muslim, was awarded a daily salary of forty akçe.[20]

Nonetheless, medicine was accepted as a possible career for *dhimmi*s by their future Muslim employers. It was seen as socially legitimate for a patron to open his household to a *dhimmi* physician. We do not find many *dhimmi*s in non-medical roles at court. Apparently, a patron could scarcely have made a Jew a member of his intimate retinue unless he filled the role of a personal physician.

From the *dhimmi*s' point of view, medicine was a venue through which aspiring non-Muslims could rise to social and economic greatness in and out of court. Career paths based on religious training and scholarship were naturally closed to them. Medicine and religious beliefs could be in conflict with each other, as, for example, when a *dhimmi* doctor prescribed an alcoholic medication to a Muslim patient.[21] Nevertheless, in contrast to judgeship, a medical practice was a feasible career for a *dhimmi*. To Muslims, a religious–juridical career was more lucrative in comparison to a medical one,[22] and therefore there was a real opportunity for *dhimmi*s in the medical field.

What services could physicians offer their patrons? Why were patrons keen to have physicians around them, so much so that sometimes the patron's bedside was crowded? The typical description of the papal bed in the Renaissance also fits some medieval Muslim rulers. Although numbers are not always specified in the sources, the picture of several doctors vigilant by their patron's sick bed is familiar.

Michael Chamberlain's monograph deals with knowledge as social and cultural capital used by Damascene notables.[23] Although of marginal status, medicine was part of *'ilm* ('knowledge'), and as such a topic of interest to many. Thus patrons who were associated with medical men and knowledge could use that as a means to earn a reputation for themselves as patrons of learning.[24] It is worth noting here that one could be involved with medicine in two ways. Mamluk and Ottoman biographical dictionaries differentiated between a scholar of medicine and a medical practitioner. Although the two groups overlapped considerably, there were many who studied medicine without practising it or who practised it only as a side occupation. Theoretical medicine was one topic among various non-religious subjects like mathematics and astronomy studied by *'ulama'*, scholars of Islamic religion, just as there were physicians who were noted for their practice – not for their scholarly work. It seems, in fact, that references to scholars who were not physicians but who wrote books on medicine are far more frequent than references to professional physicians.[25] This may be due to a bias on the part of the editors of biographical dictionaries: they took an interest in medicine as an intellectual activity and tended to ignore what they regarded as a mere practical craft. Therefore, the ideal type of a physician as it emerges from these compilations is more one of a scholar of medicine – the physician–philosopher or the physician/judge – than one of a successful practitioner. In reality, however, some of the most brilliant careers were the product of a good medical practice which made no major contribution – real or imagined – to the advancement of medical knowledge. Court physicians can be more aptly described as *practitioners*, for whom medicine was not an intellectual activity but more a craft (*sina'a*).

There were other considerations than knowledge which urged patrons to invite physicians to their court. The foremost was medical treatment. Scholarly activity was welcome, but patrons wanted to make sure that their doctors could indeed cure them and their household members when needed. The quality of medical services also had political and diplomatic aspects. Ibn Saghir was the Head of Physicians under Sultan Barquq (r. 1382, 1390–99). According to Ibn Iyas, he was sent in 1392–93 to the Ottoman Sultan Beyazid I (r. 1389–1402), who through an embassy had asked that a good physician be sent to him. Ibn Saghir died abroad on that mission the following year.[26] Good and trusted physicians were a rare commodity and could be used as gifts in the international arena. The Ottomans, as was noted earlier, took with them Egyptian medical doctors when they returned from Cairo to Istanbul in 1517.

For their part, too, physicians were drawn to patrons. Medicine was a good springboard for access to a patron: medical treatment required direct contact with the patron himself. Yet physicians who aspired to a successful career at court had to offer more than medical knowledge. 'What appear as credentials were tokens not only of an individual's acquisition of the texts carried by his *shaykh*, but of the whole complex of manners, moral conduct, deportment and scripted forms of self-presentation that in sum made up the notion of adab'.[27] Physicians at court demonstrated wit and good nature. Biographical dictionaries describe physicians at court as good-looking people and skilled debaters who provided intellectual entertainment and stimulation for their patron. Examination of the skills and knowledge of various physicians competing among themselves for their patron's favour was a public affair.

By becoming courtiers, members of the inner circle around the patron, counted among his intimate companions, they could enhance their prospects. Here we meet physicians playing a role not very different from other courtiers: giving an intimate service to the patron, not unlike the dresser or the jester. At the same time, although it was very important to be fluent in court etiquette, the physicians' fate was based not only on their social skills but on a combination of professional – here medical – and social skills. In that respect court physicians were different from other courtiers whose main role at court was to entertain the patron. Entertainment for doctors was not the aim but a means to achieve their end – keeping the patron healthy and happy with their services.

Behrens-Abouseif claims that being an eminent physician was not sufficient for social status. To secure one's career, it was necessary to acquire prestige and material gains through religious or administrative office which one's connection with the court made possible.[28] In that sense a medical career was only one step on the social ladder. Ibn al-Ukhuwwa (d. 1329) explains that the representation of non-Muslims in the medical profession out of proportion to their numbers was because a medical career did not lead to high administrative and prestigious positions and therefore appealed less to ambitious Muslims.[29] Although in Mamluk Egypt, other career paths perhaps yielded a higher percentage of success (measured in materially and socially rewarding bureaucratic posts), a medical career too could lead to appointments secured by palace connections. Ibn al-Nafis (d. 1288), who is known for his theory of pulmonary circulation, was the Chief Physician in Egypt under Baybars (r. 1260–77) and worked in a hospital. He also taught Shafi'i law in a *madrasa*. He became rich and had a luxurious house in Cairo. He left his house, his fortune and his books to the Mansuri hospital.[30] Fath Allah, who started his career as Head of Physicians, was nominated *katib al-sirr* under Barquq: he was the confidential secretary at the imperial council (*diwan*) in charge of the secretariat and the correspondence of the sultan. It was a position of power which made its holder feared and courted by the highest ranking persons.[31] It is worth remembering, however, that many physicians led their careers entirely within the medical field, as private physicians, working in hospitals or teaching, and when they put their hand to other types of trade, it was rarely on the grand scale we see here.

Life at court was far from easy. A warm personality and good looks amounted to nothing if one's capabilities could not back up one's claim to mastery of medicine. A successful physician had to be cunning, crafty and quick with his thinking in order to save his patient in a situation where normal doctors would fail. There was no room for error. Success in treatment was all important. Physicians at court had to demonstrate a 100 per cent success rate. They had to have *hiyal*. In contrast to *hiyal* in the legal context, here it does not mean an intellectual solution but a very practical treatment. In the medical context *hiyal* means the doctor's ability to apply tricks and devices not known to other physicians in order to treat someone successfully.

The physicians who formed the top medical–social echelon belonged to a household or court and drew their salaries from it. As court dependants, they were a group in between the *khassa* – elite members – on the one hand, and the *'amma* – the common people – on the other. They were in a sort of limbo: they belonged to both groups but in fact were alien to each. Our physicians tended to originate socially from the *'amma*; they worked their way up, but they shared the life of the court with the elite. Physicians were among the associates of important figures: their patron, and his advisors and companions. Some physicians became very intimate themselves with their patrons.

Speaking of physicians in later medieval England, Carol Rawcliffe claims 'that the practice of medicine brought enviable rewards and privileges to the select few who rose to particular eminence is beyond doubt; and even the moderately successful were able to accumulate enough trappings to guarantee comfort if not wealth'.[32] Pre-modern Muslim societies had similar phenomena. Economically, while physicians in Muslim courts were not necessarily rich, having a fixed salary relieved them of the need to compete with other healers for clients. Financial survival in the private market could be very brutal. They were working for a salary but they enjoyed many social and economic privileges.

Yet whatever privileges they did succeed in acquiring were achieved by individuals in specific circumstances rather than being something they were entitled to by their job description. Having access to a patron, directly or via other members of the household, also meant power, that is participation in decision-making. However, power could prove to be a double-edged sword. Sometimes physicians had to pay with their positions, at times even with their heads, because of political upheavals (I deal with this aspect of medical court life in a separate study).

It is worth remembering the case histories of the less fortunate cited in this essay. Indeed, intellectual reputation and material gain could be achieved also by medical men of humble origins – a medical career was a possible aid to social climbing. But real success was nevertheless the lot only of a select few. Many practising doctors secured no more than a modest competence. Moreover, patronage in itself was not enough to guarantee success, especially lasting success. Success at court depended on the caprices of a patron, and as a result it could be short-lived and end tragically. Not surprisingly, there were physicians who chose to avoid the hassle of court life and turned down official posts and membership in an elite group in return for peace of mind. And success in general – at court and elsewhere – was not always what it was thought to be. It did not always bring physicians respect.

Notes

1 Doris Behrens-Abouseif, *Fath Allah and Abu Zakariyya: Physicians under the Mamluks* (Cairo, 1987), pp. 21–5.
2 Ahmad b. Mustafa Ṭāşköprüzāde, *al-Shaqa'iq al-Nu'maniya* (Süleymaniye Kütüphanesi, Esad Ef. 2308), 170; M. Tayyib Gökbilgin, *XV–XVI Asırlarda Edirne ve Paşa Livası* (İstanbul, 1952), pp. 488–9; Abdülhāk Adnan Adıvar, *Osmanlı Tüklerinde İlim* (İstanbul, 1991), pp. 65–7; Esin Kâhya and Ayşegül D. Erdemir, *Bılımın Işığında Osmanlıdan Cümüriyete Tıp ve Sağlık Kurumları* (Ankara, 2000), pp. 157–61.
3 Behrens-Abouseif, *Fath Allah*, p. 11.
4 S. D. Goitein, *A Mediterranean Society: The Jewish Communities of the Arab World as Portrayed in the Documents of the Cairo Geniza* (Berkeley, CA, 1967–71), vol. 2, pp. 257, 380; vol. 1, p. 78.
5 E. Ashtor, 'The Diet of Salaried Classes in the Medieval Near East', *Journal of Asian History*, 4 (1970), pp. 11, 13.
6 Başbakanlık Osmanlı Arşivi (The Prime Ministry Archives, Istanbul), mühimme defteri 80, p. 550, item 1293.
7 Zahir al-Din al-Bayhaqi, *Ta'rikh hukama al-Islam*, (ed.) Muhammad Kurd 'Ali (Damascus, 1988), p. 56.
8 Ibn Iyas, *Bada'i' al-zuhur fi waqa'i' al-duhur* (Cairo, 1403/1983), vol. 1b, p. 462.
9 Miri Shefer, 'Medical and Professional Ethics in Sixteenth-Century Istanbul: Towards an Understanding of the Relationships between the Ottoman State and the Medical Guilds', *Medicine and Law*, 21 (2002), pp. 307–19. For famous rivalries among physicians in previous centuries, see Ibn Abi Usaybi'a, *Uyun al-Anba' fi Tabaqat al-Atibba* (Beirut, 1965), pp. 242–6; Joseph Schacht and Max Meyerhof, *The Medico-Philosophical Controversy Between Ibn Butlan of Baghdad and Ibn Ridwan of Cairo* (Cairo, 1937); Michael W. Dols, *Medieval Islamic Medicine: Ibn Ridwân's Treatise 'On the Prevention of Bodily Ills in Egypt'* (Berkeley, CA, 1984), pp. 54–66; Lawrence I. Conrad, 'Scholarship and Social Context: A medical case from the eleventh-century Near East', in Don Bates (ed.), *Knowledge and the Scholarly Medical Traditions* (Cambridge, 1995), pp. 80–104.
10 Rifki Melül Meriç, 'Osmanlı Tababeti Tarihine ait Vesikalar', *Tarih Vesikaları*, 1/16 (1955), pp. 37–113; 2/17 (1958), pp. 267–93.
11 Michael Chamberlain, *Knowledge and Social practice in medieval Damascus, 1190–1350* (Cambridge, 1994), pp. 136–7.
12 Conrad, 'Scholarship and Social Context', pp. 91–2, 97.
13 Muhammad Amin b. Fadlallah al-Muhibbi, *Ta'rikh khulasat al-athar fi a'yan al-mi'a al-hadiya 'ashara* (4 vols; Cairo, 1284H), vol. 2, pp. 240–2; Muhammad b. Mustafa Rashed, *Tarīh-i Rāshed* (6 vols; Istanbul, 1282H), vol. 1, p. 96; Adıvar, *Osmanlı Tüklerinde İlim*, pp. 122–3, 131–2; Kâhya and Erdemir, *Bılımın Işığında Osmanlıdan Cümüriyete Tıp ve Sağlık Kurumları*, pp. 179–84.
14 Goitein, *Mediterranean Society*, vol. 2, p. 245.
15 Najm al-Din al-Ghazzi, *al-Kawakib al-sa'ira fi a'yan al-mi'a al-'ashira* (ms. H. Hüsnü Paşa 876 in the Süleymaniye Library, Istanbul), fol. 225b. See also Adıvar, *Osmanlı Tüklerinde İlim*, pp. 115–16; Kâhya and Erdemir, p. 162; Uriel Heyd, 'Moses Hamon, Chief Jewish Physician to Sultan Suleyman the Magnificent', *Oriens*, 16 (1963), pp. 152–70.
16 Emir Çelebi, *Enmüzej al-Ṭibb* (British Library, Or. 7282), fol. 8; Adıvar, *Osmanlı Tüklerinde İlim*, pp. 128–9; Kâhya and Erdemir, pp. 173–4.
17 Behrens-Abouseif, *Fath Allah*, pp. 12–13; Samira Jadon, 'The Physicians of Syria during the Reign of Salah al-Din 570–98 AH 1174–93 AD', *Journal of the History of Medicine and Allied Science*, 25 (1970).
18 'Ayn-i 'Ālī, *Qavānin-i 'Āl-i 'Ūhmānī der Ḥulaṣat-i Maḍāmi-i Defter-i Divān* (İstanbul, 1979), p. 94; Heyd, 'Moses Hamon', pp. 157–8; Bernard Lewis, *The Jews of Islam* (Princeton, NJ, 1984), p. 214 n. 29.

19 Tāşköprüzāde, *al-Shaqā'iq al-nu'maniyya*, fols. 100a–1a; Heyd, 'Moses Hamon', p. 154; Bernard Lewis, 'The Privilege Granted by Meḥmed II to His Physician', *Bulletin of the School of Oriental and African Studies*, 14 (1952), pp. 550–63; Adıvar, *Osmanlı Türklerinde İlim*, 53; Kâhya and Erdemir, pp. 132–3.

20 Başbakanlık Osmanlı Arşivi (The Prime Ministry Archives, Istanbul), mühimme defteri, 108, item no. 1204 [19 zū al-ḥijja 981 (11 April 1574)].

21 See for example how Maimonides solved this moral problem: Max Meyerhof, 'The Medical Work of Maimonides', in S. W. Baron, (ed.), *Essays on Maimonides* (New York, 1966; reprint. 1941), pp. 284–5; Goitein, *Mediterranean Society*, vol. 2, p. 578 n. 84.

22 Behrens-Abouseif, *Fath Allah*, p. 12.

23 Ibid., p. 19.

24 Nicolas Vatin, 'Les médicins au chevet des sultans ottomans (XVᵉ–XIXᵉ siècles)', *Wiener Zeitschrift für die Kunde des Morgenlandes*, 89 (1999), pp. 225–51.

25 Doris Behrens-Abouseif, 'The Image of the Physician in Arab Biographies of the Post-Classical Age', *Der Islam*, 66 (1989), pp. 331–43.

26 Behrens-Abouseif, *Fath Allah*, p. 7. For diplomatic missions of physicians in previous centuries, see Ibn Abi Usaybi'a, *'Uyun al-Anba'*, p. 407; Muhammad M. Ahsan, *Social Life under the Abbasids* (London, 1979), pp. 42–3; Eliyahu Ashtor, *The Jews of Moslem Spain*, 2 vols, trans. from Hebrew Aaron Klein and Jenny Machlowitz Klein (Philadelphia, PA, 1973), vol. 1, pp. 177–81; Jamal al-Din al-Qifti, *Kitab akhbar al-'ulama' bi-akhbar al-hukama'* (Cairo, n.d.), p. 209; Bernard Lewis, 'The Sultan, the King and the Jewish Doctor', *Islam in History: Ideas, Men and Events in the Middle East* (London, 1973), pp. 166–76.

27 Chamberlain, p. 107.

28 Behrens-Abouseif, *Fath Allah*, p. 24.

29 Ibn al-Ukhuwwa, *Ma'alim al-qurba fi ahkam al-hisba*, (ed.) and trans. Reuben Levy (Cambridge, 1938), p. 166 (in Arabic numerals; Arabic text), pp. 56–7 (in Latin numerals; English translation).

30 Max Meyerhof, 'Ibn al-Nafîs', *EI²*, vol. 3, pp. 897–8.

31 Behrens-Abouseif, *Fath Allah*, p. 20.

32 Carol Rawcliffe, 'The Profits of Practice: The Wealth and Social Status of Medical Men in Later Medieval England', *Bulletin (Society for the Social History of Medicine)*, 34 (1984), p. 28.

11 Evliya Çelebi on ˈimarets

Amy Singer

[handwritten annotations: "public Kitchens" and circle around "imarets"]

Among those who recorded their observations of the Ottoman Empire, the seventeenth-century traveler Evliya Çelebi holds a unique place. From his forty-odd years of traveling the length and breadth of the empire, Evliya compiled the *Seyahatname*, ten volumes of first-hand observations and descriptions peppered with anecdote, hearsay, borrowed information, and myth. Traveling frequently in the retinues of high-ranking men of state, and sometimes on his own, he visited a great many towns of the empire in Anatolia, the Balkans, and the Arab provinces, and ventured beyond the boundaries of the empire as well. Among his observations in each place, Evliya recorded the number of public buildings: mosques, *medreses* (colleges), *mekteb*s (primary schools), baths, markets, hospitals, fountains, and ˈimarets (public kitchens). It is the last which concern us here.[1]

The present article constitutes the first step in a large project to investigate the phenomenon of the Ottoman ˈimaret, an institution perhaps unique to the Ottomans in its proliferation and purpose. The word ˈimaret itself is originally the Arabic word ˈimara meaning "habitation and cultivation" or "the act of building, making habitable, bringing into cultivation." In the Turkish form it refers either to a mosque complex (*külliye*) or to a public kitchen; both meanings are used throughout the Ottoman period, and continue to be used in scholarly writings on the Ottoman Empire. The word kitchen here refers to kitchens built for public purposes whose clientele might include any and all of those referred to under the rubric *fakir* (poor) as well as an extensive list of other deserving persons. ˈİmarets were found throughout the empire, usually as part of endowed foundations (*vakif/waqf*), dispensing food daily. The genesis of the ˈimarets is as yet untraced, and although one may point to individual antecedents, the widespread appearance of this institution seems to have no immediate parallel in Middle Eastern, Muslim, or world history in the pre-modern period.[2]

From his own description, Evliya was obviously impressed by the ˈimarets as well as with the Ottomans for establishing them. He says: "I, this humble one [Evliya], have traveled for 51 years and in the territories of 18 rulers [and] there was nothing like our enviable institution. May the beneficence of the House of Osman endure until the end of days!"[3] Thus it may be that Evliya took particular care to note these kitchens wherever he found them. At the same time, he himself may have been a client at numerous ˈimarets during his travels, making his interest, both practical and scholarly.

Little focused research has been done on the ʿimarets, thus most questions about them remain to be answered.[4] As a first step, a comprehensive catalogue of ʿimarets in the Ottoman empire may reveal patterns of ʿimaret formation, location, and beneficiaries. For all their record-making, however, this kind of list is not one which the Ottomans compiled, though they did preserve extensive records of individual institutions.[5] This is where Evliya becomes important. From his *Seyahatname*, it is possible to cull a list of ʿimarets, which, because of the extent of his travels, serves as a first approximation of a catalogue. Clearly, Evliya has his limits as a source. His accuracy fails at times; he did not visit all the places he describes; and, while in some cases he relies on second-hand evidence, including earlier chronicles, in others he falls back on invention.[6] Moreover, Evliya wrote in the mid-seventeenth century, and thus may easily have missed older institutions that disappeared before he had a chance to observe or hear of them; obviously, he would not have recorded those built after his time. Thus once an initial list is compiled it will have to be modified through the use of a variety of other sources.

Reading through large parts of the *Seyahatname*,[7] it becomes evident that Evliya had every intention of providing an accurate notation of buildings in each town he visited. Frequently his entries follow a pattern, describing first mosques (large Friday *cami*ʾs and smaller *mescid*s), then medreses, and so on through a list of building types. He often noted, for example, that while there was a mosque and a bath in some town, there existed no medrese, hospital or public kitchen.[8] Evliya's good intentions are obvious, yet his execution often fell short, so that some entries list building types followed by blank spaces where he failed to fill in the number of each type and their names. Overall, however, he did specify dozens if not hundreds of institutions, and so justifiably serves as a point of departure for this study.

In the present discussion, several points will be considered in light of the evidence from the *Seyahatname*. First, what does *ʿimaret* mean? Evliya used a number of terms for this institution and perhaps referred to more than one institution with overlapping terms. It is therefore useful to sort them out, to decide what they mean and to what extent they overlap. Second, what functions did the ʿimarets serve and what did this service include? Third, whom did they serve? Finally, from Evliya's numerous editorial remarks, one may begin to understand how the ʿimarets fit into the socio-economic fabric of the towns in which they were located. Ultimately, a comprehensive reading of Evliya allows for a mapping of ʿimarets across the Ottoman empire and also provides a quantitative measure of ʿimaret-building as well.

Terms

One of the more valuable contributions Evliya makes to our study of ʿimarets is his naming of the kitchens. When he uses "ʿimaret" on its own, the meaning is potentially in either of the two senses discussed earlier. Thus he says of the külliye of Selim I in Istanbul: *ve bir ʿimaret-i itˁamı ve bir darüʾ ż-żiyafe-i ʿulema ve suhtevat meʾkeli ve bir mihmansarayi vardır… Ġayrı medaris timarhane misillü ʿimaretler yokdur.*[9] At the end of this passage, "İmaretler" clearly means "buildings" or "institutions," while the expression "ʿimaret-i itˁamı" (ʿimaret of feeding) refers to a specific kind of building, one connected to food.[10] The common term "darüʾż-żiyafe" (house of feast) also appears in this passage, possibly as a synonym for "`imaret-i it`ami," possibly as a distinct term, pointing to the existence of separate eating facilities for the ülema and the students. The list of four terms – `imaret-i it`amı, darü'ż-żiyafe, me'kel*, and *mihmansaray* – suggests that they may each be distinct institutions; however Evliya sometimes seems to use them as synonyms in different places throughout the text.

In the course of his listings, Evliya provides an extensive lexicon of terms, with many permutations. One notes the following: *matbah-ı it`am `imaret* (`imaret of the kitchen of feeding);[11] `*imaret-i et`am ve darü'ż-żiyafe* (`imaret of feeding and house of feast) at Sultanahmet in Istanbul;[12] `*imaret-i ta`am* (`imaret of food/a meal) at Eyüb in Istanbul;[13] `*imaret-i ıt`amı* at Üsküdar;[14] `*imaret-i darü'l-it`amı* in Silivri;[15] *bir darü'l-it`am-ı daru'z-ziyafe `imareti* at the complex of Sokollu Mehmed Paşa in Budin;[16] `*imaret-i darü'z-ziyafe* in Baghdad;[17] *darü'l-et`am-ı `imarat* in Bitlis;[18] *darü'z-ziyafe-i `imarat-ı et`ime* in İmadiyye;[19] *tekye-i `imaret-i it`am* (dervish lodge of the `imaret of feeding); `*imaret-i fukaralar* (`imaret of the poor) in Bursa;[20] *me'kel-i darü'ż-żiyafat-ı at`am-ı `imarat* (refectory of the house of feasts of feeding of the `imaret); `*imaret-i me'kel* (`imaret of the refectory) in Berat;[21] and `*imaret-i darü't-ta`am* (`imaret of the house of food) in Urfa.[22] These variations all convey the common sense of a place where food is served, although in some cases the literal meaning appears convoluted.

Alongside the kitchens there might be adjunct institutions such as storehouses for provisions (*kilar*), bread ovens (*furun*), and refectories (*me'kel*) where people were actually served. Such auxiliaries seem most often to be part of the largest complexes. The Hatuniyye in Trabzon had a bread oven (*bir ekmek furunu*), a large storehouse (*kilar-ı azim*), and a special dining space for the poor, dervishes and students (*ve matbahına muttasıl cemi'i fukara ve suhtevata ma'kel-i it'amı var kim talib-i ilme mahsus darü'z-ziyafedir*).[23]

Although one thinks of `imarets as discrete institutions, this is not always the case. Foreign travel accounts contain descriptions of `imarets that seem to confuse them with *hans* or *caravansarays*.[24] On the the other hand, the term `imaret may have been far more elastic than we imagine. Encountering an `imaret, a stranger might understandably confuse it with a caravansaray, both having kitchens and distributing food free of charge. Evliya contributes to the confusion, in passages like the following one ostensibly describing an `imaret in Hersek: *bir imaret darü'l-it`am bina edüp hala cemi`i ayende vü revende müsafirin ü mücavirinleri mihmansarayda meks edüp mihmandarlar karbansarayın her ocağına bir sini ta`am çobra ve adem başına birer nan-pare ve şem`-i revgan getirirler ve her at ve deve başına birer tobra şa`ir getirüp mihmandarlar hizmet ederler, evkaf-ı azimdir.*[25]

> He built a house of feeding, an `imaret. Now all those going and coming, the travelers and sojourners, stay at the guest house. The hosting attendants bring to every [guest room, each with a] hearth, a tray with soup, a loaf of bread, and a candle. And they bring one bag of oats to each horse and each camel. The hosting attendants serve; it is a great waqf.

Throughout his narrative Evliya mixes and matches the lexical elements with no system immediately apparent. From the juxtaposition of terms in single sentences, it is, however, possible to confirm that most of the terms refer to public kitchens.

Yet the multiplicity of terms suggests that perhaps there were many different kinds of institutions originally or perhaps that they had different names depending on the region in which they were found and whether they were urban or rural. To add to the confusion, translators of Evliya over the years, stretching back to the early part of the nineteenth century, have not always been consistent or distinctive in their rendering of the various terms.

The institutions described as `imarets (in one phrase or another) could be very distinct one from the other. They differed in size, in menu, and in clientele. This is made clear first in the chapter in Book One of the *Seyahatname* on the *matbah-ı it`am `imaret* in Istanbul. Under this heading, Evliya lists three major categories of institutions. Of the first he says:

> In order to give generously the very greatest benefaction first to the strangers and the poor and the weak, the food/benefaction of the `imaret of the new palace is abundant all the months of the year, morning and late afternoon, [to] the rich and the poor, the elite and the common people, three times each, every day.[26]

This "new palace" to which Evliya refers is the Topkapı Palace built by Mehmed II, "new" because it was the second palace he built after the conquest of Istanbul.[27]

The second category of kitchens includes fourteen külliyes of Istanbul. Finally, still under the same heading, Evliya names the *tekke*s (sufi lodges) as a third category: "In addition to these, in how many hundreds of tekkes are there kitchens of Kaykavus."[28] Kaykavus was a legendary Iranian king, renowned for his great generosity.[29] In Menzil-i Nallıhān, Evliya describes a place as *matbah-ı Keykavus-misal bir imaret-i darü'z-ziyafe*, an `imaret having a kitchen like that of Keykavus.[30] Throughout his travelogue, Evliya points to tekkes which step into the role of `imarets, as needed. For example, in Diyarbekir, he says:

> In olden times there were seven public kitchens (`*imaret-i da[r]ü'z-ziyafesi*) distributing free meals. The waqfs with which they were endowed, however, have fallen into decay as a result of corruption, so that now only the public kitchen (`*imaret*) of the Great Mosque remains. However, the tekke of the shaykh of Urmia provides the poor more abundantly with food than the public kitchens do, and the same is true of the other tekkes.[31]

Three rather different types of institutions, an imperial palace, kitchens attached to mosque complexes, and dervish lodges, all fall under Evliya's general heading of `"imaret". Moreover, he points to a fourth group of kitchens, those of the large households (*hanedan*) in many towns, which host travelers as generously as the `imarets, where these do not exist or are insufficient. In Bitlis, he explains:

> Formerly the soup kitchens of Sheref Khan and Khatuniyye and Khusrev Pasha were operative, dispensing nourishment to all travelers and visitors. But now their *evkaf* have fallen to ruin, and they dispense soup only for Ashura and during the nights of Ramazan. But in fact there is no need for them, since all the houses have open doors and host wayfarers like public banquet halls (*daru'z-ziyafe gibi*).[32]

Strictly speaking, the kitchens of substantial households were not `imarets. Evliya's discussion of these kitchens and those of the palace does, however, point to the overlap between the generous and formal hosting practised by the rich and powerful, and the distributions made under the rubric of charity implied by the endowed `imarets. Common to all the kitchens is the free distribution of food to needy and/or deserving people.

Founders

Of the three types, it is the `imarets of the sultans, the second group, that wins Evliya's particular admiration. These distributed "a loaf of bread and a cup of soup . . . continuously . . . to the poor and destitute, young and old, and to the traveler twice a day, each day, up until this one."[33] A large number of these endowments was established by sultans, as well as their mothers, daughters and sisters, in Istanbul, Bursa and Edirne, the Ottoman capitals. However, Evliya finds imperial `imarets in other towns of Anatolia, such as Konya, Manisa, Silivri, Trabzon, and Amasya.[34]

Sultans were not the only ones to found `imarets. Evliya recorded `imarets bearing the names of a variety of important and wealthy people. In the towns of Anatolia and the Balkans the founders included Hersekzade Ahmad Paşa (Hersek),[35] Kara Piri Paşa, a vizier of Selim I (Silivri),[36] Koca Derviş Mehmed Paşa, a vizier of Suleyman I (Sofya),[37] two `imarets of Hayreddin Paşa'nın and one of Balabanoğlu in Iznik,[38] and one of Sokollu Mehemmed Paşa in Edirne.[39] Some bore the names of historical personages and some rare few left no individual person's name associated with them. We may assume, however, that all of the founders were people of wealth, since the initial outlay for construction and the endowment needed to ensure the running of an `imaret required substantial capital.

Clients

Evliya's descriptions give only a general sense of who ate at the `imarets. (Other sources fill in some of the details in this regard.[40]) He does make clear, nonetheless, that not all `imarets served the same clientele, nor was it necessarily their purpose to do so. The common and regular diners at `imarets included scholars, students, travelers, dervishes, and indigents. Evliya tells us that the kitchens at Topkapı Palace fed "the rich and the poor, the elite and the common people" (*bay u gedaya ve has [u]* `*ama*), and that the `imarets of large imperial mosque-complexes in Istanbul served the elite and the common people, the poor and destitute, young and old, and the traveler (*has [u]* `*ama . . . fukara ve mesakine ve pir civane ve ayende ve revendeye*).[41] This inclusive spirit is clearly formulaic, repeated to describe `imarets all over the empire. Yet it alerts us to the idea that these `imarets were not solely, nor perhaps even principally established to serve the indigent.

`İmaret clients everywhere often included travelers, those "coming and going" (*ayende ve revende*), as, for example, at the `imarets of Eyüp, Mihrimah in Üsküdar,[42] İmadiyye,[43] Trabzon,[44] Bursa,[45] Menzil-ı Nallıhan,[46] Urfa,[47] and Kayseri.[48] Some `imarets were closely attached to medreses and apparently catered primarily to their staff and students, as appeared to be the case at the medrese of Selim I (Istanbul);

perhaps there were separate kitchens for the medrese and for other clients.[49] This is clearly so in Van, where the Gāzi Hüsrev Paşa medrese had its own ʿimaret for learned men (*danişmend ve ulema*), serving also the righteous poor (*suleha fukaralara*), possibly referring to sufis in particular.[50] The medrese of Sultan Hüseyn-i Adil in İmadiyye also had an in-house kitchen, called *darüʾz-ziyafe*, to serve the students in their rooms, as well as a few travelers (perhaps housed there?).[51] At the Hatuniyye in Trabzon, a separate refectory existed especially for those "seeking knowledge" (*kim talib-i ilme mahsus darüʾz-ziyafedir*), the sufis and the students.[52]

Although some formulaic descriptions of the clients occur very frequently, others appear more rarely, suggesting that they relate directly to the specific location described. Amasya boasted ten ʿimarets in Evliya's time, including one belonging to the Mevlevîhâne, which gave food to the poor in addition to the dervishes there (*dervişanlarından maʿada fukaralara niʿmeti mebzuldur*).[53] Elbasan and Ohrid also each had a *tekye* ʿ*imareti*.[54] In Trabzon, the Hatuniyye ʿimaret gave food to the usual customers, and in addition specifically mentioned the boatmen (*keştibân*).[55] One is not surprised to find such a group in this coastal town of the Black Sea, but one wonders what privilege or weakened condition added them to the ʿimaret's roster.

Moving south and east, to the Kurdish regions of Anatolia, Evliya notes the ʿimarets of Cizre. The one located in the fortress, he says, welcomed all comers, twice daily, except for the Yezidi Kurds who are refused ("*İlla Yezidi Kürdlerine bir dane-i darı ve dürü vermeyüp Yezidileri redd ederler*").[56] Finally, at the other end of the empire in the Balkans, several entries specifically list Muslims, Christians and Zoroastrians (*cemiʿi Müslim ü gebr ü tersaya*) as being the regular clients of the ʿimarets.[57] In Elbasan, Magians (*muğana*) were included as well.[58]

Distributions

Most typically, ʿimarets regularly served soup (*çobra, çorba*) and bread (*ekmek, nan*) to their clients. In some places, the fare was more extensive, as in Budin, where a tray of rice and stew was served in addition to the soup and bread.[59] On the night of Friday (i.e. Thursday evening), richer dishes were often served, most commonly *dane* (a meat stew) and *zerde pilav* (a sweet rice dish).[60] Unfortunately, Evliya does not provide the kinds of extensive recipes and food lists found in waqfiyyas or the accounts registers of endowments.[61] Most of the ʿimarets served food all year round, daily, morning and evening (*mah-u sal biʾl-guduv veʾl-asal ... be-her ruz merreteyn*).[62] Others, for lack of funds, functioned only on Fridays and holidays like Ramadan and Ashura.[63]

A number of the ʿimarets supplied not only food, but also candles.[64] Presumably, these offered their clients a bed for the night, for which they needed light. A place like the ʿimaret of Mihrimah Sultan on the quay at Üsküdar distributed candles as well as food, and stipulated in addition, according to Evliya, that guests were welcome for only three days.[65] This final condition is one generally encountered in hans, caravansarays, and even village guest houses. In addition to people, some of the ʿimarets also fed animals. In Hersek, in Budin, and at the ʿimaret of Mihrimah Sultan in Üsküdar, each beast received a sack of food.[66] Generally, facilities for animals are associated with hans or caravansarays. The overlap of functions may be particular to these two endowments, but is also indicative of the fluidity of their nature.

* * *

Evliya's references, from something more than half of his oeuvre, provide an extensive, though far from exhaustive, picture of `imarets in the mid-seventeenth century Ottoman world. In addition to the list of institutions and, for the most part sketchy, details on each one, Evliya also compares the `imarets with other institutions providing food, such as the caravansarays, the sufi tekkes, and private homes. By doing this he points to the tradition of hospitality of which the `imarets were certainly a part, and suggests that certain ambiguities existed as to their particular character. From Evliya's descriptions, we also understand that the `imarets were shaped by their locations, despite the fact that many were imperial institutions, endowed from the Ottoman capital. Thus the fact that Christians, Zoroastrians, and Magians were allowed to eat at some `imarets in the Balkans, while the Yezidis were pointedly excluded from one in eastern Anatolia, helps to map the boundaries of local society and culture.

By way of a preliminary conclusion, we can suggest that the `imarets were another of the institutions that established a shared culture across the Ottoman empire. Evliya expects to find them in the towns along his route, and when they are absent he notes this, as well as the alternate locations for receiving a meal. More than has perhaps been indicated in writing on `imarets in the past, one may note that they served travelers as a matter of course, alongside the local poor and students. In addition to completing the survey of `imarets in the empire, future research must also take up the elastic notion of need and worthiness, to understand more fully the role of the `imarets.

Preliminary list

Name of `imaret	Location
Fatih Sultan Mehmed Han	Istanbul
Bayezid II	Istanbul
Selim I	Istanbul
Süleyman I	Istanbul
Şehzade Mehmed	Istanbul
Ahmed I	Istanbul
Haseki Sultan	Istanbul (Avret Pazarı)
Vefa Sultan/Şeyh Ebü'l Vefa	Istanbul
Emir Buhari	Istanbul
Kariye	Istanbul
Eyüp Sultan	Istanbul (Eyüp)
Şehzade Cihangir	Istanbul (Tophane)
Mihrimah Sultan	Istanbul (Üsküdar)
Valide Sultan (Nurbanu)	Istanbul (Üsküdar)
Valide (not clear whose)	Istanbul (Üsküdar)
Şeyh Mahmud Efendi	Istanbul (Üsküdar)

(continued)

Name of `imaret	Location
Evliya says total = 11	Istanbul (Üsküdar)
Evliya says total = 19	Istanbul
Hayreddin Paşa	Iznik (two are listed with the same name)
Hayreddin Paşa	Iznik
Eski `İmaret	Iznik
Yeni `İmaret	Iznik
Orhan Gazi	Iznik
Balabanoğlu	Iznik
Eşrefzade'nin Tekye	Iznik
Sultan Orhan Gazi	Bursa
Gazi Hudavendigar	Bursa
Yıldırım Bayezid	Bursa
Çelebi Sultan Mehmed—Yeşil İmaret	Bursa
Yıldırım Han	Bursa
Emir Sultan aka Şemseddin Memed b. Ali	Bursa
Koca Murad Han	Bursa
Evliya says total = 21, for the fukara	Bursa
Evliya says total = 2	Kala-i Havik, formerly Ladik, near Amasya
Mustafa Paşa	Gebze
Evliya says total = 10	Amasya
Bayezid II	Amasya
Mevlevihane	Amasya
Pir İlyas Dede	Amasya
Mehmed Paşa	Amasya
Bayezid Paşa	Amasya
Yorgoç Paşa	Amasya
Gök	Amasya
Hatuniyye	Amasya
Çöplüce	Amasya
Hersekzade Ahmed Paşa	Hersek
Bayezid II	Edirne
Sokollu Mehmed Paşa	Budin
`imaret	Köstebek Hani village
Nassif Paşa `imaret	Menzil-i Nallıhan
Meyyitoğlu Gazi Mehmed Beğ	Konis, near Filibe
Bayezid Han	Berat
Uzkurli	Berat
Aziz Efendi	Berat
Hünkar	Elbasan
Sinan Paşa	Elbasan
Tekke	Elbasan
Ohrizade	Struga
Okhrizade	Ohrid
Tekke cami	Ohrid
`imaret	Ohrid
Kaçar Beğ	Şerbetin
Kara Piri Paşa, vizier of Selim I	Silivri
Süleyman I	Silivri
Fatih Mehmed	Silivri
....	Filibe

Name of `imaret	Location
Koca Derviş Mehmed Paşa (vizier of Süleyman)	Sofya
convent of Kilghra Sultan	mouth of Danube
Abdulkadir-i Cilani	Baghdad
Şehabeddin-i Süreverdî	Baghdad
İmam-ı A`zam (Süleyman I)	Baghdad
İmam Musa	Baghdad
`imaret	Nejef
Şah Yakub	Tebriz
Sultan Mütevekkil	Tebriz
Zübeyde Hatun	Tebriz
Sultan Hasan	Tebriz
Great Mosque	Diyarbekir
Evliya says total = 6	Diyarbekir
Ibrahim Halil	Urfa
Eskicami (mu`attal)	Malatya
Şeref Han	Bitlis
Hatuniyye	Bitlis
Hüsrev Paşa	Bitlis
`imaret	Van (Tebriz kapısı)
Ulucami (Sultan Çoban Şah)	Van
Gazi Hüsrev Paşa	Van
Evliya says total = 700	Kazvin
Sultan Hüseyn-i Adil	İmadiyye
Evliya says total = 6	İmadiyye
Hatuniyye	Trabzon
Fatih Mehmed	Trabzon
Pir Dede Sultan Tekyesi	Merzifon
Evliya says total = 2	Köprü
İmaret han	Kal`a-i Köprü
Ahund Hanım Cami	Kayseri
Hacci Kılıç	Kayseri
Evliya says total = 40	Kayseri
Süleyman I	Konya
Paşa saray	Aksaray
Karamanoğlu Ibrahim Beg	Aksaray
Kızıl Medresesi	Sivas
`imaret	Çanlı Kenise
Lala Mehmed Paşa	Marmara kasaba
Sultan Murad III	Manisa
Sultaniyye (Hafsa sultan)	Manisa
Hatuniyye (Husnişah Hatun)	Manisa
Ali Beg (son of Timur Taş)	Manisa)____ these two may be one
Timur Taş Paşa (vizier of Murad III)	Manisa)
Ulu Cami	Manisa
`imaret	Sinop
Koyun Baba, built by Bayezid II	tomb near Bolu
Ziyaretgah-i Mama Hatun	Mamkhatun

Notes

1 On Evliya Çelebi, see J. H. Mordtmann and H. W. Duda, "Ewliya Čelebi," in *EI²*, II: 717–20.

2 E. W. Lane, *An Arabic-English Lexicon* (London, 1863–93), p. 2156; Cl. Huart, "ʿimāret," in *EI²*, vol. II, p. 475; Hans Wehr, *A Dictionary of Modern Written Arabic (Arabic–English)*, 4th edn, edited by J. Milton Cowan (Wiesbaden, 1979), s. v.; and Z. Pakalin, *Osmanlı Tarih Deyimleri Ve Terimleri Sözlüğü* (Istanbul, 1946), vol. II, pp. 61–3.

3 Evliya Çelebi, *Evliya Çelebi Seyahatnamesi, 1. Kitap: Istanbul*, prepared by Orhan Şaik Gökyay (Istanbul, 1996), p. 132(a).

4 See Amy Singer, "Imarets," in *The Turks*, edited by Hasan Celâl Güzel, C. Cem Oğuz, and Osman Karatay (Ankara, 2002), vol. 3, pp. 657–64, for a review of published research on the topic.

5 Amy Singer, *Constructing Ottoman Beneficence: An Imperial Soup Kitchen in Jerusalem* (Albany, NY, 2002), pp. 11–12, 104, 181, n. 4.

6 On the sources used by Evliya in his first volume, see Meşkûre Eren, *Evliya Çelebi Seyahatnâmesi Birinci Cildinin Kaynakları Üzerinde Bir Araştırma* (Istanbul, 1960).

7 This article is based on the first four volumes of the transliterated *Seyahatname*, currently being prepared by a team of scholars in Turkey and published by the Yapı Kredi Yayınları. In addition, existing translations, in particular those in the series published by Brill in Leiden having the transliterated and translated texts on facing pages, were also used. Both of these series have the advantage of being indexed, making the present project realistic as a beginning to a much larger study, instead of being a long-term project in itself.

8 For example, Evliya specifically says there was no ʿimaret in the Istanbul suburbs of Arnavutköy, Tarapia, Beykoz and Kanlıca, on which see Evliya Çelebi, *Evliya Çelebi Seyahatnamesi, 1. Kitap: Istanbul*, pp. 193, 196, 199. Beyond the capital, he continues to observe the absence of ʿimarets, in places such as Amasra, Mudurnu, Kayacık, Kars, Erceyş and Van, for which see Evliya Çelebi, *Evliya Çelebi Seyahatnamesi, 2. Kitap*, prepared by Zekeriya Kurşun, Seyit Ali Kahraman, and Yücel Dağlı (Istanbul, 1999), pp. 43, 169; Korkut M. Buğday (ed. and trans.), *Evliyā Çelebis Anatolienreise: Aus dem Dritten Band des Seyāhatnāme* (Leiden, 1996), p. 304; Nuran Tezcan, *Manisa Nach Evliyā Çelebi: Aus dem Neunten Band des Seyāhatnāme. Übersetzung und Kommentar* (Leiden, 1999), p. 56; and Evliya Çelebi, *Evliya Çelebi Seyahatnamesi, 4. Kitap*, prepared by Yücel Dağlı and Seyit Ali Kahraman (Istanbul, 2001), pp. 101(b), 113(b).

9 Evliya Çelebi, *Evliya Çelebi Seyahatnamesi, 1. Kitap: Istanbul*, p. 62.

10 Dankoff, in his translation of passages about Albania, renders ʿimaret either as "public building" or as "soup kitchen," on which see Robert Dankoff and Robert Elsie (eds), *Evliyā Çelebi in Albania (Kosovo, Montenegro, Ohrid)* (Leiden, 2000), pp. 48–9, 98–9, 132–3, 136–7, and 112–3.

11 Evliya Çelebi, *Seyahatname, 1. Kitap*, p. 132(a).

12 Ibid., p. 88.

13 Ibid., p. 169.

14 Ibid., p. 203. After using the specific term to introduce the topic, Evliya then uses the shorter "ʿimaret" in referring to the different kitchens he discusses.

15 Evliya Çelebi, *Evliya Çelebi Seyahatnamesi, 3. Kitap*, prepared by Seyit Ali Kahraman and Yücel Dağlı (Istanbul, 1999), p. 171(a–b).

16 Ibid., p. 270(a).

17 Evliya Çelebi, *Seyahatname, 4. Kitap*, p. 255(a).

18 Evliya Çelebi, *Evliya Çelebi in Bitlis*, trans. R. Dankoff (Leiden, 1990), pp. 146–7.

19 Evliya Çelebi, *Seyahatname, 4. Kitap*, p. 317(b).

20 Evliya Efendi, *Narrative of Travels in Europe, Asia and Africa in the Seventeenth Century*, translated by Joseph von Hammer (London, New York: Oriental Translation Fund; Johnson Reprint Corporation, 1834; 1968 reprint), vol. II, p. 9.

21 Dankoff and Elsie, *Evliyā Çelebi in Albania*, pp. 121 (120).

22 Buğday, *Evliyā Çelebis Anatolienreise*, p. 50.

23 Evliya Çelebi, *Seyahatname, 2. Kitap*, p. 52(a–b).
24 See J. Wild, *Neue Reysbeschreibung eines gefangenen Christen* (Nurnbert: B. Scherff, 1613), p. 190, as quoted in R. Dozy, *Supplément aux dictionnaires arabes*, 2nd edn (Paris, 1927), vol. II, p. 171.
25 Evliya Çelebi, *Seyahatname, 3. Kitap*, p. 7(b).
26 Evliya Çelebi, *Seyahatname, 1. Kitap*, p. 132(a).
27 On Topkapı see Gülru Necipoğlu, *Architecture, Ceremonial and Power, The Topkapı Palace* (Cambridge, MA, 1992).
28 Evliya Çelebi, *Seyahatname, 1. Kitap*, p. 132(a).
29 See Cl. Huart, "Kaykā'ūs," *EI²*, vol. 4, p. 813.
30 Evliya Çelebi, *Seyahatname, 2. Kitap*, p. 243(b).
31 Martin van Bruinessen and Hendrik Boeschoten (trans. and eds), *Evliya Çelebi in Diyarbekir* (Leiden, 1988), pp. 165 (164).
32 Evliya Çelebi, *Evliya Çelebi in Bitlis*, pp. 146–7.
33 Evliya Çelebi, *Seyahatname, 1. Kitap*, pp. 132(a).
34 On the patronage of these royal women, and the absence of comparable patronage by any men of the Ottoman dynasty other than the sultans, see Leslie P. Peirce, *The Imperial Harem: Women and Sovereignty in the Ottoman Empire* (New York, 1993), pp. 198–212. For the individual institutions, see the list at the end of this article.
35 Evliya Çelebi, *Seyahatname, 3. Kitap*, p. 7(b).
36 Ibid., p. 170(a–b).
37 Ibid., p. 224(a–b).
38 Ibid., p. 9(a).
39 Ibid., p. 270(a).
40 For a more detailed discussion, see Singer, *Constructing Ottoman Beneficence*, pp. 62–5.
41 Evliya Çelebi, *Seyahatname, 1. Kitap*, p. 132(a).
42 Evliya Çelebi, *Seyahatname, 3. Kitap*, p. 7(b).
43 Evliya Çelebi, *Seyahatname, 4. Kitap*, p. 317(b).
44 Evliya Çelebi, *Seyahatname, 2. Kitap*, p. 52(a–b).
45 Ibid., p. 15 (a).
46 Ibid., p. 243(b).
47 Buğday, *Evliyā Çelebis Anatolienreise*, p. 50.
48 Ibid., p. 128.
49 Evliya Çelebi, *Seyahatname, 1. Kitap*, p. 62.
50 Evliya Çelebi, *Seyahatname, 4. Kitap*, p. 125(a).
51 Ibid., pp. 314(a), 317(b).
52 Evliya Çelebi, *Seyahatname, 2. Kitap*, p. 52(a–b).
53 Ibid., p. 97(a).
54 Dankoff and Elsie, *Evliyā Çelebi in Albania*, pp. 173 (172), 215 (214).
55 Evliya Çelebi, *Seyahatname, 2. Kitap*, p. 52(a–b).
56 Evliya Çelebi, *Seyahatname, 4. Kitap*, p. 325(b).
57 Evliya Çelebi, *Seyahatname, 3. Kitap*, p. 270(a) and Dankoff and Elsie, *Evliyā Çelebi in Albania*, pp. 173 (172), 215 (214).
58 Ibid., pp. 173 (172).
59 Evliya Çelebi, *Seyahatname, 3. Kitap*, p. 7(b).
60 See the examples in Trabzon and Üsküdar: Evliya Çelebi, *Seyahatname, 2. Kitap*, p. 52(a–b); Evliya Çelebi, *Seyahatname, 1. Kitap*, p. 203.
61 For examples of these, see Singer, *Constructing Ottoman Beneficence*, pp. 58–62.
62 Buğday, *Evliyā Çelebis Anatolienreise*, p. 50.
63 Evliya Çelebi, *Evliya Çelebi in Bitlis*, pp. 146–7.
64 Evliya Çelebi, *Seyahatname, 3. Kitap*, pp. 7(b), 270(a).
65 Evliya Çelebi, *Seyahatname, 1. Kitap*, p. 203.
66 Evliya Çelebi, *Seyahatname, 3. Kitap*, pp. 7(b), 270(a); Evliya Çelebi, *Seyahatname, 1. Kitap*, p. 203.

12 Great fire in the metropolis

The case of the Istanbul conflagration of 1569 and its description by Marcantonio Barbaro

Minna Rozen and Benjamin Arbel

Research on fires and their repercussions in Istanbul from 1453 to 1918 shows that in every century almost no part of Istanbul and Galata was spared from devastating fires.[1] The fire described in Barbaro's account, published here for the first time, is just one of many fires that consumed large parts of the Ottoman capital. Selaniki Mustafa Efendi documented 17 major fires in Istanbul during the 37 years described in his history (1563–1600).[2] In 1757, a fire that began in the quarter of Cibali on the Golden Horn spread in 10 directions and destroyed half the area of Istanbul *intra muros*, consuming on its way 150 mosques, 130 *medreses*, 335 mills, 36 bath houses, 34,200 shops, and 77,400 houses.[3] During the second half of the nineteenth century, there were no fewer than 229 fires in Istanbul, which destroyed 36,000 houses.[4] Big conflagrations seem, therefore, to be a recurrent phenomenon in metropolitan life, whose impact on the city and its inhabitants must have been considerable.

Venetian *Bailo*s, the Republic's permanent representatives in Istanbul, are known as sharp observers of Ottoman realities, and their despatches also include many details on developments in the empire's capital. At least two sixteenth-century eyewitness reports by Venetian *Bailo*s on great fires in Istanbul are available: the first (included in the diaries of Marino Sanuto), describing the fire that broke out in late August 1515,[5] and the one, hitherto unpublished, on which we focus here, concerning the great fire that broke out on 28 September 1569.[6] The latter description, which is of special interest, is published here and integrated into a wider documentary and historical context, with the aim of evaluating its place in the urban development of the great city in general, and of its Jewish community in particular, and analyzing the functioning of the Ottoman system of government as reflected in this event.

Confronting great fires

Fires in an urban setting have been an ever-present phenomenon in the history of civilization. The fear of conflagrations, as well as the efforts of urban authorities to take measures against them, have left many traces in historical sources.[7] Large and densely inhabited cities were (and still are), however, particularly vulnerable to outbreaks of fire. Some of these extensive conflagrations have left long-lasting marks on the society, the economy and, of course, on the urban landscape of the cities involved.

The dubious "honorary" title "The Great Fire" is thus given to such events in Rome in 64 CE,[8] in Salonika in 1545,[9] in London in 1666,[10] in Chicago in 1871,[11] in Boston in 1872,[12] and again in Salonika in 1917,[13] and this is certainly not an exhaustive list.

Fires, like other catastrophes such as war, plague, floods, and earthquakes, offer the historian not only a dramatic setting for a historical narrative but also an opportunity to investigate aspects of material life, demographic patterns, level of institutional organization, mentalities, and many other aspects of human existence in the past.

The constant threat of fire in premodern and early modern cities was an inevitable consequence of the material culture of those periods. In regions where timber was easily and abundantly available, building materials, especially of private dwellings, were made up predominantly of wood (as can still be seen in many parts of Istanbul today). Under such circumstances, such activities as lighting, heating, and cooking could be very dangerous. The great fire that consumed the entire Imperial kitchens at the Topkapı palace started when the oil in a frying pan in the main kitchen ignited (1574).[14] Of far greater political and social consequence was the great fire in Salonika (1917), believed to have been started by a humble housewife living in the dense Jewish quarter near the port, whose attempt to fry some eggplants resulted in an upset pan and an event which changed the history of Salonika.[15]

Private activities were not the only ones in which the use of fire endangered the city. Many branches of industrial activities that were carried out within the city walls necessitated the use of fire; some were particularly dangerous in this respect. In Venice, for instance, after several fires caused by the city's glass furnaces, all furnaces of the important glass manufacture were moved to the island of Murano, where they are still functioning since the thirteenth century, an early example of a high degree of environmental consciousness. Baking, another activity susceptible to fire accidents, could not be similarly excluded from towns, and bakeries constituted a permanent danger (the Great Fire of London is believed to have started in a bakery). Hay, concentrated in great quantities within the city compound for feeding horses and other transport animals, was, of course, another dangerously combustible material. Other materials, such as tallow, oil, spirits, hemp, timber, coal, and paper, which were stocked in various parts of town, not to mention gunpowder, were also susceptible to accidents. The great density that characterized the center of big cities, particularly during periods of demographic expansion, such as the sixteenth century, was, of course, a problem both as a factor favoring the outbreak and the quick spread of fire and as an obstacle to the effective operation of fire squads.

The fight against fire in premodern cities included precautionary measures, organization of teams that were expected to present themselves on short notice as fire squads, and methods implemented in the attempt to arrest the propagation of fire and finally extinguish it. However, the effectiveness of all these measures seems to have been rather limited. In republican Rome, the night guard of the *tres viri capitales/tres viri nocturni* was also responsible for fire control, having under its supervision persons who were stationed near city gates with water buckets, slaves, carriages, and horses. This proved highly inadequate, therefore extinguishing fire in the city was often left to private entrepreneurs. At the beginning of the first century

(6 CE), Augustus organized a special fire brigade, the vigils, who were stationed in the vicinity of dangerous areas and also patrolled the city during the night, an institution that survived up to the fourth century. These cohorts were equipped with buckets, pumping engines, ceiling and grappling hooks, mattocks, axes, and mats, as well as ballistrae, probably for making firebreaks. Householders were also required to keep a supply of water ready for this purpose, and there is evidence of the use of special fire-fighting equipment in private houses.[16]

The chronicles and statutes of medieval urban communes attest to a great variety of arrangements in this respect. The fire squads of late medieval Florence, for instance, comprised 4 officers, 40 men, 2 lantern carriers, 20 water carriers and a notary. Once fire had been discovered, the parish campanile was used to put everything in operation. All the city's builders and carpenters, as well as those of its rural surroundings, were obliged to hurry to the site of the fire and start demolishing the buildings around it. Town criers had to spread the information to those who remained unaware of the alarm. When the fire broke out at night, all citizens were expected to put lights at their windows to facilitate rescue operations. Property saved from burning and destroyed houses was carried to the parish church or another safe place by men specially elected by the local population for this purpose. In fifteenth-century Venice, every parish priest had to keep 10 axes, 10 buckets with swing-bars, and 20 pails in his house. In the following century, the task of extinguishing great fires in that city was left to the workers of the big shipyard, the Arsenal, which, with its manufactories of gunpowder, and its great concentration of highly combustible material, such as timber, canvas, and pitch, constituted in itself a highly risky industrial area.[17] In early modern London, there were statutes obliging parishes to provide buckets, axes, ladders, squirts, and fire hooks. In Ottoman Istanbul, this obligation was mainly held by the corps of the Janissaries, whereas nightguards were described by a seventeenth-century traveler as knocking at the walls of private houses with iron sticks to remind their inhabitants of the dangers of fire.[18]

As attested in the former paragraph, the equipment for fire extinction in medieval Europe was not very sophisticated. Balestracci even suggests that medieval Europe lost some technical expertise that had been put to use on such occasions in Antiquity. The employment of water pumps is only attested in Europe in the sixteenth century. In fact, the main strategy employed in fighting fire in an urban setting was pulling down buildings to impede the spread of the flames.[19] In London in 1666, gunpowder was even used for making firebreaks.[20]

Material destruction seems to have constituted the main damage of great fires. Human victims were not so numerous, especially when compared to other disastrous events. The London Great Fire of 1666 was said to have destroyed some 373 acres inside the city walls, 63 outside, 87 churches, and 13,200 houses, but the number of Londoners who were definitely known to have been killed was only 6 or 8.[21] Unlike earthquakes or wars, fires allowed many people enough time to run for their lives.[22] The number of 250 victims of the Great Fire in Chicago in 1871, when the city's population reached 334,000 souls, is considered to be exceptionally high.[23] But the material consequences, especially on the individual level, were immense. People could lose all their belongings overnight, and the prospects of material recovery were normally not very bright.[24] Premium insurance existed already from the fourteenth century, but it normally covered nothing but losses related to the movement of goods on land and sea. It was only in the seventeenth century, in places like London, where building regulations reduced the risk of fire, that fire insurance could develop.[25] But that was not possible earlier, let alone in places where such regulations were non-existent or ineffective. Consequently, in the immediate aftermath of big urban fires, many people must have gone bankrupt. It is difficult to trace the consequences of a great fire on the individual level (though one such case is presented later), but we can be sure that such an event constituted a terrible trauma in the lives of many human beings.

Another typical consequence of great fires is the search for culprits. Beside the usual references, particularly by members of the religious establishment, to a fire as a chastisement from God for human sins, there is an inherent tendency under such circumstances to lay the blame for the catastrophe on foreigners. After the London fire, Dutch and French were arrested as suspects. The great fire that destroyed the Venetian Arsenal in 1569 was attributed to Jewish agents of Don Joseph Nasi.[26] And, as will be seen below, Persians were suspected of being behind the Istanbul fire of 1569. Interestingly, those who were institutionally responsible for extinguishing the fire were sometimes accused of kindling it. Cassius Dio writes that during the great fire in Rome, soldiers and members of the night watch, instead of putting out the conflagration, kindled it all the more.[27] Similar accusations were raised against the Ottoman Janissaries on several occasions.[28] The role attributed to the ruler in such circumstances depended on his public image. He may be described as a self-sacrificing benevolent prince who does not mind mingling with simple people engaged in fighting the fire, as in the case of the London fire of 1666, or he could be accused of kindling it, as in the case of Emperor Nero in 64 CE.

Theoretically, at least, great fires can be a turning point in the history of great cities, since they offer a rare opportunity for a new start in urban planning and re-construction. But the implementation of such a change, especially in a pre-modern or early modern context, depended on many factors, such as the government's order of priorities, its organizational capacities, the interaction between private and public interests, conservative mentalities, the availability of material resources, etc. In the few cases in which such a change occurred, the great fire could constitute an important turning point in the social, economic, and cultural life of the city: the new urban landscape reflected or created new architectural tastes; the use of new materials encouraged the development of economic activities related to their importation, production, and transportation, prompting a rise in the importance of certain building professions and professional organizations; bigger stone or brick buildings sometimes (but not necessarily) meant improved living conditions; broader streets and alleys facilitated the use of carriages, and hence created new acoustic and hygienic problems; sometimes the new urban landscape reflected or created a new ethnic and political balance; and last but not least, modern urban planning could mean lesser prospects for new conflagrations.

Following the great destruction in 64 CE, Nero tried to rebuild Rome on a more rational basis, but apparently without great success.[29] In early modern London, similar efforts seem to have achieved greater success, since the 1666 fire is considered by many historians to be the birth certificate of modern London, with the substitution of stone and brick for wood, the widening of streets etc. Some 9000 houses were rebuilt during the twenty-five years following this traumatic event.[30] The old medieval landscape of the French town of Rennes was replaced by a system of straight streets and stone buildings following the fire of 1720, which destroyed nearly the entire town center. The rebuilding of the town was accompanied by transformations in the social composition of various parts of the urban space.[31]

Recording the great fire

Written records of great fires are of various sorts. The great fire of Nero's Rome is described post factum by Roman historians, such as Cassius Dio, Tacitus, and Suetonius.[32] Many medieval chronicles include detailed descriptions of fires, but most of them occurred in small towns.[33] Of the one that destroyed London in 1666, there are several reports in contemporary newsletters. A rare poem in Yiddish vividly describes the fire that broke out at Rialto, the commercial center of Venice, in 1514.[34] But among the early events of this kind, the direct eyewitness report, such as the one we publish here, seems to be rather rare. Nevertheless, comparing texts from different eras describing such events, one is struck by their similarity. Literary critics would probably suggest that we are dealing here with a literary topos, repeating itself again and again in ancient Rome, early modern Venice, Istanbul, and London and most probably on other occasions as well. Similar claims have been raised, for example, regarding Boccaccio's description of the Black Death in Florence, with reference to Thucydides' similar description of the Plague that ravaged Athens in 431/430 BCE. But Boccaccio could not have known Thucydides' text, which was only translated into Latin in the fifteenth century. Similarly, it is unlikely that the Jewish author who wrote the poem on the fire in Rialto, or Marcantonio Barbaro, the Venetian diplomat who described the Istanbul fire of 1569, used an ancient model for their description. It is more reasonable to conclude that dramatic events of this kind have similar characteristics, leading to similar reactions and consequences.

While Barbaro's description, being the immediate eyewitness testimony of a serious observer, should be considered as a reliable source for the depiction of the 1569 fire, this document casts a shadow on another source in which the fire is described, namely Selaniki Mustafa Efendi's history.[35] As already noted, Selaniki relates in his book the story of many fires which occurred in Istanbul during the years he worked in the imperial service. According to him, the fire of 1569 lasted one night and one day (*bir gün, bin gice [sic]*),[36] whereas according to Barbaro the 1569 fire lasted from the first hour after sunset of 27 September, through the whole of the next day until the following morning, and was still not totally extinguished in mid-October.[37] Another fire which occurred in 1589 lasted, according to Selaniki's description, 24 hours.[38] Although the 1569 fire destroyed no smaller area than the 1589 fire,[39] Selaniki's rendition of the 1569 fire stresses the administrative changes which followed the fire, rather than the damage caused by it. On the other hand, his description of the 1589 fire recalls several details of Barbaro's description of the 1569 fire. Describing the later event (1589), Selaniki emphasized the damage done not only to the Jewish neighborhoods, but also to synagogues, mosques, hamams, and other public buildings, as well as to Jews and Muslims, and in doing so, he used expressions very similar to those of Barbaro and other eye witnesses of the fire.[40] Comparing Barbaro's description of the 1569 fire as well as other descriptions of the same event with Selaniki's depiction of the two conflagrations – 1569 and 1589 – the reader is drawn to the conclusion that Selaniki's descriptions were not always written immediately after the events, but rather later, using written material he had access to and notes prepared by himself years before the final compilation of his work. He may even have edited his original rendition of events according to written or oral information he acquired later on.[41] All that could have caused confusion of details of the two events, and the "refashioning" of their characteristics.

Istanbul on the eve of the fire

Marcantonio Barbaro's account of the Great Fire of 1569 is an important source not only for the fire but also for the portrayal of the capital on the eve of Sultan Selim II's reign. Yet any single description, however interesting it may be, can hardly do justice to this magnificent city, dramatically situated on two continents, and two major waterways, the so-called "Threshold of Felicity," the "Well-Protected Istanbul," or the "City of the World's Desire." Descriptions of various facets of the capital are included in sixteenth-century diaries, dispatches, and travelogues, such as Rabbi Mosheh Almosnino's *Extremos y Grandezas de Costantinopla*,[42] and works by Benedetto Ramberti (1534),[43] Nicolas de Nicolay (1551–52),[44] Pierre Belon (1553),[45] Hans Dernschwam (1553–55),[46] Ogier Ghiselin de Busbecq (1554–62),[47] and many other diplomats, merchants, and travelers.[48] Much like some travelogues, some of the famous maps of this period actually copy one another, and should be treated with caution,[49] but the data which can be drawn out of maps like that of Matrakçi Nasuah (1535)[50] and the panorama of the city drawn during this period,[51] are not negligible. Various studies of the urban history of the city are based partly on such sources, and partly on the study of Ottoman sources,[52] providing a fairly good picture of the fabulous metropolis. The data on the spatial structure of the city included in Marcantonio Barbaro's account of the Great Fire enrich this picture, adding to it accuracy and color.

Approaching the metropolis

In the mid-sixteenth century, any voyager sailing to Istanbul from the south would make his way through the Dardanelles, where his first station would be Gelibolu (Gallipoli), then he would pass to Tekirdağ, the island of Marmara, from whence the wind would bring him to the port of Silivri. Sailing near Florya, he would be able to enjoy the beauty of this small port crowned with forests of cypress trees. He would now continue toward the port of Yeşilköy, where the old walls could still be seen from the sea. From this point, our imaginary traveler would reach the walls of Istanbul. The first sight his eyes would meet would be the castle of Yedikule ("the seven towers" in Turkish), once the Golden Gate, the imperial entrance to the Byzantine city.[53] The castle consisted of four towers in the Theodosian wall and three towers built inside the walls by Mehmet the Conqueror. The actual entrance to the city, in the Byzantine period as well as in Ottoman times, was a small gate to the north of the castle. The Byzantine eagle above its arch attests to its origins.[54] However, a foreign traveler usually would not use this gate. By taking the sea road, he would most probably avoid the odor of the slaughterhouse outside the castle of Yedikule,[55] and would sail along the walls of the city toward Sarayi Burnu, the majestic meeting point of the Golden Horn, the Bosphorus and the Sea of Marmara. This point, the site of the ancient Byzantine acropolis, was chosen by Mehmet the Conqueror as the ideal place for his new palace. A massive wall stretched from the Byzantine sea walls along the Golden Horn to those along the Marmara coast, thus separating the grounds of the Imperial palace from the city. The palace itself was built on the highest point of the acropolis, and the slopes were planted with trees and flowers. Our traveler would pass this delightful site, and through the greenery of the Imperial parks he would be able to perceive the beautiful pavilions with their colonnaded verandas.[56] If the weather allowed it, he would soon make his way toward Galata, where most ships sailing from Europe to these waters would anchor.

Galata–Pera

Galata or Pera (Greek = "beyond," namely, the other side, as viewed from Constantinople) had initially been built by the Genoese. Surrendering without a fight to the Ottomans during the conquest of Constantinople, the city continued an uninterrupted economic and social existence through the next generations.[57] The Genoese had fortified Galata as they expanded their government in the city. As can be seen from the Buondelmonte map (of 1422) at the end of the Byzantine era, the main Genoese quarter of Galata was surrounded with walls on all sides. The rest of the town was fortified landwards, with the Galata Tower at the highest point.[58] The walls were partly destroyed by the Ottomans after the surrender of the town – but soon walls surrounding Galata from all sides were re-built by them. The walls were again renovated after the earthquake of 1509, as can be seen in the city plan of Matrakçi Nasuah.[59] The areas from the Galata Tower westward down to the Azap Kapısı (the Mariners' Gate) were inhabited by Muslim sailors, most of them Algerians, other mariners and soldiers.[60] In the sixteenth century, the San Polo and Domenico church in this area was converted into a mosque – the Şeyh Arap Camii.[61] On the western side of the Azap Kapısı, Selim I (1512–20) had started to expand the Ottoman shipyard (*terzhane*), which reached its full size at the time of Rüstem Paşa (1544–50).[62] Three main roads led from the Galata Tower toward the sea gates; one, Perşembe Pazarı (Thursday Market), led to the quay (*iskele*) of Yağ Kapanı (The Oil Scale), the second led to the gate of Balık Pazarı (The Fish Market), and the third led to Karaköy. During Rüstem Paşa's tenure as Commander of the Imperial navy (*Kapudan Paşa*), he destroyed the old Genoese church of San Michele, and built a covered market (*bedestan*) and a *han* between the Yağ Kapanı and Balık Pazarı, near the old Genoese *loggia* (Turkish = *lonca*).[63] Another important quay was that of Karaköy.

A traveler sailing from darülharb (non-Muslim territory), as well as many Greeks who reached the city, would probably anchor at one of these quays. Coming through the Yağ Kapanı iskelesi, he would pass the mosque built in the 1530s by Ibrahim Paşa outside the wall,[64] would enter the gate of Balık Pazarı, and would pass the customs, the bazaar, and into the *han*. By then he would be inside the Christian quarters of this town. An Italian would probably anchor at the Karaköy iskelesi[65] and find his way to the "new lodge" (*Yeni Lonca*), the *Palazzo del Comune* or the Frankish han as it was called by the Ottomans (now in Voyvoda Caddesi).[66]

The Frankish parts of Galata of that time still retained their Italian division into *contrade*, each one belonging to a different Catholic nation. Most of the Italians lived in the area between Yağ Kapanı and Karaköy, around the Galata Tower, although in the period under discussion many of the affluent families among them moved to the area outside the walls in what would become the quarter of Beyoğlu.[67] These mansions were surrounded by exceptionally vast gardens.[68] The Italian architecture of this part of the city was very distinct.[69] The houses were built of stone, in a Venetian or Genoese style, and the streets were paved, though quite poorly. The area between the tower (*Küle Dibi*) and the church of Aya Yorgi up to Yüksek Kaldırım was inhabited by Greeks, and so was the sea shore along the Mumhane street.

Jews began settling in Galata in the mid-sixteenth century, following the influx of the Portuguese Jews escaping from the persecution of the newly established Inquisition in Portugal (1536). These former *marranos* lived near Karaköy. The richest among them began building or buying houses (*köşk*) in the "vineyards of Pera," where foreign diplomats and rich Christian merchants were settling, while others acquired shore palaces (*yalı*) further north on the Bosphorus, in Kuruçeşme, Beşiktaş, and Ortaköy.[70] Armenians inhabited the area from Yüksek Kaldırım to the Tophane gate.[71] No formal segregation can be observed, and almost everywhere ethnically mixed streets could be found.

Like his predecessors, Bailo Marcantonio Barbaro lived in his residence inside the walls, but well before that (at least from the 1520s), the Venetian diplomats also used a summer mansion (that also served as a refuge in times of pestilence) "in the Vineyards" (*alle Vigne*). Soon after the Cyprus War (1570–73), the permanent residence was removed to the latter building.[72] Marcantonio Barbaro tells us that his residence was situated on a hill "in front of the center of Constantinople, all of which is the most beautiful and most built area of the city." From the windows of his chambers he could see the incredible sight of the Great Fire.[73] Bertelè suggested that the embassy within Pera was situated near the old Genoese tower and the former palace of the Genoese *Podestà*.[74] In fact, anywhere under the tower, between the *Yeni Lonca* and the churches of San Pietro and San George that served the Catholics in the city, could be a place matching Barbaro's description.

It should be noted that Venice held in rent another impressive piece of property in Istanbul itself. This was a spacious mansion built of stone, which was the property of Mosheh (Moses) Hamon, Sultan Süleyman the Magnificent's physician. The mansion was situated inside the Jewish quarter, and was mainly used as a dwelling place for the Venetian ambassadors who arrived in the city for special missions every now and then, since the *Baili* usually resided in Pera, and went to Istanbul only on official business. This mansion in Istanbul was burnt down with all the rest of the Jewish quarter in the Great Fire.[75]

Istanbul

Having concluded his business in Galata, the foreigner would set out to explore the marvels of the city seen "from beyond." He would either use the services of a small *kayık*, a boat carrying one or two passengers, or sail in a larger boat, the *pereme*, in the company of other passengers. Magnates, ambassadors, and noblemen had such private boats at their service.[76] The normal landing place was the Iştira, the main landing quay of Istanbul, where one found oneself immediately in the midst of the crowded masses running around their business. This is more or less the area of Eminönü and where the Yeni Camii would be built later on (1596–1660). The area on the shore-line from the walls of the Imperial palace until the Iştira (literally "buying," mean-ing commercial area) and beyond, comprised under the Byzantine government Genoese and Venetian quarters. Later on, Jews were allowed to settle in this place, which became known as the Byzantine *Giudecca*. Under the Ottomans this area became the main dwelling place of Jews, brought here from all parts of the Ottoman lands immediately after the conquest. Their numbers increased even further from 1492 onward, when many expellees from Spain and later on immigrants from Portugal joined them.[77]

Most of the transferees from Anatolia and the Balkans who were to repopulate and rebuild the empty and devastated city were settled in a trapezoid-shaped area formed by Eminönü, Sirkeci, Tahtakale, and Mahmud Paşa (today the area between and around the Galata Bridge and the Atatürk Bridge); some settled to the north of Mahmud Paşa in Zeyrek. The existence of this settlement is corroborated by Hebrew, European, and Ottoman sources.[78] The 1495 register of the *vakıf* of Mehmed II men-tions many locations where Jews were living. Identifiable, in addition to the Edirne (Karaite) quarter near present-day Eminönü, are Balık Pazarı to the north of the Spice Market (Mısır Çarşısı); Zindan Hanı, in what is now a garden, closer to the Atatürk Bridge; Sarı Demir, on the way to Un Kapanı; Tahtakale, in the vicinity of the present-day neighborhood of the same name; the area behind Zindan Hanı near Edirne Kapı; Sirkeci; and in the other direction from Eminönü toward Sarayburnu.[79]

According to Rabbi Mosheh Almosnino's description, in the 1560s it was an overpopulated area with no vacant plots for building; the only possibility was to build additional stories. The result was an area of narrow streets bordered by multiple-storeyed wooden houses.[80] The Ottoman authorities were well aware of the danger stemming from this development. A *ferman* issued on 23 Ramazan 966 (June 29, 1559) described how the Jewish community was constructing tall buildings, huts and shops joined to the city walls or very near them, and warned that a fire could break out in this concentration of wood and timber, to the detriment of the Muslims of Istanbul.[81]

Almosnino asserted that the upper storeys in these buildings were considered to be the best. The windows were normally open to the northerly winds (*tramontana*), but only occupiers of the top floors could enjoy the fresh air. The lower storeys and one-storey houses were cold in winter and hot in summer, dark and unfit for human habitation. Since there was no drainage system, the residents of these buildings threw human waste onto the lower stories; as a result, the bottom floors and the street itself were always foul smelling.[82] Imperial orders to clean the streets, if ever given regarding this area, could not solve the problem of drainage.[83] Naturally, the rich lived upstairs and the poor downstairs. The top floors were also less densely occupied. In a fairly rich household, the masters lived upstairs in spacious comfort, while the servants and the female slaves lived on the lower floors, one family to a room. Consequently, being poor also meant living with dirt, foul smells, and greater exposure to diseases.[84]

The trapezoidal area defined above, which constituted the main dwelling place of the Istanbul Jews, falls in its entirety inside the burnt area as conveyed to us by Barbaro: "longitudinally from the walls of the Grand Seigneur's palace to under Sultan Süleyman's mosque, and in latitude, from the Bedestan down to that part of the sea separating Pera and Constantinople, in a circumference of about 3 to 4 miles." His statement (even if exaggerated) that not even two Jewish houses survived the fire, reinforces this picture of the Jewish presence in the area described earlier. The impression made by the description of the fire should not delude the reader. The area around the Iştira was the central dwelling place of the Jews of Istanbul at that period, but their dense neighborhoods were just islands in the midst of the Muslim city around them.

Although the most important change from the Byzantine to the Ottoman era was the Ottoman tendency to settle in and develop the areas outside the city walls, it is the city *intra muros*, particularly the area along the walls of the Imperial palace from the Golden Horn to the direction of the Marmara coast, that was developed since the Ottoman conquest of Constantinople as the main center of the Muslim component of the city in all possible aspects: administrative, religious, and commercial.

Any person making his way on the shore from the Iştira and the Balık Pazarı, to Odun Kapısı (The Wood Gate), where construction material was unloaded from the ships and sold to contractors and private builders, could stop at the Rüstem Paşa mosque built in 1561 by this Grand Vizier and son-in-law of Süleyman the Magnificent, admire the bluish Iznik tiles with which it is decorated, and do some shopping in the commercial complex under it.[85] He might then go further on to Un Kapanı (The Flour Scale), where grain from all over the empire was unloaded for the hungry bellies of Istanbul's inhabitants. In fact, all these docks and the commercial centers around them retained their original functions from the Byzantine period. If he did not continue further to Cibali, the Greek neighborhood of Fener, the small Jewish neighborhood of Balat, toward the Muslim neighborhood of Eyüp outside the walls, he could turn back from Odun Kapısı, and pass between Tahtakale Hamamı, and the Rüstem Paşa mosque, where he would take the Uzun Çarşı road, the Byzantine *Makron Embolon*, and continue walking in this major thoroughfare, once connecting the harbor with the *Mesa*, now connecting it with the Divan Yolu (The Imperial Council Road), which follows partly the same Byzantine major thoroughfare, the *Mesa*. Walking this way, he could make a stop at the Süleymaniye complex of buildings, with its elegant mosque built by Sinan for Süleyman the Magnificent in the 1550s and the commercial and social institutions adjacent to it.[86] From there, reaching the Bedestan, built on the site of the Byzantine Forum of Constantine, where at that period one could already see both the old and the new Bedestans, he could buy anything he could imagine: beautiful pieces of jewelry, pearls, textiles, and other luxury goods coming from all over the world.[87] From here the way led to the Mahmud Paşa complex of mosque, hamam, commercial center, and the Kürkçü Hanı (The Furriers Han), all built by the Grand Vizier Mahmud Paşa between 1463 and 1470.[88]

Alternatively, instead of entering this busy commercial area, which actually creates a natural continuation from the docks and the Iştira area toward the inside of the city, one could choose another trail altogether and opt for the administrative center, adjacent to the imperial palace. In order to do so, one would leave the Grand Bazaar, and instead of going eastward, our stroller would turn westward toward the Beyazit complex of the mosque and the associated pious foundations built by Beyazit II between 1501–06.[89] From this point, walking through what is now the Yeniçeri Caddesi to the Divan Yolu, he would get to Aya Sophia. Walking to the south from the Aya Sofia, westwards from the Hippodrome he would see the magnificent mansion of Ibrahim Paşa, Sultan Süleyman's Grand Vizier and brother-in-law, completed in 1523. Since Ibrahim Paşa's execution in 1536 it belonged to the Sultan and was probably used as a court of justice.[90]

These are just landmarks on the way of the pedestrian. On his way he would pass Muslim residential neighborhoods of wooden houses, most of them of two storeys, the richer ones having a courtyard and a garden to themselves, the others having dwellings not much different from the *yahudihane*, that characteristically overpopulated courtyard around which many Jewish families lived. The closer these neighborhoods were to the harbor, the denser they became, and although Jews and Christians were not allowed to dwell close to a mosque (each neighborhood had its own mosque), the extremely dense Jewish courtyards were actually integrated into the Muslim residential fabric. These parts of the city were ethnically Islamic, with dots of Jewish presence. The Christian–Greek presence marked other parts of the city *intra muros*, those of Fener, on the way between Cibali and Balat, and Kumkapı near Yedikule.

The impact of the fire on the Jews of Istanbul

Barbaro's description makes it quite clear that the Jews of Istanbul were among the main victims of the 1569 Great Fire. Hebrew sources allow us to follow the impact of this traumatic event in some specific cases. First and foremost was the immediate physical and moral blow connected with the feeling that one's world has suddenly collapsed. Barbaro's description of Jewish and Muslim survivors of the fire walking in the streets crying and moaning, grieving the destruction of their worldly belongings, and looking for their beloved ones who had disappeared in the tumult of the fire, is corroborated by a memoir left for us by Rabbi Yitzhaq ben Avraham 'Aqrish in his introduction to the book "Three Interpretations on *Canticum Canticorum*," printed by Ya'abetz's publishing house.[91] 'Aqrish had a painful personal history. Having been expelled from Spain (1492) and later on from Naples (1541), he settled in Egypt, where he was supported by the leader of Egyptian Jewry, Rabbi David Ibn Zimrah, until the latter departed for Jerusalem in 1553. 'Aqrish left Egypt and settled in Istanbul, but his scholarly work there was interrupted by the fire. His personal experience of the Great Fire deserves citation:

> ...and I had set out and came to *Qostandinah*, a great city of many people, a metropolis of Israel, and its inhabitants great men, wise and sage, people of great name, may the Lord guard them and redeem them. And I have been living here, doing my work, the work of God, and I have not been cheating in my work either. And one day, a day of misfortune and storm,[92] a day of curse and rebuke, *Qostandinah* has been burnt, and everything in it, all her palaces aflame, all houses full of beauty and precious objects. And the great fire was burning day and night, and no one could extinguish it. And myself in the midst of the conflagration, close to the altar,[93] a place from which the fire started, may the altar be the atonement of all the children of Israel. And I have escaped like a bird from the trap, leaving my house, and all my books dear to my heart have been burnt, and no one could save them, since I myself am lame. And I have been lying stranded on the beach, five days and five nights, and no one was looking for me, and so were many others like me. I saw the earth in utter chaos, and the birds wandered away, and all the land turned into a desert and wasteland, and its name would be from now on "Conflagration."[94] And the people were going to and fro, one looking for his wife, the other looking for his sons and daughter[s?], and one departs from his brother. I was crying for my house, for my wife and for my daughter, and especially for my precious and priceless books. And after five days I went to the mansion of the lady called Kira Esther, may she be blessed of all females, the widow of Eliyah Handali, may he rest in paradise,[95] since she gave rescue and comfort to many, both rich and poor, as she had also assisted me before the fire with her donations and presents. And upon arriving at her house, I found my wife and daughter there, and some of my books, which my wife and my brother were able to save, and I found consolation with the books; although they were not many, they were among the best. Only one in fifty remained. One month later I returned to *Qostandinah*,[96] to a place that the havoc did not reach, called Kastoria,[97] where I found a few people from the Holy Congregation of Romania,[98] and I have been staying with them for four years, naked and needy, feeding on meager bread and scanty water.[99]

The immediate havoc caused by the Great Fire created practical problems but also new opportunities. One of the main immediate problems concerned those people who were sub-tenants of Jews who themselves held their property in rent from Muslims with a right to protected tenancy according to the Jewish law of *hazaqah*. Such sub-tenants had to wait until their Jewish landlord came to a new agreement with his Muslim landlord, and for the reconstruction itself, only hoping that subsequently the rent would not be raised. Most people in this condition found shelter in other dwellings that were suited to their meager means, as did Yitzhaq ben Avraham 'Aqrish. Jews who were direct lessees of a property owned by a Muslim landlord were confronted not only with the possible financial loss caused by the need to find provisional housing, but also with the rise in rent which followed reconstruction.

On other occasions, the landlords had totally new ideas as to the future use of the place, as happened to three Jews who by virtue of their *hazaqah* shared a courtyard that belonged to an Islamic religious endowment (*vakıf*). Following the 1569 fire, the trustee of this endowment decided to rebuild the place in a way that would connect it to a caravanserai (*kervanserayi*). His plan was to turn the place into a housing complex for Muslims (the author used a combination of Turkish and Judeo-Spanish to describe the architectonic nature of this proposed building: *odas* – rooms) and a mosque. When he started to implement his plan, one of the three Jews, who was a famous physician, procured a judicial writ (*pitqah* = Hebrew, literally a piece of paper) stating that since he was a physician and his services were much needed, the place should be rebuilt in its pristine form, so that he could continue to live there and give his services to his Muslim patients. But the trustee succeeded in turning the place into a religious college (*medrese*), which made it difficult to implement the wording of the court order. Ottoman grandees were called to intervene and arranged a compromise between the trustee and the Jewish physician, according to which only a small part of the courtyard would be taken in order to enlarge the caravanserai, and the rest would be rebuilt and given to the physician, who would divide it among the former tenants, or let it to whomever he wished. However, the two other *hazaqah* owners sued the physician in the rabbinical court, claiming that this would cause them to lose their *hazaqah*, and that their plots would be diminished, simply because of the physician's bad luck that his apartment bordered the caravanserai.[100]

Another kind of difficulty was posed by the destruction of public buildings. Whereas synagogues were hastily rebuilt in order to avoid loss of the right to use them, other public buildings had to wait until some great donor contributed toward their reconstruction. The fortunes and misfortunes of one such building are documented due to the dispute concerning the cause that the buildings were supposed to support. The property was a plot of land sold to the Jews of Istanbul by the Sultan, with the purpose of creating a public welfare trust. The plot had included a court-yard surrounded by a three-storey building, with two floors inhabited by poor people who were supported by the congregations of Istanbul, and the third floor housing a school for poor children. Until 50 or 60 years prior to the dispute in question (1529–39) the school had operated in this building. At a certain point, a separate building was constructed for the school, and its former premises were rented to the Bodon Congregation (of Jews hailing from Buda in Hungary). Twenty years after the Great Fire (1589), the renowned benefactor Don Shelomoh Ibn Ya'ish decided to contribute the money needed toward the reconstruction of the burnt building.[101] This started a great dispute over the question what kind of welfare was meant in the original endowment: support of the poor, or support of Torah scholars? Apart from its testimony to cooperation among the numerous Jewish congregations in Istanbul even before 1539, this document displays very vividly the impact of fires in general, and the 1569 fire in particular, on the life of the Istanbul community.[102] In this case, the fire meant that for twenty years both causes, support of the poor and study of the Torah, were denied a great deal of the financial resources earmarked for them.

Due to the migration inside the city of fire survivors unable to return to their original neighborhoods, Spanish Jews were forced to mingle with Greek-speaking congregations and vice versa. This process was one of the causes which led eventually to the disappearance of most of the Romaniot characteristics in Istanbul Jewish society. However, although the Great Fire of 1569 had an indisputable effect on the map of Jewish settlement, long after the fire at least 60 percent of the Jews of Istanbul were still clustered in the trapezoidal area burnt in 1569. This is portrayed very clearly by the information on reconstruction of the burnt area by Jews and for Jews. Moreover, the 1595–97 register of the *vakıf* of Mehmet II[103] records that the core of this Jewish settlement was still the quarters of Balık Pazarı and Babı Orya (Porta Horaia), located a little way further into the Golden Horn, a short distance from the spot indicated on the Buondelmonte plan of the city (1422) as the *Porta Iudea*. The Gate of the Jews, or *Porta Ioudaika*, the Gate of the Jewish Quarter, is still indicated as *Yahudi Kapısı* or *Çıfıt Kapısı* in the seventeenth century, although there is no evidence that the *Yahudi Kapısı* and the *Porta Iudea* were located in exactly the same place. Sources from the end of the seventeenth century onward mention the fires which destroyed these areas (1595, 1660) and eventually gave the Ottomans an excuse to relocate the original inhabitants elsewhere, especially to Hasköy.[104]

The 1595–97 survey was initiated after the fire of 1589, which again destroyed the Jewish neighborhoods, and another fire which broke out in 1594 in the nearby neighborhoods of Sinan Paşa Türbesi (the mausoleum of Sinan Paşa) and Tavuk Pazarı (The Chicken Market).[105] Most probably the aim of this survey was to check the feasibility and cost of removing the Jews dwelling in this area, where later on the Yeni Camii and other public buildings would be built. In other words, it took thirty more years and at least another fire for the Ottoman state to come up with the idea of replanning this part of the city, and two major fires besides that of 1569 (1589, 1660), to implement this plan.

It is interesting to compare the impressions derived from the foregoing documentation concerning the repercussions of the 1569 fire and those which followed it until 1660 with Rhodes Murphey's impressions, based on material gleaned from the *sicil* registers. Entries written down some thirty-eight years after the 1569 fire confirm the picture drawn by the Hebrew sources, and even strengthen it; several decades after the fire, burnt down houses and public buildings were not yet reconstructed. Yet the detailed manner in which trustees of religious foundations took care of rebuilding destroyed assets, and their precision in following the founders' wishes, led Murphey to conclude that the *evkaf* system was a tool for preserving the spatial and social fabric of the city, thus preventing the speculative misuse of fires.[106] On the other hand, from the Hebrew documents emerges the picture of trustees trying their best to change the pre-fire situation, even when not deviating from the original wishes of the founder and benefactor. For the Jewish doctor whose passage to the residences of his Muslim patients was blocked, the situation was not as before, and it was only thanks to the appreciation of his special services that he succeeded in defending his interests.[107] For thousands of Jews who had to leave Eminönü for Hasköy and Balat after 1660, their whole world had changed.

Fires and court politics

One of the outcomes of almost every fire that broke out in Istanbul was the reassessment of what could or should have been done in order to prevent it, or to facilitate its extinction. Earlier fires had already resulted in various edicts aimed at reducing the danger to the city and its dwellers. One of these was the *ferman* issued on 23 Ramazan 966 (29 June 1559), mentioned earlier, which forbade the Jewish community to construct tall buildings, huts and shops joined to the city walls or very close to them.[108] In 1568, just a year before the Great Fire, it was prohibited to build in Istanbul projecting windows and other structures protruding above the streets, in order to avoid the spreading of fire from one building to the other. The Great Fire itself was followed by a number of edicts to that effect, one prohibiting the construction of buildings above the height of two storeys (mentioned in Barbaro's account) and one promulgated in 1572, ordering Istanbul's inhabitants to keep water buckets and ladders in their houses for emergency escape.[109] Later development indicates that such precautions were unable to diminish the number of fires in the city. It was built of wood, it was dense, and no human skill or intelligence could overcome this combination.

Some observations on the political and social culture of the Empire are called for at this point. Ottoman political culture was imbued with ideas and practices derived from other eastern Empires that preceded it, combined with elements originating from the nomadic culture from which the Ottomans came. Cardinal among the "imperial" ideas was the notion that the state, including all its landed property, belonged to the ruler. Another cardinal concept, stemming from the nomadic culture, was the ideal of loyalty to the family and total obedience to its head. The combination of these two concepts may help to explain the management of the capital during the Great Fire. It should be borne in mind that this situation is but one case among several. Until the *Tanzimat* reforms of the nineteenth century, the city's management did not change very much.

Besides his imperial, administrative and military functions, the Grand Vizier held the responsibility for the capital. In other words, his was the onus to make sure that this great metropolis functioned from the municipal point of view. The Grand Vizier, his *kayamakam* (substitute) and the *bostancʹbaşı* (chief imperial gardener and person in charge of municipal security) – were simultaneously the sultan's *kul*s and the central functionaries in charge of the management of the capital. The *kul* was, in essence, the Sultan's slave, brought up to serve the state in the highest offices. He shared only part of the disadvantages of slavery.[110] An important feature of his status was the assumption that his allegiance to the sultan was total. The fact that the Grand Vizier was simultaneously the highest official in the state, the sultan's slave, and personally responsible for the functioning of the capital conveys very clearly the nature of the Ottoman world and its capital.[111]

Moreover, all these threads of allegiance were further tied up by matrimonial alliances. Many (if not most) Grand Viziers were connected to the imperial family by marriage, either to the Sultans' daughter or to the Sultan's sister. The Grand Viziers themselves made sure that functionaries on whose performance they depended would be subject to them not only through the hierarchy of authority and power, but also by family ties. This double or even triple cord of imperial and patriarchal authority, combined with servitude, may have reduced initiative but certainly ensured obedience and loyalty.[112] Thus, the main protagonists of the Great Fire were all connected to one another through family ties. The Grand Vizier Sokollu Mehmet Paşa was married in 969 (1561/62) to the daughter of Selim II, Esmakhan.[113] At the same time, Cafer Ağa, the *ağa* of the Janissaries, who according to custom was in charge of extinguishing fires in the city, was Sokollu Mehmet Paşa's son-in-law.[114] All this dense network of allegiances was not enough to ensure the city's functioning, as was seen in the case of the Great Fire.

An interesting picture emerges when we juxtapose Barbaro's account with those of Selaniki and another Ottoman source cited by Inalcik. Although Selaniki tells us laconically that due to the illness of Cafer Ağa, he was replaced by Siayavuş Paşa, Barbaro allows us a glimpse into the hidden world of the court intrigues. His rendition of the affair alludes to something more serious than the illness of the poor *ağa*. His father-in-law, the Grand Vizier, did not bother to accept the Janissaries' signals, which would have enabled them to start their rescue operations. Thus the replacement of Cafer Ağa was also an expression of dissatisfaction by the Sultan with the performance of his Grand Vizier. The whole affair seems to have been not only a metropolitan calamity but also a family affair.

Whereas Barbaro relates the rumors that Persians set the fire, the Ottoman source cited by Inalcik alludes to the propagation of the fire by the Janissaries themselves (a possibility mentioned by Barbaro only with respect to the future behavior of the Janissaries).[115] Such occurrences were not rare, and in general they could suggest that the Janissaries were underpaid and discontented. In other words, the administration was not performing well.[116] Thus, Barbaro's report, according to which the fire caused Sokollu's opponents in the court to raise their voice, seems very plausible, although the question remains why he himself did not accept the Janissaries' signal; was it an expression of incompetence or negligence, or was he himself signaling something to the Sultan?

Bailo Marcantonio Barbaro and his dispatches

Our descriptions of the Great Fire of Istanbul in 1569 appear in two letters written by a Venetian diplomatic representative in the Ottoman capital. The Venetian Republic is rightly considered to be a pioneer in Western diplomatic tradition. During the Renaissance, the Republic was among the first states to keep a network of resident ambassadors abroad. Venetian ambassadors were elected from among the most prepared and refined members of Venice's patriciate. The final reports (*relazioni*), which they presented in writing to their Senate at the conclusion of their mission, were considered already during the sixteenth century as models for imitation, and were published and studied throughout Europe.[117] However, their routine dispatches, sent to Venice during their term of office, are of no less interest, as demonstrated in the texts we are publishing here.

Among the various posts in the Republic's diplomatic network, the office of *Bailo*, first in Byzantine Constantinople and later in Ottoman Istanbul, was considered the most prestigious as well as the most difficult. During the sixteenth century in particular, the ups and downs in Venice's power and wealth depended greatly on the Republic's relations with the Ottoman Empire. In this relationship, the *Bailo*'s ability to transmit to his government accurate and useful information and his capacity to represent Venetian interests in Istanbul were of the utmost importance. Patricians who were elected to this post were therefore experienced and talented personalities.[118]

Marcantonio Barbaro, *Bailo* in Istanbul between 1568 and 1574 and the author of the descriptions published here, was born in Venice in 1518 to a patrician family that could already boast of famous members, such as the humanists Ermolao and Francesco Barbaro, or the great traveler and diplomat Giosafat Barbaro.

Marcantonio continued the family's tradition of combining involvement in Renaissance culture with engagement in public affairs. From the early stages of his adulthood he was repeatedly elected to public offices, serving, for instance, as member of the Collegio (the governing committee of the Venetian Senate), as ambassador to France, as *Riformatore* of the University of Padua, and in other magistracies. He also maintained close contacts with artistic and literary circles, and his family's villa at Maser, designed by Palladio and painted by Veronese, is undoubtedly one of the most beautiful monuments of the Venetian Renaissance.

Barbaro's service as *Bailo* in Istanbul coincided with an extremely difficult period in Venice's relationship with the Ottoman empire. He had been elected to his post in the spring of 1568, and reached the Ottoman capital in August of the same year, around the time when tension between the two states was gaining momentum. When war finally broke out in May 1570, Barbaro was put under house arrest in his official residence, situated on the hillside at Pera, opposite Istanbul across the Golden Horn, without any possibility to leave the place for about three years. During the whole period of the so-called War of Cyprus he nevertheless succeeded in maintaining contacts with the Grand Vizier, Mehmet Sokollu, by the intermediary of his Jewish physician Solomon Ashkenazi, as well as with Venice. He later negotiated the terms of the peace agreement, which was finally concluded in the spring of 1573, but only a year later was he able to return to Venice, where he was received with great honors.[119]

The two texts published here for the first time are excerpts from Barbaro's letter-book, containing copies of the dispatches that he sent to the Venetian government during his long term of office in the Ottoman capital. The writing of such dispatches was one of the main occupations of any Venetian representative abroad. They were often written on a daily basis, and sometimes even more frequently.[120] They reflect the consciousness of Venetian governing circles regarding the importance of information, any kind of information, and not necessarily that directly associated with diplomatic and political relations between states. Marcantonio Barbaro's letter-book, bound in two big volumes that are kept in the manuscript collection of the Biblioteca Nazionale Marciana in Venice, has the advantage of being much better preserved than the dispatches that were actually sent and received in Venice, for the physical condition of the latter often leaves much to be desired, as they were subject to wear and tear on the way between the two capitals. Some dispatches never even reached their destination and can therefore only be read in this letter-book.

Needless to say, Barbaro's letters constitute an excellent source, enabling us to follow day-by-day Venice's relations with the Ottoman Empire during the stormy period around the War of Cyprus. But Barbaro was also an acute and curious observer of life in the Ottoman capital, and his letters contain much important information on Ottoman affairs that cannot be found in other sources. They present aspects of Ottoman reality as perceived by a very keen, experienced, and well-informed observer.

Barbaro's description of the great fire that broke out in Istanbul on 28 September, 1569 and was still not totally extinguished by mid-October is, to the best of our knowledge, unparalleled in its detail and insight by any other known source – either Ottoman or Western – providing an excellent example of the great historical value of his dispatches.

Barbaro's eyewitness testimony is also interesting in a more personal respect. The fire broke out in the Jewish quarter, and many of its victims were Jews. During that pre-war period, Jews were often considered by Venetians as treacherous collaborators with the Ottomans against Venice. The Jews of Istanbul in particular, being the principal rivals of Venetians in the trade with the Ottoman capital, had already been the target of fierce attacks by some former Venetian Bailos, and even at the beginning of Barbaro's term of office, when a fire broke out near his residence, it was rumoured in Venice that it was a Jewish act of sabotage.[121] It goes without saying that the Muslim inhabitants of the Ottoman capital were also considered by many Venetians and other Westerners as their archenemies. Yet in Barbaro's description, we find no trace of these attitudes, and he expresses his compassion for all the victims of the fire, regardless of their religious affiliation.

This aspect of Barbaro's report is even more noteworthy if compared to the account of the same event sent to Vienna by the agents of the Habsburg emperor in Istanbul. According to one such dispatch, probably written by the Imperial ambassador Wyss, Christians and Turks who had fled to Jewish houses during the fire were killed by the Jews, who also crucified a young Christian boy and sacrificed him.[122] We do not know whether such rumors circulated in Christian milieus of the Ottoman capital. Accusations of Jews in times of calamities are well known in European history, and it could well be that similar ones popped up on this occasion too. Yet no trace of them can be found in Barbaro's description, a fact that should not remain unnoticed.

Appendix: Marcantonio Barbaro's descriptions of the Great Fire of 1569

Transcription

Letter from Pera, 1 October 1569[123]

Serenissimo Principe etc. Io vorei poter hora pienamente esprimer alla Serenità vostra con la presente quello che con vista miserabilissima è successo questi giorni qua, accioché almeno in qualche parte la potesse rapresentarsi nell'animo un'accidente tanto meraviglioso et spaventevole. Ma temo che si come li proprii occhi, certissimi testimonii di noi medesimi, non hanno potuto talmente assicurarsi, che non ci sia parsa più tosto sogno che vera visione, quella che habbiamo veduta, così la ben espressa verità da me non sarà bastante a farla comprender a Vostra Serenità et a vostre Signorie Eccellentissime di quel modo che disidererei, et che è stato in effetto. Con tutto ciò non debbo restar di darle conto con ogni verità di quello che è avenuto.

(f. 193) Et primo, per maggior intelligentia sua voglio dirle, che mai questa grandissima città di Costantinopoli, fabricata sopra diverse colline in forma triangolare, è stata ripiena di fabriche et habitationi, et fatta ricca con la rovina di tante provintie, massime a quella parte che è incontro Pera; vostra Serenità creda che la si trovava hora nel maggior colmo che la sia stata già molti anni. E vero che si può dir che la sia quasi tutta fabricata di legname. Perchè oltra l'ordimento delle case, che è di legname (eccettuando però le moschee, bagni et qualche palazzo di Bassà, che sono fatte di muri al modo di Christianità) anco quelle poche muraglie, colle quali vanno tessendo essi legnami, sono tutte fatte di qualdrelli di terra cruda mescolati di paglia; che quasi si può dir che il tutto sia di legname.

Ritrovandosi adunque al presente ogni casa arrida et secca per l'estate, et per esser cinque mesi che non ha piovuto, si attaccò il fuoco mercore, che fu alli XXVIII del passato, nella prima hora della notte, in quella parte della città più folta et più ripiena di fabriche et di ricchezza, ove habitavano li Hebrei, che è all'incontro di Pera. Il qual fuoco si allargò talmente in un momento, et si fece così grande che ben si poteva dir: "et nox sicut dies illuminabitur," andando da ogni parte le grandissime fiamme, che pareva che dal cielo piovesse il fuoco. La qual vista, accompagnata da innumerabili cridi di quei infelici homini et donne, che si vedevano abrusciar le proprie sustantie, con pericolo anco di perder li figlioli et le proprie vite, rendeva a tutti un spavento et una pietà infinita.

Vi concorse a questo incendio il Magnifico primo Bassà (f. 193v) con tutti li altri suoi collega ancora, con quelle provisioni di gente et d'altro che seppero immaginarsi; né quelle giovorono a ponto, perché essendo mal essercitate, et facendosi il fuoco ogn'hora maggiore, si destese in diverse parti con tanta furia et con tanto spavento d'ogn'uno, che fermamente si può tener che mai più d'arecordo d'huomeni o d'historie si sia veduta cosa tale.

Qusesto horrendo spettacolo non poteva esser in più commoda vista alla mia stantia di quella che è stata, perché essendo essa posta in collina in contro la mità di Costantinopoli, scopre tutta intiera la più bella, et più fabricata faccia della città, che è quella, a ponto, nella qual era attaccato il fuoco, cioè per longhezza dalla muraglia del seraglio del Serenissimo Signor fin da sotto la moschea di Sultan Suleiman, et per larghezza dal Besestano fin a questo mare che separa Pera da Constantinopoli, circuito veramente di più di tre in quatro miglia; ma quello che importa, tutto pieno di case grandi et botteghe con diverse robbe et mercantie, intanto che essendo questa parte la più populata et ricca di tutto 'l resto, si può dir con verità che più della mità di Constantinopoli si sia abrusciato, come particolarmente si potrebbe veder sopra un minuto ritratto di tutto Constantinopoli, cavato dal naturale, che ho mandato alli miei colle navi partite ultimamente di quà, che a quest'hora deveno esser gionte in quell'Illustrissima città. Et vostra Serernità sia certa, che in tutto 'l sopradetto spatio, per il longo et per il largo, non vi è restato un solo palmo di casa che si possa abrusciare che son sia stata in tutto consumata dal fuoco, perché il vento, soffiando hora (f. 194) da una parte hora dall'altra, ha talmente fatto ricercar dal foco detto circuito, che non è meraviglia se il tutto è stato abrusciato.

Et per il vero non si può immaginar manco intelligentia, né maggior negligentia, di quella che si è veduta qua in questa occasione tanto importante. Perché al numero delle genti, et agl'altri rimedii che haverebbono potuti havere, massime con la presentia di tutti li Bassà et altri grandi della Porta, si doverebbe havervi rimediato in un'hora. Et in questo proposito voglio dir a Vostra Serenità che vanno fin al cielo li gridi et lamentationi contra il Magnifico Mehemet Bassà. Perché essendo solito quando si accende fuoco d'importantia, che li Gianizzeri portano all'hora al Magnifico Bassà o al loro Agà un segnal d'un fazzoletto o altro, per mostrar che siano presenti, et dapoi andando a riconoscer ogn'uno il suo segno, vengono gratificati con qualche accrescimento di soldo, in questa occasione il predetto Magnifico Mehemet non ha voluto accettar alcun segnal da essi Gianizzeri. Li quali, non lo potendo dar anco al loro Agà, per esser in termine di morte, si alterorono talmente, che per instantia che li fusse fatta non volsero più metter mano in agiuto. Per il qual disordine, essendo la città restata in descrittione del fuoco, non è meraviglia se è causato tanto notabil danno, perché esso durò non solamente tutta la notte et tutto il giorno da poi, facendosi sempre maggiore, in modo che adombrava il sole, che con color quasi sanguino oscurava tutta la terra, ma continuò anco tutta l'altra notte seguente, nella quale si dilatò in diverse parti in un'istesso tempo, che certo è cosa impossibile d'immaginarsi, nonché di poter (f. 194v) descriver la rapresentatione veduta da tutti noi, stando alle nostre fenestre di casa.

Da questa mottione et confusione, et dalla sopradetta mala satisfattione di Gianizzeri, si stette anco in estremo travaglio che tutto 'l resto della città non andasse a sacco. Pur per gratia di Dio non successe altro. Ma mentre che la seconda notte il foco, con maggior furia che mai, faceva progressi grandissimi, minacciando di continuar a brusciar tutta la città, il Serenissimo Signor, presentendo il disordine di Gianizzeri per la poca gratitudine del Magnifico Bassà, et perché anco il loro Agà, che è genero del detto Bassà, non vi si trovava per la sua infirmità, vinto dal sdegno mandò nella mezza notte a far saper ad esso Bassà di haver levato il grado d'Agà di Gianizzeri a predetto suo genero, et di haverlo dato a Schiaus, capo della stalla et delli capigi bassi, che è tanto favorito di sua Maestà. La qual cosa ha dato grandissimo smacco ad esso Magnifico Bassà, et aperto maggiormente la strada alle mormorationi contra di lui, havendo hora li suoi emuli et nemici largo campo di cargargli la mano adosso. Mandò anco all'hora ordine Sua Maestà, che fusse promesso certo poco augumento di soldo alli gianizzeri che si diportavano bene. Colla qual provisione dicono che inanimitisi, operorono in modo che cominciorono ad avanzar in qualche parte il fuoco, se ben a me par che non dalle loro provisioni, ma che dal vento proprio sia venuto il rimedio; perché voltandosi et spingendo la fiamma verso la parte che già era abrusciata, finalmente non havendo più che brusciare, circa 'l mezo giorno seguente da se medesimo si estinse, che certo se'l vento da Tramontana, over da (f. 195) Levante, havesse continuato a soffiar gagliardamente come l'haveva principiato, non è dubio che tutta la potentia del mondo non bastava a rimediare che tutta questa grandissima et famosissima città non cascasse in cenere.

Il principio di detto fuoco è venuto, per quello che per il più si dice, da un fornaro, se ben s'è sparsa una voce, etiamdio fra grandi, che'l sia stato acceso a posta in più d'un loco da alcuni Persiani, et che ne sia preso uno. Ma però fin qua non se ne ha maggior certezza.

Il danno che ha causato questo memorabil incendio è stato infinito et incredibile, et spetialmente fra Hebrei, perché non essendo in tutto Constantinopoli restate due case di detti Hebrei che non siano abrusciate. Habitando loro in questo circuito che si è abrusciato, tutti hanno sentito, parte per il fuoco et parte per li latrocini, notabilissimi danni. Et molti anco hanno perduto tutto quello che havevano, in modo che hora è lachrimosissima vista veder tante infelici et numerose famiglie di putti et donne di Hebrei et Turchi andar per le strade piangendo et cridando, con poco o niente di sostantia da potersi sustentare. Da quel danno ne parteciperanno anco li nostri mercanti, perché restando distrutti li detti Hebrei, che levano per ordinario tutte le loro robbe et mercantie a tempo quattro e sei mesi, molti di essi nostri mercanti conveniranno restar tocchi, seben chi più et chi manco, da questa rovina.

Gratie etc.

Da Pera, a primo ottobre 1569

Letter from Pera, 15 October 1569[124]

[following his reference to an explosion and fire at Tana]

...Si ragiona anco che si sia abrusciata la contia delli Hebrei in Salonichi, et medesimamente in Bursia sia stato un altro grande incendio. Ma però di Salonichi (f. 204) et di Bursia se ne ha ancora tanta certezza quanto si ha della Tana. Qui si sta in gran dubio che sia attaccato volontariamente il fuoco et in Constantinopoli, et anco qui in Pera, dicendosi che terza notte el fu attacato in tre o quatro lochi qui in Pera, se ben vi fu rimediato senza danno. Per il che si fanno molte provisioni et guardie, et tutta la notte in Constantinopoli et qui in Pera caminano li subassi con grosso numero di gente per causa di questo sospetto. Et hanno fatto levar a tutte le botteghe certi coperti, over sporti fuori delle case et boteghe, di tavole, che occupavano tutte le strade, et erano un' esca da far correr il fuoco da un capo all'altro della città, acciò che in esse tavole non fusse attaccato il fuoco. Et hanno comandato anco espressamente che nel fabricar questo spaccio che s'è abrusciato, ogn'un slarghi le strade mezzo brazzo per banda, et che non si possi alzar le fabriche in più di dui solari alti solamente VIII piedi l'uno, perché li Gianizzeri hanno detto che per l'altezza delle case, in occasion di fuoco quelle non si possono ruinare per estinguerlo. Li qual Gianizzeri restano tuttavia malissimo satisfatti, perché, come dissi, creato che fu nel furor del foco passato il novo loro Agà, et desmesso il genero del Magnifico Mehemet Bassà, li fu data promissione, perché si affaticassero, d'accrescimento di soldo, et speravano che nelli divani passati li fusse effettuata tal promessa. In modo che non si essendo fatto altro, stanno in dubio che li sia mancato. Per il ché si teme, che in ogni minima (f. 204v) occasione di fuoco o altro, essi faranno qualche motto. Anzi, che la faranno nascer per haver modo di vendicarsene.

La rovina del fuoco passato è stata veramente grandissima, et per ancora in qualche parte arde tuttavia il fuoco, che par inestinguibile, con tutto che siano 18 giorni che lui si attaccò. Et io, che sopra il loco proprio ho voluto veder questa rovina, l'ho conosciuta per il vero maggior assai di quella che la estimai quando ne dei conto a Vostra Serenità, essendo il circuito dell'abrusciato poco meno di quatro miglia quasi in forma circulare, con rovina di 20 moschee, 15 sinagoghe d'Hebrei, et 12 bagni publici, et d'infinite fabriche grandissime, et fra le altre di quella casa del Medico Amon, che soleva esser habitation delli Clarissimi Ambascaitori di Vostra Serenità che vinivano qui, che certo era fabrica di consideratione, massime rispetto al paese. Et se ben hanno in molte parti principiato a refabricare, et che hora pari che si redefichi una nova città, con tutto ciò in molti anni non si ridurà a gran comparatione quel loco, come l'era prima che 'l si abrusciasse.

Translation

Letter from Pera, 1 October 1569

Serene Prince etc. With the present letter I would now like to be able to convey fully to your Serenity the most miserable sight that has been revealed here during these days, so that you will be able, at least partly, to imagine in your mind such a marvelous and terrifying event. Yet I am afraid that since our own eyes, those trustful testimonies of ourselves, could not assure us that what we have seen was not a mere dream impression, but a reality, I am afraid that presenting the truth to you in good writing would not be sufficient to make your Serenity and Your Excellencies understand it in the way I would wish you to, and to grasp it as it really happened. With all that, I must not abstain from reporting truthfully what has happened.

(f. 193) And Firstly, for your better understanding, I would like to tell you that this enormous city of Constantinople, built on various hills in a triangular shape, had never been so fully built, populated, and enriched by the ruin of other provinces, especially that part facing Pera. Your Serenity should believe that presently it has been at its highest peak since many years. Truly, one may say that it is almost entirely built of wood. Because besides the structure of the houses, which is all wood (except for the mosques, the baths and a few palaces of pashas built of stone walls as in Christendom), those few walls with which this wood is covered, are also made of bricks of plain earth mixed with straw. Thus, one may say that everything is made of wood.

Since there has been no rain for five months, all these houses were arid and dry when fire broke out on Wednesday, the 28th of the past month (September), at the first hour of the night.[125] This happened in the most crowded, most densely built and richest part of the city, where the Jews were living, just opposite Pera. The fire spread so quickly and became so big that one could say: "And the night has become like day in its brightness." Flames propagated in every direction, and it seemed as if a rain of fire was showering from the sky. This sight, accompanied by innumerable cries of miserable men and women who saw their belongings ablaze, and their life and that of their children in danger, brought terror and boundless pity to everybody.

His Excellency the Grand Vizier[126] (f. 193v) and all his colleagues assembled there, assisted by men and by any possible means; but these were of no avail, since they had no practice, and the fire only expanded every hour in several directions with such fury, and to such terror of everyone, that it can be stated firmly that never before has something like that been seen or memorialized in history.

This horrendous spectacle could not have been better observed than from my dwelling, since it is situated on the hillside opposite the centre of Constantinople, where the most beautiful and most densely built area of the city is spread out. Fire broke out precisely in that part, spreading, longitudinally, from the walls of the Grand Seigneur's palace[127] to under Sultan Süleyman's mosque,[128] and in latitude, from the Bedestan down to that part of the sea separating Pera and Constantinople, in a circumference of about 3 to 4 miles. But more importantly, all this area was full of big houses and shops with various goods and merchandise, so that being more densely populated and richer than all the rest of the city, one could truly say that over one half of Constantinople has been consumed. That can be seen especially in a detailed picture of the whole of Constantinople, drawn from nature, which I have sent to my family by the ships that have recently left this place, and should by now have reached that most illustrious city [Venice]. And your Serenity can be assured that every single inflammable house within the aforementioned space, in width and length, was burned to ashes, because the wind, blowing alternately from different directions, caused the fire to reach every corner within that circumference, and it is no wonder that all has been burnt down.

And truly, one cannot imagine an action of lesser intelligence or of greater negligence than what has been seen on this important occasion. For considering the number of people involved and the other means that could have been employed, particularly in view of the presence of all the pashas and other magnates of the Porte, one could expect to put it under control within an hour. In this respect I would like to tell your Serenity that blames and complaints against his Excellency Mehmet Pasha are reaching the sky. For usually, when a great fire breaks out, the Janissaries bring a handkerchief or another sign to the Grand Vizier or to their Ağa,[129] to indicate their presence, and afterwards, each one turning to identify his own sign, they are gratified with raises in their pay. This time, however, his Excellency Mehmet[130] refused to accept any sign from these Janissaries. The anger of the latter, who could not give it even to their Ağa, he being on his deathbed, was so great that, when requested to help, they refused to collaborate. Because of such disorder the city remained at the mercy of the fire, and it is no wonder that so much damage has been done, for the conflagration continued not only the whole night and the entire following day, increasing incessantly so as to dim the sun and to cast an almost blood-red color over the entire city, but also continued all through the following night, spreading at the same time in different directions, which is undoubtedly difficult to imagine, and even more so to describe, but this spectacle was witnessed by all of us, as we were watching it from our windows.

In view of this commotion and confusion, and the dissatisfaction of the Janissaries, there was also great fear that all the rest of the city would be sacked. But by God's grace, no further incidents occurred. However, while during the second night the conflagration, with greater vigor than ever, was advancing tremendously, threatening to burn the entire city, the Most Serene Seigneur, having heard about the Janissaries' dissent caused by the lack of generosity on the part of the Illustrious Pasha, and since their Ağa, son-in-law of the said Pasha, was absent owing to his illness, [the Seignor] was so upset that he sent a message at midnight to inform that Pasha that he deprived his son-in-law of the office of Ağa of the Janissaries, nominating in his place Siyavuş,[131] head of the stables and of the *kapıcı başıs*,[132] who was greatly favoured by his Majesty. This caused considerable humiliation to the Illustrious Pasha, and opened further the way for complaints against him, since his rivals and enemies felt free to hurt him. His Majesty also issued an order, promising a certain rise in the allowance of well-behaved Janissaries. It is claimed that, being encouraged by this provision, the Janissaries started to act effectively, gaining ground against the fire, but I believe that remedy arrived not through their actions, but rather because of the wind, which turned in such a direction that it pushed the fire towards that part of the city that had already been burnt, so that after not having anything more to consume, it was extinguished by itself about the middle of the following day; there is no doubt that if a northerly or easterly wind had continued to blow as in the beginning, the entire world would not have been able to prevent the descent into ashes of this great and most famous city.

It is generally believed that the fire started in a bakery, though there is a rumor, also spread among important people, that it had been intentionally ignited in more than one place by a few Persians, and that one of them has been caught. But to date, there is no confirmation of that.

The damage caused by this memorable fire has been boundless and incredible, especially among the Jews, for in the whole of Constantinople there have not remained even two houses of Jews that have not been burnt. Having all resided within that area that has been burnt, all of them have suffered enormous damage, either by the fire or by theft. Many of them have lost whatever they had possessed, so that now it is heartbreaking to witness so many desperate Jewish and Turkish families with children and women weeping and crying while passing in the streets, with nothing or very little to support themselves. Our own merchants will also be hurt, for these Jews usually buy their goods and merchandise on credit for four or five months, so that many of our merchants, to a greater or smaller extent, will have to incur losses because of their ruin.

Thanks, etc.

In Pera, on the 1st of October 1569

Letter from Pera, 15 October 1569

(following his reference to an explosion and fire at Tana)[133]

...It is also said that the Jewish quarter in Salonika has been burnt, and that another great fire has likewise broken out in Bursa. But the degree of certainty with respect to these occurrences in Salonika and Bursa is similar to the one regarding Tana.[134] It is strongly suspected here that both in Constantinople and in Pera the fire was the consequence of deliberate action, and indeed during the third night fire broke out here in Pera at three or four places, but without causing any damage. Therefore many provisions and security measures are being taken, and all through the night, both in Constantinople and in Pera, the *subaşıs*[135] are patrolling with a great number of men because of this suspicion. And, as a measure against fire, they have caused all shops to remove certain wooden coverings that are used outside houses and shops over the street, for those allowed the fire to run all through the city. They have also issued an order to the effect that when re-building new construction in the devastated area, streets should be enlarged by half a yard (*brazza*) on each side, and the houses should not have more than two storeys of eight feet each, because the Janissaries claimed that the height of the houses rendered it difficult to ruin them, when fighting the fire.[136]

These Janissaries, however, remain highly dissatisfied, since, as I have mentioned, a new Ağa was nominated to replace the son-in-law of his Excellency Mehmet Pasha, and they were promised a raise in their pay as recompense for their efforts. However, the expectation that this promise would be put into effect in one of the recent meetings of the Divan[137] has not materialized, and they are suspecting that nothing will be done. Therefore it is feared that on the next occasion of a fire or any other event, they will be the cause of some trouble, or even that they will set a fire themselves as a form of revenge.

The damage of the last fire has really been tremendous, and in some parts of the city it is still not totally extinguished. Thus it seems to be inextinguishable, since it has been 18 days since its outbreak. I myself, having inspected the ravage in situ, have discovered that it is much greater than what I estimated when reporting about it to your Serenity. The circumference of the devastated area is a little less than four miles, in a nearly circular form. The destroyed buildings include 20 mosques, 15 Jewish synagogues, and 12 public baths, as well as innumerable large buildings, among them the house of the physician Amon,[138] where the honorable ambassadors of your Serenity used to reside on their missions here, an impressive building, especially in this country. And although rebuilding has already started in many parts, and one gets the impression that a new city is being constructed, many years will pass before a place comparable to the one existing before the fire will arise.

Notes

1 A. M. Schneider, "Brände in Konstantinopel," *Byzantinische Zeitschrift*, 41 (1941), pp. 382–403; Mustafa Cezar, "Osmanlı Devrinde İstanbul Yapılarında Tahribat Yapan Yangınlar ve Tabii Âfetler," *Türk San'atı Tarihi Araştırma ve İncelemeleri*, I (1963), pp. 327–414; N. Atasöy, "The Survival of Iznik Pottery in Turkey," in N. Afasöy and J. Raby (eds), *Iznik* (London and New York, 1989), pp. 16–17. See also D. Kuban, *Istanbul – An Urban History: Byzantion, Constantinopolis, Istanbul* (Istanbul, 1996), pp. 297–8, 352, 384; K. Kuzucu, "Osmanlı Başkentinde Büyük Yangınlar ve Toplumsal Etkileri," in K. Ç. C. Oğuz (ed.), *Osmanlı Toplum*, vol. 5 (Ankara, 1999), pp. 687–9. For fires in Byzantine Constantinople, see also F. W. Unger, *Quellen der byzantinischen Kunstgeschichte* (Vienna, 1878), pp. 74–91; and T. F. Madden, "The fires in Constantinople, 1203–1204," *Byzantinische Zeitschrift*, (84/85), (1991/2), pp. 72–93.
2 Selaniki Mustafa Efendi, *Tarih-i Selaniki* (Istanbul, 1989), vol. 1, pp. 76, 213, 221, 246, 269, 285, 316, 385, 416; vol. 2, pp. 505, 601, 604, 640.
3 Findikli Süleyman Efendi, *Mir'âtü't-tevârih*, (ed.) M. Aktepe, vol. 2, A (Istanbul, 1980), pp. 9–10.
4 H. Inalcik, "Istanbul," *EI²*, vol. 4 (Leiden, 1978), p. 237.

5 Marino Sanuto, *I diarii*, vol. 21, (ed.) F. Stefani, G. Berchet, and N. Barozzi (Venice, 1887), col. 162.

6 See the appendix.

7 E. G. D. Balestracci, "La lotta contro il fuoco (XII–XVI secolo)," in *Città e servizi sociali nell'Italia dei secoli XII–XV*, dodicesimo convegno di studi (Pistoia 9–12 ottobre 1987) (Pistoia, 1990), pp. 417–38.

8 Cassius Dio, *Roman History*, 62, ch. 16–18.; Tacitus, *Annales*, XV, 35–44; Suetonius, "Life of Nero," ch. 38. See also Z. Yavetz, *Claudius and Nero* (Tel Aviv, 1999), Annex No. I ("The Fire that Ignited the Imagination"), pp. 143–60 (in Hebrew).

9 Rabbi Yosef Ibn Lev, *Responsa*, vol. I (Jerusalem, 1959), no. 62; ibid., vol. III (Benei Beraq, 1988), no. 42.

10 S. Porter, *The Great Fire of London* (Stroud, 1996).

11 H. Kogan and R. Cromie, *The Great Fire: Chicago 1871* (New York, 1971).

12 A. Mitchel Sammarco, *The Great Boston Fire of 1872* (Dover, NH, 1997).

13 Douglas Walsh, a British soldier stationed in Salonika during the "Great Fire" of 1917, claimed that since the sixteenth century the city had experienced fifteen major fires: D. Walsh, *With the Serbs in Macedonia* (London, 1920), p. 36. This alleged score is definitely too modest. During the sixteenth century, three major fires broke out within 26 years (Rabbi Shemuel de Medina, *Responsa*, Hoshen Mishpat (Lvov, 1862), no. 438), two of which were the major fires of 1522 (ibid., no. 262) and 1545. During the eighteenth century, three major fires (1734, 1759, 1776) occurred in Salonika (E. Bashan, "A Jewish Economic Elite in eighteenth-century Salonika. New Documents on the Burla Family (1763–1793)," (in Hebrew) in M. Rozen (ed.), *The Days of the Crescent: Chapters in the History of the Jews in the Ottoman Empire* (Tel Aviv, 1996), p. 194, note 2.

14 Selaniki Mustafa Efendi, *Tarih-i Selaniki*, vol. 1, p. 90.

15 Walsh, *With the Serbs in Macedonia*, p. 36. On the results of the fire, see note 31.

16 O. F. Robinson, *Ancient Rome. City planning and Administration* (London and New York, 1992), pp. 105–10; R. Sablayrolles, *Libertinus miles. Les cohortes de vigiles* (Rome, 1996).

17 Balestracci, "La lotta," pp. 433–7; F. C. Lane, *Navires et constructeurs à Venise pendant la Renaissance* (Paris, 1965), p. 176; E. Concina, *L'arsenale della repubblica di Venezia* (Milan, 1984), pp. 155–6.

18 T. Bertelè, *Il palazzo degli ambasciatori di Venezia a Costantinopoli e le sue antiche memorie* (Bologna, 1932), p. 273, n. 43. For further details on the Ottoman anti-fire regulations, see below, pp. 148, 158.

19 Balestracci, "La lotta," p. 436.

20 *The London Gazette*, Monday September 3 to Monday September 10, 1666: Internet site.

21 R. Porter, *London: A Social History* (Cambridge, MA, 1995), p. 87; Porter, *The Great Fire*, p. 56.

22 See for example, Findikli Süleyman Efendi's description of the 1757 fire in Istanbul (*Mir'âtü't -tevârıh*, vol.2, A, pp. 9–10).

23 Madden, "The Fires," pp. 86–7.

24 See below, and compare with Medina, *Responsa*, Hoshen Mishpat, nos. 94, 262, 438; Rabbi Yitzhaq Aderabi, *Responsa Divrei Rivot* (Sadilkov, 1833), no. 266; Rabbi Shelomoh Ben Avraham Ha-Kohen, *Responsa*, vol. 1 (Jerusalem, 1961), no. 36.

25 P. Earle, *The Making of the English Middle Class. Business, Society and Family Life in London, 1660–1730* (London, 1989), p. 78. The first successful fire insurance office was opened in 1681.

26 B. Arbel, *Trading Nations. Jews and Venetians in the Early Modern Eastern Mediterranean* (Leiden, 1995), p. 63.

27 Cassius Dio, loc. cit.

28 Inalcik, "Istanbul," p. 248.

29 Robinson, *Ancient Rome*, pp. 19–20, 35–6, 63–4.

30 Earle, *The Making of the English Middle Class*, pp. 22, 207.

31 Histoire de la France urbaine, vol. 3. La ville classique, de la Renaissance aux Révolutions, (ed.)
     E. Le Roy Ladurie (Paris, 1981), pp. 436, 461–3; on major changes following the 1890
     fire in Salonika see M. Anastassiadou, Salonique, 1830–1912: Une ville ottomane à l'âge des
     réformes (Leiden, 1997), pp. 361, 382–3; R. Molho, "Jewish Working-Class
     Neighborhoods Established in Salonika Following the 1890 and 1917 Fires," in
     M. Rozen (ed.), The Last Ottoman Century and Beyond: the Jews of Turkey and the Balkans,
     1808–1945 (Tel Aviv, 2003) vol. 2, pp. 173–94; G. Hadar, "Aspects of Jewish Family
     Life in Salonika,1900–1943" (PhD thesis, Haifa University), 2003, pp. 36–43. On the
     repercussions of the 1917 fire, see ibid., pp. 54–75, 152–4; Rozen, The Last Ottoman
     Century, vol.1 (Tel Aviv, 2003), ch. 9, and the bibliography.
32 See note 8.
33 Balestracci, "La lotta," passim.
34 Ch. Shmeruk, "The Poem on the Fire in Venice by Eliyahu Bachur," Kovetz 'al Yad, new
     series, (1966) 6(16), pp. 343–68 (in Hebrew).
35 Selaniki Mustafa Efendi, Tarih-i Selaniki, vol. 1, pp. 76–7.
36 Ibid., p. 76, and compare with Barbaro.
37 See note 125. Cezar ("Yangınlar," p. 332, n. 1) comments that Ottoman historians, like
     'Ali (1541–1600), Peçevi Ibrahim (1574–1649/50), and Karaçelebi Zâde 'Abd al-'Aziz
     (1592–1657), wrote that the fire lasted for one week. The two latter authors, who were
     not yet born at the time of the fire, must have gleaned their information from sources
     other than Selaniki. Discrepancies exist between various Ottoman sources regarding the
     exact date, and even the year of the fire. 'Ali, the only one of them who was alive (though
     still a young man) at the time of the fire, dated it to 1571! Rhodes Murphey, relying on
     a sicil record from 1017 (1607), also suggests 1570 or even 1571 as the year of the Great
     Fire ("Disaster Relief Practices in Seventeenth-Century Istanbul: A Brief Overview of
     Organizational Aspects of Urban Renewal Projects Undertaken in the Aftermath of
     Catastrophic Fires," in Ali Çaksu (ed.), International Congress on Learning and Education in
     the Ottoman World, Istanbul, 12–15 April 1999 (Istanbul, 2001), n. 6, p. 49). The Bailo's
     eyewitness account is confirmed by the report of the Imperial ambassador, writing on
     3 October, who also dated the outbreak of the fire to 27 September 1569 (Schneider,
     "Brände," p. 391).
38 Selaniki Mustafa Efendi, Tarih-i Selaniki, vol. 1, p. 213.
39 That is according to Barbaro's description (see the Appendix), and thus Atasöy's map, in
     "The Survival of Iznik Pottery," p. 16, should be corrected.
40 Selaniki Mustafa Efendi, Tarih-i Selaniki, vol. 1, p. 213.
41 On Selaniki's methods of work see the introduction to Mehmet İpşirli's edition of his
     History. Cf. Mehmet İpşirli, "Mustafa Selānikī and his History," Tarih Enstitüsü Dergisi
     (1970), 9, pp. 429–33, 438–9.
42 Mosheh Almosnino, Divrei Yemei Malkhei Otoman (History of the Ottoman Kings), Milan,
     Ambrosian Library, Ms. No. 126 (Sup. 35) (consulted in the Institute of Microfilmed
     Hebrew Manuscripts, National and University Library, Jerusalem, no. 12037). Written
     in Judeo-Spanish in Hebrew characters, the manuscript is divided into three parts. The
     first section of the third part, entitled Extremos y Grandezas de Constantinopla, contains
     a vivid description of the city in 1566. The first and second parts of the History of the
     Ottoman Kings and the third part's first section were translated into Spanish by Ya'aqov
     Cansino of Oran on the basis of a later manuscript. They were printed anonymously as
     Extremos y Grandezas de Constantinopla (Madrid, 1638). On this work, see also M. Rozen,
     A History of the Jewish Community in Istanbul – The Formative Years, 1453–1566 (Leiden,
     2002), pp. 41–2, 64, 98–199, 218–19, 273–4.
43 Benedetto Ramberti, Libri tre delle cose de' Turchi (Venice, 1539).
44 Nicolas de Nicolay, Les navigations, peregrinations et voyages faits en la Turquie, (eds)
     M.-C. Gomez-Géraud and S. Yérasimos (Paris, 1989).
45 Pierre Belon, Les Observations de plusieurs singularitez & choses mémorables trouvées en Grèce,
     Asie, Judée, Egypte, Arabie, etc. (Paris, 1555).

46 Hans Dernschwam, *Tagebuch einer Reise nach Konstantinopel und Kleinasien (1553/1555)*, (ed.) F. Babinger (Munich and Leipzig, 1923).

47 Ogier Ghiselin de Busbecq, *The Life and Letters of Ogier Ghiselin de Busbecq*, (ed. and trans.) C. T. Forester and F. H. Blackburne Daniell, 2 vols (London, 1881).

48 For a catalog of sixteenth-century travelogues of Istanbul, see S. Yérasimos, *Les voyageurs dans l'Empire ottoman, XIVe–XVIe siècles: bibliographie, itinéraires et inventaire* (Ankara, 1991).

49 Cf. for example, the Vavassor map, drawn around 1490 (reprinted in H. Inalcik, "Ottoman Galata, 1453–1553," in *Varia Turcica* 13 (*Colloque Galata*) (Istanbul and Paris, 1991), plan II, p. 111 with the anonymous Venetian map drawn between 1566–74: *Maps of Istanbul from the Middle Ages to the Present Day* (Istanbul, 1990), no. 11, pp. 72–3. Notice the Vavassor map (no.10, p. 71), dated there to 1558.

50 Ibid., p. 69; Sebastian Münster's map (1550) ibid., no. 9, p. 70.

51 Melchior Lorichs' panorama drawn in 1559, reproduced by M. And, *Istanbul in the Sixteenth Century: The City, The Palace, Daily Life* (Istanbul, 1994), pp. 18–21.

52 For the urban history of Istanbul in the sixteenth century according to travelogues and European accounts see S. Yérasimos, "Galata à travers les récits de voyages (1453–1600)," in *Varia Turcica* 13 (*Colloque Galata*) (Istanbul and Paris, 1991), pp. 117–30; And, *Istanbul*. For such studies based on Ottoman documents see Ö. L. Barkan and E. H. Ayverdi (eds), *İstanbul Vakıfları Tahrîr Defteri 953 (1546) Târîhli* (Istanbul, 1970); H. Inalcik, "The hub of the city: the Bedestan of Istanbul," *International Journal of Turkish Studies* 1 (1980), pp. 1–17; Inalcik, "Galata," pp. 17–117. For an overall survey of Istanbul's urban landscape during the sixteenth century, based on a wide variety of sources, see Kuban, *Istanbul*, pp. 246–86.

53 Nicolay, *Les navigations*, pp. 103–20. Cf. Ambassador Piero Zen's account of his itinerary to Istanbul as summarized by Marino Sanuto: 'Itinerario di Pietro Zeno, oratore a Costantinopoli nel MDXXIII, compendiato da Marino Sanuto', in R. Fulin (ed.), *Diarii e diaristi veneziani* (Venice, 1881), p. 108.

54 Ibid., pp. 120, 127; *Domenico's Istanbul*, trans. and comments M. Austin (ed.), Geoffrey Lewis (Warminster, 2001), pp. 2–4, 58–60; And, *Istanbul*, p. 67; Hillary Summer-Boyd and John Freely, *Strolling Through Istanbul* (Istanbul, 1989), pp. 371–4.

55 *Domenico's Istanbul*, pp. 78–9.

56 On the site of the Topkapı Palace and its view from the sea, see Nicolay, *Les navigations*, pp. 127–8; Freely, *Istanbul*, pp. 69–70. For sixteenth-century paintings of the Palace and its surroundings, see And, *Istanbul*, pp. 99–117.

57 On the conquest of Galata see G. Pistarino, "The Genoese in Pera – Turkish Galata," *Mediterranean Historical Review*, 1 (1986), pp. 63–85; Inalcık, "Galata," pp. 17–31; Rozen, *History*, pp. 12–15.

58 For Buondelmonte's enlarged map of Galata, see Kuban, *Istanbul*, p. 187.

59 On the earthquake, see Nicolay, *Les navigations*, 125–6; And, *Istanbul*, p. 95, citing Marino Sanuto, *I Diarii*, IX (Venice, 1883), col. 261. For the Matrakçi Nasuah enlarged plan of Galata, see Kuban, *Istanbul*, p. 233; And, *Istanbul*, p. 26.

60 Yérasimos, "Galata," p. 119; Inalcık, "Galata," pp. 54, 67.

61 Inalcik, "Galata," pp. 67–8, 89.

62 On the development of the Imperial dockyard, see ibid., p. 53. Cf. the Lewenklaw panorama prepared around 1586 (Österreichische Nationalbibliothek, Codex Vindobonensis 8615, reproduced by And, *Istanbul*, pp. 70–1).

63 Inalcik, "Galata," p. 90; Yérasimos, "Galata," p. 119.

64 Yérasimos, "Galata," p. 119.

65 Inalcik, "Galata," p. 36.

66 Ibid., p. 90.

67 Yérasimos, "Galata," p. 118.

68 Marcantonio Pigafetta, *Itinerario* (London, 1585), p. 114 (cited by Yérasimos, "Galata," p. 117).

162　*Minna Rozen and Benjamin Arbel*

69 Pigafetta, *Itinerario*, p. 114, cited by Yérasimos, "Galata," p. 126.

70 Rozen, *History*, pp. 60–1.

71 Bertelè, *Il palazzo*, pp. 81–98, 125–30; T. Bertelè, "Palazzi veneti a Costantinopoli," *Atti della XXVI riunione della Società italiana per il progresso delle scienze* (Venice, 1937), pp. 3–4; Inalcik, "Galata," pp. 42–3; Yérasimos, "Galata," p. 119.

72 Yérasimos, "Galata," pp. 123–4.

73 See the Appendix.

74 Bertelè, *Il palazzo*, p. 3.

75 See the Appendix. Cf. Pietro Zen's account of 1523. He was first settled in a house the location of which fits the house of Hamon as described here, where all the Ottoman dignitaries came to salute him. It was within a short ride from the Palace of the Grand Vizier Ibrahim Paşa (Sanuto, "Itinerario," p. 108). Bailo Andrea di Priuli lived in Pera (ibid., p. 118).

76 Nicolay, *Les navigations*, p. 144. See also M. Mazak, *Eski Istanbul'da Deniz Ulaşımı* (Istanbul, 1998), pp. 30–1.

77 S. Yérasimos, "La communauté juive d'Istanbul à la fin du XVIe siècle," *Turcica* 27 (1995), pp. 101–30; Rozen, *History*, pp. 55–61.

78 For traditions on the existence of this settlement, see H. Inalcik, "Jews in the Ottoman Economy and Finances, 1450–1500," in C. E. Bosworth, C. Issawi, R. Savory, and A. L. Udovitch (eds), *The Islamic World from Classical to Modern Times: Essays in Honor of Bernard Lewis* (Princeton, NJ, 1991), p. 513; U. Heyd, "The Jewish Communities of Istanbul in the Seventeenth Century," *Oriens* 6 (1953), p. 311.

79 Heyd, "Jewish Communities," p. 311.

80 Almosnino, *A History of the Ottoman Kings*, p. 188.

81 A. Refik Altınay, *Onuncu Asr-ı Hicride İstanbul Hayatı* (2nd edn) (Istanbul, 1987), pp. 87–9.

82 Almosnino, *History of the Ottoman Kings*, pp. 188–9.

83 See, for example, Refik Altınay, *Onuncu Asr-ı Hicride İstanbul Hayatı*, p. 99.

84 Almosnino, *History of the Ottoman Kings*, pp. 188–94.

85 On the Rüstem Paşa mosque and commercial center, see Kuban, *Istanbul*, pp. 271–3.

86 On the *Süleymaniye* see *Domenico's Istanbul*, pp. 4, 61–2; Kuban, *Istanbul*, pp. 251–61; And, *Istanbul*, pp. 47–51.

87 And, *Istanbul*, pp. 81–6; Kuban, *Istanbul*, pp. 225–6; Inalcik, "The Hub of the City."

88 Kuban, *Istanbul*, pp. 213, 280; Freely, *Istanbul*, pp. 172–6, 179.

89 On the Beyazit mosque and its functioning as a welfare and commercial centre, see *Domenico's Istanbul*, pp. 3–4, 61; Kuban, *Istanbul*, pp. 241–3.

90 Freely, *Istanbul*, pp. 123–7; Kuban, *Istanbul*, pp. 248, 281, 288, 299, 314, 430.

91 Avraham Ya'ari reckoned that the year of publication should be between 1575–78: A. Ya'ari, *Hebrew Printing in Istanbul* (Jerusalem, 1967), p. 122 (in Hebrew).

92 In the original the wording is סוכה, which has no meaning here. It is most likely a misprint for סופה.

93 It is difficult to ascertain what 'Aqrish meant by "altar" (in Hebrew: *mizbe'ah*). He explains that since the heart of the fire was in the midst of the Jewish quarter, it might have been pre-ordained by God to atone for the sins of Israel (according to *Mekhilta de-Rabbi Shim'on Bar-Yohai*, ch. 20, verse 22: "An altar means atonement").

94 Instead of Constantina.

95 (Greek for Lady). A title given to women (usually Jewish) who rendered all kinds of services to the women of the imperial harem (Rozen, *History*, pp. 203–7). Esther Handali was already active before 1566. She may have been the woman mentioned by Busbecq as the friend of Rüstem Paşa's wife (Mirhimah, daughter of Süleyman the Magnificent and Hurrem Sultan), whom he met in June 1560. Thus, Mirhimah was Selim II's sister (Busbecq, *The Life and Letters*, 1, p. 282); Esther Handali served Nur-Banu, the *haseki* (favorite concubine) of Selim II, before his accession to the throne. She continued her service to Nur-Banu during the reign of Selim II (1566–74), and later when Nur-Banu

became *valide sultan*, the mother of Murad III (1574–95). On the figure of Nur-Banu, see B. Arbel, "Nur Banu (*c.*1530–83): A Venetian Sultana?" *Turcica* 24 (1992), pp. 241–59; S. A. Skilliter, "The Letters of the Venetian Sultana Nur-Banu and Her Kira to Venice," in A. Gallotta and U. Marazzi (eds), *Studia Turcologica Memoriae Alexii Bombaci Dicata* (Naples, 1982), pp. 515–35.

96 Which means that this grand lady lived in Galata or Ortaköy.

97 This Greek-speaking (Romaniot) congregation was founded by Jews who had been deported by the Ottomans from Kastoria (now in Greece), in order to repopulate the conquered capital. This congregation was located at Balat (see Rozen, *History*, pp. 57–8).

98 That is, of Greek-speaking Jews.

99 Ya'ari, *Hebrew Printing*, pp. 122–3.

100 Rabbi Yosef Ibn Lev, *Responsa*, vol. 3 (Benei Beraq, 1988), no. 42.

101 A Portuguese "New Christian," also known as Alvaro Mendes, who had made a fabulous fortune from diamond quarrying in India, and became an influential personality in the Portuguese, English, and French courts. Immigrating to the Ottoman empire in 1585, he became involved in Ottoman relations with Western Europe and was nominated by Murat III as Duke of Mytilene (Lesbos): Cecil Roth, *The House of Nasi: The Duke of Naxos* (Philadelphia, PA, 1949), pp. 205–14, 247; L. Wolf, "The Jews in Elizabethan England," *The Jewish Historical Society of England, Transactions* (1928), 11, pp. 24–32, 56–91; Don Shelomo was a generous sponsor of books, rabbinical colleges and welfare institutions in the Holy Land and in the main cities of the Ottoman Empire.

102 Rabbi Betzalel Ashkenazi, *Responsa* (Venice, 1595), no. 13; Rabbi Eliyahu Ibn Hayim, *Responsa* (Jerusalem, 1960), no. 84.

103 See Yérasimos, "La communauté," pp. 121–5.

104 On these quarters, see A. Galanté, *Histoire des juifs de Turquie*, 1 (Istanbul, n.d.), pp. 25–7. On Jews living in Arabacılar Meydanı (near Balık Pazarı), see Rabbi Tam Ibn Yahya, *Responsa, Tumat Yesharim* (Venice, 1622), no. 74. For later sources on this quarter, see John Sanderson, *The Travels of John Sanderson in the Levant 1584–1602*, (ed.) W. Foster (London, 1931), p. 81; E. Çelebi Kömürciyan, *İstanbul Tarihi* (Istanbul, 1988), pp. 9, 11, 14–15, 91; Evliya Çelebi, *Seyahatname*, vol. 1 (Istanbul, 1896), pp. 413–14; cf. A. Refik Altınay, *Hicri On İkinci Asırda Istanbul Hayatı* (Istanbul, 1930), p. 88.

105 Selaniki Mustafa Efendi, *Tarih-i Selaniki*, vol. 1, pp. 213, 385.

106 Murphey, "Disaster Relief," pp. 45–7.

107 See note 100.

108 Refik Altınay, *Onuncu Asr-ı Hicride İstanbul Hayatı*, pp. 87–9.

109 Ibid., pp. 89–91.

110 On the *kul*, see H. Inalcik, *The Ottoman Empire. The Classical Age 1300–1600* (London, 1973, repr. 1975), pp. 65, 77, 84; C. V. Findley, *Bureaucratic Reform in the Ottoman Empire: The Sublime Porte 1789–1922* (Princeton, NJ, 1980), pp. 13–5.

111 On the concept of the Turkish-Muslim city and the management of the capital, see Kuban, *Istanbul*, pp. 203–5; in the seventeenth century, see Mantran, *Istanbul dans la seconde moitié du XVIIᵉ siècle* (Paris, 1962), pp. 123–77.

112 Findley, *Bureaucratic Reform*, pp. 32–3.

113 G. Veinstein, "Sokollu Mehmed Pasha," *EI²*, vol. 9, p. 737.

114 Compare Barbaro (in the Appendix) with Selaniki Mustafa Efendi, *Tarih-i Selaniki*, vol. 1, pp. 76–7. On Sokollu's reliance on family networks, see Veinstein, "Sokollu," p. 738.

115 Cf. Inalcik, "Istanbul," p. 248.

116 Ibid.

117 G. Mattingly, *Renaissance Diplomacy* (London, 1963), pp. 108–13; A. Ventura, "Introduzione," in A.Ventura and A. Segarizzi (eds), 2nd edn, *Relazioni degli ambasciatori veneti al senato* (Rome and Bari, 1976), pp. vii–x, xvii; D. Queller, *Early Venetian Legislation on Ambassadors* (Geneva, 1966); D. Queller, "The Development of Ambassadorial Relazioni," in J. Hale (ed.), *Renaissance Venice* (London, 1973), pp. 174–96.

118 C. A. Maltezou, *Ο θεσμός του Κωνσταντινουπόλει Βενετού Βαΐλου (1268–1453)* (Athens, 1970); D. M. Nicol, *Byzantium and Venice* (Cambridge, 1988), pp. 181, 191–2, 199–201, 289–91; H. Brown, "Venetian Diplomacy at the Sublime Porte during the Sixteenth Century," in his *Studies in the History of Venice* (London, 1907), vol. 2, pp. 1–38; Bertelè, *Il palazzo*, op. cit.; B. Simon, "I rappresentanti diplomatici veneziani a Costantinopoli," in *Venezia e i Turchi* (Milan, 1985), pp. 56–69; C. Coco and F. Manzonetto, *Baili veneziani alla sublime Porta* (Venice, 1985); E. R. Dursteler, "The Bailo in Constantinople: Crisis and Career in Venice's Early Modern Diplomatic Corps," *Mediterranean Historical Review* 16(2), (2001), pp. 1–30.

119 On Barbaro's role during the War of Cyprus, see also B. Arbel, "Venezia, gli Ebrei e l'attività di Salomone Ashkenasi nella guerra di Cipro," in G. Cozzi (ed.), *Gli ebrei e Venezia* (Milan, 1987), pp. 163–97; B. Arbel, *Trading Nations, ad vocem*.

120 Mattingly, *Renaissance Diplomacy*, pp. 110–12.

121 Arbel, *Trading Nations*, pp. 8–11, 13–28, 62, 117, 140.

122 Schneider, "Brände," p. 391 (Flamma in aedibus Judaeorum est nata, et in raris illis, quae reliquae fuere Hebraeorum domibus reperti sunt aliquot Turcae et Graecj ab ipsis Hebraeis interfecti nec non iuvenis aliquis Christianus, cruci affixus et sacrificatus). Interestingly, the eminent nineteenth-century historian, Joseph von Hammer, cites another report to Vienna of the same event, in which the killing of Jews and the crucifixion of a Christian boy are attributed to the Janissaries (Noctu ingens incendium, in quo Mohammed P. periclitatus lapsis, in Hebraeorum aedibus Flamma erupit, aliquot Hebraei ibidem conventi a Janicsaris interfecti et juvenis Christianus crucifixus). Cf. J. von Hammer Purgstall, *Geschichte des Osmanischen Reiches*, 10 vols (Pest, 1827–35), vol. 3 (1828), p. 528. The citation from this dispatch is omitted from the second edition of the same work: J. von Hammer Purgstall, *Geschichte des Osmanischen Reiches*, 2nd edn, 4 vols (Pest, 1840), vol. II, p. 376. Both von Hammer and Schneider only give short excerpts from these reports.

123 Biblioteca Nazionale Marciana, Venice, Ms It.VII 390–391 (8872–73), vol. I, fols 192v–195r.

124 Ibid., fols 203v–204v.

125 The Venetian "day" started after sunset of the previous day. Thus, the fire actually broke out on the evening of 27 September, according to our modern system. See note 37.

126 The Grand Vizier at that time was Sokollu Mehmet Paşa, who served under three consecutive sultans: Süleyman I, Selim II, and Murat III (June 27, 1565–October 12, 1579). On him and his tenure as Grand Vizier see Veinstein, "Sokollu," pp. 735–42.

127 Built initially between 1459 and 1478, with many additions made until the nineteenth century. For illustrations of the walls of the Imperial compound from this period, see And, *Istanbul* pp. 99–107. For an architectonic history, see Kuban, *Istanbul*, pp. 220–3.

128 The Süleymaniye was built for Sultan Süleyman I by the famous court architect Sinan. For Sinan's work in general and the architectonic description of the Süleymaniye in particular, see Kuban, *Istanbul*, pp. 255–69. For sixteenth-century pictures of the mosque, see And, *Istanbul*, pp. 46–9.

129 The commander-in-chief of the janissaries: M. Ç. Varlık, "Ottoman Institutions of the XVIth Century and Sultan Süleyman the Magnificent," in M. Ç. Varlık *et al.* (eds), *The Ottoman Empire in the Reign of Süleyman the Magnificent* (Ankara, 1988), pp. 66–7.

130 The Grand Vizier.

131 Cf. Selaniki Mustafa Efendi, *Tarih-i Selaniki*, vol. 1, p. 77.

132 The Imperial Gate Keepers. In this case the functionary in question was the *çauş başı*, chief of the Imperial messengers, in charge of prevention and punishment of delinquencies in the capital: H. A. R. Gibb and H. Bowen, *Islamic Society and the West* (Oxford, 1969), vol. 1, pt. 1, p. 119.

133 Tana – the town at the mouth of the Don river, in the north of the Sea of Azov.

134 Von Hammer wrote that the great fire in Istanbul "served as a signal for fires in several other cities around the empire," but it remains to be clarified whether these reports about

other conflagrations were mere hearsay or a reflection of reality. See von Hammer, *Geschichte*, vol. 3 (1828), p. 528.

135 Functionaries charged with policing the city (Gibb and Bowen, *Islamic Society*, pp. 119, 154–5).

136 Imperial edicts aimed to prevent fires in the city promulgated both before and after the fire (1559–72); see in Refik Altınay, *Onuncu Asr-ı Hicride İstanbul Hayatı*, pp. 87–92.

137 The Imperial Council. See Varlık, "Ottoman Institutions," pp. 35–42.

138 The famous Mosheh Hamon, the Sultan's Physician. On the man and his family, see Rozen, *History*, pp. 208–9, 211–13, and the bibliography in the notes. On this house, see pp. 141–2.

13 Futuh-i Haramayn

Sixteenth-century illustrations of the Hajj route

Rachel Milstein

A poetical description of holy Arabia in Persian, titled *Futuh al-Haramayn*, was dedicated by Muhyi al-Din Lari (or Farsi, d. 933/1526–27) to Sultan Muzaffar b. Mahmud Shah of Gujarat in 911/1505–06.[1] At that time, the sultans of Gujarat were involved in the power struggles between the Mamluks of Egypt and the Portuguese navy around the Arabian and Indian coasts, following the discovery of the sea route to Asia by Vasco da Gama.[2] As a token of commitment to Mecca, one of the Gujarati sultans built a large *madrasa* there, with a Sufi lodge.[3] The international struggle was decided by the Ottomans, who took over the Mamluk Empire in 1516–17 and chased the Portuguese from the Arabian Sea in 1541.[4] The Ottomans restored order in the Arabian peninsula, ensured safe pilgrimages under their patronage, reconstructed the water systems, set up new foundations, and sent money and gifts to the local dignitaries. Consequently, many more pilgrims from all over the Muslim lands performed the Hajj, and those who could afford the outlay, purchased Hajj certificates or other written souvenirs in Mecca.[5] In this context Lari's poem became popular, and was extensively copied and lavishly illustrated.

This chapter is a study of sixteenth-century illustrated manuscripts of *Futuh al-haramayn*. Although this text, along with others, continued to be copied and illustrated in the following centuries, I have limited my discussion to the formative period, when both architecture and painting in Ottoman Arabia were at their peak. My list of twenty-odd manuscripts is certainly not exhaustive, and more will most likely emerge in future, but it suffices for an evaluation of the phenomenon and its popularity.

Manuscripts and text

The manuscripts, with bibliographical references, are listed in an appendix. More than half of them have been described briefly in catalogs of libraries and exhibitions, with some discussions of text and illustrations in the publications by Barbara Schmitz *et al.*, and by Carol Fisher and Alan Fisher. One outstanding manuscript (Haifa, NMM), which I analyzed in a previous paper, will serve as a point of reference for some historical aspects which are not taken up here. In a paper by Hassan el-Basha, illustrations of the Prophet's mosque in Medina demonstrate the value of art as a historical source.

The manuscripts are small and slender, measuring between 21.5 cm and 24.5 cm in height, and between 14 cm and 16 cm in width, with 1 or 2 slightly larger exceptions. They contain between 40 and 60 folios; 2 or 3 are thicker. Within rulings, the poem is inscribed in black ink in 2 to 4 columns, often interrupted by inscriptions of Qur'anic verses, prayers, or titles of chapters, written in red or yellow across the width of the page. Fifteen to twenty illustrations of the sites visited on the Hajj route are interpersed in the text; the total of 24 illustrations in NMM is exceptional. A lavishly illuminated head title on the first written page (*'unwan* or *sarlawh*) usually contains the names of the poem and the poet. The folios, in quires of 8 to 10, are made of various types of paper – from Oriental paper of various degrees of fineness, to European paper with or without water marks; one example is on very fine paper, probably made of rice.

Fifteen manuscripts are dated, between 1544 and 1600, and the others can be ascribed to the same period on stylistic grounds. Twelve colophons state that the manuscripts were copied in Mecca. Even more precisely, one was made in *madrasa-ye akbari* (IO Isl. 2344), another was signed in front of the Black Stone (SP 1389), and a third was deposited in the collection of the Haram. One unusual manuscript was copied in Istanbul (Qustantiniyya, SP 1514), another can be ascribed to India, according to the quality of the paper and the style of the illustrations (SP 1340). Of three manuscripts which found their way to India (IO Isl. 2344; IO Isl. 887; and Or. 11,533), the last two may have been painted by an Indian hand. In another manuscript with a similar style, the identifying inscriptions around the images were deliberately effaced, and replaced by another hand.

Nine names of scribes and painters appear in the colophons, half of them either from Iran or the Indian peninsula. As they signed their work in Mecca, we may conclude that they were *mujawirun*, Muslims from other countries who settled in the Holy City, making their living by producing pilgrims' souvenirs. That many of them were not accomplished scribes, we can see from their poor writing and the several copying mistakes. One scribe, Sayyid 'Ali al-Husayni of NMM, tells the readers of what he called *Shawq-namah* that he wrote the text and painted the illustrations. Another, Mula Salih, is described in a note at the end of P. 237 as illuminator and painter, this probably meaning that someone else copied the text. 'Uways al-Harawi, the scribe of LAM, may have been the same person as Ways(i) al-Harawi of HM, and in this case the difference in painting styles between the two items may indicate either different painters, or different models. All in all, the manuscripts constitute a close group and testify to an intense Meccan book production, which brought together scribes and illuminators from various countries, and resulted in a distinctive style of copying and painting.

Lari's text was composed in ornate language, abounding in repetitive and rather banal, highly sentimental metaphors of a religious nature. It describes in full the rituals of the Hajj, obligatory and customary, in their correct order. The sites visited are treated more briefly, described with exaggerated spiritual eloquence, but almost without concrete details. Grammatically weak, the poet's language is not always easy to understand: this probably accounts partly for the inconsistencies among the various copies. Comparison between the manuscripts reveals two main textual variants, with different opening lines. The smaller group, which includes the very early items, or those copied outside Mecca, may represent an early line of copying, which later disappeared from the Meccan scene, but continued in other production centers. Other than that, all the manuscripts contain, fully or partially, the same text, although no two items are identical. Many lines are scrambled, and the order of the verses inverted within the *bayt*. Words which the copyists could not decipher were replaced or erroneously transcribed. Two copyists, Ghulam Sayyid 'Ali in AIA and al-Husayni in NMM, attributed the text to themselves, the latter adding a long introduction and several paragraphs in prose, with important topographic and historical information. His manuscript is also unique in the number of illustrations and the concrete informative value of his drawings and identifying inscriptions.

Illustrations, sources, and style

The cycle of illustrations is basically the same in all the manuscripts, although two minor sites in the vicinity of Mecca, Mud'a, and Shubayka, are less popular than the others. The Haram of Jerusalem, which is not included in the text, was nevertheless depicted at the end of some six manuscripts. Two others end with an image of the Prophet's sandals, which may be connected with Jerusalem, since a domed structure commemorating the Prophet's footprint is depicted in Or. 11,533. Lari's text may have been originally arranged according to the topographical or geographic order of the sites, which are thus illustrated in the early manuscripts. The later manuscripts, on the other hand, follow the order of the Hajj rituals, thus depicting Muzdalifa and Mina after 'Arafat, in spite of their greater proximity to Mecca. This new orientation induced a re-arrangement of the text, and this may have produced incoherence in the textual order of many manuscripts.

At all events, within the individual manuscripts the illustrations adhere to the textual order so neatly that when there is not enough space for an illustration immediately after the proper description, some verses are inscribed in a diagonal line, to fill the space and allow for placing the miniature on the next page. To make their compositions informative, the painters used certain visual conventions with adjoining inscriptions. Comparing the forms of the objects and the identifying inscriptions helps in decoding the sign language, which in most cases is very simple. Thus we learn that a perfect circle, a square, and a stepped form are three kinds of water reservoirs, the round being a deep pit (*bi'r* or *chah*), the square a large and shallow pool (*birka*), and the stepped form a stepped deep tank (*çeşme*). The inscriptions are either in Persian or in Arabic, and sometimes a mixture of the two. In one manuscript the illustrations are followed by longer explanations in Osmanli, perhaps a later addition made for an individual patron.

In certain cases the terms used in the inscriptions are interchangeable. Thus *qubba*, *gunbad*, *qabr*, and *mashhad* do not correspond systematically to the forms of mortuary monuments or to the individuals buried in them. On the other hand, the size, form, and decoration of a monument can reflect its relative importance. Certain components seem to represent particular architectural styles, so that changes in the form of individual monuments in earlier and later manuscripts can tell us something about reconstructions at the site. The degree of faithfulness to the physical realities of the sites, both natural and man-made, depends on the individual painter and the relative date of the manuscript. We can easily distinguish a more variable, informative, topographical orientation, with some inclination to naturalism, in the earlier manuscripts, as against a highly decorative, repetitive, and symbolic style in the later ones.

The two earliest dated manuscripts, Or. 3633 and NMM, are unusual in their realism, and in the amount of information they transmit. Both are close in style to another document, a Hajj certificate in a form of a large rotulus, which was copied at Mecca in 951/1544–45 by Abu Fadl Sinjari, for a proxy of the late Ottoman prince Shehzade Mehmet (H. 1812).[6] It has been suggested that the illustrations were added in Istanbul, as the style clearly reveals an acquaintance with Ottoman geographical manuscripts.[7] I believe it was illustrated in Mecca. The style, which differs in detail from that of metropolitan manuscripts, resembles the early Meccan manuscripts and seems to have influenced them. For example, the debt of Or. 3633 to the roll is reflected in the horizontal format of the illustrations, which in the other *Futuh* manuscripts are mostly vertical. In NMM, a large inscription on a red ground above the illustration of Jerusalem is undoubtedly a reminiscence of H. 1812. The stylistic and informative similarity between the roll and this manuscript is such that one wonders if Sayyid 'Ali al-Husayni, the scribe and painter of NMM, was not the illustrator of H. 1812, or at least his close pupil. Certain stylistic conventions typical of H. 1812 reappear in later manuscripts, such as tree leaves shaped as groups of three triangles in IO Isl. 887, and three floating lamps attached to the tops of minarets in R. 917 and IO Isl. 887. On the basis of this debt to the Hajj roll, we shall consider it here as the first item in our group, although it does not illustrate Lari's text.

In function, content, and format H. 1812 continued an older tradition of illustrated Hajj certificates which had been signed in Mecca between the twelfth and fifteenth centuries. A treasure of Ayyubid rolls with an illustrated cycle of the Hajj sites, a few Mamluk rolls with concise images of the harams in Mecca and Medina, and some paper talismans with depictions of Mecca, Medina, and 'Arafat, was found in the Great Mosque of Damascus, and is now kept in the Museum of Turkish and Islamic Art in Istanbul.[8] The Ayyubid illustrations include 'Arafat, Muzdalifa, Mina, Mecca with the *mas'a*, Medina, and Jerusalem, according to the order of the Hajj rituals. Each site features only the most important symbolic details, with no hint of topographic location or physical resemblance to the actual structures. In spite of this, the full and comprehensible cycle of images clearly served as a model for the sixteenth-century illustrations. From Mamluk times, besides the poor thirteenth-century examples in Istanbul, we know only one complete roll, a sumptuous Hajj certificate made in 836/1432 for Maymuna bint Muhammad b. 'Abd Allah al-Zardali.[9] The even more concise and symbolic style of its illustrations had no impact on our group. Only the image of the Prophet's sandals, to which an inscription attributes a talismanic role, is repeated in H. 1812, and occasionally reappears in the Meccan manuscripts (IO Isl. 887 and NYPL).

The influence of the thirteenth-century rolls on H. 1812 and the *Futuh* manuscripts is attested by the double circles which denote water reservoirs, tree trunks resembling columns with bases and capitals (roll no. 53/19, and ms. SP 1389), and the neutral bands of double contours that frame the colored architectural units. These two parallel contours systematically extend beyond the wall height, then end abruptly above roof level. This style, so characteristic of the Ayyubid rolls, recalls the calligraphic practice of drawing rulings around texts. Other calligraphic practices commonly found in both Ayyubid and Ottoman groups are delicate blue linear ornaments, which in the *Futuh* manuscripts figure on roof tops. All this may suggest that the new Meccan style was developed by calligraphers, such as Sayyid 'Ali of NMM.

We see, then, that the sixteenth-century illustrations drew on iconographic and stylistic elements from a dormant, older tradition, which was enriched by the new Ottoman vogue of cartographic painting, as in the city-scapes of Matrakçi Nasuh,[10] or the sea and port maps by Piri Re'is.[11] The influence of Matrakçi is seen, mainly in H. 1812 and the earlier *Futuh* manuscripts, in the summary line drawing, with some thin coloring of selected elements, in groups of overlapping buildings, in placing monuments on long, flat or stepped, raised bases, terminating façade walls with large colored horizontal bands and diagonal awnings, suggesting three dimensions and internal spaces by black shadings and diagonal lines, filling landscapes with tufts and trees, designing palm trees with heavy bunches of dates, and depicting mountains vertically and even upside down.

The *mélange* that issued from the two sources was developed in the later manuscripts into a new style, much more decorative, in which the objects, mainly architectural surfaces, were broken up into many units of strong, contrasting colors, to a point where the entire composition looks like the embroidered or patchwork fabrics of Hijazi dresses. No less than textiles, these strong and angular patterns recall the Arabian wall paintings, made by women, in which simple geometric patterns are repeated endlessly in rhythmical groupings and double-contours of strong color.[12] Painters turned mountains into decorative surfaces raised on bases like buildings in Matrakçi's style. They combined fantastic crenellations with decorative domes, gave spandrels undulating and cusped contours, and designed unrealistic patterns for the shafts of minarets. These later artists abstained from any indication of three-dimensionality or volume, renounced groupings and overlapping, and instead dispersed the decorative elements in symmetrical or rhythmic arrangements in spacious compositions. They usually placed monuments in the illustrations without any sense of topography, and economized on details of a sociological nature. The few exceptions among the later manuscripts were painted outside Mecca (SP 1514 in Istanbul; SP 1340 in a provincial Indian centre).

The illustrated sites: realities, legends, and visual expressions

Besides individual stylistic peculiarities, the illustrations of the specific sites differ from one manuscript to another in some architectural details. Small as they are, these differences may be valuable evidence of building activity in that period. In a pioneering experiment in that direction Emel Esin endeavored to date the Ottoman revêtement of the Dome of the Rock in Jerusalem according to an illustration of the site in the Hajj certificate H. 1812.[13] Her conclusions were misleading since she interpreted a single illustration without considering the stylistic features of the entire cycle, but the attempt opened up a new scholarly vista. A more successful study of the architectural history of the Prophet's mosque in Medina, based on several illustrations, was published by Hassan el-Basha.[14] I myself have studied the historical, technical, sociological, architectural, and topographical information which can be collected from NMM, which space does not allow me to repeat here. But I would like to call the reader's attention to two recurrent points. One is the painters' lively awareness of architectural reconstructions and additions in the sites, which they document at once. The second is the great importance of mountains, trees, and water installations, probably of immemorial sanctity, that had become associated with Islamic history and myth, thus being converted to the new religion.

In the following pages I will present the architectural components and characteristics, including certain renovations, of the sites along the Hajj route. The differences among the manuscripts are due both to changes in the sites and to the visual models and tendencies of the individual painters.

1. The Haram of Mecca   The enclosure of the Meccan mosque is always portrayed as a vertical rectangle, east being at the base. This orientation shows the door in the east wall of the Ka'ba (Figure 13.1), and the black stone at the south-east corner. The Ka'ba itself, slightly above the center, is seen covered in a black *kiswa*, with a golden band below the roof. Only in one case (P. 237) is the *kiswa* of a multi-colored zigzag pattern, introduced by the Ottomans at an unknown date. In some illustrations, the cubic shrine appears raised on a sort of pedestal, an artistic convention which seems to confer sanctity on important monuments and even on holy mountains in some of the manuscripts. All the images include the venerated gilded water spout (*mizab*) which in 960/1552–53 was replaced by a silver one and was sent to the Ottoman royal treasury in Istanbul.[15]

The circumambulating space (*mataf*) around the Ka'ba, including the low wall *al-hatim* around the so called *hajar Isma'il*, is surrounded by a high circle of metal, with lamps suspended from it, within which the ground is paved with cut stones. This pavement was renovated by order of Sultan Süleyman, and in a few manuscripts it is clearly distinguished from the pebbled ground of the rest of the courtyard.[16] Somewhat below the Ka'ba, the illustrations present the mythic stone called *maqam Ibrahim*, within a decorative pavilion;[17] the Zamzam well under a two-storey pavilion; and a pulpit on four wheels, beside a large *minbar* of multi-colored marble, made by order of Sultan Süleyman.[18] An isolated stone arch at the lowest point of the *mataf*, titled "the gate of Bani Shayba," "the old *al-salam* gate" (in P. 237), "the arch of Abu Talib" (in IO Isl. 877), or simply "arch" (*taq*), is probably a vestige of an early Haram gate, which served medieval pilgrims as a main entry to the enclosure.[19]

A pavilion on the roof over the Zamzam well provided a place of prayer for the chief *mu'adhdhin* of the Haram, or for the assistant of the Shafi'i *imam*, who himself occupied the most venerated location around the Ka'ba, behind Maqam Ibrahim. The three other *imams* and their assistants who, with the Shafi'i *imam*, led the service in turn, performed their prayers in other small monuments around the *mataf*. The Ottomans, followers of the Hanafi school of law, added a second floor to the

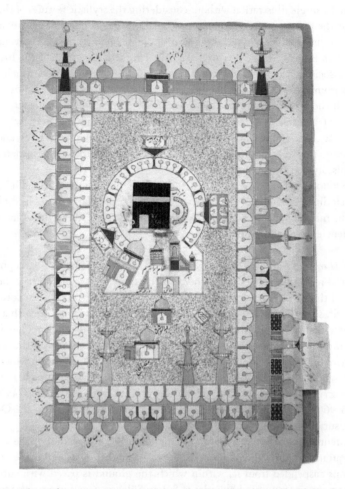

Figure 13.1 The Ka'ba in Mecca – Jerusalem, L. A. Mayer Museum, Ms. 34–69, fol. 21b.

maqam hanafi on the right of the Ka'ba, while the *maqam hanbali* on the left, and the *maqam maliki*, pictured above the Ka'ba, kept their traditional single floor.[20] Two other domed buildings of a practical nature, depicted below the Ka'ba, are a treasury of olive oil or carpets, and a store for drinking water (*sabil siqaya, siqayat 'Abbas*, or *khawd kawthar*).

The open court of the Haram is surrounded by single or double arcades, and a wall with some 17 gates of 1 to 5 arched openings. Bab Ibrahim, in the western, upper part of the composition, is usually depicted as taller and larger than all the rest, which differ in the order of their names, but not in location and number of openings. A comparison between the manuscripts suggests the following order: In the north wall, the first gate is called *al-'atiq* ("the old"), or *'ajala* ("cart") in the earliest manuscripts, and *sadda* ("the blocked") in the later ones. The change in name shows that sometime between 1569 and 1573 this gate was closed. It is followed by *al-basita* (or *satiyya* or *basitiyya*), *al-nadwa*, *ziyada*, *durayba*. In the east wall – *al-salam, al-nabi* (or *jana'iz* – "funerals"), *al-'Abbas, 'Ali*. In the south wall – *bazan, baghla* ("dung"), *safa, jiyad* (or *ajyad*), *al-rahma, shurafa', Bani Tamim, Umm Hani*. In the west wall – *al-wida'* (or *darura*), Ibrahim, and *al-'umra*.

The number of minarets around the enclosure increases from six in the early manuscripts to seven in the later ones (except IO Isl. 887, which followed an early model). According to written sources, the seventh minaret was built by order of Sultan Süleyman in 973/1565–66 between *bab al-salam* and *bab ziyada* in the northern wall, near a new *madrasa* of the four law schools.[21] Our miniatures confirm these dates with remarkable precision, since IM, from 976/1568–69, is the first to depict the seventh minaret and the new *madrasa*. In another renovation, carried out by order of Sultan Selim II in 1573, a series of domes replaced the timber roofs of the galleries around the Haram.[22] This too is documented with precision, as in 1568–69 (IM) the galleries are seen covered by a flat roof, while in 1573 (LAM) they are topped by domes. Comparison of the written and the visual evidence not only confirms the historical information, but also helps us date the manuscripts or their models.

2. The Mas'a   At the end of the visit within the holy enclosure, the pilgrims trot up and down (*sa'y*) between Safa and Marwa along a road (*mas'a*) which stretches between the west façade of the Haram and a block of public buildings (Fugure 13.2). Two pairs of green milestones on either side of the road, which in some manuscripts is called a market (*suq*), punctuate the running part of the ritual. Some of the early illustrations also depict Mt Abu Qubays behind the three arches which mark

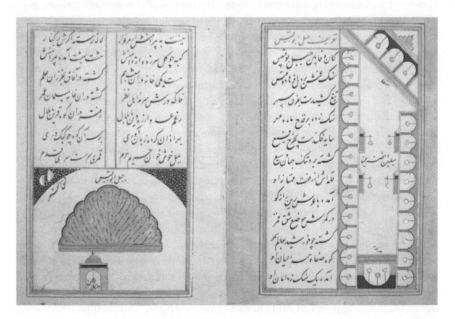

Figure 13.2 The Mas'a and Mt Abu Qubays – Jerusalem, L. A. Mayer Museum, Ms. 34–69, fols 23b–24a. (Photograph by David Silverman, Israel.)

Mt Safa and stand diagonally or at a right angle to the other end of the *mas'a*. Occasionally, a holy tree is linked by an inscription to 'Ali, or to a spring of water (*'ayn*), and a bazaar, a *ribat* named Tabrizi, and a *madrasa* of Sultan Süleyman appear, with individual characteristics, in NMM. The date of this manuscript, 1558–60, is obviously the *terminus ante quem* of these monuments.

3. *Mt Abu Qubays*   The tallest mountain in the region, stretching behind Mt Safa, Jabal Abu Qubays is venerated by Muslims primarily on account of a miraculous episode from the Prophet's hagiography, known as *shaqq al-qamar* (the cleaving of the moon). But legends and rituals that apparently infiltrated into the Muslim era testify to the earlier sanctity of this mountain. The scribe and illustratior of NMM, in a paragraph which he added to Lari's original text, tells that

> At the top of Jabal Qubays there is a cave called "the cave of the forty people," where the Prophet was seated. The sign of this is a black stone, on which a date is written in Kufic script. Above the cave is placed the kneading trough of Fatima, in which she kneaded dough. In that place the Prophet and his family ate when a table descended from heaven. And now, every Saturday, people make a visit to this place, taking with them a stew of animal heads and small animals. On that same mountain, in the side of Shi'b 'Ali, there is a well and a site called *shaqq al-qamar*.[23]

The two halves of a cloven moon are seen either together, or placed apart in the two upper corners of the composition. The blue sky, dotted with stars, is generally shaped as an arch, with round or ornamental spandrels, under which the mountain stands on a raised pedestal, like a venerated statue. In an extreme case of this symbolic presentation (Or. 343) a small starry arch completely frames the mountain, thus separating it from a domed monument, identified as the place of 'Umar's conversion to Islam, which shares the pedestal. In the other manuscripts, the domed monument, known as *Bayt al-Khayzuran*, is located at the foot of Mt Abu Qubays, which gradually develops from a rather naturalistic mass of rocks into a conglomerate of a decorative pattern.

4. *Suq al-Layl (night market)*   This Mecca neighborhood, where the Prophet and some members of his family were born, is a recommended visiting site during the pilgrimage. The first and most important holy monument, where the first prayer should be performed, is the Prophet's birthplace (*mawlid al-nabi*).[24] The early image of the building as a large two-storey dwelling, with crenellations on the roof and trees in the backyard, turned into a domed monument after a reconstruction ordered by Sultan Süleyman in 964/1556–57.[25] A small enclosure beside Muhammad's *mawlid* in NMM is said to be a scene of *dhikr* on Friday night (Figure 13.3).

The other monuments in the group are Fatima's birthplace, which in some manifestations of Shi'i sentiments is seen as larger than that of the Prophet; 'Ali's birthplace; Abu Bakr's shop (*dukkan*) or birthplace; the house of Abu Talib; two stones that spoke to the Prophet (*hajarayn mutakallimayn*); and a tree that "has been preserved from the Prophet's days," above a water system. This may be the tree which, according to tradition, approached Muhammad at his command, and then returned to its place. A place connected with Abu Hurayra (or another unclear name) appears in some of the illustrations, while a large *madrasa* and shops, which were donated by one

Figure 13.3 Suq al-Layl (night market) – St Petersburg, State Hermitage Museum, Inv. no. VR-491, fol. 20a.

of the two Gujarati Sultans named Mahmud, occupy the center of the composition in the topographically inclined NMM.[26]

5. *Mud'a* In this place, between Suq al-Layl and Ma'la, prayers are answered, according to Lari, because the Prophet camped there. Not all the scribes allocated a special space for an illustration, instead annexing this site to one of the others. In any case it seems to have looked like a road between two rows of shops (*suq mud'a*). The important sites in the vicinity are: the "Inna Fatahna" mosque, with an unusually tall minaret;[27] a nearby open-air *musalla* known as the Mud'a mosque; al-Husayniyya place of prayer; the dervish lodge (*zawiya*) of shaykh 'Abd al-Qadir (Gilani?); and a domed monument, perhaps a mausoleum (*qubba*) of Shaykh Harun (the biblical figure Aaron?).

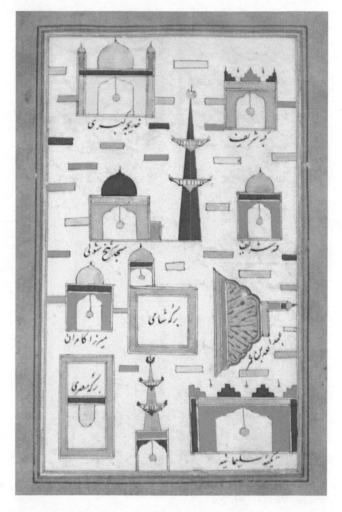

Figure 13.4 The Ma'la Cemetery – Jerusalem, L. A. Mayer Museum, Ms. 34–69, fol. 27b.
(Photograph by David Silverman, Israel.)

6. *The Ma'la cemetery*   Close to Mecca, on the way to Mina, the surroundings of the
Ma'la cemetery served as a camping ground (*manzil*) for the poor among the pilgrims.
Two large water tanks with elaborate gates, one for the Syrian caravan (*birkat shami*)
and one for the Egyptian (*birkat masri*), drew water from the surrounding mountains.
Having reconstructed the ruined wall of the cemetery (Figure 13.4) in 950/1543–44,
Sultan Süleyman built outside it a large complex consisting of a soup kitchen
(*ashkhana-ye sultani* or *takkiyyat khassiki*), with a bazaar of thirty-six shops, in the name
of his deceased wife Hasseki Sultan. The revenue from this endowment was intended
for the maintenance of the Haram in Mecca.[28] A drinking water fountain (*sabil*) was

erected by Mustafa Nasir al-Din in the name of Sultan Süleyman, with grilles around the four sides of an upper floor. The citizens of Mecca enjoyed sitting there, above the refreshing humidity emanating from the water.[29] All these installations, and a second *sabil* inside a building near the Ma'la gate, are accurately depicted in NMM and some of the others. A second monument, the Raya Mosque, was built where the Prophet is said to have fixed his banner on the day of his victorious entry into Mecca.[30] In a few illustrations this mosque is depicted in Mud'a, although Lari locates it in Ma'la.

The cemetery contained the tombs of many important figures from different periods. However, the choice of names varies from one manuscript to another, save that of the Prophet's wife and first believer, Khadija (*sitti* or *bibi Khadija kubra*), whose tomb always looks large and beautiful. Lari's text mentions khawaja Fadil 'Iyad, shaykh 'Umar 'Arabi, a spiritual leader of the Beduin, and 'Abd Allah b. 'Umar, whose tombs appear also in the illustrations. Although mentioned in the text, Ibn Zubayr and shaykh 'Ala' al-Haqq Kirmani are absent from the paintings, which instead offer a collective list of the following personalities: Shaykh al-Zamani, Shaykh Shuli (including a mosque with a tall minaret), Arghun, Shah Bik, Mirza Kamiran, Sha'ban Nuri, Isma'il Sarwal, khwaja 'Arif, Ibn amir (al-mu'minin) 'Umar, the *shurafa'* Ahmad and Muhammad of the Barakat family, and many anonymous *shurafa'*, *fuqaha'*, *mashayikh*, and simple people, arranged by ethnic group.

7. *The Shubayka cemetery* "Having said *labbayka* and resumed your way, by the time you say the *tamjid* you have reached the gate of Shubayka, at the entrance to Mecca, a cemetery where a blessed tooth of the Prophet is buried. A number of notables from Yemen are buried there."[31] An elaborate mausoleum of a Yemenite notable, shaykh Qutb 'Abd al-Kabir, is mentioned in the text and depicted in all the manuscripts, sometimes beside a second Yemenite shaykh, 'Abd Ruz. The tomb of Sultan Mahmud b. Sultan Ibrahim (of Gujarat) is seen in two illustrations, one of them being the trustworthy Hajj roll H. 1812, which depicts also the mosque of 'Aysha, a meeting point on the road (*miqat*) where the caravans came together to start the pilgrimage. Several manuscripts also locate the birthplace of 'Umar b. Abi Talib in the vicinity. NMM adds a luxurious house of the Banu Shayba clan, who hold the key of the Ka'ba, together with more modest habitations, and huts which belong to the "Meccan milkmen, who sell milk."

8–9. *Mt Nur (Hira') and Mt Thawr* Jabal Nur ("Mountain of Light") was thus named because it contains the cave of Hira', the place of Muhammad's first revelation. The cave is indicated on the mountain slope, while at the summit a domed monument may represent a visiting place. In Jabal Thawr the Prophet is said to have found shelter while fleeing from Mecca to Medina in the company of Abu Bakr. The refugees, pursued by their Meccan enemies, found a cave in the mountain, into which Abu Bakr first introduced his arm, to be confronted by a serpent. The two men then crawled through a narrow and thorny crack in the rock which in later centuries became a challenge to visitors, notably the obese.[32] Lari describes a narrow cave with a turquoise vaulting, but in the illustrations the cave, in the exact center of the mountain, looks round or triangular, with no specific coloring.

Like other holy mountains in our manuscripts, Jabal Nur and Jabal Thawr are often seen raised on a pedestal and roofed by an arch with a decorative contour. In one case even the arch rests on the pedestal (Or. 343), and in another, the domed monument is built above the arch (NYPL).

10. 'Arafat   On the day of 'Arafat, the ninth of Dhu al-Hijja, all the pilgrims perform together the ritual *wuquf* (standing in silence) and prayers at the foot of Jabal al-Rahma (Mount of Mercy), known also as Jabal 'Arafat. In the sixteenth century the *imams* gave the sermon from the *minbar* of a mosque in the southern part of the plain, and only later moved to a raised platform (*suffa*) on the mountain, below a small domed monument. Next to the mosque, identified in our manuscripts as Masjid 'Arafa, Masjid Namira, or Masjid Ibrahim al-Khalil, the area of the standing ritual (*bayn al-'alamayn*) is marked by four posts (*mil* or *hadd al-mawqif*). From the inscriptions in H. 1812 we learn that adherents of the Hanafis performed the standing on one side of the mosque, the Shafi'is on the other side (Figure 13.5).

Figure 13.5 'Arafat – Haifa, The National Maritime Museum, Inv. no. 4576, fol. 34a. (Photograph by David Silverman, Israel.)

The ground between the holy standing area and the mountain was occupied, according to the testimony of the *futuh* illustrations, by two gigantic ceremonial candelabra, one Syrian and the other Egyptian; the corresponding tents of the commanders of the Syrian and the Egyptian caravans (*mir hajj*); and the decorated *mahamil* (gift palanquins) of the two caravans. Lari tells us that in his time the Syrian *mahmal* was covered with a patchwork pattern on green atlas, while the Egyptian one was arrayed in a complete Egyptian *kiswa* (a textile cover for the Ka'ba, which was woven in Egypt after the Mongol destruction of Baghdad). His description of a black *mahmal* under a parasol, in the midst of the caravans, not confirmed by the illustrations, may in fact be a nostalgic recollection of the Hajj caravan in the time of the 'Abbasids, whose dynastic color was black. On the other hand, a third *mahmal*, which arrived from Yemen for the first time in 967/1559, that is later than the date of Lari's poem, was recorded in the NMM illustration in that same year, and then in all the later manuscripts. Strangely enough, even after the arrival of the third, Yemenite ceremonial palanquin, all these later illustrations still depict only two very high tents or parasols, that sheltered the *mahamil*, and were known as stork-tents (*khaymat laklak*).

To the north of the mountain, a building called Adam's Kitchen "has become a resting place for the poor (or mystics)." It commemorates the spot where Adam and Eve are said to have been reunited after their expulsion from Paradise, as a result of which they fell down on different parts of Earth. Close to this soup kitchen or hostel in the NMM illustration, among the pilgrims' tents and litters that stretch behind the mountain, two large tents are designated as coffeehouses (*qahwa khana*). At that time coffee had just been introduced into Arabia, and the presence of this institution in the camp of 'Arafat testifies to its popularity, and perhaps to the way it spread so quickly in the Muslim world.

Three large water tanks, each serving a different caravan, are arranged schematically in one continuum at the foot of Jabal 'Arafat in all the late manuscripts. This image, which draws on the artistic tradition of the thirteenth century Hajj documents, shows the stylistic shift of our manuscripts from a topographically inclined orientation to a symbolic arrangement.

11. Muzdalifa   The caravans with the *mahamil* leave 'Arafat after sunset for the raised eastern end of the Muzdalifa valley, a place also called *al-mash'ar al-haram*. A monument at this station had steps built over an external arch, which led to a higher level (or served as a base) for lighting devices, set behind large crenellations. An arch at the corner of the external courtyard of the monument is identified either as a *mihrab* or as a gate. The various illustrations of the site feature mainly a functional and ritualistic combination of water reservoirs and lighting devices (Figure 13.6).

12. Mina – the place of ritual sacrifice   The village or the market of Mina (Figure 13.7; see also Figure 13.12), the last camping station of the Hajj, is basically one street. In it, during *'id al-adha*, the pilgrims throw stones at three pillars, or "piles" (*jamarat*), in commemoration of Abraham and Ishmael stoning Satan, who tried to divert them from the sacrifice. The third pillar, called *jamarat al-'aqaba*, is set up on a small hillside at the end of the street, not far from the place of the sacrifice.

Following the Hajj, international commerce flourished in the many shops along the way to Masjid al-Khayf near the foot of the mountain that encircles the valley. A domed building in the open court of the mosque is said by the adjoining inscriptions

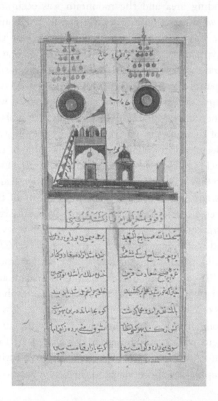

Figure 13.6 Muzdalifa – Paris, Bibliothèque Nationale de France, Supp. Pers. 1514, fol. 28a. (Photograph by David Silverman, Israel.)

to cover the site of the Prophet's tent. A small door opened from the mosque to the mountain, where a cave sheltered the Prophet during the revelation of *surat al-mursalat*.[33] The cave is seen in a corner of some illustrations, beside the rows of colorful tents. Arranged in alternating directions, the triangular shapes of the tents and the straight lines of square shops make attractive, carpet-like compositions.

13. The mountains of Mafrah   Having performed the Hajj, the pilgrims paid a visit to the Prophet's mosque and tomb in Medina. They usually chose the road of Ali's Wells, Jabal Mafrah, and the Tombs of the Martyrs, which offered an easy passage between the mountain chains, and enough water along the way. Probably thanks to the abundance of water, Jabal Mafrah assumed a degree of sanctity, and the painters depicted it in the same way as the other holy mountains. While the early manuscripts emphasize the importance of the pass by showing two separate mountains with some space between them, the later ones adhere to a symbolic image of a single mountain, with two horns flanking a deep hemispheric curve cut out of the summit. A mosque named Dhu al-Khulayfa or Masjid 'Ali is depicted in these later manuscripts below the mountain, near two water pits, which like the mosque are associated with 'Ali.

Figure 13.7 Mina – Jerusalem, L. A. Mayer Museum, Ms. 34–69, fol. 37a.

The Osmanli explanation around the painting in P. 273 says that the site is known as 'Ali's Gate, where the pilgrims take on the state of *ihram*.

14. The Prophet's Tomb-Mosque in Medina As with the Ka'ba in Mecca, some changes of detail in the otherwise frozen image of the site faithfully record contemporary restorations and alterations.[34] Like the Ka'ba, the holy enclosure is portrayed as a rectangle surrounded by arched galleries, with a changing number of minarets and gates along the façades. Only NMM, as usual, depicts the urban features of the city, with some reflection of the social structure.

A visit to the mosque always began at Bab al-Salam, in the south-west corner of the enclosure and the upper right corner in the illustrations (Figure 13.8). From there the visitor headed to the tomb chamber on the left, walking between the *qibla* wall

Figure 13.8 The Prophet's Tomb-Mosque in Medina – Haifa, The National Maritime Museum,
Inv. no. 4576, fol. 42a. (Photograph by David Silverman, Israel.)

and a low arcade that separated him from the interior of the prayer hall, called
Garden of Paradise (*rawda-ye bihisht*). The *rawda* was enlarged over the centuries, and
the low arcade is in fact a remnant of an ancient *qibla*. A *mihrab* in this wall, named
after 'Uthman b. 'Affan, was traditionally used by the Shafi'i *imams*; another, inside
the prayer hall and detached from the actual *qibla*, is called the Prophet's *mihrab*,
while a third, used by the Hanafi *imams*, is occasionally called "the new *mihrab*"
(P. 237; SP 1514). The only other object seen inside the prayer hall is a large and
elaborate *minbar*, a donation of Sultan Süleyman in 957/1550–51.[35] The manuscripts

illustrated before this date must therefore represent an earlier *minbar*, while the new one is clearly identified as *minbar jadid* in later illustrations. Between the prayer hall and the open court, a raised platform is variously identified as the balcony of important people, the place of the *mukabbirun* (those who say "Allahu Akbar" during the prayer), the *huffaz* (who recite the Qur'an), or the *mua'dhdhinun*.

To the left of the *rawda*, inside a room called the Chamber (*al-Hujra*), and roofed by the famous green dome, are the Tomb of the Prophet and two other tombs, tradi-tionally identified as those of Abu Bakr and 'Umar. Visitors can see these tombs through large windows with iron grilles, correctly portrayed in some of the manu-scripts. In front of this room, an anonymous tomb that was found under the floor during a restoration was thought to be the burial place of Fatima, after a tradition that her chamber was located in that part of the enclosure.[36] A roofed arcade in front of this tomb is believed to be the Prophet's original place of prayer, and is therefore called *ma'bad Mustafa*.

In the courtyard, two palm trees beside a venerated domed storage place for olive oil and a water pit are thought to be vestiges of Fatima's garden. A strange looking object in the centre of the court in NMM is identified by an inscription as a timer (sun dial) for prayer (*miqat-e namiaz*). The four gates of the enclosure are named al-Salam, al-Rahma, the Women, and Gabriel in all the manuscripts but the order varies from one illustration to another. The number of minarets around the court seems to have increased from 4 to 5 between 1544–45 and 1560, the dates of H. 1812 and NMM, contradicting Hassan el-Basha's contention in his important article. El-Basha did not see the fifth minaret in AIA, dated 1582, outside the Gate of Mercy, because it had been effaced, apparently during a rebinding of the quires.[37]

15. Al-Baqi' cemetery   Most of the Prophet's family members, friends and followers, were buried in the cemetery of Medina, behind al-Baqi' city-gate. Lari's text and the various illustrations differ from each other in the locations of the tombs, and in certain names, which may testify to a Sunni or Shi'i affiliation, and to the ethnic background of either painters or patrons. A collective list of the well-known names can be divided into two groups – one of those mentioned by all sources, the other of those appearing occasionally.

The first group includes: the graves or cenotaphs of 'Abbas, the Prophet's uncle, the Shi'i *imams* Hasan, Ja'far al-Sadiq and two others (Muhammad Baqir and Zayn al-'Abidin, according to some painters) in the largest and most distinguished mau-soleum of Baqi'; 'Uthman b. 'Affan, in the second important mausoleum, of which the stepped roof and the tall finial are perhaps a naive rendition of the Iraqi "sugar loaf" con-ical dome; the Prophet's infant son Ibrahim, whose tomb is identified by some people as "the house of sadness" (*bayt al-huzn*) but rejected by others; the Prophet's wives and paternal aunts are in one or two monuments; the jurist Malik b. Anas and his disciple al-Nafi', in twin mausolea in front of the gate; Halima al-Sa'diyya, the Prophet's wet-nurse, at the very end of the cemetery, not far from Fatima bint Asad, 'Ali's mother. The second group includes: 'Aqil b. Abi Talib; Khawaja Muhammad Farsi; Hadafa al-Suhaymi; Sa'd b. Waqqas; 'Abd al-Rahman 'Awn; and the Prophet's daughters.

As at other visiting sites, there are a few wells around al-Baqi', one of which is known as "the well of the seal." A very controversial tradition recounts that in this pool the third caliph 'Uthman lost the prophetic seal that passed from Muhammad to his *khulafa'*. As with King Solomon's seal, there was magic in the Prophet's seal, and losing it meant losing the Caliphate.[38] According to Lari, the well of the seal is part of the next site, Quba'.

16–17. Quba' and the "Four Mosques"   Due to their geographical proximity these two sites are not clearly distinguished from each other, and two of the mosques in them shift arbitrarily from the illustration of Quba' to that of the "Four Mosques." (Figure 13.9). Masjid Quba', outside Medina, is said to have been originally a halting place for caravans, where the Prophet, having dismounted from his she-camel, challenged his friends to try and mount it. Only 'Ali was able to make the animal march. The resting place of this camel was eventually surrounded by the court of the large mosque, but several illustrations indicate it by a schematic sign, a hallmark of the Meccan style, which designates "a place." Consisting of a horizontal bar and two shorter vertical ones, the sign resembles a horizontal grave with vertical stones above the head and the feet, or simply a horizontal rectangle, open at the top.

Many palm trees are depicted around Masjid Quba' in all the illustrated manuscripts. Two of them, unusually large and with twisted trunks, are identified as "talking palms." The word Quba' seems to have been erroneously copied as *qubba* in IO Isl. 877, thus producing a new mosque name – *Qubbat al-Islam*. This gave rise to another error, better suited to a painter of Indian origin, who named the mosque *masjid quwwat al-Islam* ("the mosque of the power of Islam") (Or. 11,533).

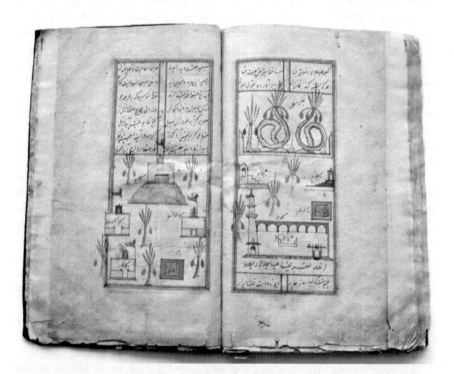

Figure 13.9 Quba' and the "Four Mosques" – Haifa, The National Maritime Museum, Inv. no. 4576, fols 45b–46a. (Photograph by David Silverman, Israel.)

Close to this large mosque are two smaller ones – Masjid Fath and Masjid Shams. The first gave its name to an entire group of small mosques, each consisting of a single covered gallery or even an uncovered *qibla* side of a small court.[39] The Fath mosque is said to be named after *surat al-fath*, which was revealed to the Prophet in this place. However, it has two other names: al-Ahzab, because the Prophet preached here before the War of the Tribes, and al-A'la, because it is built in an elevated part of the valley.[40] The other group consists of four mosques, named Masjid al-Nabi, Masjid 'Ali, Masjid Salman al-Farisi, and Masjid al-Sahaba only in NMM.

18. Uhud The last visiting site in Arabia is Jabal Uhud, where the Prophet's uncle Hamza b. 'Abd al-Muttalib and many other Muslims were killed in a famous battle against their Meccan opponents (Figure 13.10). All the martyrs were buried at the foot of the mountain, Hamza in what later became a big domed mausoleum, the others in rows of shallow graves.

On the way from Quba' to Uhud, separated from both by mountains and water tanks, stands the Double-qibla Mosque (*dhu al-qiblatayn*). It is said to be the first

Figure 13.10 Uhud – Paris, Bibliothèque Nationale de France, Supp. Pers. 1514, fol. 40a.
(Photograph by David Silverman, Israel.)

mosque established by the Prophet in the vicinity of Medina, when the Muslim prayer was still directed toward Jerusalem. A controversial tradition reports that when the Prophet was instructed to change the *qibla* toward Mecca, he rebuilt the mosque.[41] However, the illustrations depict the original *mihrab* in the courtyard, turned in the opposite direction to the new *mihrab*, which is inside the mosque.

19. al-Haram al-Sharif in Jerusalem   The text of *Futuh al-haramayn* ends after the visit to Uhud, but, following the Ayyubid Hajj certificates and the roll H. 1812, a few manuscripts include a painting of the Jerusalem haram at the end. There is much

Figure 13.11 al-Haram al-Sharif in Jerusalem – Paris, Bibliothèque Nationale de France, Supp. Pers. 1514, fol. 42a. (Photograph by David Silverman, Israel.)

affinity between the illustrations of Jerusalem in the Ottoman roll and in NMM, both in the color scheme, and in the inclusion of a large inscription of the *isra'* verse above the painting. This band suggests that Sayyid 'Ali, the painter of NMM, copied his composition from a scroll, where lines of inscriptions separate the illustrations (Figure 13.11).

In all the Jerusalem illustrations, the Dome of the Rock is portrayed on its high platform, in the center of a lower enclosure surrounded by galleries. Al-Aqsa mosque is seen in the upper part of the composition, usually above images of the eschatological Scales of Acts (*mizan al-a'mal*), and the pool of Kawthar in paradise. The name Kawthar was given to the actual ablution pool on the site, which was renovated by Sultan Süleyman, and the scales, although, of course, unseen, are represented in

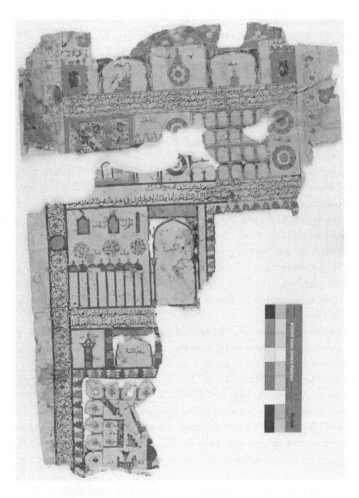

Figure 13.12 Muzdalifa, Mina, and the Ka'ba, a fragment of a thirteenth-century pilgrimage certificate – Istanbul, Türk ve Islam Eserleri Müzesi, Inv. 53/10.

the Haram by a small stone pavilion between the Dome of the Rock and al-Aqsa. The eschatological role of the Haram is further accentuated in NMM by small imaginary monuments, such as "the gate of Paradise," "the gate of Hell," and the "bridge" (*sirat al-mustaqim*). The northern arcade, or entrance porch of the Dome of the Rock, is called "the gate of the Throne," and the southern arcade, between the Dome of the Rock and al-Masjid al-Aqsa, is called "the gate of the throne of the Lord of the Worlds."

The historical meaning of the Haram is reflected in *mihrabs* associated with Adam, Nuh, 'Isa, Musa, Yusuf, Ya'qub, al-Khalil, Zakariyya, and Yahya, and with two small monuments on the raised platform of the Dome of the Rock, which are associated with King David and King Solomon, or, in one manuscript, with the landing spot of Buraq in the *isra'* (Or. 11,533).

Conclusions: a sixteenth-century Meccan school of painting

Based on both content and style, we can trace a line which brings all the manuscripts into one group and reconstructs their genealogical order. At the beginning of this line are the rotulus H. 1812 and the *Futuh al-haramayn* manuscript Or. 3633. Going by the number of minarets in Mecca, and some stylistic details, they are followed by R. 916, R. 917, NMM, and HM, which reflect Sunni sentiments. The line of Or. 3633 produced, through another branch, the non-Meccan manuscripts SP 1514 and SP 1340. The line of HM produced IM and LAM, while the decorative style of R.917 is reflected in all the others. Another early tradition is revealed in the opening lines and the illustrative details of the relatively late Or. 11,533, which may have been completed in India. The same opening lines and the lack of a Yemenite *mahmal* in 'Arafat testify to an early model for IO Isl. 877, which was copied not before 1595. The last generation within the group, *c*.1600, is represented by the simplistic style of NYPL. The manuscripts examined here thus reveal a Meccan school of painters, probably calligraphers in the first place, who used various sources in developing their own particular style, suited to non-figurative, symbolic images of the visiting sites in Arabia and Jerusalem.

The sixteenth-century artists of *Futuh al-haramayn* illustrated some other texts as well, and their compositions were soon imitated in other centers and other media. For example, an identical cycle appears in an anthology of Persian texts, copied in 990/1582 at Mecca by Mahmud b. Jan Mahmud Balkhi,[42] and in an undated *Manasik hajj* in Arabic, Persian, and Osmanli.[43] Illustrations of Mecca and Medina which reveal close acquaintance with the Meccan school were depicted in al-Tusi's *'Aja'ib al-makhluqat* of 970/1562–63, apparently in another center.[44] From the seventeenth century onward the variety of the illustrated sites was remarkably reduced, and the remaining images grew more conventional and symbolic. In the same period, the harams of Mecca and Medina were reproduced on large ceramic tiles which, unlike their contemporary manuscripts, preserved the fresh style of the preceding century.[45]

Appendix – the manuscripts

Dated manuscripts

AIA	990/1582	London, Ahuan Islamic Art, Exhibited in Riyadh, King Faisal Center for Research and Islamic Studies – copied by the scribe Ghulam 'Ali.[46]
CB	1003/1595	Dublin, Chester Beatty Library, Pers. 245 – copied at Mecca by Muhammad al-Katib of Rida.[47]
HM	970/1562–63	St. Petersburg, The State Hermitage Museum, VP 941 – copied by the scribe Vas (or Ways) al-Harawi at Mecca.[48]
IM	976/1568–69	Jerusalem, Israel Museum, 838.69 – copied at Mecca.[49]
IO Isl. 887	1103/1595(t.a.q.)	London, British Library, IO Isl. 887 – copied at Mecca.[50]
IO Isl. 2344	1006/1598	London, British Library, IO Isl. 2344 – copied in the *madrasa-ye akbari* on 9 Sha'ban, at Mecca, by the scribe Imam Quli Qandarzi (Qundarzi?) b. Dawlatqadam.[51]
LAM	980/1573	Jerusalem, L. A. Mayer Museum, Ms. 34–69, copied by the scribe 'Uways al-Harawi at Mecca.[52]
NLR	996/1588	St Petersburg, National Library of Russia, PNS 425 – dated the month of Ramadan.
NMM	966–8/1558–60	Haifa, National Maritime Museum, Inv. No. 4576 – copied and illustrated by Sayyid 'Ali al-Husayni at Mecca, under the title *Shawq-namah*.[53]
SP 1389	982/1574–75	Paris, Bibliothèque Nationale de France, SP 1389 – dated Friday of Ramadan, Muhammad Yar Badakhshani in front of the black stone at Mecca.[54]
SP 1514	984/1577	Paris, Bibliothèque Nationale de France, SP 1514–13 Shawwal, in Istanbul (*balda qunstaniniyya*).[55] After a model illustrated between 1568 and 1573.[56]
Or. 3633	951/1544	London, British Library, Or. 3633, dated 14 Ramadan, at Mecca.[57]

Undated manuscripts

NYPL	n.d.	New York Public Library, Spencer, Turk ms. 2 – copied at Mecca.[58]
Or. 343	n.d.	London, British Library, Or. 343.[59]
Or. 11,533	n.d.	London, British Library, Or. 11,533.[60]

P. 237	n.d.	Paris, Bibliothèque Nationale de France, P. 237 copied by Mulla Salih Muzahhib Naqqash of *Maqam Ibrahim* (in the Haram of Mecca) and presented as a gift to *nazir al-haramayn*.[61]
R. 917	c.1550	Istanbul, Topkapı Saray Museum, R. 917.[62]
R. 916	c.1550	Istanbul, Topkapı Saray Museum, R. 916.[63]
SP 1340	n.d.	Paris, Bibliothèque Nationale de France.

Further manuscripts, which I have not examined, are known in the scholarly literature. One, in an unknown collection, is dated to 984/1576,[64] and another, copied at Mecca in 1008/1600, is in Hyderabad, Salar Jang Museum.[65] Two undated manuscripts are in Dublin, the Chester Beatty Library (CB),[66] and the University of Michigan Library, Rare Book Room, Islamic MS 347.[67]

Notes

1 On Lari, *EI*[2], s.v. "Muhyi al-Din Lari."
2 On these struggles, see Serjeant, *The Portuguese off the South Arabian Coast*, especially pp. 160–2; On the involvement of the Gujarati sultans, see al-Nahrawali, Qutb al-Din, *Kitab al-i'lam bi-a'lam bayt allah al-haram*, Ferdinand Wüstenfeld (ed.), vol. 3 of *Chroniken der Stadt Mekka* (Leipzig, repr. Hildesheim, 1981, 1987), p. 245; on the Gujarat sultans, see *EI*[2], s.v. "Mahmud."
3 This information is obtained from one of the illustrated *Futuh al-haramayn* manuscripts. See Milstein, Rachel, "Kitab Shawq-nama," p. 298.
4 Al-Nahrawali, pp. 245–6.
5 On the Ottoman contribution to the *hajj*, see Faroqhi, *Pilgrims and Sultans*; on the ensuing building activity, see Raymond, André, "Le Sultan Süleyman," pp. 371–84; al-Nahrawali; Sabri, *Mir'at al-haramayn*.
6 This famous roll was described and illustrated in Tanindi, Zeren, "Rersimli bir Haç Vekaletnamesi (An Illustrated Hajj Vekalatname)," *Sanat Dünyamiz* (1983), vol. 9/28, p. 409. Galeries Nationales du Grand Palais, *Soliman le Magnifique*, p. 129, with an illustration of the Prophet's mosque in Medina. The collection of the Topkapı Museum contains another *hajj* certificate, E. 9518, in the form of a rotulus, dated 9 Dhu al-Hijja 950/4 March 1544, loc. cit.
7 See Atil, Esin, *The Age of Sultan Süleyman the Magnificent*. A Catalogue of an Exhibition in the National Gallery of Art (Washington and New York, 1987), p. 65.
8 The rolls were studied by Dominique Sourdel and Janine Sourdel-Thomine in "Une collection médiévale de certificats de pèlerinage," and in "Certificats de pèlerinage par procuration." J. Sourdel-Thomine published some of them in "Une image musulmane de Jérusalem," and Aksoy and Milstein published the illustrated rolls in "A Collection of Thirteenth Century Illustrated Hajj Certificates."
9 London, British Library, Add. 27566.
10 See Nasuhü's-silahi (Matrakçi), *Beyan-i menazil-i 'irakeyn*; Atil, *The Age of Sultan Süleyman the Magnificent*, pp. 79–87.
11 See for example, Özdemir, *Piri Reis*.
12 Photographed documentation of Hijazi dresses and houses, in Mauger, *Tableaux d'Arabie*, pp. 8, 166–73.
13 Esin, Emel, "Un manuscrit illustré représentant les sanctuaires de la Mecque et Médine et le dome du Mi'radj, à l'époque des Sultans turcs Selim et Süleyman Ier

(H.922–74/1516–66)," in Abdeljelil Temimi (ed.), *Les provinces arabes et leurs sources documentaires à l'époque ottomane, parties française et anglaise* (Tunis, 1984), pp. 175–90.

14 el-Basha, Hassan, "Ottoman Pictures of the Mosque of the Prophet in Madinah as Historical and Documentary Sources," *Islamic Art* (1988–89), vol. 3, pp. 227–44.

15 This event is described in Sabri, *Mir'at al-haramayn*, vol. 1v, p. 790.

16 For an eye-witness description of this reconstruction, see NMM, fols 18b–19a, translation in Milstein, "Kitab Shawq-nama," pp. 294–5.

17 On this place, see Kister, "Maqam Ibrahim," pp. 477–91.

18 Ibid.

19 In the illustrated Ayyubid *hajj* certificates, pilgrims are said to have entered through *Bab bani Shayba*. See note 8.

20 On the rivalry between the Ottoman governor and the Meccan public in this matter, see Milstein, "Kitab Shawq-nama," p. 296.

21 Sabri, *Mir'at al-haramayn*, vol. 1v, pp. 758–60, vol. 1vi, p. 916.

22 Faroqhi, Soraya, *Pilgrims and Sultans*, pp. 101–2.

23 NMM, fols 7a–8a.

24 According to al-Azraqi, *Akhbar Mekkah*, F. Wüstenfeld (ed.) (Leipzig, repr. Beirut, 1858/1964), p. 198.

25 Sabri, *Mir'at al-haramayn*, vol. 5vii, p. 1056.

26 Either Mahmud I (r. 1458–1511), or Mahmud III (r. 1537–54). See *EI*^{2}, s.v. "Mahmud."

27 The name is a reference to Qur'an 48:1: "Surely we have given you a *manifest* victory (*inna fatahna laka fath^{an}* mubin^{an})."

28 Sabri, *Mir'at al-Haramayn*, vol. 5vii, p. 1039; Faroqhi, *Pilgrims and Sultans*, p. 107.

29 Al-Nahrawali, p. 13.

30 Ibid., p. 14.

31 NMM, fol. 25a.

32 Al-Azraqi, *Akhbar Makka*, p. 205; al-Harawi, *Guide des Lieux de Pèlerinage*, p. 202; Ibn Jubayr, *Voyage*, pp. 136–7.

33 Qur'an 77.

34 The documentary value of these pictures of Medina is demonstrated by el-Basha, "Ottoman Pictures," pp. 766–9.

35 The date is given by Sabri, *Mir'at al-haramayn, al-Madina*, vol. 2ii, p. 830.

36 This information is given in al-Samhudi, p. 610.

37 El-Basha, "Ottoman Pictures," p. 228.

38 On this controversy, see al-Samhudi, pp. 942–4

39 Mostafa, *al-Madina al-Munawwara*, pp. 189–90, nos. 132–41.

40 Al-Samhudi, pp. 830–7.

41 The various opinions are presented by al-Samhudi, pp. 244–52, 795–800.

42 Harvard University Art Museum, Edwin Binney, 3rd Collection, 1985.265. See Binney, *Turkish Treasures*, No. 100, p. 154, with illustrations on p. 155.

43 St Petersburg Branch of the Oriental Institute, Russian Academy, Ms. A 1406.

44 Istanbul, Türk ve Islam Eserleri Müzesi, Env. no. T 2013; another illustrated copy of the same text, still with six minarets in Mecca, is in Istanbul, Topkapı Museum, H. 404.

45 Examples of seventeenth-century Ottoman tiles: Athens, Benaki Museum, inv. no. 124; Kuwait National Museum, LNS 60 C; tiles fixed to walls of the Rüstem Paşa camii and the Topkapi Saray in Istanbul, and many more; see Erdmann, "Ka'ba-Fliesen," pp. 192–7.

46 Riyadh, *The Unity of Islamic Art*, no. 52, pp. 68–9; el-Basha, "Ottoman Pictures of the Mosque of the Prophet," pp. 227–44; Schmitz *et al.*, p. 43.

47 Arberry, *Chester Beatty Library: Persian Manuscripts*, vol. III, pp. 22–3; Schmitz *et al.*, p. 43.

48 Amsterdam, *Earthly Art-Heavenly Beauty*, No. 16, p. 79, with an illustration of the valley of 'Arafat.

49 A description of the manuscript by Naama Brosh, in Milstein, *Islamic Painting in the Israel Museum*, 99–100, and the illustration of the Ka'ba on p. 101.

50 Schmitz *et al.*, 43; Robinson, *India Office Library*, p. 234.
51 Rieu II, p. 65; Fisher and Fisher, 46; Robinson, Basil, *Persian Paintings*, 1976, 2324; Schmitz *et al.*, p. 43; the earlier date suggested by some of these publications is contradicted by a dated colophon on fol. 41b.
52 The dating 1573 is based on the depiction of domes in the Holy Mosque of Mecca. See discussion.
53 For a detailed description and an analysis of the illustrations, see Milstein, "Kitab Shawq-nama."
54 Blochet, Edgar, *Manuscrits persans*, pp. 344–50, no. 1823; Schmitz *et al.*, p. 43.
55 Blochet, *Manuscrits persans*, vol. 3, no. 1823; Richard, *De la Bible à nos jours*, no. 142, pp. 156–7, illustrations on p. 157; Schmitz *et al.*, p. 43.
56 The dating of the model is based on the presence of seven minarets and the flat roof of the Holy Mosque in Mecca. See discussion.
57 Rieu, *Supp.* 301 p. 192; Munzawi, *Fihrist*, vol. 4, no. 32470; Titley, *Turkish Manuscripts*, no. 50, pp. 60–1; Fisher and Fisher, p. 46; Schmitz *et al.*, p. 42.
58 Schmitz *et al.*, no. I.3, pp. 42–6, figs 26–30.
59 Fisher and Fisher, p. 46.
60 Fisher and Fisher, p. 46; Munzawi, no. 32484.
61 Blochet, *Manuscrits Persans*, vol. III, p. 318, no. 1768; Schmitz *et al.*, p. 43.
62 Karatay, Fehmi Edhem, *Topkapi Sarayi Müzesi Kütüphanesi Farsçe Yazmalar* (Istanbul, 1961), vol. 1, no. 263, no. 772; Tanindi, "Islam Resimde Kustal Kent," p. 408; Munzawi, no. 32490; Galeries Nationales du Grand Palais, *Soliman Le magnifique*, p. 128, with an illustration of the Ka'ba.
63 Karatay, 771; Tanindi, 408.
64 A. Müller, *Der Islam im Morgen-und Abendland* (Berlin, 1885), pl.I. Cited by Ettinghausen, *ZDMG* 12 (1934) 115, and by Schmitz *et al.*, p. 44, note 8;
65 Ashraf, M., *A Concise Descriptive Catalogue of the Persian Manuscripts in the Sâlâr Jung Museum and Library*, vol. V (Hyderabad, 1969), pp. 21–2, no. 1687; Schmitz *et al.*, p. 43, note 3.
66 Arberry, Arthur J., B. W. Robinson, E. Blochet, and J. V. S. Wilkinson, *The Chester Beatty Library: A Catalogue of the Persian Manuscripts and Miniatures* (Dublin, 1959–62), vol. II, pp. 52–3.
67 Fisher and Fisher, pp. 98–9, no. 53.

References

Aksoy, Sule, and Rachel Milstein, "A Collection of Thirteenth Century Illustrated Hajj Certificates," in Irvin Çemil Schick (ed.), *M. Ugur Derman 65th Birthday Festschrift* (Istanbul, 2000), pp. 101–34.

Amsterdam, *Earthly Art-Heavenly Beauty: Art of Islam*, A Catalogue of an Exhibition (Amsterdam, 2000).

Arberry, Arthur J, B. W. Robinson, E. Blochet, and J. V. S. Wilkinson, *The Chester Beatty Library: A Catalogue of the Persian Manuscripts and Miniatures* (Dublin, 1959–62).

Ashraf, M., *A Concise Descriptive Catalogue of the Persian Manuscripts in the Sâlâr Jung Museum and Library*, vol. V (Hyderabad, 1969).

Atil, Esin, *The Age of Sultan Sûleyman the Magnificent*, A Catalogue of an Exhibition in the National Gallery of Art (Washington, DC and New York, 1987).

al-Azraqi, *Akhbar Mekkah*, F. Wüstenfeld (ed.) (Leipzig, repr. Beirut, 1858/1964).

el-Basha, Hassan, "Ottoman Pictures of the Mosque of the Prophet in Madinah as Historical and Documentary Sources," *Islamic Art* (1988–89), vol. 3, pp. 227–44.

Binney, Edwin, 3rd and W. Denny, *Turkish Treasures from the Collection of Edwin Binney, 3rd* (Portland, OR, 1979).

Blochet, Edgar, *Catalogue des manuscrits persans de la Bibliothèque Nationale* (Paris, 1928).

Erdmann, Kurt, "Ka'ba-Fliesen," *AO* (1959), vol. 3, pp. 192–7.

Esin, Emel, "Un manuscrit illustré représentant les sanctuaires de la Mecque et Médine et le dome du Mi'radj, à l'époque des Sultans turcs Selim et Süleyman Ier (H.922–74/1516–66)," in Abdeljelil Temimi (ed.), *Les provinces arabes et leurs sources documentaires à l'époque ottomane, parties française et anglaise* (Tunis, 1984), pp. 175–90.

Ettinghausen, Richard, "Die bildische Darstellung der Ka'aba im islamischen Kulturkreis," *ZDMG* (1932–34), vol. 86–7 (NF 11–12), pp. 111–37.

Faroqhi, Soraya, *Pilgrims and Sultans: The Hajj under the Ottomans 1517–1683* (London and New York, 1994).

Fisher, Carol G. and Alan Fisher, "Illustrations of Mecca and Medina in Islamic Manuscripts," in Carol G. Fisher and Alan Fisher (ed.), *Islamic Art from Michigan Collections* (East Lansing, MI, 1982).

Galeries Nationales du Grand Palais, *Soliman le Magnifique*. Catalogue d'une exposition (Paris, 1990).

al-Harawi, Abu al-Hasan, *Guide des Lieux de Pèlerinage*. Traduction annotée par Janine Sourdel-Thomine (Damascus, 1957).

Ibn Jubayr, *Ibn Jubayr. Voyages*. Translated and annotated by Maurice Gaudefroy-Demombynes, 2 vols (Paris, 1949–51).

Karatay, Fehmi Edhem, *Topkapi Sarayi Müzesi Kütüphanesi Farsçe Yazmalar* (Istanbul, 1961).

Kister, M. J., "Maqam Ibrahim. A Stone with an Inscription." *Le Muséon*, (1971), vol. 84, pp. 477–91.

Mauger, Thierry, *Tableaux d'Arabie* (Paris, 1996).

Milstein, Rachel, *Islamic Painting in the Israel Museum* (Jerusalem, 1984).

Milstein, Rachel, "Kitab Shawq-nâma: an illustrated tour of holy Arabia," *Jerusalem Studies in Arabic and Islam* (2001), vol. 25, pp. 275–345.

Mostafa, Saleh Lamei, *al-Madina al-Munawwara, Urban Development and Architectural Heritage* (Beirut, 1981).

Munzawi, Ahmad, *Fihrist-i nushaha-yi khatti-yi farisi*, Tehran 1930–32 (1349–1351).

al-Nahrawali, Qutb al-Din, *Kitab al-i'lam bi-a'lam bayt allah al-haram*, Ferdinand Wüstenfeld (ed.), vol. 3 of *Chroniken der Stadt Mekka* (Leipzig, repr. Hildesheim, 1981, 1987).

Nasuhü's-silahi (Matrakçi), *Beyân-i menâzil-i 'irâkeyn-i Sultân Süleymân Hân*, with introduction and notes by Hüseyn G. Yurdaydin (Ankara, 1976).

Özdemir, Kemal, *Piri Reis* (Istanbul, n.d.).

Raymond, André, "Le Sultan Süleyman et l'activité architecturale dans les provinces arabes de l'Empire (1520–66)," in Gilles Veinstein (ed.), *Soliman le Magnifique* (Paris, 1992).

Richard, Francis, *De la Bible à nos jours: 3000 ans d'art*, A catalogue of an Exhibition (Paris, 1985).

Rieu, Charles, *Catalogue of the Persian Manuscripts in the British Museum* (London, 1966).

Riyadh, *The Unity of Islamic Art: An Exhibition of Islamic art at the Islamic Art Gallery, the King Faisal Center for Research and Islamic Studies* (Riyadh, Saudi Arabia, 1405 AH/1985 AD, 1985).

Robinson, Basil, *Persian Paintings in the India Office Library: A Descriptive Catalogue* (London, 1976).

Sabri Eyüp, *Mir'at al-Haramayn* (Qustantiniyya, 1201–06/1786–91).

al-Samhudi, Nur al-Din 'Ali b. Ahmad, *Wafa' al-wafa bi-akhbar dar al-Mustafa* (Beirut, 1955).

Schmitz, Barbara *et al.*, *Islamic Manuscripts in the New York Public Library* (New York and Oxford, 1992).

Serjeant, R.B., *The Portuguese off the South Arabian Coast* (Oxford, 1963).

Sourdel, Dominique and Janine Sourdel-Thomine, "Une collection médiévale de certificats de pèlerinage à la Mekke conservés à Istanbul. Les actes de la période seljoukide et bouride (jusqu'à 549/1154)," in J. Sourdel-Thomine (ed.), *Études médiévales et patrimoine Turc* (Paris, 1983), pp. 167–273.

Sourdel, Dominique and Janine Thomine-Sourdel, "Certificats de pèlerinage par procuration à l'époque mamlouke," *JSAI* (2001), vol. 25, pp. 212–33.

Sourdel-Thomine, Janine, "Une image musulmane de Jérusalem au début du XIIIe siècle," in Daniel Poirion (ed.), *Jérusalem, Rome, Constantinople: l'image et le mythe de la ville* (Paris, 1976), pp. 217–33.

Tanindi, Zeren, "Rersimli bir Haç Vekaletnamesi (An Illustrated Hajj Vekalatname)," *Sanat Dünyamiz* (1983), vol. 9/28, p. 409.

Tanindi, Zeren, "Islam Resimde Kustal Kent ve Yöre Tavirleri," *Journal of Turkish Studies* (1984), vol. 7, pp. 407–37, fig. 11–14.

Titley, Norah M., *Miniatures from Turkish Manuscripts; A Catalogue and Subject Index of Paintings in the British Library and the British Museum* (London, 1981).

14 The forgotten province

A prelude to the Ottoman era in Yemen

Jane Hathaway

Michael Winter began publishing his pioneering work on Ottoman Egypt at a time when Egypt, after the Ottoman conquest of 1517 but before the reign of Mehmed 'Ali Pasha (1805–48), was still relatively unknown territory. His *oeuvre* has done a great deal to redress this state of affairs. Throughout its history, however, whether as an Ottoman province or otherwise, Egypt has been linked, often symbiotically, with Yemen. Nonetheless, Yemen under Ottoman rule – particularly during the first period of Ottoman rule, 1538–1636, remains as unexplored today as Ottoman Egypt was before Professor Winter launched his career. In a forthcoming book, I have reviewed the history of Yemen during this first period of Ottoman rule with reference to its effects on the political culture of Ottoman Egypt.[1] The present contribution seeks to provide a context and a framework for this initial Ottoman period by exploring Yemen's pre-Ottoman connections to Egypt.

Yemen has been a partner, silent or otherwise, in Egypt's history from remote antiquity until the recent past. Although Yemen was not, like Egypt, one of humankind's original cradles of civilization, a highly sophisticated civilization had emerged there by at least 1000 BCE. Geography and climate played no small part in this circumstance. Centuries later, Roman geographers knew Yemen as *Arabia felix*, or "happy Arabia," for, unlike most of the rest of the Arabian Peninsula, Yemen was not desert but relatively fertile, if rugged, agricultural land. Moreover, its location at the southwestern tip of the Arabian Peninsula, bordering both the Red Sea and the Indian Ocean, made it a critical axis of overseas and overland trade and gave it enormous strategic potential.

The indigenous population of Yemen belonged to a distinctive South Arabian people who differed considerably from populations farther north in the Arabian Peninsula. They spoke a southern Arabian language that, although Semitic, was written in a different script from the northern dialects that would form the basis for classical and modern Arabic, and contained a number of other distinctive features. Indeed, Irfan Shahid has argued that, from a purely linguistic standpoint, the ancient Yemenites were not, strictly speaking, Arabs.[2] Inscriptions on stone in this language remain a critical source for the ancient history of Yemen and Oman. Before the advent of Islam, southern Arabia's cultural ties to the Horn of Africa were arguably stronger than those binding the region to the northerly portions of the Arabian Peninsula.

By far the oldest trace of a highly developed civilization in Yemen is the legendary Ma'rib Dam, whose construction dates to the eighth century BCE or thereabouts. The dam ensured Yemen's agricultural prosperity for well over a millennium. Whether the dam was the work of Yemen's earliest documented kingdom, that of Saba', is not clear. Saba' did, in any case, take the city of Ma'rib, east of San'a', as its capital, from which it ruled the central portion of today's Yemen from several centuries BCE through the third century CE. Ma'rib was located along the ancient incense route that ran from what is today eastern Oman northward through the interior of the Arabian peninsula.[3] This location would have given Saba' commercial links with the northerly portions of the Arabian Peninsula and with the Fertile Crescent. Indeed, the Queen of Sheba (known in Islamic tradition as Bilqis), who, according to the Hebrew Bible (1 Kings 10:1–13), visited King Solomon in Jerusalem, is often associated with Saba'.[4] Although the Book of Kings has the Queen journeying to Jerusalem to verify the stories she has heard of Solomon's wisdom and majesty, it broadly hints that she also came to trade in the products for which Yemen was justifiably famous. Foremost among these were the legendary frankincense and myrrh, produced from the resin of two species of tree that grow in what are now eastern Yemen and western Oman.[5] In antiquity, both substances were in high demand for covering up the odors of dead bodies, as in Zoroastrianism, and for anointing religious officials and performing religious rituals, as in Temple-era Judaism.[6]

In the early centuries of the Common Era, Saba' encountered a challenge from a rival Yemeni power, that of Himyar. The Himyarite kingdom ultimately displaced that of Saba' at a time when momentous political and cultural changes were occurring in the region. Foremost among the cultural changes was the spread of Christianity, which took root in Egypt well before the Byzantine emperor Constantine declared it the state religion of the Byzantine Empire in 330 CE. Unlike the central Byzantine lands, however, Egypt persisted in adhering to Monophysite Christianity, which posits a single nature, at once human and divine, for Christ; Egyptian Christians opposed the Council of Chalcedon's ruling in 451 that Christ was dyophysite, possessing distinct human and divine natures.[7] Persecution of Egyptian monophysites by the official Chalcedonian church would later dispose the Egyptian Christians favorably toward their Muslim conquerors, whom they regarded as fellow monotheists, in contrast to the Dyophysite authorities in Constantinople.[8] From Egypt, Monophysitism spread to Ethiopia, now a Byzantine client state, and, under the influence of proselytes from the northern Arabian kingdom of Ghassan and perhaps from Ethiopia, won converts in Yemen. Najran, in the far north of Yemen, originally converted to Orthodox Christianity in the early fifth century, had by the early sixth century become a Monophysite bastion.[9]

The Himyarite rulers, however, did not adopt Christianity but, in the fifth century, converted to Judaism. Shortly thereafter, they began persecuting their Christian subjects, most of them Monophysite, supposedly in reaction to the Byzantines' persecution of their Jewish subjects. In retaliation, Monophysite Ethiopia, with the blessing of the Byzantines, invaded Yemen in 525 CE, putting an end to the Himyarite dynasty.[10] The upheaval caused by the Ethiopian occupation was compounded by a natural disaster in 550 CE, when the ancient Ma'rib Dam collapsed, destroying the basis of Yemen's prosperous agricultural economy.[11]

Yemen at this point found itself caught between two rival empires: the Chalcedonian Christian Byzantine Empire and the Zoroastrian Sasanian Empire. Yemen was a strategic linchpin between the two massive powers: a hostile Yemen would threaten the access of both to the Indian Ocean. Moreover, both the Byzantines and Sasanians needed the frankincense and, to a lesser extent, the myrrh that Yemen produced; incense was used in both Monophysite and Dyophysite church services and played an important part in Zoroastrian purification practices as well.[12]

The Sasanian emperor Khusrau I Anushirvan (r. 531–79 CE) was understandably alarmed at the extent of Byzantine influence in the Red Sea region following the Ethiopian occupation of Yemen; finally, in 570 CE, his forces invaded Yemen and ousted the Ethiopians.[13] Yemen thus became an active participant in the series of wars that engulfed the Byzantine and Sasanian empires just as Islam was emerging in the Arabian Peninsula. Not since Alexander the Great defeated the Achaemenid emperor Darius in 330 BCE had the two empires experienced such territorial flux. Anushirvan's successor, Khusrau II Parviz (r. 589–628 CE), managed to take greater Syria, including the holy city of Jerusalem, from the Byzantines in 622 CE and even occupied Egypt briefly; he was then beaten back by the Byzantine emperor Heraclius, who subsequently stormed all the way into Mesopotamia. Yemen, however, remained a Sasanian satrapate. As a result of the Sasanian occupation, Yemen acquired a population of descendants of the Persian soldiers who came to be known collectively as *Abna'*, or "sons," and who would play a not insignificant role in Yemen's early Islamic history.[14]

During these years of territorial flux, Yemen came into closer commercial and cultural contact with the more northerly portions of the Arabian Peninsula. The series of disasters that hit Yemen in the sixth century drove waves of southern Arabian tribesmen northward into the interior of the peninsula; it was perhaps during this period that the difference between northern and southern tribes became a serious source of division in the tribal politics of the peninsula. Indeed, the population of Medina, where the Prophet Muhammad founded the first Muslim community after emigrating from Mecca in 622 CE, was largely Yemeni, although we do not know when their ancestors settled there. Meanwhile, Yemen's trade with the interior of the peninsula was mushrooming. The state of war between the two empires made the sea route through the Red Sea to the Indian Ocean extremely hazardous; Yemeni goods therefore had to be carried overland by camel caravan if they were to reach Egypt or Syria. These circumstances gave Mecca, the Prophet's hometown, strategically located on the caravan route running northward from Yemen through the western Arabian Peninsula, a golden opportunity to enhance its commercial importance.[15]

Yemen in Muslim popular lore

Not coincidentally, Yemen occupies a special place in Muslim tradition. Southern Arabia was thought to have been the home of one of the indigenous Arabian prophets who preceded Muhammad: Hud, who prophesied in vain to the people of 'Ad in what is now southeastern Yemen or northwestern Oman (Qur'an 11:50–60). (Indeed, Yemeni chronicles typically report the tradition that Hud's tomb was discovered in the Hadramawt early in the Islamic period.)[16] The ancient kingdom of Himyar is romanticized in Arab folklore, although not to the extent of the pre-Islamic heroes, villains, and poets of the regions farther north. Muslim-era commentators tended to lump the varied southern Arabian civilizations together under the rubric "Himyarite," since the Himyarite was the last great southern Arabian civilization of which they knew. As Reynold Nicholson points out, the indecipherable inscriptions that the early Muslims encountered on their journeys southward were enough to prompt tales of the mysterious civilization of the south, now vanished. Sketchy tales of past greatness and disaster, furthermore, lingered in the region and were transmitted by Muslim chroniclers.[17] The catastrophic collapse of the ancient Ma'rib dam in 550 CE[18] was an obvious subject of story and verse, more so as it had occurred comparatively recently. The Himyarite kings, who took the title *tubba'*, acquired similarly legendary status. One in particular, the third-century As'ad al-Himyari, metamorphosed into a world-conquering Alexander the Great type. The honorific bestowed upon him in popular lore, Madiqarib, is in fact a corruption of the title *muqarrib* (literally, "one who draws near," evidently referring to a federator), borne by the rulers of ancient Saba'.[19] As'ad is erroneously depicted in some bodies of lore as the first *tubba'* to adopt Judaism, which these stories portray as an admirable monotheism in a sea of polytheism, and, moreover, to have been the first person ever to cover the Ka'ba, Mecca's sacred shrine, with a *kiswa*, or ceremonial cloth.[20] A far less savory character is Dhu Nuwas, putative last Himyarite monarch, who converted to Judaism and began persecuting his Christian subjects, thus, according to the legends, bringing down upon his head the Ethiopian invasion that destroyed the Himyarite monarchy in 525 CE.[21]

But above both of these monarchs, as well as all other Yemeni kings, Himyarite or otherwise, looms the figure of Sayf b. Dhi Yazan, the legendary founder of the Himyarite civilization. A series of epic adventure stories traces the exploits of this hero, who is said to have embraced the faith of Abraham and to have spread that faith into eastern Africa, converting the Sudanese and fighting those sons of Ham who would not abandon paganism. Sayf is credited with diverting the course of the Nile so that it flowed through Egypt, creating the basis for Egyptian civilization.[22] Indeed, his reputed impact on Egypt and the neighboring regions of Africa is comparable to the legendary impact of Alexander the Great (Iskandar) on Iran and Central Asia. During the Ottoman era, if we may take Evliya Çelebi as a guide, the inhabitants of Egypt's sub-provinces and their administrators still related tales of how Sayf shaped the region.[23]

Yemen under Islamic rule

Once Islam began to spread through the Arabian Peninsula, Yemen was swiftly added to the new Muslim polity. The Christians of Najran submitted to the Prophet Muhammad himself in 631 CE and were allowed to continue practicing their religion.[24] The Himyarite remnant, in contrast, rebelled following the Prophet's death in 632 CE; they were led by a member of the ancient ruling family Dhi Yazan, supposedly founded by the legendary Sayf b. Dhi Yazan.[25] 'Ali b. Abi Talib, the Prophet's son-in-law, was appointed first Muslim governor of Yemen.[26] Subsequent governors came from families of both northern Arab, or Qaysi, and southern Arab, or Yemeni, descent.[27]

Under the Umayyads and 'Abbasids, Yemen served as a way station for ships en route from Egypt to India. Trade was a key source of Egyptian influence – not only economic and political but also cultural and theological – in Yemen; hence, the coastal population of Yemen adopted the Shafi'i legal rite that evolved in Lower Egypt during the ninth century. By the same token, the Shafi'i rite spread along this oceanic route to southern India and ultimately all the way to Malaysia and Indonesia.[28] On the other hand, Yemen's distance from the central authority made it an attractive haven for militant offshoots of normative Sunni Islam, particularly the two smaller branches of Shi'ism: Isma'ili, or "Sevener," Shi'ism, and Zaydi, or "Fiver," Shi'ism. Since members of these minority sects constitute 2 of the 3 major Muslim communities in Yemen, their doctrines are worth examining.

Zaydi and Isma'ili Shi'ism

Zaydism takes its name from Zayd b. 'Ali, the fifth Shi'i imam and the great-grandson of 'Ali b. Abi Talib. In 740 CE, Zayd staged a rebellion in Kufa against the late Umayyad caliphs, not unlike the rebellion attempted in Kufa on behalf of his grandfather, Husayn b. 'Ali, six decades earlier. Although the Umayyads brutally crushed the revolt, killing Zayd in the process, support for the movement persisted in Kufa and, to some extent, Medina, and apparently spread into North Africa.[29] Nonetheless, only two lasting Zaydi political movements were founded after this defeat. The first established a state in Tabaristan, on the southern shore of the Caspian Sea, in the early ninth century; it survived, in one form or another, into the eleventh century.[30] The second and much longer-lived movement began when the imam Yahya al-Hadi (d. 911), a grandson of the Hasanid imam whose followers had first promoted Zaydism in Tabaristan, migrated from Medina to Yemen late in the ninth century, establishing his capital at the northern highland city of Sa'da.[31] It is to him that Yemen ultimately owes its Zaydi population.

Al-Hadi did not, however, found a line of imams that lasted, unbroken, for centuries. On the contrary, Zaydi theory of the imamate militates against cohesion and an uninterrupted succession of imams within the Zaydi community. Unlike Isma'ili or Twelver Shi'i doctrine, Zaydi theology posits an active, visible imam, descended from either Husayn or his brother Hasan, who is learned in the religious sciences and who publicly proves himself worthy of leading the Muslim *umma*, in battle if necessary.[32] What this has meant in Yemeni history is that scions of numerous lines of Hasanid and, less frequently, Husaynid descendants have proclaimed their *da'was*, or "calls" – occasionally simultaneously, so that the supporters of one line were obliged to fight it out with supporters of another. Thus Yemen over the centuries has seen numerous lines of Zaydi imams. The last, that of the Hamid al-Din family, ended with Imam Yahya's overthrow by republican forces in 1962.

Zaydism is generally regarded as more compatible than either of the other major branches of Shi'ism with Sunni Islam. The sect normally diverges less overtly from

Sunni practice than do Isma'ili and Twelver Shi'ism. In the first period of Ottoman rule in Yemen, it appears, Zaydis employed the same call to prayer as Sunnis; later, they began to insert the line "Come to the best of works," as do Isma'ilis and Twelvers. Unlike other Shi'is, however, they refrain from cursing the first three caliphs recognized by Sunnis – Abu Bakr, 'Umar, and 'Uthman – in their Friday sermons.[33] Zaydis, in fact, have been known to regard their religion as a fifth legal rite, or *madhhab*, alongside the Hanafi, Maliki, Shafi'i, and Hanbali rites of Sunni Islam.[34]

The two larger branches of Shi'ism, Isma'ili and Imami, or Twelver, hold that each imam possesses esoteric knowledge of the Qur'an and can recognize such knowledge in his successor, whom he must designate. The two sub-sects disagree as to which imam went into a state of occultation (*ghayba*), bringing the line to an end. Isma'ilis believe that the seventh imam, Isma'il b. Ja'far al-Sadiq, who died in 760 CE, designated his son Muhammad to succeed him, but that this son ultimately went into occultation – a transcendent state from which he will return at the end of time. A militant Isma'ili movement, vehemently opposed to the 'Abbasid caliphate, appeared only in the mid-ninth century, by which time its adherents were known as Qarmatis, after the ninth-century proselyte Hamdan Qarmat.[35] Rejecting even feigned acceptance of 'Abbasid authority, the Qarmatis removed themselves from the 'Abbasid polity, establishing small, insular settlements in remote locales; the quasi-communistic character of these settlements, each centered on an Isma'ili missionary, became a target of vehement Sunni polemic.[36]

Early in the tenth century, the leader of the central Qarmati community in Syria proclaimed himself a descendant of Isma'il and, as such, a living imam. When his home community proved reluctant to accept his claim, he turned to North Africa, where, with the help of an industrious proselyte and after overcoming considerable obstacles, he founded the Fatimid caliphate. The Fatimids set themselves up as a counter-caliphate, both territorially and doctrinally, to the 'Abbasids. By the end of the tenth century, they held all of North Africa, Egypt, Syria, and the Hijaz, including the Holy Cities.[37]

This first Fatimid caliph, commonly known as 'Ubaydallah al-Mahdi, sent a proselyte, or *da'i*, to Yemen, where Qarmati missionaries had already enjoyed success. The Qarmati effort, however, faced resistance from none other than the Zaydi imam al-Hadi, who attacked the Qarmatis from his capital at Sa'da and defeated them shortly before his death in 911.[38] He is said, in fact, to have wielded 'Ali's sword Dhu al-Faqar against them.[39] Having weathered this blow, Yemen's Qarmatis proceeded to fight it out among themselves: those who recognized the Fatimids against those who did not.[40] Only in 1038 did conditions stabilize under the leadership of the Fatimid proselyte 'Ali b. Muhammad al-Sulayhi, a member of the Hashid tribal confederation,[41] who united Yemen as never before or since. By the time of his death in 1067, 'Ali's rule extended from Mecca to the Hadramawt.[42] The local dynasty that he founded kept Yemen a staunch Fatimid ally, and therefore closely tied to Egypt, for the next several decades.[43] Thanks in large part to the efforts of Fatima Mernissi, the Sulayhids are perhaps most famous for producing two extraordinary political women: Asma' bint Shihab, the mother of 'Ali al-Sulayhi's son and successor al-Mukarram; and al-Mukarram's wife, Bint Ahmad al-Sulayhi. Following al-Mukarram's premature death, Bint Ahmad became the effective ruler of the Sulayhid domain; her strategy included marrying a series of Isma'ili missionaries. On her death in 1138, at the age of eighty-eight, Yemen disintegrated into a collection of warring regional statelets.[44]

Ayyubids, Rasulids, Tahirids, and Mamluks

The intervention in 1173 by Salah al-Din al-Ayyubi (Saladin), who had displaced the Fatimids in Egypt in 1171, returned a large part of Yemen to the Sunni fold. During a period of nominal rule by various members of the Ayyubid house, Yemen fell under the administration of a Turcoman family known as the Banu Rasul because the founder had supposedly been sent to Syria and Egypt as the representative (*rasul*) of the 'Abbasid caliph.[45] The Rasulids ruled as Ayyubid vassals until, on the death of Mas'ud al-Ayyubi in 1227, Nur al-Din 'Umar b. 'Ali al-Rasuli broke with the Ayyubids and established a wholly independent Rasulid kingdom.[46] Under the Rasulids, staunch Turcophone Shafi'is, Yemen enjoyed one of its increasingly rare periods of complete independence from Egypt – although, to be sure, the Rasulids were careful to keep in the good graces of the later Ayyubids and their Mamluk successors. The Rasulid sultans cultivated a highly sophisticated court culture; a number of the sultans were themselves poets and astronomers of some note.[47] Meanwhile, they nurtured Yemen's commercial links with India and the Far East. In the fifteenth century, in fact, the fleet of Chinese junks commanded by the famous Chinese Muslim eunuch Zheng He (Cheng Ho) arrived at Zabid.[48] However, the Rasulids never exercised total control over all of Yemen. Their stronghold was the southern coastal region, particularly the port of Zabid. The Zaydi and Isma'ili tribes of the highland interior enjoyed a large degree of autonomy.

It was perhaps somewhat ironic, therefore, that the end of the Rasulid dynasty came not at the hands of Zaydi or Isma'ili tribesmen but at the hands of an Arab Shafi'i family, the Banu Tahir. The Tahirids were Arab notables based in the Indian Ocean port of Lahaj. Taking advantage of internal divisions among the Rasulids, the Tahirids displaced them in 1454 without, however, extending their sphere of influence much beyond the southern coastal area.[49] Although the Tahirid sultans were hard put to match the intellectual sophistication of their Rasulid predecessors, they did import seminal recent works of Sunni, and more particularly Shafi'i, theology from Mecca into Yemen; these books were then endowed in perpetuity as pious foundations (*waqf*, pl. *awqaf*).[50]

The Tahirids were ruling the southern coastal region from their capital at Zabid when the Portuguese appeared in the Indian Ocean at the close of the fifteenth century. In 1513, the Portuguese, after a string of unsuccessful attacks on the Yemeni coast, took Kamran island; this prompted the Mamluk sultan of Egypt to intervene for fear the Portuguese would soon have unbridled access to the Hijaz. A Mamluk naval force proceeded to attack the Tahirids on the western and southern coasts in 1514, earning the opprobrium of Ibn al-Dayba' and other Yemeni chroniclers.[51] This was just the period when the Mamluk sultanate, itself never a formidable naval power, was accepting the aid of its more powerful Ottoman neighbor against the

Portuguese. These joint operations led to a very curious interlude in Yemeni history, during which Ottoman naval commanders, including the famous admiral Salman Reis, were, in actual fact, administering the Yemeni port cities. Al-Nahrawali refers to this period as the "era of the levends," *levend* being a common Ottoman term for a naval mercenary.[52]

Yemen under Ottoman rule

In fact, Yemen must certainly have loomed large in the Ottoman decision to conquer Egypt from the Mamluks. Mamluk ineffectiveness against the Portuguese in the Red Sea clearly alarmed the Ottomans. Yemen, after all, served as the gateway to Mecca and Medina for pilgrims coming from India, the Far East, and eastern Africa; as such, it was also the first line of defense against any threat to Egypt from those regions. The Portuguese themselves had visions of occupying Mecca and Medina on the way to their ultimate messianically inspired goal, the Christian reconquest of Jerusalem.[53]

The Ottoman conquest of Yemen and Yemen's fortunes and downfall as an Ottoman province are the subjects of another study. Here, I have sought to depict the conditions that led to this strategic way station's relatively brief incorporation into the Ottoman Empire. Yemen's historical connection to Egypt loomed large in this incorporation and largely defined Yemen's experience, both from 1538 to 1636 and from 1872 to 1918, as an Ottoman province. We can only hope that scholars of the Ottoman Empire ultimately recognize this seminal link and write Yemen into the empire's history in the same way that Michael Winter helped to write Egypt into that history.

Notes

1 Jane Hathaway, *A Tale of Two Factions: Myth, Memory, and Identity in Ottoman Egypt and Yemen* (Albany, NY: State University of New York Press, forthcoming), chapter 4.

2 Irfan Shahid, *Byzantium and the Arabs in the Fifth Century* (Washington, DC, 1989), pp. 338–9. See also Brian Doe, *Socotra: Island of Tranquility* (London, 1992), p. 27. Interestingly, this is also the conclusion of 'Abd al-Rahman b. 'Ali b. al-Dayba' (d. 1537 CE) in his *Tuhfat al-zaman fi fada'il ahl al-Yaman* (ed.), Sayyid Kusrawi Hasan (Beirut, 1992), p. 29.

3 Muhammad 'Abd al-Qadir Bafaqih, *L'unification du Yémen antique: la lutte entre Saba', Himyar, et le Hadramawt du Ier au IIIème siècle de l'ère chrétienne* (Paris, 1990), pp. 144–5. Sometime around the first century CE, San'a' displaced Ma'rib as the Sabian capital; see ibid., pp. 149–51. See also Albert Deflers, *Voyage au Yémen: Journal d'une excursion botanique faite en 1887 dans les montagnes de l'Arabie Heureuse* (Paris, 1889), pp. 15–16.

4 For another legend associated with the Queen of Sheba, see Evliya Çelebi (*c.*1611–82), *Seyahatname*, vol. X: *Mısır ve Sudan*, (ed.) Mehmed Zillîoğlu (Istanbul, 1966), pp. 647, 682.

5 John Noble Wilford, "Ruins in Yemeni Desert Mark Route of Frankincense Trade," *New York Times*, January 28, 1997, pp. B9–10.

6 Mary Boyce, *A History of Zoroastrianism*, vol. I: *The Early Period, Handbuch der Orientalistik*, Der nahe und mittlere Osten, VIII/1, instalment 2, no. 2A (Leiden, 1975), p. 304; Exodus 30:1, 7–9, 23–30, 34–8; 37:25–9; 39:38; 40:5, 27; Leviticus 2:2, 15–16; 6:8; 16:2, 12–13; 24:7; Numbers 4:16; 7:14, 20, 26, 32, 38, 44, 50, 56, 62, 68, 74, 80, 86; 16:17–18, 35;

17:5, 11–12. See also W. Gunther Plaut *et al.*, *The Torah: A Modern Commentary* (New York, 1981), pp. 636, 863 note.

7   R. V. Sellers, *The Council of Chalcedon: A Historical and Doctrinal Survey* (London, 1953), esp. pp. 103–57, 254–83.

8   Sawirus b. al-Muqaffa' (fl. 955–87), *Ta'rikh batarika al-kanisa al-misriyya/History of the Patriarchs of the Egyptian Church*, vol. III, part 1, ed. and trans. Antoine Khater and O. H. E. KHS-Burmester (Cairo, 1968), pp. 490–98.

9   Shahid, *Byzantium and the Arabs in the Fifth Century*, pp. 77, 149, 360–76.

10   Ibid., pp. 175–6; Shahid, *Byzantium and the Arabs in the Sixth Century*, I (Washington, DC, 1995), part 1, pp. 53–4, 144–7; part 2, pp. 728–31. On the Himyarites generally, see Bafaqih, *Unification*, pp. 175–93.

11   Wendell Phillips, *Qataban and Sheba: Exploring the Ancient Kingdoms on the Biblical Spice Routes of Arabia* (New York, 1955), pp. 221–3.

12   Boyce, *History of Zoroastrianism*, I, p. 304.

13   Shahid, *Byzantium and the Arabs in the Sixth Century*, I/1, pp. 365–7 (where he verifies the date of the invasion), 547.

14   See, for example, Ibn al-Dayba', *Qurrat al-ʿuyun bi-akhbar al-Yaman al-maymun*, (ed.) Muhammad b. 'Ali al-Aku' al-Hawali, 2 vols (Cairo, 1977), I, p. 163; Muhammad b. Ishaq (d. *c.*768), *The Life of Muhammad*, (ed.) 'Abd al-Malik b. Hisham (d. 834), trans. and with an introduction and notes by Alfred Guillaume (Lahore, Karachi, Dacca, 1955, 1968, 1970), pp. 30–4, cited in Qutb al-Din Muhammad b. Ahmad al-Nahrawali al-Makki (1511–82), *al-Barq al-yamani fil-fath al-'uthmani*, a.k.a. *Ghazwat al-Jarakisa wal-Atrak fi janub al-jazira*, (ed.) Jasir Hamad (Riyadh, 1968), p. 285; *EI*[1], s. v. San'a', by R. Strothmann; Robert L. Playfair, *A History of Arabia Felix, or Yemen* (Amsterdam and St Leonards, 1970; reprint of 1859 Bombay edn), pp. 72, 76–8. These *Abna'* are not to be confused with the sons of the Khurasani Arabs who participated in the 'Abbasid revolution.

15   This claim is disputed by Patricia Crone, *Meccan trade and the rise of Islam* (Princeton, NJ, 1987); see also R. B. Serjeant's highly critical review article, "Meccan Trade and the Rise of Islam: Misconceptions and Flawed Polemics," *Journal of the American Oriental Society* (1990), 110, pp. 472–86.

16   Husayn Zahir al-Zabidi, untitled history of Zabid (1609–10), Istanbul, Süleymaniye Library, MS Fatih 5374, fol. 334r; 'Abdallah Muhammad b. Ibrahim b. Battuta (1304–77), *Rihlat Ibn Battuta*, introduction by Karam al-Bustani (Beirut, 1964), p. 262; Evliya Çelebi, *Seyahatname*, vol. X, p. 693.

17   Reynold A. Nicholson, *A Literary History of the Arabs* (Cambridge, 1969), chapter 1. Yahya b. al-Husayn b. al-Qasim (1625–89) notes 'Himyarite ruins' in Sa'id 'Abd al-Fattah 'Ashur (ed.), *Ghayat al-amani fi akhbar al-qutr al-yamani*, 2 vols (Cairo, 1968), II, p. 598, while Carsten Niebuhr notes descendants of the "Toba" in Kheivan, supposedly their seat; see *Travels through Arabia and other countries in the East*, trans. Robert Heron (Edinburgh and London, 1792; reprint Beirut, n.d.), pp. 52–3. See also Deflers, *Voyage au Yémen*, pp. 69–70.

18   See "Ibn Hisham's Notes" to Ibn Ishaq, *Life of Muhammad*, pp. 693–4. The Qur'an refers to the dam break as divine punishment for the "Sabians," ingratitude to God for the bounty of their land; see sura 34:15–6.

19   The title *Madiqarib* appears as early as the sixth century BCE: National Museum, San'a', catalog 24: bronze statue of Madiqarib b. Marib from the Awwam temple in Ma'rib, 6th century BCE, bearing an inscription to Almaqah, the chief Sabean god, in exhibit "Queen of Sheba: Treasures from Ancient Yemen," British Museum, 6 June–4 October 2002.

20   Ibn Ishaq, *Life of Muhammad*, p. 7; see also Ibn al-Dayba', *Tuhfat al-zaman*, p. 29; Anonymous, *Ta'rikh San'a' (al-)Yaman*, (mid-eighteenth century), Istanbul, Süleymaniye Library, MS Ayasofya 3048, fos 164r–165r; al-Zabidi, history of Zabid, fol. 330r; (Mustafa Bey al-)Rumuzi, *Tarih-i feth-i Yemen* (to 1568), Istanbul, Topkapı Palace Library, MS Revan 1297, fol. 28r.

21 For the story of Dhu Nuwas' conversion to Judaism, see Ibn Ishaq, *Life of Muhammad*, pp. 14, 17–20. According to a 530 CE Ethiopian inscription on a stela in the National Museum, San'a', catalog 37, describing the invasion, the Himyarite king at the time of the invasion was Yusuf Asar Yathar: exhibit "Queen of Sheba: Treasures from Ancient Yemen."

22 Lena Jayyusi, translator and narrator, *The adventures of Sayf Ben Dhi Yazan: An Arab folk epic*, introduction by Harry Norris (Bloomington, 1996). M. C. Lyons, *The Arabian Epic: Heroic and Oral Story-Telling*, III: *Texts* (Cambridge, 1995), pp. 586–641.

23 Evliya Çelebi, *Seyahatname*, X, pp. 350, 613, 629, 632, 634, 690.

24 Ibn Ishaq, *Life of Muhammad*, pp. 270–7.

25 *EI*[1], s. v. San'a', by R. Strothmann.

26 Ibn al-Dayba', *Bughyat al-mustafid fi ta'rikh madinat Zabid*, (ed.) 'Abdallah al-Habashi (San'a', 1979), pp. 23–4; Ibn al-Dayba', *Qurrat al-'uyun*, vol. I, pp. 83–7.

27 G. Rex Smith, "The Early and Medieval History of San'a', ca. 622–1382," in R. B. Serjeant and Ronald Lewcock (eds), *San'a': An Arabian Islamic city* (London, 1983), p. 53.

28 On the rise, spread, and practices of the legal rites, see Joseph Schacht, *An Introduction to Islamic Law* (Oxford, 1964; reprint 1995), chapter 9.

29 Paul E. Walker, "Qayrawan in Revolution: Local Perspectives on the Assumption of Power by the Fatimids in 909," paper delivered at the Middle East Studies Association conference, Chicago, December 1998.

30 Wilferd Madelung, *Religious trends in early Islamic Iran* (New York, 1988), pp. 87–90; Bertold Spuler, *History of the Muslim World, I: The Age of the Caliphs*, trans. F. R. C. Bagley, paperback edn. (Princeton, NJ, 1995), pp. 66–7; Farhad Daftary, *The Isma'ilis: their history and doctrines* (Cambridge, 1990; reprint 1995), pp. 339, 371, 373, 448–49.

31 Ibn al-Dayba', *Qurrat al-'uyun*, I, pp. 167–9; Madelung, *Religious trends*, pp. 87–8. Madelung explains that al-Hadi even visited Tabaristan before his relocation to Yemen and attracted numerous Tabari Zaydis to Yemen as his supporters.

32 Madelung, *Religious Trends*, pp. 86–7; Daftary, *Isma'ilis*, pp. 69–70, 74–6, 166; Paul Dresch, "Imams and tribes: the writing and acting of history in Upper Yemen," in Philip S. Khoury and Joseph Kostiner (eds), *Tribes and State Formation in the Middle East* (Berkeley, CA, 1990), p. 266; Nahida Coussonnet, "Les assises du pouvoir zaydite au XIIIe siècle," in Michel Tuchscherer (ed.), *Le Yémen, Passé et présent de l'unité, Revue du Monde Musulman et de la Méditerranée* no. 67 (Paris, 1994), p. 30; François Blukacz, "Le Yémen sous l'autorité des imams zaidites au XVIIe siècle: Une éphémère unité," in Tuchscherer (ed.), *Le Yémen*, p. 40; Bernard Haykel, "Al-Shawkani and the jurisprudential unity of Yemen," in Tuchscherer (ed.), *Le Yémen*, p. 56; Manfred Kropp, "The realm of evil: the struggle of Ottomans and Zaidis in the 16th–17th centuries as reflected in historiography," in B. Knutsson, V. Mattsson, and M. Persson (eds), *Yemen: Present and Past* (Lund, 1994), p. 90.

33 Spuler, *Age of the Caliphs*, p. 67. See also al-Nahrawali, *al-Barq al-yamani*, pp. 59, 184, 188.

34 Fuad Ishaq Khuri, *Imams and Emirs: State, Religion, and Sects in Islam* (London, 1990), p. 123; Kropp, "Realm of evil," p. 90; al-Nahrawali, *al-Barq al-yamani*, p. 59; Haci 'Ali, *Ahbar ül-yamani* (1666–67), Süleymaniye Library, MS Hamidiye 886, fol. 202r. There was an attempt by the Ottomans in the eighteenth century to designate Twelver Shi'ism as a fifth "Ja'fari" *madhhab*, after Ja'far al-Sadiq. This, however, occurred in the context of political negotiations with Fath 'Ali Shah of Iran and was ultimately unsuccessful.

35 Daftary, *Isma'ilis*, pp. 102–7.

36 Shihab al-Din Ahmad al-Nuwayri (1279–c.1332), *Nihayat al-arab*, Paris, Bibliothèque Nationale, MS Fonds Arabe 1576, fos. 48b–49b, in Bernard Lewis (ed. and trans.), *Islam: From the Prophet Muhammad to the Conquest of Constantinople*, II: *religion and society*, paperback edn (New York and Oxford, 1987 [1974]), pp. 63–5.

37 On the Fatimid caliphate, see Heinz Halm, *The empire of the Mahdi: the rise of the Fatimids*, trans. Michael Bonner (Leiden, 1996); Daftary, *Isma'ilis*, pp. 126–274.

38 Ibn al-Dayba', *Qurrat al-'uyun*, vol. I, pp. 178–220; Daftary, *Isma'ilis*, p. 118.

39 C. van Arendonk, *Les débuts de l'imamat zaidite au Yémen*, trans. Jacques Ryckmans (Leiden, 1960), p. 221.

40 Ibn al-Dayba', *Qurrat al-'uyun*, I, pp. 202–27; Daftary, *Isma'ilis*, pp. 131–2.

41 *EI²*, s. v. 'Hashid wa-Bakil', by G. Rentz.

42 Ibn al-Dayba', *Qurrat al-'uyun*, vol. I, pp. 241–50; Yahya b. al-Husayn, *Ghayat al-amani*, I, pp. 237, 253–7; Daftary, *Isma'ilis*, pp. 209–10.

43 Ibid., pp. 247–372; Ibn al-Dayba', *Bughyat al-mustafid*, pp. 46–50; Yahya b. al-Husayn, *Ghayat al-amani*, vol. I, p. 295.

44 Fatima Mernissi, *The Forgotten Queens of Islam*, trans. Mary Jo Lakeland (Minneapolis, 1993), chapters 7–8.

45 'Ali b. al-Hasan al-Khazraji (d. 1410), *The Pearl-Strings: A History of the Resuliyy Dynasty of Yemen*, trans., introduction, annotations, index, tables, and maps by Sir J. W. Redhouse; (ed.) E. G. Browne, R. A. Nicholson, and A. Rogers, E. J. W. Gibb Memorial Series, 2 vols (Leiden and London, 1906), I, p. 75; Yahya b. al-Husayn, *Ghayat al-amani*, I, p. 419; Abu 'Abdallah al-Tayyib b. 'Abdallah b. Ahmad Abu Makhrama (1465–1540), *Ta'rikh thaghr 'Adan wa-tarajim 'ulama'iha*, (ed.) 'Ali Hasan 'Abd al-Hamid, 2nd printing (Beirut and Oman, 1987), p. 205.

46 Al-Khazraji, *Pearl-strings*, I, pp. 81–91; Ibn al-Dayba', *Qurrat al-'uyun*, I, pp. 413–22; II, pp. 1–3; Ibn al-Dayba', *Bughyat al-mustafid*, p. 81; Yahya b. al-Husayn, *Ghayat al-amani*, I, pp. 418, 420–1; *EI¹*, s. v. "Rasulids," by A. S. Tritton.

47 Daniel Martin Varisco, *Medieval agriculture and Islamic Science: The Almanac of a Yemeni Sultan* (Seattle, 1994); Yahya b. al-Husayn, *Ghayat al-amani*, I, pp. 476–7; II, p. 527.

48 Hikoichi Yajima (ed.), *A chronicle of the Rasulid dynasty of Yemen from the unique MS Paris no. arabe 4609* [i.e. Bibliothèque Nationale, MS arabe 4609] (Tokyo: Institute for the Study of the Languages and Cultures of Asia and Africa, Monograph Series No. 7, 1976), pp. 105, 114, 145; Ibn al-Dayba', *Qurrat al-'uyun*, II p. 123; id., *Bughyat al-mustafid*, p. 104; Yahya b. al-Husayn, *Ghayat al-amani*, II, p. 565.

49 Ibn al-Dayba', *Qurrat al-'uyun*, II, pp. 144–235; id., *Bughyat al-mustafid*, pp. 124–214; Yahya b. al-Husayn, *Ghayat al-amani*, II, pp. 585–650.

50 Ibn al-Dayba', *Qurrat al-'uyun*, II, pp. 193–4; id., *Bughyat al-mustafid*, pp. 213–14; Yahya b. al-Husayn, *Ghayat al-amani*, II, pp. 622–3: Muhammad b. Bahadir al-Zarkashi's (1344/5–92) fourteen- (Yahya has twenty-four)-volume hadith collection, and Ibn Hajar al-'Asqalani's (1372–1449) commentary on al-Bukhari's *Sahih*, one of the six canonical Sunni collections of hadith.

51 Ibn al-Dayba', *Qurrat al-'uyun*, II, pp. 216–35; Yahya b. al-Husayn, *Ghayat al-amani*, II, pp. 630–1, 640–54; al-Nahrawali, *al-Barq al-yamani*, pp. 16–32. See also M. Yakub Mughul, "Portekizli'lerle Kızıldeniz'de Mücadele ve Hicaz'da Osmanlı Hâkimiyetinin Yerleşme hakkında bir Vesika," *Belleten* (1965), 2(3–4), p. 39.

52 Al-Nahrawali, *al-Barq al-yamani*, pp. 32–59; Yahya b. al-Husayn, *Ghayat al-amani*, II, pp. 668–85. Al-Nahrawali mistakenly gives Salman's name as Süleyman. M. Yakub Mughul has published a letter dated 25 Rebiülevvel 923/17 April 1517 from Salman Reis to Selim I, then in Egypt (Topkapı Palace Archives, E. 8337), along with commentary; see "Portekizli'lerle kızıldeniz'de Mücadele," pp. 37–47. *Levend* can refer to any type of mercenary; however, it is frequently applied to naval personnel. See the references to *levendler-i donanma-ı Hümayun* ("*levends* of the imperial navy") in Istanbul, Başbakanlık Arşivi, Kamil Kepeci, Kahve Rusumu 4519 (1129/1717). See also Gustav Bayerle, *Pashas, Begs, and Effendis: A Historical Dictionary of Titles and Terms in the Ottoman Empire* (Istanbul, 1997), p. 102; Mughul, "Portekizli'lerle Kızıldeniz'de Mücadele," p. 46; Riza Nour, "L'histoire du croissant," *Revue de turcologie* (1999), 1, 3 (February), pp. 88, 317.

53 Sanjay Subrahmanyam, "Du Tage au Gange au XVIe siècle: Une conjoncture millénariste à l'échelle eurasiatique," *Annales: Histoires, Sciences Sociales* (2001), 56(1), pp. 52–4, 77–81. I am grateful to Geoffrey Parker for calling my attention to this article.

15 Islam in the Sudan under the Funj and the Ottomans

Gabriel Warburg

My interest in the process of Islamization in Sudan during the Funj Sultanate and under Ottoman rule was evoked by more contemporary events. Studying the Sudan during the twentieth century both under colonial rule and since independence, I became rather puzzled by the central role played by what was known as "Popular Islam" not only in the social and cultural make-up of the country, but also in its politics. The two major Islamic movements which flourished both during the Condominium and since independence, namely the Khatmiyya and the Ansar, seemed to be able to pull the strings of any political movement or party which sought to play an independent role in the emerging state. My quest for an answer was at first limited to the more immediate and contemporary circumstances. The fact that Sudan was ruled during the first half of the twentieth century by two colonial powers, one Christian and one Muslim, seemed to solve part of the problem. It enabled each of the two Muslim movements to seek the support of one of the antagonistic co-domini, England or Egypt. Thus the Ansar because of their hatred of the Egyptians favored the British, whilst the Khatmiyya because of antagonism with the Ansar adopted the motto "the enemy of my enemy is my friend" and took shelter behind Egypt. Consequently, these two "popular Islamic sects," as they came to be known in Anglo-Egyptian discourse, seemed to reign supreme in Sudanese society and politics despite the anti-sectarian policy of the colonial rulers. An additional answer could be sought in the complexity of the religious and ethnic composition of the country. With approximately one-third of the Sudan lying south of latitude $10\,°N$, the population of which was mostly of African descent and non-Muslim, it seemed natural that Muslim movements with a missionary zeal would seek to play a prominent role in attempting its Islamization. This tendency was strengthened by British "Southern Policy," seeking to stop Islam from penetrating into these "closed districts" and inviting Christian missionaries to undertake the education of southern children in order to prepare the ground for their proselytization. Once again the fact that there were two colonial patrons with opposing aims, one Christian and one Muslim, enabled Muslim movements in the North to exploit this antagonism in order to further their own goals. Finally, I was, of course, aware that both the first colonial period, the so-called "Turkiyya" in the years 1821–25, as well as the Mahdist movement which ruled in Sudan from 1885–98, left their marks on the Sudanese scene and especially on its Islamic character. However, the more I studied pre-Condominium Sudan, the more I realized that the roots of the influence of Sufism or Popular Islam, which later was abbreviated as "Sectarianism," lay in the pre-colonial period when the Islamization of Sudan took place. I therefore decided to devote this paper to that period and to the failed attempts undertaken under Turco-Egyptian rule to bring Sudanese Islam into line with Azharite concepts of so-called Islamic orthodoxy.[1]

Holy families and Sufism under the Funj

The great success of Sufism and of the Holy Families in the Funj Sultanate of Sinnar, between the fifteenth and eighteenth centuries, is one of the main reasons leading to Sudan's Islamization. Sufi shaykhs and Muslim "holy men" had a large following in Sudan for a number of reasons.[2] First, although the process of Islamization by Muslim jurists (*fuqaha'*) had started earlier, Sufism was by far more popular and easier to comprehend than its orthodox counterpart. Second, by the sixteenth century Sufism had reached a rather low ebb and was tainted with many superstitions. Paradoxically, this paved the way for its absorption into a superficially Islamized population, such as that of the Sultanate of Sinnar, and made it much easier because local customs and superstitions were simply assimilated by the sufi orders. Third, the saint cult and *baraka* (divine blessing) were both inheritable and appealed to Sudan's tribes since they offered the population popular intermediaries with God. Consequently, the *fuqara'* (dervishes), or *fikis* (a corruption of *faqih*, Muslim jurist), as they were locally known, were better understood and more popular than the learned and knowledgeable *fuqaha'* or *'ulama'*. In his article on the role of the *'ulama'* in spreading Islam in the Sudan, Muhammad Ibrahim Abu Salim states that in the Sudan, unlike in some other Muslim states, there was no indigenous class of *'ulama'* who could fulfill special religious, cultural, or social functions. The Sudanese *'alim* was consequently first and foremost a loyal member of a Holy Family or a sufi order since Sufism was regarded in Sudan as the confirmed path to Muslim piety. Sudanese esteem, as far as men of religion were concerned, therefore preferred *tasawwuf* (mysticism) over *'ilm* (science; learning). The Sudanese *'alim* was, in most cases, a sufi who having memorized the Qur'an had decided to devote himself to further religious studies while maintaining his sufi beliefs and loyalties.[3]

Among those who introduced Islam into the Funj Sultanate there were holy families who had settled among the tribes, established their own Qur'an schools, and gained both influence and wealth.[4] The Awlad Jabir were one of these holy families who played an active role in the Islamization of Sudan from the beginning of the Funj Sultanate. They established schools in the Nilotic Sudan as well as in Dar Fur and Wadai and accumulated considerable wealth as well as social standing. The graduates of their schools became *'ulama'* in various parts of Sudan.[5] The Awlad Jabir also provide a good example of the accumulation of wealth and economic power in the hands of some of the holy families. Like many riverain tribesmen stemming primarily from the Ja'aliyyin and the Danaqla, who were driven from the Nile Valley to seek their fortunes in western Sudan, the Awlad Jabir too established branches of their family in Dar Fur and Wadai probably as part of this migration. But unlike the riverain tribal migrants who sought occupation primarily in trading, the Awlad Jabir, apart from their Islamic teaching, enhanced their position as major landowners and administrators. Their estates differed in size and value and in some cases included whole villages, as well as numerous slaves.[6]

Another holy family which illustrates the religious, social, and economic impact of these holy men was the Majdhubiyya. They were a family of *fuqara'*, residents of al-Damir situated on the Nile north of Omdurman, which was the center of the Ja'aliyyin tribe. As part of the Ja'aliyyin, the Majadhib claimed descent from 'Abbas, the Prophet's uncle. The founder of the Majdhubiyya was a Ja'ali *faqih*, Hamad ibn Muhammad al-Majdhub (b. 1693/94), who studied the Maliki legal treatises in Sudan and later made the pilgrimage to Mecca, where he studied and joined the Shadhiliyya sufi order. Upon his return he reorganized the community of al-Damir which was thereafter dominated by him and his offspring. The Funj Sultanate of Sinnar was in decline during that period but Islamic beliefs and institutions had gradually overcome traditional African ones and consequently al-Damir, under the influence of the Majadhib, became a flourishing religious center. When Bruce visited it in 1774, he described it as "a town *belonging* to Fakir Wed Madge Doub" [*sic* wad Majdhub], who is worshipped by the Ja'aliyyin. When, some forty years later, in 1814, Burckhardt visited the town, he wrote that all power was still vested in al-Faqih al-Kabir, while *baraka* was no longer confined only to the head of the Majadhib but had spread to other members of the family and even to some who were not directly related to it. Many of these *fuqaha'* had their own chapels next to their houses. But, according to Burckhardt "Friday prayers were always performed in the great mosque" of the Majadhib which also included a *madrasa* (a school of Islamic studies). The emphasis was on the training of students in Islamic law from as far West as Kordofan and Dar Fur. The teachers were mostly Majadhib *'ulama'* who had studied in Cairo or Mecca. Al-Damir thus became a well-known center for the administration of justice, in accordance with Islamic law. The office of *al-faqih al-kabir* (the great jurist) remained hereditary within the Majdhubiyya and his powers were considerable. Opposition to the Majadhib, even among the nomads in the vicinity of al-Damir, seems to have been negligible and their power, though derived from their religious standing, soon embraced all aspects of al-Damir's political, social, and economic life.[7] All this came to an end as a result of the Ja'aliyyin uprising against Turco-Egyptian rule in 1822 following which the Majadhib, who played a part in the revolt, had to escape from that region together with the Ja'aliyyin.

In order to comprehend the Islamic background of the Mahdiyya and the Weltanschauung of Muhammad Ahmad, its founder and first leader, an understanding of Sudan's larger sufi brotherhoods is also required. The intellectual innovations of the eighteenth- and nineteenth-century sufi orders, primarily attributed to Shaykh Ahmad ibn Idris, are not the concern of the present study and are probably not of particular relevance to the impact of the sufi heritage in Sudan on the Mahdiyya.[8] It is, however, relevant that some of these orders, notably the Sammaniyya and the Khatmiyya in the case of Sudan, introduced new organizational structures which paved the way for the winning of cross-tribal support within wider territories. This pattern of expansion entailed the incorporation of pre-existing religious centers into this new *tariqa* network. The Sammaniyya was the first of these new "supra-national" sufi brotherhoods. Muhammad b. 'Abd al-Karim al-Samman (1718–75), the founder of the new order, was initiated into the Khalwatiyya while on a visit to Cairo in 1760. Both he and his successors continued to live in al-Madina and it was through their *khulafa'* that their message was propagated in Indonesia, Malaysia, and Sudan. One of their *khulafa'* was Ahmad al-Tayyib wad al-Bashir, who had been initiated into the order while on a pilgrimage to al-Madina, in about 1764. Upon his return to Sudan he succeeded in recruiting Sudanese followers especially in the Gezira, south of Omdurman, where the Hamaj Regent Nasir b. Muhammad Abi Likaylik, joined the newly founded Sammaniyya order and granted Ahmad al-Tayyib an estate. Furthermore, several of the religious shaykhs of the earlier sufi orders such as the Halawiyyun, the Ya'qubab, and the Qadiriyya, also joined the Sammaniyya. The importance of this development lay in the fact that the prevailing trend in Sudanese Sufism had been one of small and rather diffused orders which had wielded little influence outside their limited circle of tribal followers.[9] The arrival of these more centralized and better organized supra-national orders, of which the Sammaniyya was a forerunner, helped to create an Islamic network whose impact transcended tribal or regional boundaries and hence had wider political implications. However, the Sammaniyya lost its impact soon after its founder's death. Ahmad al-Tayyib al-Bashir died in 1824, shortly after the Turco-Egyptian conquest of Sudan, without nominating his successor (*khalifa*). Consequently the followers of the order split into several groups under the leadership of rival *khulafa'*: Muhammad Sharif Nur al-Da'im (d. 1908–09), al-Qurashi wad al-Zayn (d. 1878), and Ahmad al-Basir (d. 1830). Thus the Sammaniyya, instead of assuming the stature of a centralized order with branches in several regions, split into numerous autonomous sub-orders due to clashes of personalities as well as diverse ethnic and regional loyalties.[10]

The Khatmiyya was another such supra-national order and its subsequent history differed from that of the Sammaniyya. It was first introduced into Sudan by Muhammad 'Uthman al-Mirghani (1793–1852), a member of a Sharifian family who had studied under Ahmad ibn Idris. He toured the Funj Sultanate of Sinnar on al-Idrisi's behalf, in 1815–19, namely on the eve of its conquest by Muhammad 'Ali's Egyptian army. In 1816 he entered Sinnar, the capital of the Funj Sultanate, and ini-tiated students into his embryonic Khatmiyya order.[11] Following the death of Ibn Idris, in October 1837, Muhammad 'Uthman sent his son Muhammad al-Hasan to found a Khatmiyya branch in Sudan and, for a variety of reasons mentioned later, gained immediate government support from the newly established Turco-Egyptian administration. Al-Sayyid al-Hasan al-Mirghani was of Sudanese origin. He was born in Bara in Kordofan in 1819 and was later sent to Mecca where he memorized the Qur'an and studied a wide range of Islamic topics with his father. Following his grad-uation, he was ordered by his father to return to Sudan, which was already ruled by Muhammad 'Ali's agents, and act as his *khalifa* in that country. Sayyid al-Hasan started an intensive missionary campaign in the riverain and eastern regions of northern Sudan. He appointed agents from among Khatmiyya supporters, including several contemporary holy men as well as followers of the Shadhiliyya order, who transferred their allegiance to him. The Khatmiyya's great success in Sudan was probably the product of a number of causes. First, due to its superior organization it was able to face challenges to its influence and did not suffer from internal splits like those which, as noted earlier, afflicted the Sammaniyya. Second, the Khatmiyya was one of the first among the new sufi orders of the Idrisi tradition to arrive in Sudan and hence its message was more coherent and less tainted by local superstitions. Third, and probably most important, Sayyid al-Hasan exploited the fact that the older and smaller sufi orders had been largely discredited and partly destroyed by Sudan's Egyptian rulers. He thus came to the riverain tribes, such as the Sha'iqiyya, as the charismatic holy man in whose *tariqa* they could find a substitute for their traditional institutions and superstitious *fikis*. Finally, the Khatmiyya benefited from its association with Sudan's new rulers, namely the Turco-Egyptians, whose conquest of Sudan coincided with the expansion of their *tariqa*. In this respect it is important to note that al-Sayyid al-Hasan associated with the Turco-Egyptian rulers at the explicit wish of his father.[12] Thus on the eve of the Turco-Egyptian conquest, the political, economic, and social power of the new sufi orders and the well-established holy families was superior to that of central government in the disintegrating Funj Sultanate which was conquered by Egypt in 1820–21.

Sufism and orthodox Islam under Turco-Egyptian rule: 1820–81

The annexation of Sudan by Egypt was undertaken in two stages. The first stage, in 1820–22 under Muhammad 'Ali the Ottoman Wali of Egypt and Egypt's de facto ruler until 1848, embraced primarily the central northern Sudan. The second stage of this conquest was completed under his grandson, the Khedive Isma'il, during the 1870s when he extended Egyptian rule to the Great Lakes in Central Africa and to Bahr al-Ghazal and Dar Fur in Western Sudan. In Sudanese history this period became known as the "First Turkiyya." The term Turkiyya is not really arbitrary since Egypt itself was an Ottoman province, ruled by an Ottoman (Albanian) dynasty. Moreover, most of the high officials and army officers serving in Sudan were of Ottoman rather than Egyptian origin. Lastly, though Arabic made considerable headway during the second half of the nineteenth century in Sudan's daily administrative usage, senior officers and officials communicated in Ottoman Turkish, since Turkish was the language of the ruling elite even though their superior – the Khedive – was of Albanian origin. The Egyptian army brought with it three *'ulama'* belonging respectively to the Shafi'i, Hanafi, and Maliki schools. Of the three only the Maliki *qadi*, Ahmad al-Salawi, played a significant role since most of the Sudanese were followers of the Maliki *madhhab*. He supported their schools (*kuttabs*), befriended their *'ulama'* and granted young Sudanese graduates employment opportunities in the newly founded *shari'a* courts and in other government offices. He was also the first to encourage Sudanese *'ulama'* to put pen to paper and consequently we have to thank him for Ahmad Abu 'Ali's history of the Kings of Sinnar, known as "The Funj Chronicle" (*kitab al-shuna*), which has remained a primary source for the study of that period.[13]

But although the conquered regions of northern Sudan were already Arabized and superficially Islamized, the new rulers badly needed a local elite with whom they could communicate and whom they could trust to act on their behalf in fulfilling certain administrative functions, hitherto unknown in the newly annexed territories. The elite of Sudan at the time of the invasion consisted primarily of two elements: tribal shaykhs and heads of holy families and sufi orders. The Ottoman–Egyptians viewed neither of these groups as trustworthy, since both were naturally loyal to their local adherents and in the case of the sufis and *fikis*, their mysticism – tainted with local superstitions – was abhorrent to the new rulers. They therefore looked for possible allies who seemed to be more dependable and hence trustworthy.

Among the tribal population their choice fell on the Sha'iqiyya, one of the northern riverain tribes whose villages were spread along the Nile south of the Egyptian border. They had fought against the Egyptian army when it first invaded northern Sudan, in 1820, but following their defeat had become trustworthy allies of the new rulers. The Sha'iqiyya supplied the government with irregular soldiers (*bash buzuq*) who acted as tax collectors among the other tribes and were in return exempt from taxation. Military raids led by the Sha'iqiyya became a regular method of tax collection, hated and feared by the other tribes. Another tribe whose interests seemed at first to coincide with those of Sudan's new rulers were the Ja'aliyyin, who were leading *jallaba* (traders) and hence benefited from the newly established order. The Ja'aliyyin *jallaba*, as well as traders from other riverain tribes, engaged in barter trading especially during slack agricultural periods when their small farms could be left in the hands of their families and their slaves. They initially welcomed Turkish rule since in addition to security it also led to greater prosperity through the establishment of military posts and improved communications. However, heavy taxation soon drove many of the smaller riverain farmers from their lands, since they were in no position to pay the taxes. Furthermore, shortage of cash with which to pay these taxes forced them to hand over their cattle and their house slaves on whom their agricultural production depended. The Egyptian historian Muhammad Fu'ad Shukri thus lists the heavy taxes, which in numerous cases exceeded the value of the taxed article, as a major cause for discontent which led to the Ja'aliyyin revolt in 1822–23. He also emphasized the brutality and corruption involved in the extraction of these taxes by the Sha'iqiyya tax collectors. In fact the mass escape of oppressed peasants who could not pay their taxes from the riverain regions to Dar Fur, the Nuba Mountains and Bahr al-Ghazal, in the western Sudan, created a new class of migratory *jallaba* who thrived in these regions and became involved in the trade in ivory and slaves. Most of them made their livelihood as small merchants hoping to return to their homes once they became rich. But this happened only to few of them, primarily to those who engaged in large-scale trade in ivory or slaves. Others became peddlers and middlemen and could barely make ends meet.[14]

The Turco-Egyptian conquest established a relatively modern administrative system in Sudan with which neither the old holy families nor the sufi orders could compete. Within the traditional Islamic elite there consequently emerged a feeling of frustration and hostility, leading to identity or solidarity transcending both tribes and villages, against the Turks as the common enemy. Those who rebelled like the Ja'aliyyin or the Majdhubiyya suffered defeat. Others who collaborated, like the Sha'iqiyya and the Khatmiyya sufi order, managed to break out of their confined regions and became part of the new state system, creating centralized organizations throughout the Sudan.[15]

The Khatmiyya was, as mentioned earlier, the only well-organized sufi order which collaborated with the Turco-Egyptian rulers and did not denounce them as alien conquerors. Not unlike the government, the Khatmiyya encouraged a more centralized "orthodox" Islam rather than the diffused *fiki*-oriented sufism, which had prevailed in Sudan until its arrival. It therefore found in the Turco-Egyptian rulers natural allies. The religious centers of the Khatmiyya were tolerated and even subsidized by the new rulers who also exempted the Khatmiyya shaykhs from taxation. As for the older generation of sufi orders, several methods were employed to undermine their leadership, though with varying degrees of success. The introduction of Shari'a courts alongside government-supported *khalwas* or *kuttabs* (Qur'an schools), was aimed at curtailing the sufi hold over their adherents. In certain cases, sons of sufi leaders were sent to al-Azhar to study and were later appointed to government posts as teachers or *qadis*. However, the Turkiyya failed in its attempts to replace sufi orders or local *fikis* with its newly imported Azharite *'ulama'*. This was the result of the popularity of local holy men among the rural population. The *fuqara'*, as they were called, did not fill merely a religious function, they also played a dominant social role in the spheres of education and health within their societies. Hence, even after the introduction of Azharite educated *'ulama'*, *shari'a* courts under government control, government-run schools, and modern clinics, the majority of the rural people continued to prefer their local "holy men" (*fikis*), since they were imbued with *karama* (saintliness) and *baraka* (blessing). People who suffered from government oppression, taxation and forced labor could hardly be expected to trust the Azhari *qadi* or *'alim*, both of whom were government employees. Instead they remained loyal to the *fuqara'* who had healed them and guided them through previous calamities, and who shared similar interests.[16]

Relations between the Khatmiyya and the government were not always cordial and after al-Sayyid al-Hasan's death, several Khatmi agents were arrested and their privileges were abolished. Thus, when we attempt to explain the success of the Khatmiyya's missionary campaign, we need to place more emphasis on the appeal of its spiritual message, on the one hand, and on the charisma of al-Sayyid al-Hasan, on the other. Sayyid al-Hasan died on 18 November 1869 and his son, Sayyid Muhammad 'Uthman II, was recognized by the family and the principal agents of the Khatmiyya as his successor. He had to face several challenges following his appointment. There was, as mentioned above, a change in the attitude of the government toward the order which brought about the arrest of several Khatmiyya leaders and the cancellation of their privileges. This affected especially the northern regions of Dongola and Berber, both strongholds of the Khatmiyya. Luckily for Sayyid Muhammad 'Uthman II, the change in government policy was a temporary setback and after 1873 the government's cordial relations with the Khatmiyya order were resumed.[17] A further challenge to the Khatmiyya emerged at that time due to the arrival in the Sha'iqiyya region of numerous additional followers of Shaykh Ibn Idris who founded the new Ahmadiyya Idrisiyya order in that region. Al-Mirghani wrote a pamphlet in which he claimed that the Khatmiyya was the "seal" (*al-khatm*) of Sufism, namely the ultimate *tariqa*, and that he was the last of the *awliya'* from whose descendants the expected *mahdi* would appear.[18] It is therefore hardly surprising that when Muhammad Ahmad made his manifestation as *al-mahdi al-muntazar* (the expected Mahdi), in June 1881, Sayyid Muhammad 'Uthman II sent out messages in which he denounced the Mahdi as an impostor and the Mahdiyya as a "blind and deaf [agent of] sedition whose advocates are at the gates of hell."[19] This denunciation of Muhammad Ahmad's claim to be the *mahdi* was a natural outcome of the Khatmiyya's claim that its shaykhs belonged to the ranks of *qutb al-aqtab* (the sufi "pole of poles") and *khatm al-wilaya al-muhammadiyya* ("seal of the representation of Muhammad"), on the basis of direct prophetic sanction.[20] According to some accounts, the Mahdi even offered to make Muhammad 'Uthman II one of his four *khulafa'* but the latter declined. Instead he helped to recruit anti-Mahdist forces among his followers in eastern Sudan. In June 1884, when it became clear that the Mahdiyya was gaining ground, he escaped with his younger son 'Ali al-Mirghani via Massawa to Sawakin, from where they proceeded to Egypt and continued to make propaganda against the Mahdiyya until the Mahdist state was destroyed in September 1898. It is therefore no wonder that when the Khatmiyya headquarters near Kassala were conquered by the Mahdist amir 'Uthman Diqna, its central mosque and al-Sayyid al-Hasan's tomb were both destroyed.[21]

Muhammad Ahmad b. 'Abdallah, the future *mahdi*, was initiated into the Sammaniyya at an early stage of his life. Muhammad Sharif, the founder's grandson, was one of his first sufi teachers but, following a dispute, he expelled him from the order. Muhammad Ahmad then transferred his allegiance to al-Qurashi wad al-Zayn, a Sammani shaykh of a rival branch, and later married his daughter. He stayed with his new teacher until 1878 and helped to erect Shaykh Qurashi's tomb following his death in that year. It is consequently of no wonder that the Sammaniyya under al-Qurashi and Ahmad al-Basir, to whom Muhammad Ahmad remained loyal, joined the Mahdiyya at the outset, while his first Sammani teacher Shaykh Muhammad al-Bashir continued to oppose him. The Mahdi inadvertently benefited from the fragmentation of the Sammaniyya since in a centralized order under one Shaykh recognized by all followers, he would probably not have succeeded in his initial claim to the Mahdiship. The Mahdiyya needed a centralized Islamic structure to enable it to spread its message. But, unlike the Khatmiyya, Mahdist revivalism was intertwined with the social and economic transformation of the state, which made cooperation with the rulers impossible. The socio-economic policies adopted by the Turco-Egyptian rulers, especially with regard to the slave trade, played into the Mahdi's hands since because of them the people of Sudan were "ready to hear and participate in the mission of 'reviving' Islam in their area."[22]

Although the "civilizing mission" of Khedive Isma'il included the introduction of "orthodox" Islam into the newly acquired regions, he seems to have been primarily motivated by political and economic ambitions rather than by religious zeal. With the aim of acquiring regions on the Red Sea, Isma'il exploited the threat of Christian missionaries in order to convince the Sultan to cede them to permanent Egyptian rule. Similarly, his establishment of Shari'a courts in Sawakin and its hinterland, with Azhari *qadis*, probably stemmed from his desire to subjugate the semi-pagan Beja and introduce orderly government, rather than from the purely religious belief in the superiority of orthodox Islam. Khedive Isma'il and his Armenian prime minister Nubar Pasha had both been educated in France and were imbued with its secular ideology. They sought to create a Europeanized Egyptian empire in Africa, in which Islam would play a role but would never be allowed to interfere with Khedive Isma'il's political and modernizing ambitions. Yet this so-called "civilizing mission" by which Islam was granted only a limited political role came to an end as the result of Egypt's bankruptcy and the consequent decline in the efficiency of Turco-Egyptian administration after the mid-1870s. Furthermore, Egyptian rule had expanded the means of communication and brought security to Sudan. It thereby enabled small merchants and preachers, such as the future *mahdi* Muhammad Ahmad, to travel to western Sudan with relative ease. The anti-Turkish message which the future *mahdi* and other holy men preached was aided by the rapid social and economic decline and the growing oppressiveness of the rulers. It thus appealed to an ever-expanding audience. Muhammad Ahmad, like other sufi leaders, tribal shaykhs, and merchants, although a "non-nationalist," was expressing the anti-Turkish feelings of a large segment of the population.[23] The Sudan was ready for a jihad led by a *mahdi* against "corrupt" and un-Islamic Turkish rule, just as Egypt, hit by bankruptcy, was ready for the 'Urabi revolt which led subsequently to the British conquest of the Nile Valley.

Sufis and *'ulama'* under the Mahdi: 1881–85

Muhammad Ahmad b. 'Abdallah, the Mahdi of nineteenth-century Sudan, was the founder of an Islamic messianic movement who sought to implement pure uncorrupt Islam, under the banner of revivalism and renewal (*ihya wa-tajdid*). Our interest in the Mahdi, in this study, concerns primarily his sufi background and the question whether the Mahdist movement can be seen as a continuation of the traditions introduced into Sudan by the holy families mentioned earlier. Muhammad Ahmad received his early religious education from his father, a Dongolawi ship-builder, who had moved to Karari with his family to further his business. Following his father's untimely death, he entered a local Qur'anic school. His mother Zaynab (?) and two of his brothers were by that time also in Karari, where they carried on the business of building boats and barges started by their father and cared for the young Muhammad Ahmad.[24] Following his memorizing of *sura* 114 of the Qur'an, which was a normal feat for Muslim boys,[25] the young Muhammad Ahmad proceeded northwards to Berber, half-way between Omdurman and Dongola, to continue his studies under the *faqih* Muhammad al-Khayr 'Abdallah Khojali. He studied there for three years and established close relations with members of the local Majdhubiyya holy family. Following several years of "theological and juristic" study, Muhammad Ahmad returned to Khartoum where he joined the Sammaniyya sufi order, while studying with Shaykh Nur al-Da'im.[26]

According to Schoenfeld, it was at that time that Muhammad Ahmad started his travels to Sennar, Kordofan and Darfur in order to spread the Sammani message. He next moved to Aba Island on the White Nile where he led a very puritanical life. Two of his brothers joined him there and pursued their previous trade as barge-builders, while he himself cultivated a small plot of land growing the little food he required.

It was there that he met 'Abdullahi al-Ta'aishi, who arrived from Darfur to join him and who later became his Khalifa. 'Abdullahi was so impressed by Muhammad Ahmad's holiness, personality and his words of wisdom that he "was content to simply look at him and listen to his teaching." Only after several hours of listening in awe did he dare to ask to be allowed to become one of Muhammad Ahmad's disciples.[27] Muhammad Ahmad's early education was therefore quite typical of that of other children born in the riverain Sudan. This involved memorizing the Qur'an and subsequently, if demonstrating both interest and talent, moving on to nearby holy men in order to undertake further studies. In the case of Muhammad Ahmad these holy men, or *fuqaha'*, included teachers belonging to two of the best known holy families, the Majdhubiyya and the Sammaniyya.

The most comprehensive biography of the Mahdi is the *sira* – or biographical chronicle – describing the life and the campaigns of Muhammad Ahmad al-Mahdi, as written by Isma'il b. 'Abd al-Qadir, one of his contemporary adherents – on orders from the Mahdi's Khalifa 'Abdullahi al-Ta'aishi. The *sira*, in a condensed version translated and annotated by Haim Shaked, is of great significance since it presents us with a Sudanese nineteenth-century point of view of both the Turkiyya and the Mahdist state.[28] The Mahdi, as *khalifat rasul allah*, played a central role within the Mahdist movement. Without the attributes of a *mahdi*, which Muhammad Ahmad and his adherents were convinced he possessed, such a movement could not have started let alone succeeded. Mahdism was consequently modeled, to a large extent, on the historical heritage of the Prophet and the four just Caliphs (*al-khulafa' al-rashidun*), which was the only period in Islamic history when the *umma* was undivided and followed a path leading to the establishment of a just community of believers, based on the Qur'an and the *Sunna*. Muhammad Ahmad projected himself as having been appointed to the supreme succession (*al-khilafa al-kubra*) as Successor of the Apostle of God (*khalifat rasul allah*), where his leading disciples were the successors of the rightly-guided caliphs (*al-rashidun*). Three of these were appointed soon after his manifestation. 'Abdullahi b. Muhammad al-Ta'aishi's status was recognized in his title of *Khalifat al-siddiq*, that is the successor of Abu Bakr. An early follower of the Mahdi, 'Ali b. Muhammad Hilu ('Ali wad Hilu) was appointed the successor of 'Umar (*khalifat al-faruq*), and the Mahdi's young son-in-law, Muhammad Sharif b. Hamid, was appropriately named the successor of 'Ali (*khalifat al-qarrar*). The appointment of the successor of 'Uthman was offered by the Mahdi, in May 1883, to the contemporary head of the Sanusiyya sufi order, Muhammad al-Mahdi, whose co-operation Muhammad Ahmad was anxious to obtain, but the offer was ignored.[29]

When announcing his manifestation, on 29 June 1881, Muhammad Ahmad based his claim largely on his reputation as a sufi shaykh of the Sammaniyya order, with considerable following in the White Nile region. The Sammaniyya had predicted that the *mahdi* would be one of its adherents and one of its leaders, Shaykh al-Qurashi Wad al-Zayn, had stated that his tomb would be erected by the future *mahdi*. Thus, following his death in 1878, his pupil and follower, Muhammad Ahmad b. 'Abdallah, erected the tomb and subsequently advised Shaykh Muhammad al-Tayyib al-Basir and other Sammani leaders to free themselves "of all worldly affairs and be in readiness for a Godly mission." On the day of his manifestation, Muhammad Ahmad wrote once again to Shaykh al-Basir informing him that the Prophet had instructed him to shoulder the honorable mission of the expected *mahdi*. In his letter the future Sudanese Mahdi described a vision in which the Prophet Muhammad addressed him and several saints, mostly of the Sammaniyya order, telling them that "whoever does not regard his [Muhammad Ahmad's] Mahdiship as true is an unbeliever in God and His Apostle."[30] It was further emphasized that the Mahdi's office was eternal since, like the Prophet, he was created out of the "sacred light of God." Moreover, the announcement, which was made during a prophetic colloquy (*hadra nabawiyya*), emphasized that Muslims who did not follow the Mahdi or who rejected his mission were heretics. The Mahdi therefore claimed to possess all the requirements and attributes (*al-shurut wal-awsaf*) demanded of the historic *mahdi*, according to the Maghribi school. Muhammad Ahmad claimed that as the Mahdiyya was one of the pillars of Islam, those who refused to follow him were *kuffar* (unbelievers). His doctrine and judicial verdicts thereby became infallible.[31]

The Mahdi styled himself the Prophet's successor, but did not attempt to cite proof-texts from the Qur'an or the hadith (traditions) to buttress his claim. It was only in later letters that such texts were cited but even then Muhammad Ahmad's sufi background remained predominant. This was used against him by both Egyptian and Sudanese *'ulama'* who ridiculed him for failing to comply with the criteria indicated in the traditions regarding the expected *mahdi*. Moreover, the *'ulama'* also attacked Muhammad Ahmad for declaring jihad against the Turks, which they viewed as a reprehensible slaughter of Muslims.[32] The *'ulama'* who opposed the Mahdi based their arguments primarily on the absolute legitimacy of Ottoman rule, which embodied the Caliphate to which all Muslims owed unquestionable obedience. They rejected Muhammad Ahmad's claims to the Mahdiship, declaring that since there was a legitimate Caliph in office "a *bay'a* (oath of allegiance) to another person was null and void and had no effect whatsoever." Muhammad Ahmad refuted these arguments, stating that the office of the Caliphate had ceased to exist long ago and the present rulers in Turkey and Egypt must be deposed since they had "turned away from the law of the Lord of the messengers."[33] Isma'il b. 'Abd al-Qadir, the author of the Mahdi's biography, ridiculed the anti-Mahdist claims of Egyptian *'ulama'* and compared their support for 'Urabi's revolt with their rejection of the Mahdi's mission. The fact that they issued *fatwas* against the Khedive Tawfiq and his allies "rendered the fighting against the Turks obligatory on all Muslims, let alone the Mahdi, whose very mission was to do away with the Turks."[34] It is also significant that the author portrayed the Turks as *a'da' al-din* (enemies of faith), and even as enemies of God and *kuffar*, while the Christians in general and the British in particular were treated with more respect. His portrayal of Turkish wickedness reiterated many of the Mahdi's own criticisms of Sudan's foreign rulers, evident in this message:

> [The land] was filled with oppression and tyranny by the Turks, who profaned the sacrosanctities of the Religion and imposed the poll-tax on the Muslims. Falsity and infamy spread amongst them and they obeyed Satan and rebelled against the Merciful [God]. They hastened to obliterate the traces of Islam and they did not fear Allah ...[35]

In his paper on revolutionary aspects in the Mahdi's ideology, Muhammad Sa'id al-Qaddal emphasized the fact that the Mahdi divided the world into two: that of the Mahdiyya and that of the Turkiyya. The dividing line between them was the acceptance of the Mahdi's *da'wa*. All those who refused were unbelievers (*kuffar*) and hence belonged to the non-Muslim Turkish world whose blood should be shed in the forthcoming jihad and whose possessions were legal booty for the community of true believers. According to al-Qaddal, the purpose of this revolutionary approach was rather pragmatic since the Mahdi had to overcome the Turco-Egyptian enemy and total jihad was both justified and necessary under these circumstances. However, as in many revolutionary ideologies, this too proved to be an obstacle in later developments since it dictated the perpetuation of jihad against both Egypt and Ethiopia, even after the enemy had been expelled from Sudan's boundaries. Consequently, this endless war undermined the economic and political stability of the Mahdist state leading to military defeats and economic disaster. In the final analysis, al-Qaddal concludes, this ultimately facilitated the European penetration into the region.[36]

Faithfulness, as expressed in the Mahdist *bay'a*, was based on the oath of allegiance, first enunciated by the Prophet. It later was adopted with certain variations also by the heads of numerous sufi orders. However, the Mahdi realized at an early stage that he had to define his movement and its supporters in a distinctive way so as to differentiate between them and the many other sufi orders scattered throughout Sudan. Although in the initial stages of his movement the support of the sufi shaykhs and their followers was essential, it later became intolerable since in the Mahdiyya there could be only one central authority, the Mahdi and later the Khalifa 'Abdullahi. The Mahdi's followers, who in the early stages of the revolt were still called *fuqara'* or *darawish*, following sufi custom, were thereafter renamed *ansar* in line with the precedent of the Prophet's supporters. The Mahdi's ostensible reason in issuing this decree was that since his followers were promised paradise as a reward for their faithful devotion and willingness to die in jihad, they could not go by their previous sufi titles, which indicated poverty and humility. However, those who refused to join the Mahdi continued to be known as *fuqara'* or *darawish* since they did not deserve paradise.[37]

As noted, sufi traditions played a predominant role in Sudanese Islam. However, the new sufi orders, founded since the eighteenth century, were more outgoing and missionary in their approach but, at the same time, less flexible in their attitude to pre-Islamic traditions or local superstitions. Their emphasis on the *da'wa* also helped them to go beyond the older established orders. It was thus crucial for the Mahdi to gain the support of these well organized and centralized orders, especially during the early stages of his movement, since he could exploit their organizations in order to spread his own *da'wa* among their members. First he relied on the support of his fellow members in the Sammaniyya and he convinced some of the order's shaykhs to attend his colloquy. He then recruited followers of the Tijaniyya and Isma'iliyya orders, when he set out to spread his mission in the Western Sudan. The Isma'iliyya order in Kordofan is a good example of this wise policy, since it was from Jabal Qadir in southern Kordofan that the Mahdi intended to start his jihad. Led by Muhammad Isma'il al-Makki, the Isma'iliyya, which had been oppressed by the Turkish administration, embraced the Mahdi as the expected savior even before his manifestation as *al-mahdi al-muntazar*. This support, combined with that of the powerful Baqqara tribes in Kordofan and Dar Fur, provided the Mahdi with the popular base required for his campaigns in the West. As to the eastern Sudan, the Majdhubiyya, which had also suffered from Turkish oppression ever since the Ja'aliyyin rebellion in 1822, helped him in gaining support among the Beja tribes in the Red Sea region.[38] When the Mahdist troops threatened al-Qadarif in April 1884, the Majadhib were allegedly involved in bringing about the peaceful surrender of the town. Initially, the Mahdi permitted the continuation of Qur'anic education in al-Qadarif, but in his letter to Ahmad b. al-Hajj 'Ali al-Majdhub he clearly stated that precedence had to be given to the jihad and that the study of the Qur'an was only allowed as long as the Mahdist amir responsible for the area did not personally go on a military campaign.[39] Ahmad b. Hajj 'Ali al-Majdhub served as imam and teacher in al-Qadarif for some time after the Mahdist revolt. However, continuing war, drought, and hunger led to a disruption of studies and the school had to be closed. Among the Mahdi's early adherents there were, not surprisingly, many sufi shaykhs and members of their orders who believed that the Mahdist militant brand of popular Islam would help them to get rid of the alien *'ulama'*, imported by the Turco-Egyptian rulers from al-Azhar, and thus help them to regain their previous standing. The Khatmiyya was the only large and important sufi order which did not join the Mahdi despite his repeated appeals. It rejected him, first, because of its claim regarding the status of Muhammad 'Uthman al-Mirghani II, who was created out of the Prophet's light and thus was superior to the impostor Muhammad Ahmad. Second, as part of the new urban class, the social and economic interests of Khatmiyya adherents were largely linked with those of the Egyptians. Offshoots of the Khatmiyya such as the Isma'iliyya in Kordofan as well as Khatmiyya adherents in Western Sudan were, as mentioned, among the early supporters of Muhammad Ahmad al-Mahdi. But although most of the Khatmiyya leaders and their followers believed in the coming of a *mahdi*, they refused to recognize Muhammad Ahmad as such. The supreme Shaykhs of the order, Muhammad 'Uthman II and Muhammad Sirr al-Khatim II, persisted in their anti-Mahdist propaganda throughout the existence of the Mahdist state, both within the Sudan and in Egypt. Muhammad 'Uthman II used the Khatmiyya headquarters near Kassala as an anti-Mahdist center and traveled throughout the region in order to gather as many anti-Mahdists as possible around him. Even General Charles Gordon, during his last mission in Sudan in 1884–85, used Muhammad 'Uthman II in order to correspond with the outside world from the besieged Khartoum. But finally Muhammad 'Uthman was forced to withdraw, first to Sawakin and later to Egypt, where he died in 1886. His son Sayyid 'Ali al-Mirghani later settled in Cairo, with Sirr al-Khatim II, to study at al-Azhar. Following their departure from Sudan, al-Bakri al-Mirghani became the leader of the Khatmiyya at Kassala where he and his followers swore allegiance to the Mahdist state, now led by the Khalifa 'Abdullahi. However, al-Bakri continued to oppose the Mahdiyya and even took part in military actions against the Ansar. Several prominent Khatmiyya leaders, including Maryam bint Hashim al-Mirghani, were imprisoned during the Mahdiyya and remained under arrest until after the Anglo-Egyptian conquest.[40] The Mahdist state later turned even against its most loyal sufi allies since it refused to tolerate their divided loyalties and demanded complete submission first to the Mahdi and later to the Khalifa. In a proclamation issued by the Khalifa, early in 1884, he denounced, in the Mahdi's name, all sufi orders as divisive and called upon their adherents to disband them and grant their undivided loyalty to the Mahdiyya.[41] The Mahdi himself also dealt in some detail with the relationship between Sufism and the Mahdist *da'wa*. He compared sufi beliefs to "water wells" from which the adherents drank so as to quench their spiritual thirst. However, now that a great sea of water, namely the Mahdiyya, had engulfed all these small wells it no longer made sense to drink from them since they were now within the (spiritual) sea of the Mahdiyya. Quoting from Ahmad al-Tayyib w. al-Bashir, the Mahdi expressed this in a letter to the Sammaniyya Shaykh, Muhammad al-Tayyib al-Basir.[42] The stage of cooperation with friendly sufi orders had thus come to an end and the Mahdist theocracy was well on its way.

The Mahdi styled himself the Prophet's successor but as noted did not attempt to cite proof-texts from the Qur'an or the hadith to buttress his claim. This can be explained partly by Muhammad Ahmad's sufi background. His was a charismatic leadership in which *baraka*, implying an active power of holiness, played an important role. The citing of texts from the hadith was therefore of lesser significance to him and to the majority of both sufi shaykhs and followers in Sudan, than to his antagonists the Azhar-trained *'ulama'*. The Mahdi denounced them as evil (*'ulama' al-su'*), because of their exclusive dependence on the written texts and their failure to accept him. He stated that "texts cannot bind God's will" and accused them of having become subservient to forms while ignoring the content. He did not forgive them for allying themselves with non-Muslims and acting in defiance of Islam at the behest of their alien masters. According to the Mahdi they refrained from implementing the *shari'a* and even sanctioned the breaking of the fast of Ramadan by the pro-government troops in Khartoum, so that they could fight against the Ansar. Their excuse was that the Prophet had sanctioned the conquest of Mecca under similar circumstances. The Mahdi stated that he did not oppose the *'ulama'* for their learning but for their subservience to texts which they misused to denounce his mission and to justify their support of a corrupt government. In other words, he contended that most *'ulama'*, limited by their scientific methods, lacked the tools inherent in Sufism to comprehend his mission.[43] It is noteworthy that his opponents among the *'ulama'* did not reject the idea of a *mahdi* but concentrated on proving that Muhammad Ahmad was a pretender (*mutamahdi*). They did not denounce the concept of the *mahdi* as heretical, probably because this belief prevailed in Sudan's sufi traditions. On the other hand there were according to al-Sadiq al-Mahdi, the Mahdi's great grandson, many *'ulama'* both in Sudan and Egypt who justified the Mahdi's call for a jihad against the Sultan (*al-khuruj 'ala al-sultan*) for the following reasons. First, they regarded Khedive Tawfiq as a collaborator with British colonialism and therefore as unfit to rule. Hence the Mahdi, like 'Urabi in Egypt, had a duty to fight against the Egyptian attempt to conquer Sudan. Second, every Muslim had a duty to rise up against the Ottoman Sultan 'Abd al-Hamid II who had betrayed Islam through his support of Christian foreigners. The prerogative of Muslim unity and submission to the legitimate ruler, therefore, no longer applied and the Mahdist uprising was fully justified. Third, Islam required an active leader who would implement the laws of religion. It was immaterial whether this role was fulfilled by the Mahdi of Sudan or by someone else. Among the *'ulama'* who sent messages of support to the Mahdi was Shaykh Ahmad al-'Awwam, one of Ahmad 'Urabi's supporters, who had been exiled to Sudan and was later imprisoned in Khartoum by General Gordon. His message of support was sent to the Mahdi from the besieged city in 1884 but failed to reach him until after the Mahdist conquest of Khartoum in January 1885.[44] Similar views were expressed by Jamal al-Din al-Afghani and Muhammad 'Abduh and published in their journal *al-'Urwa al-Wuthqa* while they lived in Paris.[45]

The Mahdi and his *ansar* had meanwhile undertaken the *hijra* to Jabal Qadir in the Nuba Mountains in order to escape from government revenge, just as the Prophet and his followers had undertaken the *hijra* to Yathrib (Medina) in flight from their enemies some 1250 years earlier. The Mahdi's call for jihad was also modeled on that of the Prophet. It was a holy war seeking to convince the unbelievers, whether corrupt Muslims, Christians, or pagans, that there was only one just cause. Those who refused to join the true religion, as propagated by the Mahdi, were imprisoned, killed in battle, or exiled from Sudan. They included many of the leading *'ulama'*, as well as heads of sufi orders and tribal shaykhs. However, the jihad aimed to liberate not only Sudan but all the domains ruled by the corrupt Ottoman Sultan, starting in Egypt.[46] Although the pre-*hijra* stage was largely dominated by Muhammad Ahmad's sufi allies, headed by Muhammad al-Tayyib al-Basir and the Sammaniyya order, the post-*hijra* stage diminished the sufi connection and strengthened the position of the western tribes, such as the Baqqara, on the one hand, and the Nuba kingdoms, on the other. The alliance with King Adam 'Umar, the independent ruler of Jabal Taqali, was crucial in enabling the safe arrival of the Mahdi and his followers at Jabal Qadir, on 1 November 1881 (7 Dhu al-Hijja 1298). Thus the western regions became the main source of Mahdist support already at an early stage of the movement and its natural area for gaining new adherents and additional territories was in Dar Fur and Bahr al-Ghazal, while the Nile regions and the Gezira had to wait for a later stage. It was in the West that the Mahdi's Ansar had their first decisive military triumphs in December 1881 and May 1882.

Following the victory over Yusuf Hasan al-Shalali, on May 30, 1882, the Mahdi declared the implementation of his governing laws. In a way, this may be viewed as the beginning of independent Sudanese statehood. It was at Jabal Qadir that he organized his government and appointed his *khulafa'* to govern in various regions. He also divided the army into three commands or flags, the red flag under Muhammad Sharif his cousin, the green, under 'Ali wad Hilu, and the blue (or black) flag, under 'Abdullahi al-Ta'aishi; in addition there was the white command flag, carried by the Mahdi's brother Muhammad 'Abdallah. He appointed his close friend Ahmad Sulayman as head of the newly constituted treasury (*amin bayt al-mal*) while Ahmad Jubara was named *qadi al-Islam*.[47]

Although the Mahdi's early victories over government troops were viewed as the final proof of the validity of his mission, he soon met with a new obstacle. Government troops were capable of prolonged resistance in fortified positions and an attempt to storm El-Obeid (al-Ubayyid) the provincial capital of Kordofan, on

8 September 1882, was a complete failure. Thereafter the Mahdi relied upon siege tactics, and the tribal forces were supplemented with a corps known as the *jihadiyya*, largely recruited from captured government troops of southern Sudanese origin and of the ex-slave armies, also southerners, who had joined the Mahdi with their previous commanders. They were provided with firearms, which the Mahdi was anxious to keep out of the hands of the undisciplined tribal warriors. The surrender of El-Obeid, on 19 January 1883, gave the Mahdi an urban administrative center and Kordofan formed the first nucleus of a territorial Mahdist state. In the meantime, khedivial control had been further weakened by the British occupation of Egypt, in September 1882, and the reluctance of the British government to undertake any further administrative or military commitments in Sudan. An Egyptian expeditionary force was, however, organized with Colonel William Hicks, a retired Indian Army officer, as chief of staff. Advancing through difficult terrain from the White Nile into Kordofan, it was annihilated by the Ansar at Shaykan, on 5 November 1883. The Mahdi was now the master of the West. Dar Fur and Bahr al-Ghazal were evacuated or surrendered by their European governors, the Austrian, Rudolf von Slatin, and the Italian, Romolo Gessi, in December 1883 and April 1884 respectively.[48] Meanwhile, 'Uthman Diqna, a descendant of a mercantile family in Sawakin, had been sent in May 1883 to raise the revolt among the Beja of the Red Sea province, a mission in which he was supported by the influential leader of the disgruntled Majdhubiyya holy family, Shaykh al-Tahir al-Majdhub. Consequently, by the end of February 1884 the Red Sea region was under Mahdist control and only Sawakin remained in Egyptian hands.[49] The Ansar were now rapidly closing in on Khartoum. 'Uthman Diqna's success closed the route from the Red Sea to the Nile, while the fall of Berber to an army of Ansar, in May 1884, put an end to traffic along the Nile to Egypt. Military pressure on Khartoum itself was increasing, and between April and October 1884 the Mahdi brought up his main forces from El-Obeid to Omdurman where they set up camp opposite the capital. Weakened by siege, the city fell on 25 January 1885, Gordon Pasha, the governor-general, being killed in the fighting.[50]

From his new seat of government in Omdurman, legislation was undertaken by the Mahdi after the fall of Khartoum. He revised some of his earlier formulations and intended to compile them into a comprehensive body of law, a task that was, however, interrupted by his sudden death. In order to achieve his goals the Mahdi had to create a unique legal methodology that provided him with unlimited authority to enact positive rules without interference from orthodox *'ulama'*. This implied meeting custom and tribal law half-way while maintaining puritanism in matters pertaining to morality and ethics. It also enabled a charismatic leader, like the Mahdi, to out-maneuver his antagonists and solve the daily political and social problems within the Mahdist theocracy, without undue interference. "The Mahdi's legal methodology, though simple and unsophisticated, seems to have been effective in enabling him to achieve his goals. He ignored all schools of law (*madhahib*) and disregarded their legal literature, thus releasing himself from the burden of *taqlid*, and the positive law as consolidated within these schools."[51] The Mahdi acknowledged three sources of law, in the following order: the Sunna, the Qur'an, and the *ilham* (inspiration) transmitted to him by the Prophet. In this he agreed with other reformist or revivalist movements, such as the Wahhabiyya and the Sanusiyya, who emphasized the Sunna and the Qur'an as sources of law, and replaced *qiyas* (analogical reasoning) with direct inspiration (*ilham*) from the Prophet. Since such inspirations were not subject to the *ijma'* (consensus) of the *'ulama'* this gave him greater freedom in establishing the Islamic law in accordance with the dictates of his movement. *Ijtihad* (independent judgment), in which customary law also played a significant role, was preserved for the Mahdi alone. It was a personal *ijtihad* in which *ilham* (inspiration) played a role exceeding that allowed by analogical reasoning (*qiyas*). To this, one should add the impact of the Mahdi's sufi background, first within the Sammaniyya order and later through the teachings of Ahmad ibn Idris, both of which influenced his judgment. Ibn Idris also influenced the Mahdi's thinking through his emissary 'Abdullahi al-Dufani, who was one of Muhammad Ahmad's teachers prior to his proclamation as Mahdi.[52]

Finally, it is important to re-emphasize that in the Mahdiyya there could be no separation between religion and state. The Mahdist state embraced all matters pertaining to government or administration and rejected any attempt to regard political matters as being separate from religion. The creation of an Islamic society was ordered by God and it could not be regarded as a political entity, such as a kingdom or a *bashawat*, both of which were by definition divorced from religion. The mistaken attempt to separate religion from state was, according to the Mahdi, the reason for the deterioration of the Turkish Empire and the Egyptian Khedivate. The bases for a righteous Islamic society were asceticism and the renunciation of worldly things (*taqashshuf wa-zuhd*). Muhammad Ahmad's inclination to abolish the sufi orders and the four schools (*madhahib*) of Sunni Islam probably preceded his manifestation as *mahdi* and was part of his belief in the unity of God (*tawhid*). It implied the inseparable basis of the Mahdist state which was to be founded solely on the Prophet's principles. The first written expression we have to this effect is the Mahdi's letter to Shaykh Muhammad al-Amin al-Hindi, written in Sha'ban 1299 (June–July 1882), in which he urges him to follow only the Qur'an and the Sunna. After the *hijra* to Jabal Qadir, where sufi traditions were much weaker than in the Nile Valley, total opposition to the four Sunni schools (*madhahib*) and the sufi orders (*turuq*) prevailed in the Mahdi's writings. In a letter written to *al-faqih* Balal Sabun and his followers the Mahdi explicitly stated that the Qur'an and the Sunna were the sole source of all that mattered regarding *tawhid* and *fiqh*.[53] But, according to Abu Salim, the most elaborate treatment of this subject is to be found in an undated letter written by the Khalifa 'Abdullahi to the Mahdi's followers in the first few months of 1884 (mid-1301 AH). In this letter the Khalifa explicitly reminds them that the Mahdi has ordered all followers to abolish the sufi orders since he is the "Seal of all the Saints" (*khatim al-awliya'*).[54]

In conclusion, it seems clear that sufism, as introduced into Sudan by holy families and numerous sufi shaykhs during the Funj Sultanate, was the main source of Islam in Sudan and that despite attempts undertaken during the first Turkiyya to undermine it and replace it with orthodox Islam as practised in Egypt, it survived into the twentieth century. The Mahdiyya in effect started off by exploiting Sufism against the "evil *'ulama'*" imported into Sudan by the Egyptians. Although it later turned against the sufi shaykhs in order to establish its exclusiveness as the sole source of Islamic legitimacy and power, it re-emerged in twentieth-century Sudan in a form not dissimilar to other sufi orders. All the attempts undertaken against Sufism during the Condominium (1899–1955) failed to diminish its centrality and thus the two leading religious movements, the Khatmiyya and the Ansar, maintained their position as political power brokers until the end of the twentieth century. All attempts to challenge their centrality, undertaken primarily by the military, with or without civilian backing, have failed so far.

Notes

1 Parts of this chapter first appeared in my book: *Islam, Sectarianism and Politics in Sudan, from the Mahdiyya to the Present* (London, 2003).

2 Yusuf Fadl Hasan (ed.), *Sudan in Africa* (Khartoum, 1971), pp. 73–86; also P. M. Holt, "Holy Families and Islam in the Sudan," in P. M. Holt (ed.), *Studies in the History of the Near East* (London, 1973), pp. 121–34.

3 Muhammad Ibrahim Abu Salim, "Dawr al-'ulama' fi nashr al-Islam fi al-Sudan," in Muddathir 'Abd al-Rahim and al-Tayyib Zein al-'Abdin (eds), *Al-Islam fil-Sudan, buhuth mukhtara min al-mu'tamar al-awwal li-jama'at al-fikr wal-thaqafa al-Islamiyya* (Khartoum, 1987), pp. 31–42.

4 For details see the contemporary chronicle written by *katib al-shuna* known as The Funj Chronicle; see P. M. Holt, *The Sudan of the Three Niles, the Funj Chronicle* (Leiden, 1999); also P. M. Holt, "Holy Families."

5 For details of their history and their religious teachings, see P. M. Holt, "The Sons of Jabir and their Kin: A Clan of Sudanese Religious Notables," in Holt (ed.), *Studies*, pp. 88–103; and id., "Holy Families."

6 R. S. O'Fahey and M. I. al. Abu Salim, *Land in Dar Fur, Charters and Related Documents from the Dar Fur Sultanate* (Cambridge, 1983), pp. 18–9; see also H. Klein, "The Awlad Jabir and their Land 1720–1900," unpublished MA thesis, University of Haifa, 1984 (Hebrew).

7 J. Spaulding, *The Heroic Age in Sinnar* (East Lansing, 1985), pp. 173–4, quoted from J. Bruce, *Travels to Discover the Source of the Nile*, 2nd edn (Edinburgh, 1805), p. 451; and J. L. Burckhardt, *Travels in Nubia*, 2nd edn (London, 1822), p. 236.

8 R. S. O'Fahey and B. Radtke, "Neo-Sufism Reconsidered," *Der Islam* (1993) 70/1, pp. 52–87; also R. S. O'Fahey, *Enigmatic Saint: Ahmad Ibn Idris and the Idrisi Tradition* (London, 1990).

9 For details see Ali Salih Karrar, *The Sufi Brotherhoods in the Sudan* (London, 1992), esp. pp. 42–72.

10 Karrar, *Sufi Brotherhoods*, pp. 43–8.

11 For details see O'Fahey, *Enigmatic Saint*, pp. 142–9.

12 Karrar, *Sufi Brotherhoods*, pp. 75–6; according to Karrar neither Ibn Idris nor Muhammad 'Uthman al-Mirghani had previous relations with rulers but his orders to al-Hasan stated explicitly that he should establish close relations with the Turks and not follow in his footsteps in this respect.

13 Abu Salim, "Dawr al-'ulama'," p. 81.

14 Muhammad Fu'ad Shukri, *Al-Hukm al-Misri fil-Sudan, 1820–1885* (Cairo, 1947), pp. 221–42; J. Spaulding, "Land Tenure and Social Class in the Northern Turkish Sudan," *International Journal of African Historical Studies* (1982), 15/1, pp. 7–19; also A. Bjorkelo, "Turco-Jallaba Relations 1821–1885," in L. O. Manger (ed.), *Trade and Traders in the Sudan* (Bergen, 1984), pp. 84–9.

15 J. O. Voll, "Islam and Stateness in the Modern Sudan," McGill University, CDAS, Discussion Paper No. 4 (Montreal, March 1983), pp. 15–18.

16 Mohammad Said al-Gaddal, "Religion in a Changing Socio-Political Structure: A Case Study of Islam in Nineteenth Century Sudan," in M. W. Daly (ed.), *Modernization in the Sudan. Essays in Honour of Richard Hill* (New York, 1985), pp. 51–3.

17 Karrar, *Sufi Brotherhoods*, pp. 86–7, 88–91.

18 O'Fahey and Radtke, "Neo-Sufism," p. 82; a similar claim was made by al-Qurashi wad al-Zayn, a Shaykh of the Sammaniyya, a few years later, see below.

19 O'Fahey and Radtke, "Neo-Sufism," p. 83, quoted from the Bergen photographic collection; NI 298, 15/26; for further details on the Khatmiyya's relations with the Mahdiyya see Karrar, *Sufi Brotherhoods*, pp. 93–102.

20 Cited in O'Fahey and Radtke, "Neo-Sufism," p. 67

21 Dhaher Jasim Muhammad, The Contribution of Sayed 'Ali al-Mirghani, Leader of the Khatmiyya, to the Political Evolution of the Sudan, 1884–1968, unpublished PhD dissertation, University of Exeter, 1988, pp. 3–12.

22 J. H. Voll, "Revivalism and Social Transformation in Islamic History," *Muslim World* (1986), 76, the passage quoted is from pp. 177–8.

23 Voll, "Islam and Stateness," p. 19.

24 Na'um Shuqayr, *Jughrafiyya wa-ta'rikh al-Sudan*, 2nd edn (Beirut, 1967), p. 322.

25 Sura 114 is the last sura of the Qur'an. Suras 113 and 114 are known as *al-mu'awwidhatan* (*awwadha* = to invoke the protection [of God]; to hang an amulet [on a child]); these *suras* were short and easy to memorize and regarded as crucial for young children since they invoked the protection of God from all ills and evils.

26 E. D. Schoenfeld, *Die mohammedanische Bewegung im aegytischen Sudan* (Berlin, 1905), p. 69; see also R. Hill, *A Biographical Dictionary of the Sudan*, 2nd edn (London, 1967), pp. 260–1; Hill states that Muhammad al-Khayr was earlier known as Muhammad al-Dakkayr. He later was appointed by the Mahdi as Mahdist amir and was governor of Berber and the Ja'aliyyin until his death in 1888; according to Ibrahim Fawzi, Muhammad Ahmad moved to Khartoum with his brothers and studied under several teachers including Shaykh Sharaf al-Din 'Abd al-Sadiq. He later moved to the Jazira and studied *fiqh* with Shaykh al-Amin al-Suwaylah b. Muhammad at the Wad 'Isa mosque; see I. Fawzi, *Kitab al-Sudan bayna yaday Ghurdun wa-Kitshener*, two volumes (Cairo, 1319/1901–02), I, pp. 70–2; according to A. B. Theobald, *The Mahdiyya* (London, 1951), pp. 27–8, Muhammad Ahmad joined the Sammaniyya while studying under Shaykh Muhammad Nur al-Sharif, one of the leaders of the Sammaniyya, in a village north of Khartoum.

27 Schoenfeld, *Bewegung*, p. 71; quoting R. C. Slatin, *Fire and Sword in the Sudan*, p. 122 [p.129 of the English edn]; according to Na'um Shuqayr 'Abdullahi lost consciousness for more than an hour as a result of this meeting; when he finally got to his feet to shake Muhammad Ahmad's hand, he again became unconscious. Shuqayr, *Ta'rikh*, pp. 327–8; Aba Island became the spiritual center of the twentieth-century Ansar.

28 H. Shaked, *The life of the Sudanese Mahdi. A Historical Study of kitab sa'adat al-mustahdi bi-sirat al-Imam al-Mahdi by Isma'il b. 'Abd al-Qadir* (New Brunswick, NJ, 1978); the author of this biography was born in El-Obeid in 1844 and was a grandson of Isma'il al-Wali, head of the Isma'iliyya and one of the Mahdi's first supporters; a copy of the manuscript is in the Sudan Archive at Durham University Library.

29 P. M. Holt, "Al-Mahdiyya" *EI²*, vol. 5, pp. 1248–9; according to some sources the title of Khalifat 'Uthman was also offered to Muhammad 'Uthman al-Mirghani II, who ignored the honor.

30 Quoted from P. M. Holt, "Islamic Millenarianism and the fulfillment of Prophecy," in *Essays in Honour of Marjorie Reeves* (Essex, 1980), pp. 340–1; P. M. Holt, *The Mahdist State in the Sudan 1881–1898*, 2nd ed (Oxford, 1970), p. 105; see also *Manshurat al-imam al-mahdi*, vol. II (Khartoum, 1963); M. I. Abu Salim, *Al-athar al-kamila lil-imam al-Mahdi*, 7 vols (Khartoum, 1990–94), vol. I, pp. 76–83; Shuqayr, *Ta'rikh*, p. 643.

31 Ahmed Uthman Ibrahim, "Some Aspects of the Ideology of the Mahdiya," *Sudan Notes and Records* (1979), 60, pp. 30–2, quoting from *Manshurat*, I, 12; thus a wife who had embraced Mahdism would be granted a divorce on the grounds that her husband, who had rejected the Mahdi, was an unbeliever.

32 Holt, "Islamic Millenarianism," pp. 342–6; for details of this controversy see Shuqayr, *Ta'rikh*, pp. 651–4.

33 Rudolf Peters, "Islam and the Legitimation of Power: the Mahdi Revolt in the Sudan," *XXI. Deutscher Orientalistentag, 23.–29. März 1980, Ausgewaelte Votraege*, (ed.) F. Steppat (*ZDMG* Supplement V), pp. 409–20, at pp. 414–15.

34 Shaked, *Sudanese Mahdi*, p. 93, quoted from pp. 108–9 of the manuscript.

35 Shaked, *Sudanese Mahdi*, pp. 202–3, quoted from the *Sira*, 12/11–15.

36 Muhammad Sa'id al-Qaddal, "Al-ru'ya al-thawriyya fi fikr al-Mahdi 1884–1885," in 'Umar 'Abd al-Raziq Naqr (ed.), *Dirasat fi al-mahdiyya* (Khartoum, n.d. [1983?]), pp. 74–88.

37 Abu Salim, *Al-Athar*, II, pp. 310–12, quoting messages addressed to *al-ahbab*, in March–April 1884; J. S. Trimingham, *Islam in the Sudan*, 2nd impression (London, 1965), pp. 150–7; E. L. Dietrich, "Der Mahdi Mohamed Ahmed vom Sudan nach Arabischen Quellen," *Der Islam* (1925), 24, pp. 199–288.

38 R. Hill, *Egypt in the Sudan 1820–1881* (London, 1959), p. 127; see also Abu Salim, *Al-Athar*, I, pp. 76–81, in which the Mahdi orders Muhammad al-Tayyib al-Basir to apply the bay'a to his brethren in the Sammaniyya order and to make the *hijra* to Jabal Qadir; Karrar, *Sufi Brotherhoods*, pp. 93–102; see also Nels Johnson, "Religious Paradigms of the Sudanese Mahdiyah," *Ethnohistory* (1978), 25/2 pp. 159–78.

39 Abu Salim, *Al-Athar*, IV, 212.

40 Karrar, *Sufi Brotherhoods*, pp. 99–102.

41 Abu Salim, *Manshurat al-Mahdiyya* (Beirut, 1979), pp. 61–5; the Mahdi also banned the use of sufi flags and forbade their ceremonial *dhikr*.

42 Abu Salim, *Al-Athar*, I, p. 78; al-Sadiq al-Mahdi, *Yas'alunaka 'an al-mahdiyya* (Beirut, 1975), p. 173.

43 Sadiq, *Yas'alunaka*, pp. 225–6; Abu Salim, *al-Haraka al-fikriyya fil-mahdiyya*, 3rd edn (Khartoum, 1989), pp. 80–1; Holt, *Mahdist State*, p. 108.

44 Muhammad Ibrahim Abu Salim, "Nasihat al-'Awwam wal-'alaqa bayn al-thawratayn al-mahdiyya wa'l-'urabiyya," unpublished text; I am grateful to Prof. R. S. O'Fahey of the Department of History at the University of Bergen for enabling me to use his copy of Abu Salim's manuscript.

45 Al-Sadiq al-Mahdi summarized the views of the *'ulama'* opposing the Mahdi in *Yas'alunaka*, pp. 145–9, and of those supporting him on pp. 149–53; in Muhammad Ibrahim Abu Salim and K. S. Vikør, "The Man Who Believed in the Mahdi," *Sudanic Africa* (1991), 2, pp. 29–52, the authors tell of a Moroccan *'alim*, Ahmad b. 'Abdallah al-Fasi, who expressed his pro-Mahdist views in 1888–89, and rejected all doubts raised against the Mahdi by Azhari and Sudanese *'ulama'*; on al-'Awwam's message see Abu Salim, *Haraka*, pp. 67–71; Abu Salim states that al-'Awwam, 'Abduh, and al-Afghani did not support the Mahdi's religious message but welcomed his military victories over British forces; see Abu Salim, "Nasihat al-'Awwam," which deals with the relationship between the two revolts. On al-'Awwam see also J. Hunwick and R. S. O'Fahey, *Arabic Literature in Africa*, I (Leiden, 1994–95), pp. 332–3.

46 Abu Salim, *Al-Athar*, I, pp. 153–4.

47 Abu Salim, *Haraka*, pp. 19–23; for the Mahdi's letter to Muhammad Ra'uf see Abu Salim, *al-Murshid ila watha'iq al-mahdi* (Khartoum, n.d.), p. 12, document 19.

48 R. Hill, *Slatin Pasha* (Oxford, 1965), pp. 18–20; H. Keown-Boyd, *A Good Dusting* (London, 1986), pp. 17–18.

49 H. C. Jackson, *Osman Digna* (London, 1926), pp. 24–8.

50 Keown-Boyd, *Good Dusting*, pp. 71–4.

51 A. Layish, "The Legal Methodology of the Mahdi in the Sudan, 1881–1885, issues in Marriage and Divorce," *Sudanic Africa* (1997), 8, pp. 37–66, at p. 39.

52 Layish, "Legal Methodology," 44.

53 Abu Salim, *Haraka*, pp. 44–5; the letters are quoted from id. *al-Murshid*, document 44 on p. 24, and document 879 on p. 412.

54 Abu Salim, *Haraka*, pp. 45–8; the Khalifa's letter refers exclusively to the Tijaniyya order.

16 Observations on some religious institutions in Damiette and Faraskur in the eighteenth century

Daniel Crecelius

Judges (*qadi*s) throughout the Ottoman Empire played an important role in the creation, management, and overall supervision of the *awqaf* (pious endowments) of their Muslim community.[1] They "tested" new *awqaf* in their courts, registered validated *awqaf* in their carefully prepared registers (*sijillat*), and supervised the supervisors (*nuzzar*; sing. *nazir*) of both *awqaf khayriyya* and *ahliyya*.[2] They frequently heard complaints from worshippers that the *nazir* was withholding funds for the services, salaries or upkeep of the religious structure for which he was responsible, judged cases from competing parties pertinent to the supervision of *awqaf*, or listened to the complaints of beneficiaries that the *nazir* was not distributing benefits properly or was not maintaining the income-producing value of the properties endowed to support the *waqf*. In Egypt, for instance, the *Qanunname-i Mısır* of Sultan Sülayman al-Qanuni specifically ordered that an inspector (*nazir*) and clerk (*katib*) sent from Istanbul annually should check the accounts of the *awqaf* through the *qadi* to make certain that their expenditures were according to the stipulations set out by the donors. This official was charged with broad authority to inspect these *waqf* properties and to assure their maintenance and repair.[3] In the absence of these officials from Istanbul, the local *qadi* assumed responsibility for maintaining the structure of *awqaf* in his jurisdiction. It does not appear that the practice of sending officials from Istanbul on an annual basis was maintained; nor did the *qadi* always exercise effective supervision of *awqaf* in his jurisdiction. There are numerous cases of citizens or beneficiaries of *awqaf* lodging complaints in the *qadi*'s court against negligent or corrupt supervisors. Many of these cases indicate that for decades, the *nazir*s did not file reports on the income and expenditures of the *awqaf* they supervised.

During his brief stint as governor of Egypt in 1193/1779, Isma'il Pasha[4] sent an order to the *qadi* of Damiette chastising him for not carrying out his duties in providing accounts of the *awqaf* of his district. He commanded him to undertake a survey of the physical condition of the religious institutions under his jurisdiction and to supervise necessary repairs to the structures.[5] The *qadi*, in turn, ordered the supervisors of both *awqaf ahliyya* and *awqaf khayriyya* in Damiette and its surroundings to provide accounts of the *awqaf* they supervised. Isma'il Pasha remained less than one year as governor and only a few of the *nazir*s of Damiette's mosques, schools, and tombs submitted the requested accounts. The accounts that were submitted for the period, recorded in the exceedingly rich registers of the Damiette court, form the basis of this study.

The Damiette *sijillat*, especially the ones from the sixteenth century, have been badly damaged by water and wear and are exceedingly difficult to read. Even the registers from the eighteenth century show some damage. Their spines have been broken at one time and the pages became loose. When they were rebound, pages were frequently reassembled out of order. In some instances, the second part of a case appears among the pages of a register from an earlier year and the first page of the same case is bound among the pages of a later year. Nevertheless, I have been able to extract from these registers a total of ninety one accounts, both *awqaf ahli* and *khayri*, for the period 1164–1218/1750–1804.[6] This study focuses only on the thirty five complete accounts of *awqaf khayriyya* to elucidate the range and condition of religious institutions in Damiette in the eighteenth century.

Damiette, which sits along the eastern shoreline of the eastern, or Damiette, branch of the Nile a short distance from the Mediterranean Sea, has been an important entrepot linking Egypt with the ports of the Levant and Anatolian coastlines in particular and the eastern Mediterranean in general.[7] Like the other major Egyptian cities, it was host to a broad range of nationalities. It was largely destroyed during the Crusader invasion of the eastern Delta and rebuilt, hence its religious structures are not as old as those of other Egyptian towns and cities.[8] Although the town and the surrounding area were dotted with mosques, schools, and *zawiyas*, it was possible to piece together full accounts only of the following ten religious structures from the registers of Damiette:

Zawiyat Shaykh Ahmad ibn Fadl	Zawiyat Ibn Wakil al-Sultan
Jami' Muhammad Çorbaji in Faraskur	Jami' al-Kawundaki in Faraskur
al-Madrasa al-Mu'ayyaniyya	al-Madrasa al-Nasiriyya
Masjid al-Mu'allaq	Jami' al-Zikwi
al-Madrasa al-'Utbaniyya (al-'Atabani)	Zawiyat Ibn Nuwayr Bahr

This list is not long because few of the supervisors responded to the *qadi*'s demand for an accounting. Moreover, Isma'il Pasha did not remain long enough as governor to enforce his demand for the accounts.[9] None of these institutions, with the possible exception of the Madrasa al-Mu'ayyaniyya, appear today as they are described in the documents of the eighteenth century. Some, such as the Masjid al-Mu'allaq, have disappeared. The majority of these institutions was given substantial renovations by Egypt's revolutionary government; in many cases the old institutions were knocked down to make way for entirely new structures. In Faraskur, for instance, the Jami' Muhammad Çorbaji was completely renovated in 1971, while the Jami' Kawundaki was demolished and an entirely new mosque, the largest in Faraskur, was built on its site. In Damiette, the Madrasa al-Nasiriyya has been entirely rebuilt and a separate building was constructed near it for the *zawiya* of Ibn Nuwayr. The Matbuli Madrasa was built entirely new in 1978 and the Jami' al-Zikwi (al-Bahr), which is the most important mosque in Damiette at present, has been replaced by a lovely, modern structure overlooking the Nile where it makes a major bend. The Madrasa al-'Utbaniyya (al-'Atabani), which is on a main street called Shabatani and sits one block away from the Jami' Badri, which was next to the disappeared Musallimiyya, has also been renovated to the point that its early origins have been entirely obscured. The large Mu'ayyaniyya *madrasa*, built by the Mamluk sultan Qa'it Bey, stands in ruin today, but still offers the visitor a good idea of its original size, splendor, and significance.

The supervisors of Damiette's religious institutions

It would appear from the limited data at our disposal that the supervision of Damiette's religious institutions was generally in the hands of a small circle of high-ranking religious and military officials or their male children. The supervisor of the important Jami' al-Kawundaki in Faraskur in 1190/1776–77 was Shaykh 'Ali, the son of the deceased Muhammad al-Hajji from Jirbas, and the *nazir* of the mosque of the deceased Muhammad Çorbaji in the same town was al-Hajj Ahmad Iwaz al-Sittal. Neither of these two administrators seems to have any significant connection to nearby Damiette. The supervision of Damiette's main religious institutions, however, was in the hands of a small group of individuals.[10]

It is not surprising to find that officials of the central government played an important role in the supervision of the most important mosque/*madrasa* in Damiette. Beginning with the earliest year of our data (1168/1754–55) and continuing to the end of our period of survey (1208/1793–94), the Madrasa al-Mu'ayyaniyya's supervisor was the chief Ottoman judge (*qadi al-qudah*) in Cairo.[11] He appointed as local agent (*wakil*), however, the amir Ibrahim Çorbaji Mustahfazan al-Qanili. It was not unusual for the top-ranking Ottoman religious officials and officers of the (now Mamluk-dominated) Ottoman *ocak*s (military units) serving in Egypt to claim the supervision of important religious institutions, especially when the *awqaf* of these institutions produced significant income. Among the expenditures from the income of the Madrasa al-Mu'ayyaniyya, for instance, was an item for 5,000 *nisf fidda*s in salary for the *nazir*, in this case the chief *qadi* of Cairo, and 1,500 *nisf fidda*s for his agent in Damiette, the amir Ibrahim Çorbaji.[12] These salaries were larger than those paid to the full-time employees of the *madrasa*.

The supervision of virtually all of the large delta-based *awqaf* of the medieval Mamluk sultans had fallen to the Mamluk beys during their period of resurgence under Ottoman rule. *Awqaf* were seen as a source of income and even smaller religious institutions came to have supervisors from the middle levels of dominant military units. The supervisor of the long-established Madrasa al-Barquqiyya, for instance, was 'Uthman Agha al-Malatili, the *dizdar* (commander) of Damiette's fort.[13] It should not be forgotten that the founders of many public *awqaf* stipulated in their endowment deeds that the supervision should be given to the chief judge, a particular local mufti or whoever held the *mashyakha* of the particular institution for which the endowment was originally established.

When we look at the supervision of the small number of *madrasa*s, mosques, and *zawiya*s in Damiette for which we have data, the dominance of a handful of individuals becomes apparent.

For the years 1168–69/1754–56 the *nazir* of the small Masjid al-Mu'allaq was Shaykh Shihab al-Din Ahmad al-Faraskuri al-Shafi'i.[14] Years later, however, the supervision had been assumed by Shaykh 'Ali, the son of the deceased al-Qadi Hasan al-Shafi'i. Shaykh 'Ali perhaps "inherited" supervisions from his father, who apparently was a judge in Damiette, for 'Ali appears as *nazir* of a number of Damiette's religious institutions, including one-third of the supervision of the Zawiyat Ibn Wakil al-Sultan,[15] and the full supervision of al-Madrasa al-Nasiriyya and the Zawiyat Ibn Nuwayr which was inside the Madrasa al-Nasiriyya.[16]

It is interesting that Shaykh 'Ali ibn al-Qadi Hasan al-Shafi'i held one-third of the supervision of the Zawiyat Ibn Wakil al-Sultan while the other two-thirds was held by Shaykh Muhammad, called Yunis, and his brother Shaykh Ibrahim, the sons of Shaykh 'Abd al-Karim, known as Ibn 'Allam al-Manzili, the Shafi'i mufti. The Shafi'i mufti and his sons held an even larger range of supervisions of Damiette's religious structures. The Zawiya of Shaykh Dhahir al-Din and his brother Shaykh Shihab al-Din, the two sons of Shaykh Ahmad ibn Fadl, was supervised by Shaykh 'Abd al-Karim al-'Allami, the Shafi'i mufti in 1168–69.[17] Years later, his two sons are cited as *nazir*s of the Zawiya of their own deceased father. Shaykh 'Abd al-Karim, known as Ibn 'Allam al-Manzili al-Shafi'i, was also cited as supervisor of the mosque of Hasan al-Tawil.[18]

In addition to their supervision of *awqaf*, trained men of religion might hold teaching positions within a *madrasa*, might act as imams or preachers in a mosque, or might recite portions of the Qur'an at tombs, in mosques and schools, or during special nights of the religious calendar. In addition to their duties as supervisors, Shaykh Yunis and Shaykh Ibrahim, for instance, also received salaries for preaching at the Madrasa al-Mu'ayyaniyya.[19] The former Hanafi mufti, Shaykh 'Abd al-Raziq al-Qashimi, received salaries for reading the Qur'an in the Jami' al-Zikwi, al-'Utbaniyya, al-Shabtaniyya, al-Musallimiyya, the Zawiyat Sidi Abi al-'Abbas al-Hariti and inside the tomb of Sidi Fatih Abi al-'Ata.[20]

Another family, not clearly identified with a particular office, accumulated a number of supervisions of Damiette's public religious institutions. In 1168 Shaykh Hasan ibn al-Shaykh 'Ali al-Raziqi al-Rifa'i and the children of his brother Shaykh Marzuq are cited as supervisors of the Madrasa al-'Utbaniyya. In 1180/1766–67 the supervision was still divided between Shaykh Hasan and the children of his deceased brother Shaykh Marzuq, but Shaykh Hasan must have died without heirs by 1189/1775–76 when three children of Shaykh Marzuq are cited as the supervisors of the Madrasa al-'Utbaniyya.[21]

On 25 Jumada I 1192/21 June 1778 a letter arrived from the governor in Cairo announcing the appointment in Cairo of Shaykh Hasan al-Kafrawi as Shafi'i mufti.[22] He, in turn, appointed Shaykh Muhammad al-Danjihi as Shafi'i mufti in Damiette.[23] In addition to the other important administrative functions he quickly assumed, Shaykh al-Danjihi acquired the supervision of the most important mosque in Damiette, the Jami' al-Zikwi, or Jami' al-Bahr because of its location along the Nile bank.[24]

It is to be expected that the supervision of Damiette's major religious institutions was held by the town's leading religious officials, the chief judge, the shaykh holding the most important position in the town's major mosque or *madrasa*, or, above all, by the Shafi'i mufti. Shaykh Danjihi's notices of appointment, for instance, emphasize that he was the spokesman (*mutahaddith; mutakallim*) for all the men of religion in Damiette, making him the most influential religious leader in this important port.[25]

Properties owned by the *awqaf*

The accounts from the Damiette *sijillat* reveal that the bulk of income for the ten religious institutions came from urban commercial properties. The smaller institutions, the *zawiya*s, were supported by only a few properties immediately adjacent to the institutions or facing them on the same street. Several of the mosques owned so few properties and had such small incomes that they could barely sustain their functions and/or personnel.

The Zawiya of Ibn al-Nuwayr inside the Madrasa al-Nasiriyya received income in the two years 1194–95/1780–81 from only three shops, half of a place for washing chickpeas, and from a plot (*sahha*) on which were two shops. It had the modest income of 3,140 *nisf fiddas* for the two-year period.[26]

The Zawiya of Ibn Fadl owned six properties in 1168/1754–55, but by 1192/ 1778–79 it cited revenues from only four of these properties. The previous year it had a modest income of only 1,360 *nisf fiddas* from one-fourth of a *bustan*[27] and two halls (*qa'a*s).[28] Without sufficient resources at his disposal, the supervisor offered one of the halls rent free to 'Ali Katkhuda in 1193/1779 in exchange for the new tenant making necessary repairs to it.[29]

The Zawiyat Ibn Wakil al-Sultan in the Suq al-Khila'iyyin, on the other hand, owned ten shops next to the *zawiya*, a *mastaba*, a storeroom (*hasil*), and three empty plots. In 1192/1778–79, these properties produced an income of 3,216 *nisf fiddas*, while in 1196/1781–82 the *waqf* received an income from these properties of 3,734 *nisf fiddas*.

Several of the mosques and *madrasa*s of Damiette appear to have been in dire financial straits, for their expenses were far greater than their income. They owned so few properties that it was extremely difficult for their supervisors to work their way out of the substantial debts the institutions carried.

The Masjid al-Mu'allaq reported an income of only 1,080 *nisf fiddas* for the two years 1168–69/1754–56 and only 2,140 for the two years 1194–95/1780–81. Its income came only from two *qa'a*s and a shop beneath the small mosque. In both periods, it had expenses at respectively 31 and 165 percent greater than income. Its *nazir*, Shaykh 'Ali the son of the deceased al-Qadi Hasan al-Shafi'i, had recently made extensive repairs to it.

The Madrasa al-Nasiriyya on the Nawari canal had an income of only 15,000 *nisf fiddas* for the eight *hijri* years 1188–95/1774–81 and expenses of 28,226 *nisf fiddas*. Its modest income of just under 1,900 *nisf fiddas* a year came from 3 shops, one-half of a *tabaqa* (a floor in a tenement), 2 *qa'a*s, 2 storage areas, 15 open plots, 3 of which were vacant, and 15 *bustan*s.[30] At the end of 1195/1781 its *nazir* was owed 2,822 *nisf fiddas*, or more than a full year's income.

The largest, best endowed, and functionally the most important religious institutions in Damiette were the Madrasa al-Mu'ayyaniyya, the Jami' al-Zikwi, also known as Jami' al-Bahr, and the Madrasa al-'Utbaniyya. These larger institutions not only derived income from far more properties than the ones mentioned above, but also appear to have owned a better quality of income-producing property.

For the period 1168–1211/1754–97 the supervisor of the Madrasa al-Mu'ayyaniyya in the Suq al-Aruzz reported incomes from between 33 and 37 urban properties, including a bathhouse (*hammam*) and a place for grinding coffee (*madaqq al-bunn*), 49–50 urban plots, and 25–50 *bustan*s. The Jami' al-Zikwi (al-Bahr) for the four years 1191–94/1777–80 reported an income of 15,462 *nisf fiddda*s from the Wikalat al-Jibn near the mosque, of 13,500 *nisf fidda*s from one-half of the Wikalat al-Fajwa in the same area, and 2,120 from the Wikalat al-Shirbini. Six of its properties were vacant. It also owned 15 *bustan*s and over 50 plots, many of which were vacant.[31] The Madrasa al-'Utbaniyya[32] in 1168/1754–55 reported an income of 11,319 *nisf fidda*s from a total of 35 properties belonging to its *waqf*. It owned all or part of 18 shops located in the Suq al-Haririyyin facing the *madrasa*, the Suq al-Husuriyyin, and the Suq al-Khashshab. Income from these properties, four of which had no income, dropped to 9,872 *nisf fidda*s in 1189/1775–76.[33]

There are two accounts for religious institutions in Faraskur, a short distance south of Damiette on the same bank of the Nile, recorded in the *sijillat* of the Damiette court. The mosque of Muhammad Çorbaji owned 23 storage spaces, 2 coffeehouses, 4 residences (a *dar* and three *buyut*), a farm (*dawwar*), 5 plots of land, a small *wikala*, and a residence and a room above the *wikala*. It reported incomes of 10,872 and 8,109 *nisf fidda*s for 1192/1778–79 and 1196/1781–82 respectively. Its expenses exceeded income by only 15 and 3 percent for the 2 years, so that among the 10 institutions surveyed it appears to be the one least burdened by debt.[34] This is probably owing to its recent founding by a member of the military establishment, who endowed for its support a significant number of commercial and residential units in Faraskur.

The Jami' al-Kawundaki in the period 1188–90/1774–76 reported sizable incomes from thirty five properties. Its largest assets appeared to be the Wikalat al-Ghilal in Faraskur and a threshing wheel (*da'ira*). It also reported owning eight empty plots from which no income was derived.[35]

It appears from this brief survey of the properties included in the *awqaf* of the religious institutions of Damiette and Faraskur that the bulk of the income of these institutions came from urban commercial properties. Many were attached to the institutions, in the same block of buildings, or near to them in the same street. Most owned shops and storage areas which produced modest incomes; all seemed to own empty plots on which commercial activities could take place. Structures might even be erected on these plots and rents paid to the *waqf* by the persons building on the plots. *Wikala*s, or shops and storage areas in these commercial structures, appear to have produced the greatest income. Since Damiette was surrounded by a rich agricultural zone, it is not surprising to find many agricultural plots and (fruit) trees included in Damiette's *awqaf*. Unfortunately, the court documents do not tell us where these *bustan*s were located, their size, or the individual rents of each *bustan*. Some might even have been small plots of fruit-bearing trees in the town itself. The Jami' Muhammad Çorbaji was the only institution reporting income from two coffeehouses and the two Faraskuri mosques also reported significant income from ownership of farmland.

The properties included in the *awqaf* of the religious institutions of Damiette appear therefore to be rather homogeneous. The majority were commercial properties, usually shops, and storage areas. *Wikala*s were sources of significant income for some of these institutions. Residences are not included in great number in these *awqaf*, and only rarely did these *awqaf* own commercial assets such as water wheels, ovens, or mills.

Economic condition of the ten religious institutions

Table 16.1 synopsizes the accounts, reducing them to totals for income and expenditures for the years cited. The years in which there is an excess of income over expenditures are few. Far more common were the years in which the *nazir* was required to spend more than the income from the *waqf*'s properties. The final column of this table expresses the surplus of income or excess of expenditure as a percent of income.

Table 16.1 Awqaf Khayriyya of Damiette – income and expenditures

Name of institution	Year AH	Income nisf fiddas	Expenses nisf fiddas	Balance nisf fiddas	Deficit/ surplus (%)
Zawiyat Shaykh	1168–69	2,800	2,767	+33	+1
Ahmad Ibn Fadl	1187	1,360	2,382	−1,022	−175
	1189	1,360	2,313	−953	−170
	1190	1,360	2,273	−913	−167
	1191	1,360	2,164	−804	−159
	1192	2,506	2,992	−486	−119
	1193	1,360	1,541	−181	−113
	1194	1,360	1,391	−31	−102
	1196	1,360	1,388	−28	−102
Zawiyat Ibn Wakil	1190	3,500	7,528	−4,028	−215
al-Sultan	1191	3,119	7,194	−4,075	−230
	1192	3,216	4,075	−859	−127
	1195	3,224	2,963	+261	+8
	1196	3,734	10,746	−7,012	−187
Zawiyat Ibn Nuwayr	1194–95	3,140	3,742	−602	−119
Jami' al-Kawundaki	1188	31,475	42,075	−10,600	−134
in Faraskur	1189	30,815	31,850	−1,035	−103
	1190	86,038	22,924	+63,114	+74
Jami' Muhammad	1191	10,872	12,544	−1,672	−115
Çorbaji in Faraskur	1196	8,109	8,320	−211	−103
al-Madrasa al-'Utbaniyya	1168	11,319	10,121	+1,198	+11
(al-'Atabani)	1180	11,256	11,121	+135	+1
	1189	9,872	10,140	−268	−103
al-Madrasa	1189	31,657	32,688	−1,031	−103
al-Mu'ayyaniyya	1190	32,027	33,624	−1,597	−105
	1191	32,027	37,338	−5,311	−117
	1192	32,247	42,658	−10,411	−132
	1197	33,126	35,555	−2,429	−107
	1207	32,024	32,251	−227	−101
	1208	28,381	29,487	−1,106	−104
	1211	27,814	41,530	−13,716	−149
al-Madrasa al-Nasiriyya	1188–95	15,000	28,226	−13,226	−188
Masjid al-Mu'allaq	1168–69	1,080	1,415	−335	−131
	1194–95	2,140	5,680	−3,540	−265
Jami' al-Zikwi (Jami' al-Bhar)	1192–94	62,596	105,836	−43,240	−169

It would appear that the Muslim religious institutions of Damiette were not in a strong economic position in the period under survey. There is even some evidence of decline during the roughly half century bracketed by the available accounts. In 1168–69/1754–56 the Zawiya of Shaykh Ahmad ibn Fadl and the Madrasa al-'Utbaniyya actually reported a surplus of income over expenditures (1 and 11 percent respectively), whereas the Masjid al-Mu'allaq, a small mosque with a modest endowment of only three properties, had a deficit of 31 percent from its meager income. Thereafter, 29 of the remaining 32 accounts assembled from the scattered pages of the Damiette *sijillat* showed deficits of varying sizes. Some deficits were manageable and did little harm to the institution, but too often, the institutions, particularly the *zawiya*s with meager incomes, reported deficits of such sizable proportions that their debts to the *nazir*, who advanced them funds, were greater than the entire annual income of the *waqf*. It was often then that the supervisor had to give up some control of the institution's real assets to encourage a lessee to advance payment on a lease via the device of *ijaratayn* for the property to have needed repairs.

Income from the assets the institutions owned remained fairly constant over time, owing largely to the stability in the number of properties owned and to the long term leases the *nazir*s signed with tenants.[36] For instance, the two institutions for which we have the most accounts reported annual incomes within narrow ranges. The Zawiya of Shaykh Ahmad ibn Fadl over the period 1168–96/1754–82 had an annual income of 1,360–1,400 *nisf fidda*s, except for the year 1192/1778–79 when it had an income of 2,506 *nisf fidda*s. The Madrasa al-Mu'ayyaniyya for the years between 1189–1211/1775–97 for which we find accounts reported incomes between 27,814 and 33,126 *nisf fidda*s. However, if income remained fairly constant, inflation could pose a further threat to the economic well-being of these religious endowments.

While incomes remained fairly constant, the *nazir*s could not always control expenses. The salaries for personnel were constant, as were expenses for mats for the floors, oil for the lamps, clothes and food to be distributed on specified religious holidays, water for the cisterns, food for the oxen that drove the water wheels, and others. Necessary repairs to the institutions, and to the properties that generated the income for the *waqf*, appear scattered here and there in the available accounts. For lack of sufficient financial resources, the *nazir*s had to postpone necessary repairs to the properties owned by the *waqf* and to the institutions supported by the income from the properties.[37] During periods of extensive repair, the salaries of essential personnel were often withheld if the structure remained closed, creating savings for the *waqf* but hardship for its employees. The maintenance of the properties that produced the income for the *awqaf* was so important that many donors stated in their endowment deeds (*waqfiyyat*) that the *nazir*'s first responsibility was to maintain these properties before all else and they stipulated that income was to be spent on the upkeep and repair of the income-producing properties before any income was spent on salaries and services. It would appear that few supervisors followed these instructions closely. Over time, for lack of proper maintenance, the income-producing properties of the *waqf* and the institution the *waqf* was set up to support showed obvious signs of decay while the *nazir* tried to sustain the continuation of the institution's religious mission. The responses the *nazir*s made to these problems are not within the scope of this chapter. Long-term leases of *waqf* properties, the exchange of unproductive properties, mortgages, the giving of permission to others with sufficient capital to build on *waqf* land or to make substantial additions to existing *waqf*-owned properties brought temporary relief but long-term disadvantage to the *waqf*.[38]

Itemized expenditures of the religious institutions of Damiette and Faraskur

The financial accounts prepared by accountants (*afandis*) for the supervisors of *awqaf* give us some insight into the religious activities undertaken in each institution and their physical condition.[39] We find expenses for the *nazir*, for the specialist who prepared the account, for the witnesses to the account, and sometimes for the individual who certified the need for repair to a structure. Salaries for all the people performing religious services for the mosque, *madrasa* or *zawiya*, such as imams, *khatibs*, *mu'adh-dhins*, timekeepers, instructors of the various Islamic disciplines, Qur'an reciters, specialists who recited during the month of Ramadan, and others were listed in the accounts. The salaries for personnel who performed services for the institution, such as janitors, watchmen, carpenters, water carriers, and the like were also cited. Expenses for candles, floor mats, oil for the lamps, distributions of clothing and food during Ramadan, and the like formed an important part of an institution's total expenses. As mentioned above, the supervisors of most religious institutions had to advance money to cover the excess of expenses over income of the institutions they managed. Some *nazirs* were owed sums greater than the annual income of the properties they managed.[40] See Table 16.2.

Some of the data assembled in Table 16.2 are skewed, owing to special circumstances in the particular year for which an account is recorded. For instance, the account for the Jami' al-Kawundaki in Faraskur for the year 1190/1776–77 shows a total income, mostly from one-time payments, of 86,038 *nisf fiddas*. This sum included 16,500 *nisf fiddas* extra rent from a *wikala* which the *nazir* had obtained, another 16,000 *nisf fiddas* owed by the previous supervisor, back rent of 3,600 *nisf fiddas* for the previous 13 years, 13,486 *nisf fiddas* for back rent for the years 1183–89, back rent of 7,300 *nisf fiddas* from the year 1184 and 12,470 *nisf fiddas* for back rent of farmland for the preceding four years.[41] This account suggests that the new supervisor was more aggressive in collecting rents than the previous one had been. The incomes of the previous two years (31,475 and 30,815 *nisf fiddas*) appear to be closer to the norm. Likewise, the account for the Zawiya of Ibn Wakil al-Sultan for the year 1196/1781–82 shows that the supervisor withdrew 6,302 *nisf fiddas* that he was owed by the *waqf*, so the figure for administrative expenses is also skewed for that year. Nevertheless, some generalizations can be made from the figures assembled in Table 16.2.

Many of the items, such as salaries for the scholars who performed religious services at the institutions, or for the service personnel and supplies, were fairly constant. Yet there are years when the institution was closed for repairs (see al-Masjid al-Mu'allaq for the period 1194–95/1780–81 or the Jami' al-Kawundaki for the year 1190/1775–76) and no salaries were paid. In general, Table 16.2 shows that salaries

Table 16.2 Expenses by area in *nisf fidda*s

Name of waqf	Income by year(s) AH	Administrative expenses (%)	Salaries		Repairs (%)	Owing the nazir	Totals % of income
			Religious personnel (%)	Supplies services (%)			
Al-'Utbaniyya	1180	2,400	4,842		3,879		11,121
(al-'Atabani)	11,256.5	21.3%	43.0%		34.5%	1,680	98.8%
	1189	1,080	3,710	5,370			10,160
	9,872	10.9%	37.6%	54.4%		368	102.9%
Al-Mu'ayyaniyya	1191	6,920	17,450	8,425	902		33,697ᵃ
	32,027	21.6%	54.4%	26.3%	2.8%	5,111	105.1%
	1192	15,597ᵇ	14,685	2,876	9,500		42,658
	32,247	48.4%	45.5%	8.9%	29.5%	5,111	132.3%
Zawiyat Ibn Nuwayr	1195–95	720	240	1,360	992		3,312
	3,140	22.9%	7.6%	43.3%	32.6%	2,822	105.4%
al-Madrasa al-Nasiriyya	1188–95	2,360	5,924	16,480	4,102		28,226
	15,000	15.7%	39.5%	110.0%	27.3%	21,653	192.4%
al-Masjid al-Mu'allaq	1168–69	240		240	615		1,095
	1,080	22.2%		22.2%	57.0%	631	101.4%
	1194–95	440		740	4,500		5,680
	2,140	20.6%		34.6%	210.3%	3,540	265.3%
Jami' al-Kawundaki	1190	1,348	2,158		4,953		22,781
	86,038	1.6%	2.5%		5.8%	10,774	26.5%
Jami' Muhammad Çorbaji/Faraskur	1191	720	1,380	1900	8,544		12,544
	10,872	6.6%	12.7%	17.5%	78.6%	9,239	115.4%
Zawiyat Ibn Wakil al-Sultan	1191	1,215	1,260	804	22		3,301
	3,119	38.9%	40.3%	25.8%	0.7%	4,075	105.7%
	1192	1,395	1,215	628	28		3,266
	3,216	43.4%	37.8%	19.5%	0.8%	4,188	101.5%
	1196	6,302		763	3,572		10,637
	3,734	168.8%		20.4%	95.7%	7,012	284.9%
Zawiyat Ahmad ibn Fadl	1194	341	435	615			1,391
	1,360	25.1%	32.0%	45.2%		1,502	102.3%
Jami' al-Zikwi (al-Bahr)	1192–94		34,045	37,860		33,931	105,836
	62,596		54.4%	60.5%		54.2%	169.1%

Notes

Table 16.2 breaks down the expenses reported by the *nazir* into four broad categories. They are Administrative Expenses (consisting largely of the salary received by the *nazir*, but also including the payments to the scribes who prepared the accounts, witnesses certifying the accounts, and others); Salaries, including gifts during Ramadan, for the religious personnel (teachers, imams, *khatib*s, *mu'adhdhin*s, Qur'an reciters, etc.); Supplies and Salaries for those performing secular services for the institution, such as carpenters, water carriers, drivers of oxen for the *saqiyya*, etc.; and Repairs. The figures in the column citing the amount owed to the *nazir* by the *waqf* are not included as part of the Total column, except in the case of Jami' al-Zikwi for 1192–94 AH.

a The account claims total expenses of 37,338 *nisf fidda*s, but does not list all expenses.
b In this year, the wakil took 9,597 *nisf fidda*s owed him from the income of the *waqf*. He was still owed 5,111 *nisf fidda*s.

and the cost of supplies amounted to 50–75 percent of total expenditures.[42] Of the four areas of expense highlighted in Table 16.2, the expenses of administration and those for repairs fluctuated most widely. Administrative expenses ranged between 6.6 and 48.4 percent of income (leaving out the special cases of Jami' al-Kawundaki and Zawiyat Ibn Wakil al-Sultan). The administrative expenses for the Zawiya of Ibn Wakil al-Sultan had a particularly high rate, ranging between 38.9 and 43.4. percent.[43]

The chief *qadi* in Cairo received far more (5,000 *nisf fiddas*) for his absentee honorific supervision of the Jami' al-Mu'ayyaniyya than any other *nazir*s of religious institutions in Damiette or Faraskur received for their on-site services.

Repairs to the religious institutions or to the revenue-producing buildings that supported them appear to have been made only when absolutely necessary. The Masjid al-Mu'allaq was completely repaired by its *nazir* during the years 1194–95/1780–81, as was the Zawiya of Ibn Wakil al-Sultan in 1196/1781–82, whereas the two large town mosques, the Jami' al-'Utbaniyya and the Jami' al-Mu'ayyaniyya, on two occasions received repairs costing totals of 34.5 percent and 22.3 percent of income respectively. Many of the smaller institutions had such limited incomes that repairs were difficult to undertake. See, for instance, the income figures for al-Masjid al-Mu'allaq, the Zawiya of Ibn Wakil al-Sultan, or the Zawiya of Ahmad ibn Fadl.

Conclusions

It would appear that in the second half of the eighteenth century Damiette's Muslim religious institutions were administered by a small circle of high-ranking *'ulama'* and military officials. The case of Damiette's major mosque, the Jami' al-Zikwi, or al-Bahr, was unique. Its *nazir* was the chief *qadi* in Cairo and his agent was one of the chief military officers in Damiette. The other mosques, *madrasas* and *zawiyas* surveyed in this study were supervised by a small number of local notable religious families whose representatives either held high religious office, such as those of mufti or *qadi*, or were the sons of deceased high-ranking religious leaders. *'Ulama'* of the Shafi'i rite were predominant among this group.

The religious institutions in Damiette itself were supported by a wide range of commercial properties such as *wikalas*, shops, *hasils*, and *qa'as* from which their *awqaf* received rents. In addition, the institutions owned a large number of *bustans* and empty plots. Residences are seldom mentioned in the accounts surveyed. The two institutions in Faraskur, which was surrounded by an agricultural zone, owned a better quality of properties, including *wikalas* and farmland, and appeared to be in less financial distress than the institutions in Damiette. It may be that these institutions, being newer, suffered less deterioration to their buildings than the Damiette institutions.

The data suggest that the Muslim religious institutions in Damiette were in a period of decline. Income from their properties, many of which were vacant or did not produce income, was not sufficient to meet the on-going expenses of the institutions. Salaries and services ate up the bulk of their incomes. Even the salaries and expenses for supervision and accounting ran between 6.6 and 48 percent of total income. Little was left with which the supervisors could make necessary repairs to the religious institutions and their properties.

The figures in Table 16.1 also show that incomes from *waqf* properties either remained fairly constant or declined in the period under survey. The Jami' al-Kawundaki in Faraskur is an aberration. We find more properties un-leased or more plots not producing any income as the years go by. With very few exceptions in individual years, the *nazir* reported a (sometimes sizable) deficit of expenses over income. Some institutions owed their *nazir*s a sum greater than the annual income of the *waqf.*

The Muslim community in Damiette was served by a rather small group of large mosques and *madrasa*s and a larger number of *zawiya*s, some of which offered instruction and worship. Among mosques, only the Jami' al-Zikwi, which reported an income for the three years 1192–94/1178–80 of 62,596 *nisf fidda*s, had sufficient income to pay for salaries and services. The Masjid al-Mu'allaq had an income so low from the three small properties it owned that it could not offer a full range of religious services.

The major religious institutions of Damiette were the four or five *madrasa*s that still offered religious services and instruction. Among these, the Madrasa al-Nasiriyya had an income only slightly higher than the various *zawiya*s of the town. The Zawiyat Ibn Nuwayr inside this *madrasa* reported an income almost as great as the *madrasa*'s. We do not have an account for the Madrasa al-Madbuliyya which lay in the northern section of the town, but we do know that it continued to offer instruction, for a shaykh of the residents of the *madrasa* drew a salary. The Madrasa al-'Utbaniyya reported annual incomes of approximately 10,000–11,000 *nisf fidda*s and appears to have been one of the better supervised institutions, for it carried little debt. Its few salaried teachers, however, appear mainly to have been for the instruction of children.[44] The Madrasa al-Mu'ayyaniyya enjoyed the largest income among the religious institutions but also reported a deficit for each of the eight years for which we are able to put together an account. These were the four *madrasa*s still operating in Damiette. The Zawiya of Ibn Wakil al-Sultan also apparently offered classes, for 720 *nisf fidda*s in salary was given to a scholar who served as imam and who also offered instruction.[45] Other older institutions, such as the Madrasa al-Ridwaniyya for which no account was found, appear to have been in decline. Supervisors seldom had sufficient funds to make necessary repairs to the institutions or their income-producing properties, hence the institutions were condemned to gradual decline over time.

Despite their financial problems, religious institutions continued to function, perhaps in a reduced mode, for centuries. In 1592, for instance, the Masjid al-Mu'allaq, the Madrasa al-Musallimiyya, the Masjid of Shaykh Abu al-Nur, the mosque/*zawiya* of Ibn Nuwayrinja, the Madrasa al-Nasiriyya, and the mosque of al-Bakri had either closed completely or could no longer offer services because an officer of the Ottoman 'Azab corps had acquired their supervision and withheld all their income for a number of years.[46] Yet we find many of them still functioning in the late eighteenth century.

That religious institutions could survive over centuries through times of neglect, through a decline in income, through lengthy periods when their supervisors neglected their duties or stole from the income of their *awqaf*, says a good deal about the ability of such institutions to survive difficult times. It suggests also that looking at scattered accounts of these institutions over a period of just one year, or even a series of years within a narrow period, does not tell us the whole story of the financial situation of these institutions, some of which were "recently" created or renovated, while others supported religious services for centuries.

Notes

1 On the involvement of the state in the affairs of *awqaf*, see Muhammad 'Afifi, *al-Awqaf wal-Haya al-Iqtisadiyya fi Misr fil-'Asr al-'Uthmani* (Cairo, 1991), pp. 62–79; Richard van Leeuwen, *Waqfs and Urban Structures: The Case of Ottoman Damascus* (Leiden, 1999), pp. 86–92.

2 In the Hanafi school of law, to which the Ottomans adhered, a *waqf* was challenged, or tested, prior to its validation.

3 See *Qanunname-i Misr*, translated into Arabic by Ahmad Fu'ad Mitwalli (Cairo, 1986), p. 85.

4 Isma'il Pasha reached Cairo on 23 January 1779 and was deposed in early September of the same year. See Thomas Philipp and Moshe Perlmann (eds), *'Abd al-Rahman al-Jabarti's History of Egypt* (Stuttgart, 1994), Vol. II, pp. 80–1/Vol. II, pp. 50–1 of the Bulaq edition in Arabic.

5 See Dar al-Watha'iq al-Qawmiyya (Cairo), hereafter DWQ, Mahkamat Dimyat, Sijill 278 (1192–94 AH), p. 22.

6 Many more partial accounts were found, but it was not possible to piece them together, spread as they were over many registers, or damaged beyond repair.

7 See Daniel Crecelius and Hamza 'Abd al-'Aziz Badr, "French Ships and their Cargoes sailing between Damiette and Ottoman Ports, 1777–1781," *Journal of the Economic and Social History of the Orient* (1994), 37, pp. 251–86.

8 See Jamal al-Din al-Shayyal, *Mujmal Ta'rikh Dimyat* (Port Sa'id n.d.), pp. 40–4.

9 Mention is made in the Damiette registers of the following religious structures in the town and surrounding region. Some appear to have been in disrepair, some were inside others, most appear to have been in economic distress, but many continued to provide partial functions. One of the more intriguing is the Madrasa al-Madbuliyya which is mentioned on more than one occasion as having a shaykh of the residents (*shaykh al-mujawwirin*). No full account of this *madrasa*, which was founded by the Mamluk ruler al-Ashraf Qa'itbey for the saintly shaykh al-Salih al-Madbuli, was found. See DWQ, Mahkamat Dimyat, Sijill 8 (972/1565–66), item 615. Religious structures mentioned are the following: al-Madrasa al-Aznudiyya; al-Madrasa al-Shabtaniyya (See Sijill 116, item 311); Zawiyat Sidi Abi al-'Abbas al-Hariti; Jami' al-'Izba in the strait (*bugaz*) of the port; Jami' Shaykh 'Umar al-Mawsali in Harat al-Manshah; Jami' Sidi Hasan al-Tawil in the port; Jami' al-Arba'in to the west of al-Jabbanah; al-Madrasa al-Barquqiyya on the Khalij al-Nawari near the Qantarat al-Khawwasin. It was founded by al-Hajj Yusuf, known as Ibn al-Nar. See, for instance, DWQ, Mahkamat Dimyat, Sijill 170 (1075 AH), Item 15; Sijill 238 (1164 AH), item 63. The Madrasa al-Musallimiyya on the main thoroughfare had lost its functions and become the seat of the court (*mahkama*). See DWQ, Mahkamat Dimyat, Sijill 4 (972), items 102, 622; Sijill 95 (1056 AH), item 169.

10 Data for the Jami' al-Kawundaki in Faraskur were found in DWQ, Mahkamat Dimyat, Sijill 273 (1183), pp. 8, then 15–16; Sijill 277 (1192–93), pp. 189–90.

11 Data on the Madrasa al-Mu'ayyaniyya were found in DWQ, Mahkamat Dimyat, Sijill 246 (1169), Item 59; Sijill 273 (1183), pp. 119–20; Sijill 277 (1192–93), pp. 84, then 61, 77–8, 179–80; Sijill 279 (1194–97), p. 248; Sijill 281 (1192–97), p. 272; Sijill 282 (1197–98), pp. 267–68; Sijill 290 (1209), pp. 314–15.

12 The *nisf fidda* was the Egyptian colloquial term for the official Ottoman *para*, a small silver coin of account. Forty *nisf fidda*s equaled one piaster (*qirsh*); twenty-five thousand *nisf fidda*s equaled one Egyptian purse (*kis*). See Stanford J. Shaw, *The Financial and Administrative Organization and Development of Ottoman Egypt: 1517–1798* (Princeton, 1962), XXII; André Raymond, *Artisans et commerçants au Caire au XVIIIe siècle* (Damascus: 1973), Vol. I, pp. 34–6.

13 DWQ, Mahkamat Dimyat, Sijill 280 (1195–96), p. 175.

14 Data on the Masjid al-Mu'allaq were found in DWQ, Mahkamat Dimyat, Sijill 248 (1170), p. 248; Sijill 280 (1194–95), p. 189.

15 Data for the Zawiya of Ibn Wakil al-Sultan were found in DWQ, Mahkamat Dimyat, Sijill 275 (1190), pp. 59–60; Sijill 277 (1192–93), p. 238; Sijill 278 (1192–94), pp. 99–100;

Sijill 280 (1195–96), pp. 113–14; Sijill 281 (1192–97), p. 102; Sijill 282 (1197–98), p. 49.

16 Data on the Madrasa al-Nasiriyya can be found in DWQ, Mahkamat Dimyat, Sijill 280 (1195–96), pp. 54–5.

17 DWQ, Mahkamat Dimyat, Sijill 248 (1170), pp. 48–9.

18 Ibid., Sijill 276 (1194–95), p. 212.

19 Ibid., Sijill 277 (1192–93), pp. 179–80.

20 Ibid., p. 29.

21 Data for the Madrasa al-'Utbaniyya were found in DWQ, Mahkamat Dimyat, Sijill 248 (1170), 43; Sijill 249 (1170), pp. 173–4; Sijill 276 (1192–93), pp. 236–8; Sijill 289 (1207–08), pp. 112, 133.

22 DWQ, Mahkamat Dimyat, 276, p. 234. The next day, letters arrived from the duumvirs Ibrahim Bey and Murad Bey announcing the same news, as if validating the governor's decree. Loc. cit.

23 Shaykh Kafrawi had been one of the favorites of the amir Muhammad Bey Abu al-Dhahab, who appointed him to an important position in the mosque/*madrasa* he built in Cairo before his death in 1775. See Daniel Crecelius, "The Waqfiyah of Muhammad Bey Abu al-Dhahab, II," *Journal of the American Research Center in Egypt* (1979), XVI, pp. 130–1. His obituary is given in al-Jabarti's *History of Egypt*, Vol. II, pp. 271–5; Vol. I, pp. 165–7 of the Bulaq Arabic edition.

24 The Danjihi family was apparently a well-known religious family in Damiette. Al-Jabarti cites the obituaries of Ahmad ibn Salah al-Din al-Danjihi who died on 19 April 1769 and had been the shaykh of the Madbuliyya Madrasa and supervisor of its *awqaf*, and Shaykh Muhammad ibn Yusuf ibn 'Isa al-Danjihi al-Shafi'i, who died on 29 January 1765. See *Al-Jabarti's History of Egypt*, Vol. I, p. 529/Arabic I, p. 317, and Vol. I, p. 433/Arabic I, p. 262.

25 DWQ, Mahkamat Dimyat, Sijill 276 (1192–93), p. 234.

26 Ibid., Sijill 280 (1195–96), p. 41.

27 In the eighteenth century a *bustan* designated agricultural land surrounded by (possibly fruit) trees.

28 Data on the Zawiya of Ahmad ibn Fadl were found in DWQ, Mahkamat Dimyat, Sijill, 275 (1190), p. 12; Sijill 276 (1192–93), p. 216; Sijill 278 (1192–94), pp. 100–1; Sijill 279 (1194–97), p. 229; Sijill 280 (1195–96), p. 56; Sijill 282 (1197–98), p. 349.

29 DWQ, Mahkamat Dimyat, Sijill 276 (1192–93), pp. 101–2.

30 This *madrasa* was located in the Khatt Suq al-Hisba. The *zawiya* of Ibn al-Nuwayr was added inside it at a later date. Data on the Madrasa al-Nasiriyya were found in Mahkamat Dimyat, Sijill 280 (1195–96), pp. 54–55.

31 Data on the Jami' al-Zikwi were found in DWQ, Mahkamat Dimyat, Sijill 279 (1194–97), p. 300, then Sijill 281 (1192–97), pp. 71–2.

32 This *madrasa*, inside of which was the tomb of Sidi Fatih Abi al-'Ata, goes back to the Fatimid period. It was originally known as al-'Atabani, after Abi al-'Ata. The mosque is in the southern section of the town, near the Zikwi mosque at the point where the river bends. It stood originally near the Nile bank, but by the eighteenth century was a short distance from the river, owing to the build-up of land where the river bends.

33 Despite the stipulation made by many donors that the property belonging to their *waqf* should not be "mortgaged, leased, sold, or exchanged," in subsequent years, when the *waqf* did not have the financial resources to make necessary repairs to its income-producing property, supervisors would offer various types of leases to generate the income for the repairs. The practice was not popular with donors or beneficiaries because all too often the lessee gained control of the property through the device of a long-term lease, known as *ijaratayn*. On the various types of leases relating to *waqf* properties, see, among other sources, John Robert Barnes, *An Introduction to Religious Foundations in the Ottoman Empire* (Leiden, 1987), pp. 50–9, and Randi Deguilhem, "Waqf documents: a multi-purpose historical source – the case of 19th century Damascus," in Daniel Panzac (ed.), *Les villes dans L'Empire ottoman: activités et sociétés* (Paris, 1991), tome I, pp. 76–95.

34 Data on the Jami' Muhammad Çorbaji were found in DWQ, Mahkamat Dimyat, Sijill 275 (1190), pp. 247–8; Sijill 282 (1197–98), pp. 267–8; Sijill 284 (1201), p. 310.

35 DWQ, Mahkamat Dimyat, Sijill 277 (1192–93), pp. 189–90.

36 We see very few properties added to the *awqaf* surveyed during the roughly half a century 1754–97. On the other hand, we find an increasing number of properties reporting no income, an indication that they were falling into disrepair or, as in at least one case, a military officer paid no rent for a residence belonging to the *waqf* because he renovated the residence at his own expense. Many of the accounts also report no income from unused plots (*sahhat*) of land.

37 This contrasts clearly with the accounts from the *awqaf ahliyya* of the Damiette registers. These *ahli* accounts indicate that *nazir*s, usually the beneficiaries of their "family" *awqaf*, were able to make extensive renovations to their properties on an almost annual basis. Many supervisors reported painting their residences annually, upgrading their living quarters, or adding rooms to their existing residences but still distributed a sizable surplus to the beneficiaries of the *waqf*.

38 See, for example, the discussion on the condition of the religious institutions in Aleppo in the mid-eighteenth century and the problems related to the supervision of these institutions in Abraham Marcus, *The Middle East on the Eve of Modernity: Aleppo in the Eighteenth Century* (New York, 1989), pp. 305–13.

39 As anyone who has worked with the official accounts of the Ottoman government knows, numerous errors of addition and subtraction can be found in these records. Not all of the figures in Table 16.2 add up to the totals cited in the Damiette registers.

40 See, for example, the accounts of the Zawiya of Ibn Wakil al-Sultan, al-Madrasa al-Nasiriyya, the Masjid al-Mu'allaq, the Zawiyat Ahmad ibn Fadl, and the Jami' al-Zikwi.

41 DWQ, Mahkamat Dimyat, Sijill 277 (1192–93), pp. 189–90.

42 The small Masjid al-Mu'allaq either had no religious personnel or was closed during the four years surveyed in Table 16.2.

43 In 1196/1781–82 the *nazir* withdrew a sizable amount that was owed him from previous years, thereby making this item 168.8 percent of income.

44 DWQ, Mahkamat Dimyat, Sijill 289 (1207–08), report for the year 1180, pp. 112, 133.

45 Ibid., Sijill 275 (1190), pp. 59–60.

46 See Daniel Crecelius and Hamza 'Abd al-'Aziz Badr, "The Usurpation of Waqf Revenues in Late Sixteenth Century Damiette," *Journal of the American Research Center in Egypt*, (1995) XXXII, pp. 265–8.

17 The expropriation of the Pasha's peasants

Ursula Wokoeck

One of the products of Michael Winter's scholarly interest in Ottoman history is his *Egyptian Society under Ottoman Rule, 1517–1798*.[1] At first sight, the title may seem a bit surprising: the study covers a very long period, three centuries, but leaves out the fourth, that is, the nineteenth century, with which Winter is also well acquainted. But the study does not deal with political history alone; it has also a strong focus on society. The great wealth of information relates to pre-modern, especially urban society in Ottoman Egypt, although it does not by any means neglect the political setting.[2] If the discussion had been extended to the nineteenth century, it would have gone beyond the framework of the study. The political, social and cultural developments of that century brought a quantitative increase in change to Ottoman Egypt, which is inevitably linked with a qualitative aspect, namely the beginning of modernity. Although dating the onset of modernity has been and still is a much contested issue, there is fairly wide agreement that the eighteenth century (at least until the early 1770s) is still to be considered pre-modern.[3] Moreover, Ottoman rule over Egypt was clearly interrupted by the French occupation in 1798. Winter's study can end there, and thus avoid the thorny problems of nineteenth-century modernity.

Since it is the student's prerogative to be less prudent than her teacher, I shall try to make a tiny contribution to the modernity debate, namely the issue of property rights with regard to peasant land in the first half of the nineteenth century in Ottoman Egypt. In light of the fundamental importance of agriculture for pre-modern society,[4] changes in the land regime are seen as major indicators for the beginning of modernity, in particular in the form of the introduction of the modern concept of private property with regard to agricultural land.[5] In *The Pasha's Peasants*,[6] Kenneth Cuno provides the most pertinent and thorough study of the land regime in the Egyptian countryside. On the basis of extensive archival research (focusing on the Mansura region), the work covers a period of some one hundred years (from the mid-eighteenth to the mid-nineteenth centuries). Cuno combines a close and extremely skilful reading of the archival sources with an outline of the wider historical developments in Ottoman Egypt for the century under investigation. One of the great merits lies in the period studied. The starting point, 1740, is generally accepted to belong to the pre-modern period of Egyptian history, while its conclusion, 1858, is widely regarded as part of an era when modernity, or modernization, has already set in. That means that the transition from pre-modern to modern structures and dynamics should have occurred in the period under investigation. On the basis of his findings, however, Cuno argues that no major change can be found until 1858, and that the transition from the pre-modern to the modern period should to be sought in the later part of the nineteenth century.

More specifically with regard to peasants, Cuno begins by mapping their position in the land regime of the eighteenth century. In principle, all agricultural land was considered *miri* or *kharaj* land. The former term emphasizes that it belongs to the ruler/state, while the latter focuses on the holder's obligation to pay a tax on the produce (*kharaj*). Agrarian administration[7] mainly meant administration of *kharaj*. Cuno emphasizes that 'the right to exploit the land was left to the peasants. What was at issue was control of the surplus they produced'.[8] The land tax (*kharaj*) was collected either directly by state officials, or via intermediaries: tax farming (*iltizam*) or direct assignment to the military (*iqta'*). Although the form of tax collection may account for processes of centralization and decentralization within the Ottoman system, Cuno found no indication that such shifts altered the measure of control over peasants in eighteenth-century Egypt; no signs of developments towards 'enserfment' or 'feudalization' were found in rural society.[9] Most agricultural production was carried out by peasants, as individual (household) units within a stratified village setting.[10]

In Lower Egypt, peasant land tenure[11] was characterized by peasant households-holding rights (*tasarruf* – rendered as 'usufruct') to specific units of *miri* land, that is, 'in effect state-owned land'.[12] These rights could be sold, inherited, rented and pawned. The holders of such rights were obliged to cultivate the land and to pay *kharaj*. The failure to do so for a couple of years in succession might result in a loss of the right, if it were transferred to a more able candidate. Cuno notes that – despite the scantiness of our information – there is evidence to suggest that this kind of land regime existed throughout the Muslim period and even earlier, under Byzantine rule, when all agricultural land was considered 'state fiscal land'.[13]

The right of *tasarruf* was distinguished from the right of *milk*.[14] Apart from gardens, vineyards and orchards, *milk* was exceptional with regard to agricultural land, as reflected not only in mere quantitative terms, but also in the requirement of title deeds.[15] Moreover, *milk* was usually found among members of intermediary groups. The rights of *tasarruf* and *milk* followed distinct rules: *milk* did not entail the duty of cultivation, nor was *kharaj* payment due. *Milk* was inherited according to the rules of Islamic law, while *tasarruf* was passed on according to Ottoman *qanun* and practice, giving preference to non-division (of the work unit) and to male descendants. Furthermore, in case of voluntary alienation, *tasarruf* required – at least in principle – the cooperation of an official, while for *milk* it was a purely civil or private matter.

Against the background of the eighteenth-century situation and its dynamics, Cuno analyses the changes that began in the 1810s under Muhammad/Mehmet 'Ali[16] (r. 1805–48). Cuno argues that Muhammad 'Ali's political aims did not substantially differ from those of 'Ali Bey al-Kabir (r. 1760–72). However his strategies did, in so far as the European powers, in particular the growing European market for agricultural produce, had become a decisive factor in his calculation.[17] As for rural society proper, the 1810s brought a general recovery, which also included a 'liberation' of the peasants from their obligations towards the *multazim*. In the course of the abolition of the *iltizam* system, the peasants became 'the Pasha's peasants'.[18] In the 1820s, a change for the worse occurred, resulting in accelerated stratification among the peasantry, due to extensive redistribution aiming at the reallocation of peasant land from those unable to cultivate and pay taxes to those peasants who could do so.[19] In addition to natural disasters, the peasants' deteriorating situation can be attributed to a loss of manpower due to conscription and extensive *corvée*s for the building and maintenance of summer canals, and growing indebtedness combined with a loss of autonomy due to state intervention in production itself which stemmed from the combined effects of taxation and the monopoly system.[20]

The 1830s ushered in the appearance of what has been termed *'uhda*. This may refer to two different, though related phenomena. The common background was the growing inability of many peasants to cultivate their land and, in particular, to pay the taxes due. In the 1830s and 1840s, one variation of the term referred to the (not necessarily voluntary) assumption of responsibility by members of the elite for the arrears and current taxes of entire villages. Village *'uhda*s were tax farms.[21] A second variation of the term *'uhda* appeared in the 1830s, which referred to the contractual acquisition of *tasarruf*, entailing the responsibility (*'uhda*) for cultivation and tax payment. The difference between this practice and traditional forms of acquisition of *tasarruf* seems to lie in the emphasis on the obligation as well as in the fact that new holders might not necessarily have been peasants, in other words also townspeople. This form of *'uhda* signals the extension of the potential land tax payers to more affluent strata of non-rural society.[22]

Cuno observes that stratification is nothing new or modern in peasant society. In view of its acceleration, he considers the possibility whether quantity amounts to a qualitative change, and decides against it, on the basis of the following argument: *tasarruf* is considered a right to usufruct, not pertaining to the land itself.[23] The latter is state-owned. Muhammad 'Ali's reforms are seen as the mere realization of rights inherent to state ownership.[24] Exercising these rights had far-reaching consequences for peasants. At least temporarily, they lost a great part of their previous freedom of action with regard to decisions relating to both production proper and their relations to outsiders (marketing and finance) – entailing a higher degree of exploitation. The extent of the latter was such that large numbers of peasants were no longer able to meet their obligations (cultivation and tax payment) and lost their right of *tasarruf*, which traditionally was dependent on the fulfilment of these obligations. In that situation the government resorted to reallocating peasant land to those able to cultivate it and pay taxes. This was a traditional state prerogative (rooted in ownership), though it had previously not been exercised in such an extensive and systematic manner. Cuno argues that, although they resulted in major changes in rural society, these measures did not bring about any change with regard to the right of *tasarruf*.[25]

That very right in its traditional form was legally maintained up to and including the land law of 1858.[26] Contrary to previous studies (especially those by Gabriel Baer) which assumed that this law increased peasants' rights by granting rights of inheritance and alienation (and thus approaching private property), Cuno argues that there was no change in the concept and range of *tasarruf*, which remained as distinct from private property as it had been in the eighteenth century. The only change was a formal one: the introduction of the requirement of official written documentation for transactions. The purpose of the law was not to change the prevailing legal situation, but rather to fend off an enormous wave of law suits for reinstatement filed by peasants who had lost their land in the preceding years of crisis.[27] In Cuno's view, private property for peasant land became a possibility only under the *Muqabala* law (1871/74) and an effective reality under British occupation.[28]

There can be no doubt that Cuno's study is based on a thorough and systematic examination of pertinent archival material. Accepting these data, I would like to ask here whether his interpretation is the only possible one. The reasons for raising the question are two central arguments which might be less conclusive than Cuno seems to suggest. The first concerns the nature of *tasarruf* (and along similar lines of *iltizam*) which is considered a right to usufruct, not pertaining to the land itself.[29] To the best of my understanding, property cannot be anything but a right.[30] Thus the fact that *iltizam* and *tasarruf* are merely rights does not a priori move them to a level distinct from the one where property might be located, quite the contrary.

The second argument concerns the applicability of modern concepts to pre-modern contexts. Cuno stresses that the use of the term 'property' for pre-modern Egypt is unacceptable as being anachronistic. It is certainly plausible to call for a distinction between what is found in pre-modern Egypt and the modern concept of property. However, Cuno himself does not refrain from such anachronistic use of the concept of property. With regard to state ownership of land, matters are discussed as if the state's rights pertaining to land were indeed property in the modern sense. Although the peasants' rights are seen as something unrelated to modern property rights, pre-modern state-ownership contains at least in its potential, the comprehensive and exclusive nature of modern property. Thus Muhammad 'Ali's reforms can be seen to realise the inherent potential of full state-ownership.[31] Why should pre-modern state's rights be seen as precursors of modern rights, while that option is a priori – as a matter of concept – excluded with regard to pre-modern peasants' rights?

In order to illustrate the point at hand, comparison with a pre-modern European development may be useful. There the concept of property (in land) as an absolute, abstract, comprehensive right, from which all other rights to the object derive, can by no means be taken for granted. For example, in the German tradition,[32] the central concept expressing the relation between a person and an object is *Gewere*, the Roman legal equivalent of which has – since the fourteenth century – been considered to be *possessio*. The term *'eigen'/'Eigentum'* (in modern terminology: 'property') also referred to a person's relation to an object. The contents of *eigen* may have varied considerably, except for one requirement: *Gewere*. Generally, *eigen* means *das rechtmaessig Gehabte* (holding in rightful/lawful possession). *Eigen* may include cases of *proprietas ad dies vitae* as well as obligations to regular rent payments. Since *eigen* is not conceived as an absolute right, several persons may hold different rights to the same object as *eigen*.

Since the thirteenth century, the dominant trend in the various conceptions of *eigen* was one perceiving the term in direct opposition to *lehen* (fief). In this sense, *eigen* became synonymous to *allod*. However, also in this version, *eigen/allod* was only one of several main forms of a person's right pertaining to an object.

Against that background, the contrast to Roman law conceiving property (*dominium, proprietas*) as an absolute, comprehensive right to an object, accounts for the difficulties the commentators faced in their attempt to adapt Roman law to contemporary requirements in the fourteenth and fifteenth centuries. The solution found was an alteration of the theory, that is, the introduction of the doctrine of the divisibility of property. Thus they not only introduced next to the *dominus directus* (an owner whose right is not derived from someone else) a *dominium utile* – creating a pair that expresses the opposition between *eigen/allod* and *lehen*; but also a second pair: *dominium superium-dominium inferium* (usually *not* integrated into a *dominium plenum*). Under absolutism, jurists and theologians developed this distinction further, arguing that all property is a derivative right from a comprehensive *dominium* vested in the ruler.

The concept of undivided, absolute and comprehensive property emerged only with liberalism (in particular in its opposition to absolutism) – in the second half of the eighteenth century. Private property is seen as the 'material' expression of the free will (the essence of the individual): the privatized version of the absolutist ruler/sovereign. This change in concept resulted in the appearance of two main new battle lines: (1) A 'societal' conflict between prospective proprietors: according to the new concept, the absolute comprehensive nature of property excludes the possibility of the coexistence of several different property rights pertaining to the same object. The transition, therefore, means that one of them has to be elevated to 'the real thing', while the others are degraded to merely derivative rights. In other words, a process of expropriation of alternative owners occurs, the outcome of which depends on the actual (political, social, economic) strength of the parties concerned. (2) A 'political' conflict between private property and the state: this one has not been 'solved'; neither side has come out victorious, that is, expropriated the other. Instead, a truce has been struck based on a terminological compromise: the distinction between private and public, between property and sovereignty. Thus, property can be conceived as an abstract, absolute, comprehensive right in the societal context, while state 'infringement' on the very principle is categorized in contemporary terminology as '*Sozialbindung des Eigentums*', that is, the public liability of private property. The term allows for the distinction between *public* restrictions on ownership in fee simple, and those characterizing restricted ownership.

Although the European example can certainly not be taken as the measure of things, it nonetheless provides one possible model for a situation where the modern concept of absolute property is absent. For lack of a better alternative, it might be worthwhile to consider the 'divided property' concept with regard to pre-modern Egypt. There are three candidates for potential holders of such rights: the peasants, the intermediaries (e.g. *multazims*), and the state. For brevity's sake, the discussion here will relate only to the peasants and the state.[33] Neither has absolute property in the modern sense. The story relating the development from such a state of affairs to the introduction of a modern concept of property would have to negotiate between two potential narrative threads: one narrating the process of expropriation of either one of the pre-modern property holders, and the other recounting the compromise struck between private property and sovereignty. Since the second alternative, that is, the potential lineage of sovereignty, is usually forgotten, when focusing on the issue of private property, it may serve here as starting point.

Any interpretation proposing to see in the state's right to agricultural land a pre-modern form of sovereignty, and in *tasarruf* a pre-modern form of property, has to face the objection that there was also in pre-modern times 'real' property, namely *milk*. Cuno shows that among the *'ulama'* there were debates over whether or not peasant land had the legal status of *milk*, and that the dominant view decided against this option.[34] Furthermore, Cuno draws attention to the fact that with regard to transactions and inheritance distinct legal terms were used. Courts recorded the sale of *tasarruf* with the formula: *nazala wa-faragha wa-asqata* (to transfer, release and cede), and not as *ba'a* (to sell with regard to *milk*).[35] Inheritance was – in legal discourse – not termed *irth*, but *intiqal* (transmission).[36]

The argument concerning terminology would be conclusive, if the continuous usage of certain terms (*milk* is the modern term for property) were indicative of their equally constant meanings. Even if the field of meaning could be shown not to have changed much, this would still not prove that the exclusiveness the term enjoys today existed also in previous periods. Moreover, the strategies for ordering social practice by means of concepts may not be similar. In other words, there may have been different terms for 'the same thing'. Today, as far as terminology goes, the 'sale' of a tomato is the same as the 'sale' of an industrial plant. Considering the difference in what has to be done in order to accomplish one or the other, two different words for these transactions might not seem out of place. In this regard it is also noteworthy that – according to the court records which Cuno reviewed – the peasants usually did not bother much with legal subtleties: to sell was *ba'a*, and inheritance was *irth*, also with regard to *tasarruf*.

In addition, the field of meaning of the term *tasarruf* is by no means as narrow and clear as Cuno's interpretation implies. According to Wehr it means 'usufruct, free disposal, right to dispose, administration',[37] and according to Lane, 'the being/becoming employed to act in whatever way one pleases, according to one's own judgement/discretion/free will or as a free agent in the disposal/management of the affair'.[38] The emphasis on 'free disposal' seems to support a 'property thesis' rather than rule it out.

In the light of these arguments, one might see both *tasarruf* and *milk* as property. The difference between these two types of property is to be sought in their relation to sovereignty, that is, the standardized degree of government interference. The point at hand may be illustrated by a present-day example: hygiene inspections by government officials in private homes are usually not considered acceptable, although in private restaurants they are. The difference as such is not sufficient to question the proposition that both homes and restaurants are private property. In an 'agrarianate citied society', agricultural production provides the basis for all other activities. Seen from the centre (the state), its functioning is of vital concern. Thus it is conceivable that the state claims a greater degree of interference than in other economic or social spheres. Thus *milk* may be seen as property pertaining to objects with regard to which the state has relatively little interest in taxation nor as to how they are used, transferred or inherited. *Tasarruf* pertains to agricultural land from the produce of which the state demands the payment of *kharaj*, one of its major revenue sources. In addition, the state claims the right to demand cultivation, control over alienation and inheritance. Since non-cultivation results in the non-payment of taxes, the reallocation of land that has not been cultivated for several years in succession can be seen as the execution of a debt against the property.

As for the control over alienation, Cuno notes that the court records contain only few such cases.[39] The examples cited tell us nothing about the circumstances. Thus all that is known is that in principle such a prerogative existed. On that slim factual basis, one may speculate that the control over alienation amounts first of all to the requirement of notification about the identity of the new person liable for paying tax and about the possible disappearance of the previous holder who may have unsettled accounts. In addition, it includes the possibility of checking the qualification of the prospective new holder – comparable to the limiting effect which the requirement of business licences may have today on the sale and acquisition of businesses.

The issue of inheritance is mainly an extension of the last consideration and a question of jurisdiction. The basic prerequisite for agricultural production is the peasant household. The land held by the right of *tasarruf* belonged to a household, although it was usually recorded under the name of its head (the oldest male).[40] If inheritance were to follow *shari'a* rules (as in the case of *milk*), the result would be the division of that basic unit. By contrast, *qanun* regulations applicable to *tasarruf* favoured the integrity and continuity of the household by transferring the right to the next oldest male in it. Thus the difference does not primarily concern the question whether or not *tasarruf* can be passed on after the death of its holder, but rather the identification of the 'lineage'.

Cuno cites two legal debates among the *'ulama'* that may cast doubt on the interpretation suggested here. One is a minority opinion held by some Shafi'i and Maliki jurists in Ottoman Egypt and Syria, according to which the cultivators' land is to be considered *milk* rather than *miri*. The second debate concerns the change in the legal status of peasant land (from *milk* to *miri*) in the Hanafi view.[41] The terminology of tax versus rent (*ijara*) in this context may be less conclusive than Cuno's discussion suggests.[42] The general fields of meaning of the root as recorded by Lane are far wider than what rent signifies today in the relation to the concept of absolute private property. Moreover, in its legal usage, the meaning is related to the term *tasarruf*. Thus the argument is circular.

On the other hand, the shift from *milk* to *miri* occurred within the Hanafi *madhhab*, that is, the official *madhhab* of the Ottoman Empire, at a time when the Ottomans established their rule over rich agricultural lands in the Arab–Muslim world. The debate among the *'ulama'* which Cuno cites may not concern the question of state ownership versus private property, but rather represent an attempt at bargaining over the degree of state interference in property rights. To what extent that claim could actually be realized is still an open question. If language usage is an indication, a concept of a derivative nature of peasants' rights to land did not inspire actual terminology. In Lower Egypt, the permanence of peasants' rights to specific pieces of land was expressed in the term *athar*,[43] denoting 'something that remains, and/or is passed on'.[44] Only from 'the mid-nineteenth century onward the terms *athariyya* and *kharajiyya* were used synonymously to refer to peasant-held land, which paid the *kharaj* tax'.[45]

On the basis of the earlier discussion, it is possible to conceive of *tasarruf* as (pre-modern) property, and of state ownership as the pre-modern lineage of sovereignty. Such alternative conceptualization may have major implications for the account of the developments since Muhammad 'Ali's reign. The Pasha's claim to state ownership seems to concur with contemporary European perceptions. Under the French occupation, large parts of *miri* land became '*domaines de la République*',[46] and 'hardly any of the numerous (contemporary) accounts of (Muhammad 'Ali's) rule failed to point out that he had made himself the sole owner of the land'.[47]

At face value, this view implies the expropriation of the peasants. However, Cuno's investigation shows that the right of *tasarruf* continued to exist. There is also no firm evidence for the assumption that *tasarruf* was effectively turned into a derivative right. It is therefore arguable that the state's claim to ownership coexisted with *tasarruf*. That means that the basic constellation remains one of either 'divided property' or sovereignty versus property, and that the story of Muhammad 'Ali's reforms has to narrate the political struggle of bargaining over the limits of state interference in property rights.

In that light, this reader cannot accept Cuno's argument that the increased tax burden, the change and increase in obligatory labour services, the direct intervention in production and market relations, as well as the massive systematic reallocation of land with tax arrears did not affect the *right* of *tasarruf*. If the state increases its right of interference, the property right is affected – as is reflected in modern legal debate on the question at which point the restrictions set to private property by public interests are such that they amount to expropriation. This argument could be challenged, if the degree of interference practised under Muhammad 'Ali was merely a realization of an already existent right, as Cuno seems to hold. For example, with regard to the reallocation of land, Cuno notes that this was a traditional right of the state, though it was rarely exercised. Motivated by the extraordinary conditions of Egypt during the early parts of the nineteenth century, Muhammad 'Ali exercised that right for the first time systematically on a massive scale. Thus the novelty is merely a quantitative one. But may not quantity amount to quality?

An indication that the state policy was not simply the realization of a long-standing and accepted tradition is found in the huge number of people who apparently thought that they had some ground for reclaiming *their* land previously lost or abandoned on account of tax arrears. As Cuno points out, this enormous wave of claims was the main reason for the legislation of the land law of 1858. Such wide disagreement calls for an explanation other than a reference to tradition. Here it might be worth investigating the actual functioning of the second variety of the *'uhda* phenomenon. As Cuno shows, this institution was meant also to expand the circle of people liable (and able) to pay land tax beyond peasant society. It seems rather unlikely that some one living in town and affluent enough to take upon himself such an obligation would move to the countryside and work the land. A plausible alternative may be a sort of 'share cropping' arrangement with the peasants on the land. In actual practice, the situation may not have differed much from that under the 'fractured' *iltizam* system, which Cuno found in the eighteenth century. Peasants might therefore see themselves as holding *tasarruf* (under a sort of *multazim*), whereas the institution of '*uhda*, as Cuno discerned it in the documents, stripped them of that right.

In the light of the argument presented here, the right of *tasarruf* seems to have become more limited by 1858 than it had been in the eighteenth century. The development reflects a gradual limitation of property rights, which can also be conceived as a process of expropriation. At the same time, the land law of 1858 can also be seen as a stepping-stone in the direction of the introduction of private property in the modern sense. Though it brought no increase in peasant rights, but rather the contrary, the 1858 land law nonetheless prepared the way for the transition, in so far as it codified the newly heightened strength of the state (not only as sovereign but also as proprietor) vis-à-vis *tasarruf*. It was from this position of strength that in the 1870s (*muqabala* law), the state attempted to claim and to sell the idea that *tasarruf* was indeed distinct from property. On the basis of the eighteenth-century situation, such an assertion would have been inconceivable.

With regard to the periodization debate, the interpretation sketched here suggests relocating the 'beginnings of modernisation' to the traditional baseline, around 1800 and agreeing with Cuno's observation:

> Modern historians have tended to overlook the fact that in certain basic ways Muhammad Ali was pursuing the traditional aims of Egyptian rulers and even using some of their traditional strategies, for in the new economic and political environment of the nineteenth century these policies had a transformative impact on the economy and society.[48]

Notes

1 Michael Winter, *Egyptian Society under Ottoman Rule, 1517–1798* (London, 1992).

2 The term 'pre-modern' employed here follows Marshall Hodgson's concept of 'agrarianate citied societies'. Marshall G. S. Hodgson, *The Venture of Islam: Conscience and History in a World Civilization, vol. 1: The Classical Age* (Chicago, IL, 1974), pp. 107–9.

3 Conventionally, Egyptian (as well as much of Middle Eastern) modern history was thought to have begun with the French occupation of Egypt in 1798. See, for example, P. J. Vatikiotis, *The Modern History of Egypt* (London, 1969) (as of the second edition (1980), the title was changed to *The History of Egypt from Muhammad Ali to Sadat/Mubarak*); William R. Polk and Richard I. Chambers (eds), *The Beginnings of Modernization in the Middle East: The Nineteenth Century* (Chicago, IL, 1968). The first alternative reading tried to push the date line back into the last third of the eighteenth century, arguing that modernity commenced due to integration into the world economic system. The most outstanding contribution for Egypt is Peter Gran, *The Islamic Roots of Capitalism: Egypt, 1760–1840* (Austin, TX, 1979); and his 'Late-Eighteenth-Century – Early-Nineteenth-Century Egypt: Merchant Capitalism or Modern Capitalism?', in Huri Islamoğlu-Inan (ed.), *The Ottoman Empire and World-Economy* (Cambridge, 1987), pp. 27–41. However, subsequent research has gone in the opposite direction: locating the decisive date in the mid-nineteenth century and even beyond. One of the early studies of this trend was Ehud R. Toledano's *State and Society in Mid-Nineteenth-Century Egypt* (Cambridge, 1990).

4 See note 2.

5 According to Gabriel Baer, private ownership emerged in the course of the adoption of European law codes in the 1850s. See especially his extensive study, *A History of Landownership in Modern Egypt 1800–1950* (Oxford, 1962). An alternative reading that seemed to suggest

that already in the second half of the eighteenth century distinct indigenous developments toward private ownership (with regard to *iltizam* holders) can be discerned is found in Kenneth M. Cuno, 'The Origins of Private Ownership of Land in Egypt: A Reappraisal', *International Journal of Middle East Studies* 12 (1980), pp. 245–75; reprinted in Albert Hourani, Philip S. Khoury and Mary C. Wilson (eds), *The Modern Middle East: A Reader* (London, 1993), pp. 195–228.

6 Kenneth M. Cuno, *The Pasha's Peasants – Land, Society and Economy in Lower Egypt, 1740–1858* (Cambridge, 1992).

7 Ibid., chapter 1.

8 Ibid., p. 19.

9 Ibid., chapter 2.

10 Ibid., chapter 3.

11 Ibid., chapter 4.

12 Ibid., p. 13.

13 Ibid., pp. 18–19.

14 Ibid., pp. 74, 77, 80. The term *milk* or *mulk* came to mean private property in modern times, and is usually thought to refer to property also in pre-modern times.

15 Ibid., p. 22.

16 Ehud R. Toledano, entry 'Muhammad 'Ali', *EI²*.

17 Cuno, p. 104.

18 Ibid., chapter 9.

19 Ibid., pp. 155–6.

20 Ibid., chapter 7.

21 Ibid., pp. 157–9.

22 Ibid., p. 157.

23 Ibid., p. 81.

24 Ibid., pp. 201–2.

25 Ibid., p. 190.

26 Ibid., pp. 195–7.

27 Ibid., pp. 190–1.

28 Ibid., pp. 203–4.

29 Ibid., p. 81. With regard to *iltizam* Cuno explains: 'Though the ability to be inherited and alienated is a characteristic of property, *iltizam* rights were not rights of landownership. The characteristics of property were located in the *iltizam* itself, not in the land' (ibid., p. 37).

30 Though in everyday language land (like any other object) is said be bought or sold, all that can be bought or sold in legal terms are the (property) rights pertaining to the object. Note the difference to the concept of possession.

31 Ibid., pp. 201–2.

32 For an outline, see Dieter Schwab, entry 'Eigentum', in Otto Brunner, Werner Conze and Reinhard Koselleck (eds), *Geschichtliche Grundbegriffe – Historisches Lexikon zur politisch-sozialen Sprache in Deutschland*, vol. 2 (Stuttgart, 1975), pp. 65–115; Dieter Schwab, entry 'Eigen', in Adalbert Erler and Ekkehard Kaufmann (eds), *Handwoerterbuch zur deutschen Rechtsgeschichte* vol. 1 (Berlin, 1971), pp. 877–9.

33 The *iltizam* system was abolished in the early stages of Muhammad 'Ali's reforms, and the village *'uhda* system was much more limited in extent and relatively short-lived.

34 Cuno, pp. 22–4, 77–80.

35 Ibid., p. 82.

36 Ibid., p. 74.

37 Hans Wehr, *A Dictionary of Modern Written Arabic*, 3rd edn by J. Milton Cowan (London, 1976).

38 Edward W. Lane, *Arabic-English Lexicon*, 2 vols (Cambridge, 1984 repr. of 1874/1877 edn).

39 Cuno, pp. 35–6.

40 Ibid., p. 233 n.14.

41 Drawing on Baber Johansen, *Islamic law on land tax and tent. The peasants' loss of property rights as interpreted in the Hanafite legal literature of the Mamluk and Ottoman periods* (London, 1988).
42 Cuno, pp. 22–4.
43 Ibid., p. 66.
44 Ibid., p. 232, n. 10.
45 Ibid.
46 Ibid., p. 46.
47 Ibid., p. 204.
48 Ibid., p. 103.

Publications of Michael Winter

Books

Society and Religion in Early Ottoman Egypt: Studies in the Writings of 'Abd al-Wahhab al-Sha'rani (New Brunswick, NJ: Transaction, 1982).

Egyptian Society Under Ottoman Rule, 1517–1798 (London and New York: Routledge, 1992).

Egyptian Society Under Ottoman Rule, translated into Arabic by Ibrahim Muhammad Ibrahim (Cairo, 2001) (translation of the above).

(ed., with Hava Lazarus-Yafeh), *Islam Judaism, Judaism Islam*, (Tel Aviv: The Broadcast University and The Ministry of Defence Publishing House, 2003) (in Hebrew).

(ed., with Amalia Levanoni), *The Mamluks in Egyptian and Syrian Politics and Society* (Leiden: Brill, 2003).

To appear

(ed., with Miri Shefer), *The Ottoman Empire and the Turkish Republic. Studies in Honor of Aryeh Shmuelevitz* (in Hebrew).

Articles

"The Teaching of Islamic Religion in the Turkish republic," *Ha-Mizrah he-Hadash*, 1968, 18, pp. 223–45 (in Hebrew).

"The Mawalid in Egypt from the Beginning of the Eighteenth Century to the Middle of the Twentieth Century," in Gabriel Baer (ed.), *The 'Ulama' and Problems of Religion in the World of Islam. Studies in Honour of Uriel Heyd* (Jerusalem: Magnes Press, 1971), pp. 79–103 (in Hebrew).

"The *Ashraf* and the *Niqabat al-Ashraf* in Egypt in Ottoman and Modern Times," *Ha-Mizrah he-Hadash*, 1975, 25, pp. 293–310 (in Hebrew).

(English translation): "The *Ashraf* and *Niqabat al-Ashraf* in Egypt in Ottoman and Modern Times," *Asian and African Studies*, 1985, 19, pp. 17–41.

"Prinzipien religioeser Erziehung im Heutigen Islam," in A. Falaturi and W. Strolz (eds), *Drei Wege zu dem Einen Gott* (Freiburg: Herder, 1976), pp. 141–61.

(English translation): "Principles of Religious Education in Present-Day Islam," in A. Falaturi and W. Strolz (eds), *Three Ways to the One God: The Faith Experience in Judaism, Christianity and Islam* (New York: Crossroad, 1987), pp. 103–16.

"Ali Ibn Maymun and Syrian Sufism in the Sixteenth Century," *Israel Oriental Studies*, 1977, 7, pp. 281–308.

"Content and Form in the Elegies of al-Mutanabbi," J. Blau (ed.), *Studia Orientalia Memoriae D. H. Baneth Dedicata* (Jerusalem: Magnes Press, 1979), pp. 327–45.

"The Islamic Profile and the Religious Policy of the Ruling Class in Ottoman Egypt," in J. L. Kraemer and Ilai Alon (eds), *Religion and Government in the World of Islam* (=*Israel Oriental Studies*, 10, 1980), pp. 132–45.

"A Seventeenth Century Arabic Panegyric of the Ottoman Dynasty," *Asian and African Studies*, 1980, 13, pp. 130–56.

"Turks, Arabs and Mamluks in the Army of Ottoman Egypt," *Wiener Zeitschrift fuer die Kunde des Morgenlandes*, 1980, 72, pp. 97–122.

"'Ali Efendi's Anatolian Campaign Book: A Seventeenth Century Defense of the Egyptian Army," *Turcica*, 1983, 15, pp. 267–309.

"Egyptian Jewry in the Ottoman Period according to Turkish and Arabic Sources," *Pe'amim*, 16, 1983, pp. 5–21 (in Hebrew).

"Military Connections Between Egypt and Syria (including Palestine) in the Early Ottoman Period," in A. Cohen and G. Baer (eds), *Egypt and Palestine: A Millennium of Association (868–1948)* (Jerusalem and New York: Ben Zvi Institute and St. Martin's Press, 1984), pp. 139–49.

"Orthodox Islam and Popular Islam in Turkey and Egypt at the end of the Middle Ages," *Zemanim* (Tel Aviv), 1984, 16 (Autumn), pp. 48–57 (in Hebrew).

"The Revolt of Ibrahim Pasha, Governor of Baghdad, 1056/1646–1057/1648," *Festschrift Andreas Tietze, Wiener Zeitschrift fuer die Kunde des Morgenlandes*, 1986, 76, pp. 323–8.

"Social and Religious Reform in Later Sufism," *Ha-Mizrah he-Hadash*, 1986, 31, pp. 35–47 (in Hebrew).

"A Polemical Treatise by 'Abd al-Ghani al-Nabulsi against a Turkish Scholar on the Religious Status of the *Dhimmi*s," *Arabica*, 1988, 35, pp. 92–103.

"The Relations of Egyptian Jews with the Authorities and with the Non-Jewish Society," in Jacob M. Landau (ed.), *The Jews in Ottoman Egypt, 1517–1914* (Jerusalem: Misgav Yerushalayim, 1988), pp. 371–420 (in Hebrew).

"A Statute for the Mercantile Fleet in Eighteenth Century Egypt," *Mediterranean Historical Review*, 1988, 3, pp. 118–22.

"Saladin's Religious Personality, Policy and Image," in J. L. Kraemer (ed.), *Perspectives on Maimonides* (Oxford: Oxford University Press, 1991), pp. 309–22.

"An Arabic and a Turkish Chronicle from the beginning of Ottoman rule in Egypt," in Amy Singer and Amnon Cohen (eds), *Aspects of Ottoman History: Papers from CIEPO IX, Jerusalem, Scripta Hierosolymitana* (Jerusalem: Magnes Press, 1994), pp. 318–26.

"The Arab Self-Image as Reflected in Jordanian Textbooks," in A. Susser and A. Shmuelevitz (eds), *The Hashemites in the Modern Arab World: Essays in Honour of the late Professor Uriel Dann* (London: Frank Cass, 1995), pp. 207–20.

"Islam in the State: Pragmatism and Growing Commitment," in Shimon Shamir (ed.), *Egypt from Monarchy to Republic: A Reassessment of Revolution and Change* (Boulder, CO: Westview, 1995), pp. 44–58.

"Islamic Attitudes toward the Human Body," in Jane Marie Law (ed.), *Religious Reflections on the Human Body* (Bloomington and Indianapolis, IN: Indiana University Press, 1995), pp. 36–45.

Hebrew translation of the above in: Hava Lazarus-Yafeh (ed.), *Muslim Writers on Jews and Judaism* (Jerusalem: Zalman Shazar Center, 1996), pp. 183–93.

"Syria – from Mamluk to Ottoman rule," *Ha-Mizrah he-Hadash*, 1996, 38, pp. 26–37 (in Hebrew).

"Ottoman Egypt, 1525–1609," in M. W. Daly (ed.), *The Cambridge History of Egypt vol. 2: Modern Egypt, from 1517 to the End of the Twentieth Century* (Cambridge: Cambridge University Press, 1998), pp. 1–33.

"The Ottoman Occupation," in Carl F. Petry (ed.), *The Cambridge History of Egypt vol. 1: Islamic Egypt, 640–1517* (Cambridge: Cambridge University Press, 1998), pp. 490–516.

"The Re-Emergence of the Mamluks Following the Ottoman Conquest," in Thomas Philipp and Ulrich Haarmann (eds), *The Mamluks in Egyptian Politics and Society* (Cambridge: Cambridge University Press, 1998), pp. 87–106.

"Islamic concepts of Time," *Zemanim* (Tel Aviv), 1999–2000, nos. 68–9 (Autumn–Winter) pp. 88–99, 110–11 (in Hebrew).

"Attitudes toward the Ottomans in Egyptian Historiography during Ottoman Rule," in Hugh Kennedy (ed.), *The Historiography of Islamic Egypt (c.950–1800)* (Leiden: Brill, 2001), pp. 195–210.

"Inter-*Madhhab* Competition in Mamluk Damascus: al-Tarsusi's Counsel for the Turkish Sultans," in *Jerusalem Studies in Arabic and Islam*, 2001, 25 (*David Ayalon Memorial Volume*), pp. 195–211.

"Religious Life in Mamluk Damascus and the Limits of Religious Tolerance," in Nahem Ilan (ed.), *The Intertwined Worlds of Islam, Essays in Memory of Hava Lazarus-Yafeh* (Jerusalem: Ben Zvi Institute and Bialik Institute, 2002), pp. 211–34 (in Hebrew).

"Mamluks and Their Households in Late Mamluk Damascus: A *Waqf* Study," in Michael Winter and Amalia Levanoni (eds), *The Mamluks in Egyptian and Syrian Politics and Society* (Leiden: Brill, 2003), pp. 297–316.

"The Civic Bureaucracy of Damascus in the Late Mamluk period," *Vostok, Asian and African Studies* (St Petersburg) (February, 2004), pp. 47–66.

To appear

"Arabic Historiography during the Ottoman Period (Sixteenth–Eighteenth Centuries)," in Donald Richards and Roger Allen (eds), *The Cambridge History of Arabic Literature.*

"The Bureaucratic Elite in Mamluk Damascus," in David J. Wasserstein (ed.), *Elites in Islamic Societies.*

"Coping with a Complex Heritage: Egyptian Modernists on the Historical Caliphate," in David Menashri (ed.), *Religion and State in the Middle East. Studies in Honor of Shimon Shamir.* A Hebrew version of this to appear in Miri Shefer and Michael Winter (eds), *The Ottoman Empire and the Turkish Republic, Studies in Honor of Aryeh Shmuelevitz.*

"Sufis and fuqaha' in the Ottoman Arab World between Confrontation and Accommodation," in *Vestnik Moskovskogo Universiteta Vostokovedenie (Moscow University Journal)*, Series 13 (Oriental Studies), no. 4, December 2004.

"Turkish-Arabic Cultural Relations: Influences Between Istanbul, Cairo and Damascus (Sixteenth–Eighteenth Centuries)," *Proceedings of CIEPO (Ottoman Studies Association), London, 2002.*

Articles in the Encyclopaedia of Islam (2nd edition)

"Ma'arif (education, public instruction) – the Ottoman Empire and the Central Arab Lands," vol. 5 (1985), pp. 902–15.

"al-Sha'rani," vol. 9 (1995), p. 316.

"Ta'rikh (Arabic historiography 1500–1800)," XII (Supplement), pp. 795–9.

Index

Avaris
Yaridis